A Guide to

The Norton Reader

ELEVENTH EDITION

A Guide to
The Norton Reader

ELEVENTH EDITION

Linda H. Peterson
Yale University

John C. Brereton
Brandeis University

Anne Fernald
DePauw University

Paul Heilker
Virginia Tech

Rajini Srikanth
University of Massachusetts, Boston

W. W. NORTON & COMPANY
New York • London

W. W. Norton & Company has been independent since its founding in 1923, when William Warder Norton and Mary D. Herter Norton first published lectures delivered at the People's Institute, the adult education division of New York City's Cooper Union. The Nortons soon expanded their program beyond the Institute, publishing books by celebrated academics from America and abroad. By mid-century, the two major pillars of Norton's publishing program—trade books and college texts—were firmly established. In the 1950s, the Norton family transferred control of the company to its employees, and today—with a staff of four hundred and a comparable number of trade, college, and professional titles published each year—W. W. Norton & Company stands as the largest and oldest publishing house owned wholly by its employees.

Composition by Cathy Lombardi.
Manufacturing by Victor Graphics.
Production Manager: Ben Reynolds.

ISBN 0-393-92475-0 (pbk.)

W. W. Norton & Company, Inc., 500 Fifth Avenue, New York, N.Y. 10110
www.wwnorton.com
W. W. Norton & Company Ltd., Castle House, 75/76 Wells Street, London W1T 3QT

1 2 3 4 5 6 7 8 9 0

Contents

* Indicates selections included in the *Shorter Edition.*

HUMAN NATURE

CULTURAL CRITIQUE

PROSE FORMS: OP-EDS

SAMPLE SYLLABI

Index of Rhetorical Modes

NARRATION

Maya Angelou: *Graduation* (NR 32, SE 18, G 8)
Margaret Atwood: *True North* (NR 171, SE 90, G 44)
Mary Austin: *The Land of Little Rain* (NR 186, SE 84, G 47)
Dionne Brand: *Arriving at Desire* (NR 418, SE 241, G 110)
Lord Chesterfield: *Letter to His Son* (NR 644, G 176)
Wayson Choy: *The Ten Thousand Things* (NR 12, SE 12, G 4)
Judith Ortiz Cofer: *More Room* (NR 167, G 43)
Paul Collins: *22,000 Seedlings* (NR 782, G 203)
Annie Dillard: *Terwilliger Bunts One* (NR 151, SE 69, G 39)
Frederick Douglass: *Learning to Read* (NR 408, SE 236, G 107)
Loren Eiseley: *The Brown Wasps* (NR 74, G 17)
Anne Fadiman: *The His'er Problem* (NR 518, SE 308, G 134)
Amitav Ghosh: *The Ghosts of Mrs. Gandhi* (NR 818, G 210)
Langston Hughes: *Salvation* (NR 1125, SE 656, G 281)
Maria Laurino: *Words* (NR 498, G 129)
Chang-Rae Lee: *Coming Home Again* (NR 1, SE 1, G 1)
Fatema Mernissi: *The Harem Within* (NR 162, SE 106, G 42)
N. Scott Momaday: *The Way to Rainy Mountain* (NR 192, SE 78, G 49)
Toni Morrison: *Strangers* (NR 132, SE 74, G 35)
Farley Mowat: *The Watcher Watched* (NR 600, G 160)
John Muir: *A Wind-Storm in the Forests* (NR 583, SE 356, G 156)
Edward Rivera: *First Communion* (NR 1127, SE 658, G 282)
Scott Russell Sanders: *Under the Influence* (NR 140, SE 58, G 38)
Sonia Shah: *Tight Jeans and Chania Chorris* (NR 304, SE 210, G 77)
Gary Soto: *The Guardian Angel* (NR 80, G 19)
Fred Strebeigh: *The Wheels of Freedom: Bicycles in China*
    (NR 330, G 85)
Henry David Thoreau: *Where I Lived, and What I Lived For*
    (NR 1155, SE 674, G 288)
James Thurber: *University Days* (NR 437, SE 257, G 114)
Sallie Tisdale: *We Do Abortions Here: A Nurse's Story*
    (NR 713, SE 426, G 191)
Barbara Tuchman: *"This Is the End of the World": The Black Death*
    (NR 759, SE 453, G 199)
Alice Walker: *Beauty: When the Other Dancer Is the Self*
    (NR 68, SE 46, G 16)
E. B. White: *Once More to the Lake* (NR 82, SE 52, G 20)
Walt Whitman: *Abraham Lincoln* (NR 104, G 27)
Terry Tempest Williams: *The Clan of One-Breasted Women*
    (NR 636, SE 386, G 172)

DESCRIPTION

Edward Abbey: *The Serpents of Paradise* (NR 589, SE 362, G 158)
Mary Austin: *The Land of Little Rain* (NR 186, SE 84, G 47)
Roland Barthes: *Toys* (NR 325, G 83)
Joan Didion: *On Going Home* (NR 9, SE 9, G 2)
Annie Dillard: *Terwilliger Bunts One* (NR 151, SE 69, G 39)
Gretel Ehrlich: *Spring* (NR 575, SE 344, G 154)
Lars Eighner: *On Dumpster Diving* (NR 22, SE 27, G 7)
Nora Ephron: *The Boston Photographs* (NR 696, G 187)
Henry Louis Gates Jr.: *In the Kitchen* (NE 299, G 76)
Philip Gourevitch: *After the Genocide* (NR 812, SE 481, G 208)
David Guterson: *Enclosed. Encyclopedic. Endured: The Mall of America*
    (NR 198, SE 111, G 50)
Nathaniel Hawthorne: *Abraham Lincoln* (NR 119, G 32)
John Hockenberry: *The Next Brainiacs* (NR 982, SE 571, G 250)
Thomas Jefferson: *George Washington* (NR 116, G 31)
Jamaica Kincaid: *The Ugly Tourist* (NR 565, SE 341, G 152)
Aldo Leopold: *Marshland Elegy* (NR 613, SE 382, G 165)
Ellen Lupton and J. Abbott Miller: *Period Styles: A Punctuated History*
    (NR 529, G 139)
Nancy Mairs: *On Being a Cripple* (NR 58, SE 36, G 15)
Toni Morrison: *Strangers* (NR 132, SE 74, G 35)
George Orwell: *Shooting an Elephant* (NR 851, SE 493, G 216)
Wallace Stegner: *The Town Dump* (NR 18, G 5)
John Tierney: *Playing the Dozens* (NR 516, G 133)
John Updike: *Little Lightnings* (NR 1085, SE 645, G 271)
John Updike: *Moving Along* (NR 1087, SE 647, G 271)
Tom Wolfe: *Yeager* (NR 123, G 34)
Virginia Woolf: *My Father: Leslie Stephen* (NR 136, G 36)
Dorothy Wordsworth: *The Alfoxden Journal 1798* (NR 96, SE 352, G 24)

EXPOSITION

Essays That Compare and Contrast
Francis Bacon: *Of Youth and Age* (NR 552, SE 331, G 145)
Frances FitzGerald: *Rewriting American History* (NR 828, G 211)
Adam Goodheart: *9.11.01: The Skyscraper and the Airplane*
    (NR 292, SE 187, G 74)
Jamaica Kincaid: *Sowers and Reapers* (NR 156, G 40)
John McMurtry: *Kill 'Em! Crush 'Em! Eat 'Em Raw!* (NR 309, SE 200, G 79)
Reinhold Niebuhr: *Humor and Faith* (NR 1141, G 284)
William G. Perry Jr.: *Examsmanship and the Liberal Arts: A Study in
    Educational Epistemology* (NR 465, G 120)
Alexander Petrunkevitch: *The Spider and the Wasp* (NR 595, SE 368, G 159)
Anna Quindlen: *Between the Sexes, a Great Divide* (NR 254, SE 158, G 63)

Terry Tempest Williams: *The Clan of One-Breasted Women* (NR 636, SE 386, G 172)

Mary Wollstonecraft: *A Vindication of the Rights of Women* (NR 559, SE 337, G 148)

PERSUASION/ARGUMENT

Hannah Arendt: *Denmark and the Jews* (NR 807, SE 477, G 207)

Russell Baker: *American Fat* (NR 394, G 100)

Caroline Bird: *College Is a Waste of Time and Money* (NR 429, SE 268, G 113)

Kenneth A. Bruffee: *Binge Drinking as a Substitute for a "Community of Learning"* (NR 404, G 105)

Anthony Burgess: *Is America Falling Apart?* (NR 286, SE 181, G 73)

Edward Hallett Carr: *The Historian and His Facts* (NR 834, G 213)

Lord Chesterfield: *Letter to His Son* (NR 644, G 176)

Carl Cohen: *The Case for the Use of Animals in Biomedical Research* (NR 687, G 185)

William Cronon: *The Trouble with Wilderness* (NR 617, G 167)

Paul Fussell: *Thank God for the Atom Bomb* (NR 724, SE 434, G 194)

Stephen Jay Gould: *Darwin's Middle Road* (NR 1011, SE 600, G 255)

Stephen Jay Gould: *The Terrifying Normalcy of AIDS* (NR 720, SE 433, G 193)

Lani Guinier: *The Tyranny of the Majority* (NR 885, G 227)

Jack Hitt: *The Battle of the Binge* (NR 401, SE 207, G 103)

Molly Ivins: *Get a Knife, Get a Dog, but Get Rid of Guns* (NR 389, SE 206, G 96)

Thomas Jefferson: *Original Draft of the Declaration of Independence* (NR 871, G 220)

Thomas Jefferson and Others: *The Declaration of Independence* (NR 874, SE 513, G 220)

Martin Luther King Jr.: *Letter from Birmingham Jail* (NR 889, SE 521, G 229)

Joseph Wood Krutch: *The Most Dangerous Predator* (NR 628, G 171)

Aldo Leopold: *The Land Ethic* (NR 707, SE 420, G 189)

Michael Levin: *The Case for Torture* (NR 675, SE 407, G 182)

Abraham Lincoln: *The Gettysburg Address* (NR 561, SE 339, G 150)

Abraham Lincoln: *Second Inaugural Address* (NR 880, G 224)

Lady Mary Wortley Montagu: *Letter to the Countess of Bute, Lady Montagu's Daughter* (NR 557, SE 335, G 148)

Michel de Montaigne: *That One Man's Profit Is Another's Loss* (NR 643, SE 394, G 175)

Ngugi wa Thiong'o: *Decolonizing the Mind* (NR 1054, G 265)

Joyce Carol Oates: *Against Nature* (NR 621, G 168)

Katha Pollitt: *Does a Literary Canon Matter?* (NR 1047, SE 618, G 264)

Jonathan Rauch: *In Defense of Prejudice* (NR 666, SE 398, G 180)

Tom Regan: *The Case for Animal Rights* (NR 677, SE 409, G 183)

Adrienne Rich: *Taking Women Students Seriously* (NR 448, G 117)

Thematic Table of Contents

CRIME AND VIOLENCE

WAR AND ITS EFFECTS

ILLNESS, DEATH, AND DYING

RELIGION AND SPIRITUALITY

Preface: To the Instructor

We have prepared this *Guide* in order to offer collegial advice about using *The Norton Reader*. Occasionally, we have drawn on materials from earlier *Guides*, retaining entries we found imaginative and workable but substituting new ideas when we thought them likely to produce better classroom discussion. More often, we have written new entries, drawing on our combined experiences as writing teachers and our enthusiasm for the essays new to the eleventh edition. Not every suggestion will work for every instructor, nor will every writing assignment work for every student. But we have tried hard to be helpful—even though this has meant including more suggestions than any single instructor can use in any single class.

In conceiving the *Guide*, we have kept in mind the various kinds of writing courses for which *The Norton Reader* is well suited. One model for freshman composition calls for serious, solid essays that first-year college students will enjoy reading and writing about and that will introduce them to common topics and themes of academic life. Textbooks for such courses are often labeled "liberal arts readers" or just "college readers," suggesting that they introduce students to the college curriculum even as they improve critical thinking and writing. Whether or not you use this label, we think *The Norton Reader* ideal for such a course, and we have tried to suggest discussion questions and writing assignments that will engage students seriously with significant issues, in and out of the academy. You will find a syllabus for a version of this course, "Great Ideas and Enduring Questions," at the end of this *Guide*.

The Norton Reader works well in other kinds of writing courses, too, including those that focus on writing in the disciplines, those that address contemporary debates in North American culture, and those that focus on the essay as a form. Writing across the curriculum, one of the major pedagogical movements of the last decade, has reshaped the thinking of many of us who teach composition; it has reminded us not only of the importance of writing for learning but also of the discipline-specific nature of academic discourse. For instructors who use a writing-across-the-curriculum approach, the second half of *The Norton Reader* will prove especially valuable—as will, we hope, our suggestions in the *Guide*. We have tried to send students back to sources, for example, to see how a professional historian works or to compare the prose of a scholar writing for a lay audience versus for fellow academics. For units representing a range of discourse, we have tried to include questions that get at discourse conventions within disciplines, as well as at rhetorical options that individual writers may—or may not—choose to exercise.

If you prefer to focus your reading and writing on contemporary cultural debates, we urge you to consider a syllabus based on the "Cultural Critique" section, with additional essays from "Human Nature," "Education," "Nature and the Environment," and "Philosophy and Religion." We have labeled the section "Cultural Critique" to acknowledge that a major tradition of the essay focuses on analyzing and reforming culture, but in fact *The Norton Reader* includes essays on topics of contemporary relevance in every section—whether on ethnicity in "People, Places" and "Language and Communication," on gender in "Human Nature," on race in "Cultural Critique," or on American religions in "Philosophy and Religion." If you wish, you can build an entire course on issues of race, ethnicity, class, and gender—as we have done in another sample syllabus of the *Guide*.

If you plan to teach a course that emphasizes argument and persuasion, we encourage you to start with the "Op-Eds" prose forms. The short pieces we have included were published in major newspapers or magazines and represent what is often called "civic discourse." Each writer has taken an issue of public debate and clearly argued a position within that debate, whether on gun control (Ivins), grade inflation (Staples), the abuse of the English language (Baker), or binge drinking on college campuses (Wechsler et al., Hitt, Bruffee). For more extended arguments, the "Ethics" section is particularly useful in that it contains longer essays, but as the syllabus on "Persuasion and Argument" shows, there are examples of argument in virtually every section of the *Reader*.

Finally, *The Norton Reader* offers a superb resource for courses that focus on the essay as a literary and social genre. The early sections of the *Reader*—"Personal Report," "People, Places," "Prose Forms: Journals," "Cultural Critique"—reproduce some of the best essays and essayists of the last half-century, whereas the later sections include many fine examples of what is often called "the literature of fact." In writing the *Guide*, we have retained questions with a literary slant—questions about style, tone, persona, and rhetorical techniques—and we have suggested assignments that give students the opportunity to experiment with various forms of the essay genre. But we have also added questions that explore the personal, social, and political uses of the essay—so that students can think about how an essay situates itself in a historical moment for a specific rhetorical purpose. (For a full-scale course on the modern essay, see the sample syllabus at the end of the *Guide*.)

The arrangement of the *Guide* follows the contents of *The Norton Reader*, Eleventh Edition, and provides suggestions for teaching every selection. It can, of course, be used with the Shorter Edition, and our entries give page numbers for both editions. The Index of Rhetorical Modes (pp. xiii–xviii) and the Thematic Table of Contents (pp. xix–xxii) also cite page references for both editions (NR = Regular Edition, SE = Shorter Edition, G = Guide). The rhetorical index, intended to help instructors who prefer to organize their courses by rhetorical modes, lists most of the essays included in the *Reader*; the Thematic Index includes over half.

We hope the *Guide* will serve as a springboard for questions you may ask and for observations students may make. Entries consist of three or four parts:

1. An introduction to the essay and the author, which may be supplemented with the biographical sketches in the "Authors" section of the *Reader*.
2. Questions reprinted from the *Reader*.
3. "Analytical Considerations," which take up matters of form and content, rhetoric and style, and which are meant to help instructors plan their syllabus and class discussion.

4. "Suggested Writing Assignments," which supplement assignments in the *Reader* itself and draw on key concepts from the work, other essays related in theme or style, topics that touch students' lives, and enduring issues central to a liberal education—all with the aim of giving students provocative, wide-ranging possibilities for writing.

We hope you will find our suggestions in the *Guide* useful. They represent the collective wisdom of former authors of the *Guide*, the editors emeritii, most notably Arthur Eastman and Joan Hartman; the co-editors of *The Norton Reader* itself; our editors at Norton, Marilyn Moller, Nicole Netherton, and Julia Reidhead; and our colleagues at our home institutions and in the profession at large.

Linda H. Peterson, *Yale University*
John C. Brereton, *Brandeis University*
Anne Fernald, *DePauw University*
Paul Heilker, *Virginia Tech*
Rajini Srikanth, *University of Massachusetts, Boston*

To Students: Reading and Writing
with *The Norton Reader*

The Norton Reader includes essays on a range of subjects—some familiar, others more specialized; some personal, others highly public. You'll find the familiar and personal in sections like "Personal Report" and "People, Places," the specialized and public in sections like "Ethics" and "Science and Technology." "Personal Report" appeared in the first edition, "Nature and the Environment" in the ninth edition, and we've added "Spoken Words" to this one. Some essays—Martin Luther King Jr.'s "Letter from Birmingham Jail" and Jonathan Swift's "A Modest Proposal," for example—are constant favorites. Other essays—approximately one-quarter—are new to this edition.

The editors read widely in order to include a variety of authors writing on a variety of topics in a variety of ways. We include male and female voices; American, British, and Canadian voices; African American, Asian American, American Indian, Caribbean, and Hispanic American voices. Some essays are calculatedly challenging, others relatively simple. Some are long, others short. Although most were published recently, some are older; although most are written in English, a few are translated from other languages. What they have in common is excellence: we, as the editors, without actually defining good writing for ourselves or for each other, have agreed on the inclusion of each essay. We find their authors, sometimes well known, sometimes virtually unknown, speaking with authority and seeing with distinctive angles of vision. We find their subjects important, timely, timeless, engaging. We find their writing convincing and clear, their style lean when elaboration is not required, yet adequate to complexity.

The Norton Reader contains a large number of essays, more than any instructor will assign during a semester.. We know that there are many kinds of college writing courses; we know that instructors link reading and writing in a many different ways. We aim in *The Norton Reader* to accommodate all or most of them. We leave it to your instructors to direct you through the essays, to decide which ones to assign, and to show you how to approach them to discover their richness. We also hope you'll choose to read some extra essays on your own—essays whose titles or topics appeal to you.

READING WITH A CRITICAL EYE

Most of the essays in *The Norton Reader* originally appeared in magazines or books written for educated general readers. These essays were intended to be read by people who wanted to know—or know more—about their subjects, who knew—or knew of—their authors, or who were tempted to launch into unfamiliar subjects written about by authors they had never heard of because they encountered these essays in publications they ordinarily read. In the world outside the classroom, readers bring their own interests and motivations to the essays they read. Putting them in a textbook almost inevitably makes reading them seem artificial.

Even so, we, as editors, want to help you read these essays critically by understanding their contexts and thus making your reading process become more "real." When you begin reading an essay assigned by your instructor, we suggest using some or all of these tactics.

- Preview the essay: Think about its title, read its opening paragraph, skim the topic sentences. Look at the contextual note we have provided on the first page of each essay, and try to imagine the experience, issue, or debate that motivated the essayist to write.
- Read the questions included after the essay: Think about the issues—the topic, structure, or language—that the questions pose, or imagine a personal response to the final question—usually a writing assignment.
- Write in the margins: Note points that seem interesting and important; forecast issues that you think the writer should address; pose questions of your own. Talk back.
- Note what confuses you: In addition to points that you understand, note points that you fail to understand and save them for class discussion. Failures can be as instructive as successes, and recognizing your difficulties as a reader will help sharpen your skills.
- Summarize the essay: Write a summary of the essay in your own words in a journal or class notebook; make a list of its key points; list the questions that the essayist raises and answers.
- Keep a reading journal: Make notes about what you read; record your responses to each essay; write questions about what puzzled you and what you want to discuss with classmates.
- Reread the essay: If possible, read the essay for a second time before you discuss it in class; if you lack time, reread the key passages and paragraphs that you marked in your marginal notes. Ask yourself what you see the second time that you didn't register on first reading.

As these tactics suggest, reading need not be only a private activity; it can also become a communal and cooperative one. Sharing reading journals in class helps to demystify reading and clarify points of confusion. Discussion, in class as a whole or in smaller groups, can elucidate your own and others' interpretations of the essays, as well as differences in interpretations. What interests and motivations do we bring to particular essays? Do some interests and motivations yield better readings than others? What strategies do we employ when we read? Are there other useful ones? What meanings do readers agree about, what meanings do they disagree about? Can we account for our differences? What are responsive and responsible readings? What are irresponsible readings, and how do we decide? All these questions—and others—can emerge as private reading moves into the public arena of the classroom.

To help you read each essay, we've added some aids to explain facts and information that the original readers of these essays probably knew and that might help you comprehend the essay more readily:

- **Contextual notes:** We've placed these notes at the bottom of the first page of each essay. They provide information about when and where the essay first appeared and, if it began as a talk, when and where it was delivered and to what audience. For example, Maya Angelou's "Graduation" comes from her autobiography, *I Know Why the Caged Bird Sings*, published in 1969; after the book's popular success, Angelou continued her life story in five sequential volumes, most recently in *A Song Flung Up to Heaven* (2002). Scott Russell Sanders's "Looking at Women" appeared in the *Georgia Review*, a small circulation literary magazine, whereas John Tierney's "Playing the Dozens" was first published in the *New York Times Magazine* in a section called "The Way We Live Now." Other essays were first presented in oral form: David McCullough's "Recommended Itinerary" began as a graduation address at Middlebury College in 1986 and then was revised for an essay collection, *Brave Companions: Portraits in History* (1992); the "Cherokee Memorials," along with a dozen supporting documents, were delivered aloud as well as presented in writing to the United States Congress in 1830.

  We try to explain a little about the books, magazines, and newspapers that published these essays—for example, that the *New York Times Magazine* is a large circulation weekly magazine included with the Sunday newspaper; the *Georgia Review*, a small circulation literary journal published three times a year by the University of Georgia. As editors, we could swamp *The Norton Reader* with additional information about publication and authorship, but we prefer to include more essays and keep contextual information brief.

- **Authors' biographies:** The section called "Authors," located at the end of the volume, provides information about the men and women who wrote the essays. Putting this information at the end provides you with a choice. You may know something about an author already and not wish to consult this section. You may prefer to find out something about an author before you read his or her essay. Or you may just prefer to encounter the authors as unknowns, letting them identify themselves within the essay. Sometimes knowing who authors are and where their voices come from helps readers hear them and grasp what they say—but sometimes it doesn't.

- **Illustrations:** For this edition of *The Norton Reader*, we've added photographs, drawings, graphs, and other visuals that originally accompanied the essays. In some cases, as with Toni Morrison's "Strangers" or H. Bruce Franklin's "From Realism to Virtual Reality: Images of America's Wars," the authors began writing their essays by thinking about the photographs, pondering their significance, and interpreting the images. In other cases, such as James Thurber's "The Owl Who Was God" or Fred Strebeigh's "The Wheels of Freedom: Bicycles in China," the authors provided images to accompany their prose: in Thurber's case, his own drawing of an owl; in Strebeigh's, photographs he took during his travels in China at the time of the Tiananmen uprising. In still others, the illustrations were added after the essays were written, often by an editor responsible for seeing the work through the press, sometimes in consultation with the author.

As you look at the visual images, you might think about the ways in which they enrich, highlight, and possibly challenge the essay itself. Do the visual images primarily illustrate the essay, or do they emphasize a feature unexplained by the essayist? Do the images enrich one aspect of the writing and make that aspect clearer, or do they minimize certain aspects of the subject, perhaps aspects you find important? What do you see in the images that the essayist discusses or explains? What do you see that he or she overlooks or minimizes? We have included the images original to the essays to allow them to "speak" to each other, as they did at the time of the essays' original publication.

- **Annotations:** For many essays, we provide explanatory footnotes—a sure sign that this is an academic textbook. Most commercial magazines do not include footnotes, whereas academic writing often does. We identify footnotes the authors originally wrote themselves, in square brackets, as author's notes. But we've written most of the footnotes that help with difficult words and allusions. Our guidelines go something like this:

  1. We generally *don't* define words that appear in standard collegiate dictionaries unless they are foreign. If an unfamiliar word is central to the meaning of an essay, the author is likely to define it. If the author doesn't, you can consult your dictionary or guess its meaning from the context.

  2. We *do* provide information about most people, places, works, theories, and other unfamiliar things. For example, for Maya Angelou's "Graduation," we explain Gabriel Prosser, Nat Turner, and Harriet Tubman but not Abraham Lincoln and Christopher Columbus; we also explain Stamps (an Arkansas town) and "Invictus" (a poem).

  3. We try to explain but not interpret; that is, we give information but leave it to readers to interpret the essays by deciding how the authors frame and use that information, how it adds to their argument or expression, how it contributes to their meanings. Francis Bacon's "Of Youth and Age," for example, requires extensive annotation. It is possible to figure out from the essay itself that Julius Caesar and Septimius Severus succeeded later in life, after stormy youths; but our note actually translates the Latin quotation about Severus, confirms their late success by giving dates, and explains that Severus, like Caesar, ruled Rome. Our notes for "Of Youth and Age" measure the distance between Bacon's original readers and readers today. Bacon assumed that his readers read Latin, were familiar with ancient and European history, and were willing to take as illustrative examples of "youth" and "age" male rulers and public figures. We give dates and facts but leave you to work out the meanings implicit in Bacon's examples.

Our experience in the classroom helps us as editors to make guesses about what you know, what you don't know, and what you may need or want to know. For some essays, we've asked students who have taken our courses to read the new essays and tell us what annotations to add. But, despite our good intentions, you can be sure that we'll fail you in some places by not explaining enough or that we'll annoy you in others by explaining what you find clear. When we fail, ask your instructors for help; when we annoy, take our efforts as well intentioned.

Here's the most important point: Annotation, while it *facilitates* the making of meaning in reading, can never take its place. Reading is an active process. Experienced readers take responsibility for that action by reading critically, constructing meaning, interpreting what they read, not just by moving their eyes over the page and expecting meaning to occur automatically. If our annotations help you read critically, then use them; if they interfere, then just continue reading the main text.

- **Questions:** After most essays in *The Norton Reader* we include questions to help you become an active reader, and often these questions give directions to *do* something.

  1. Some questions ask you to locate, mark, or identify because we want you to notice the essays' structural features, the patterns that undergird and make manifest their meanings. Narrative, description, exposition, persuasion, and argument take conventional shapes—or distort them—and recognizing these shapes enhances comprehension.

  2. Other questions ask you to paraphrase meanings—that is, to express them in your own words, to extend points by providing additional examples, or to reframe points by connecting them with other essays.

  3. Still other questions ask you to notice rhetorical features that contribute to meanings: the author's choice of title or epigraph, the author's voice (or persona), the author's assumptions about audience (and how the author speaks to the audience), the author's choice of style and forms of expression. We ask you to consider the effects of these rhetorical choices.

  4. At least one question, usually the last, asks you to write. Sometimes, we ask you to demonstrate comprehension by an informed assent— that is, by bringing in something from your own experience or reading that extends an essay. Sometimes, we ak for an informed dissent—that is, by bringing in something from your experience or knowledge that qualifies the author's argument or calls it into question. Often, we ask you to compare or contrast one author's position with another's—especially when their positions seem fundamentally opposed. Or we ask you to adapt one of the essay's rhetorical strategies to a topic of your own choice and to make the essay your own by basing it on personal experience.

Readers write, writers read. The processes are connected, and we have tried to make the questions concern them both. Making meaning by writing is the flip side of making it by reading, and we hope to engage you in both processes. In neither is meaning passed from hand to hand like nickels, dimes, and quarters. Instead, it is constructed—as in the making of quilts or houses or institutions.

WRITING WITH AN ACTIVE VOICE

The process of making meaning by writing is less mysterious than the process of making it by reading. Nowadays most instructors, however they choose to link reading and writing, emphasize process and multiple products—that is, the first drafts and revisions that precede final essays. As students you may not have the time for as many as your instructor may desire, but distributing your time over several drafts rather than concentrating on a single one may turn out to be the most efficient use of your time.

Experienced writers know they can't do everything at once: find or invent material, assess its usefulness, arrange it in paragraphs, and write it out in well-formed sentences. If you try to produce a good essay at one sitting, in a single draft, you are likely to thin out your material, lock yourself into a structure you don't have time to change, and write jumbled paragraphs and clumsy sentences that won't fully convey your meaning or intention. In the end, writing several drafts—in short periods spaced over more than a day—will produce a better essay, one that is thoughtful and deserving of a respectable grade.

For an experienced writer, the process of writing an essay typically includes these steps, which we urge you to take:

- Start with brainstorming, note-taking, listing, freewriting, or whatever heuristic techniques—that is, whatever means of discovering what to write—work for you. Experiment with methods suggested in your writing class.
- Then try out what you have to say by composing a rough draft or small sections of a draft. Don't feel obliged to start with the introduction and write straight through to the conclusion. If you don't know where to begin, write a section you know you want to include, then move on to another. As you compose, you will begin to find out what you mean, what is important to your argument, what is missing, and what needs to be revised to make it make sense.
- At any point in this process, print out a clean, readable version of your draft, read it through, and make changes. Add to, subtract from, rearrange, and revise the parts of your essay.

Large and small elements of the composing process are reciprocal. Good writers work back and forth among wholes and parts, sections and paragraphs, introductions and conclusions. As shape and meaning come together, you can begin to refine smaller elements: sentences, phrases, specific words. You can qualify your assertions, complicate your generalizations, and tease out the implications of your examples. Finally, you can tinker with surface features by rewording, pruning, and correcting spelling and punctuation during the editing and proofreading processes. But so long as the larger elements of an essay need repair, it's too soon to work on the smaller ones, so save the tinkering for the end. Then, like any professional writer, you will need to stop—not because there isn't more to be done but because you have other things to do.

As a writer, you will want to enlist the aid of readers. Although writers can compose and revise alone, it's best to try our a complete draft of your essay on someone responsive to your writing. At their best, writing classes enable students to put less-than-final drafts into circulation and receive responses to them through instructor's comments, group work, and peer critique. Here are some all-purpose questions that you might use on your own, or in a peer group to discuss a draft. The questions should probably be asked in the order they appear, since they go from larger elements to smaller ones.

- Take introductions as promises and ask: "Does this essay keep the promises the introduction makes?" If it doesn't, either the introduction or the essay needs to be revised. By listening to the responses of your readers, you may discover that you've wandered off the topic and need to pull yourself back to the assigned task through substantial revision of content and organization.
- Then ask, "Does this essay include enough material?" You may feel that the essays in *The Norton Reader* are dense and overspecific; your instructors, on the other hand, may find your essays skimpy and underspecific. Good writers thicken their writing with particulars to transmit their meanings and engage readers' interest, understanding, and imagination. Good writers tend to include much evidence, to sustain multiple illustrative examples, and to provide rich detail. If your readers ask for more evidence, examples, or information, take their suggestions seriously.
- Next ask, "Does the essay interpret its material clearly and connect its examples to the main argument?" Good writers specify the meanings they derive from their examples; they don't expect the examples to speak for themselves, because examples seldom do. A case in point is the use of quotations. How many are there? How necessary are they? How well are they integrated? What analysis of commentary follows each? Good writers introduce quotations by explaining who is speaking, where the voice is coming from, and what to listen for; they finish off quotations by making connections to their own argument.
- Then ask, "Is the material in this essay well arranged?" Writing puts readers in possession of material in a temporal order: that is, readers read from start to finish. Sometimes material that appears near the end of an essay might better appear near the beginning; sometimes material that appears near the beginning might better be postponed. Transitions between paragraphs may be unclear; when they are hard to specify, the difficulty may lie in the arrangement of the material.
- Then ask, "Which sentences unfold smoothly and which sentences are likely to cause readers to stumble?" Readers who can point to what makes them stumble will teach you more about well-formed sentences than will any set of rules for forming them. If possible, ask your readers to help you rephrase a sentence or write the thought in different words.

All writers need to try out their arguments on other people before they produce a final draft. Because the world itself is complex and the people in it have varied experiences and perspectives, examples that seem to one person clear-cut may seem to another forced or exaggerated. In peer groups, listen to readers who disagree with you, who find your position slanted or overstated. Be responsive to their comments, and qualify your interpretations or further explain points with which they don't concur.

Both reading and writing, then, can and should be shared. Collaborative exercises can create communities of active readers to discuss the essays of professional writers in *The Norton Reader*, as well as one another's writing. Learning to become a responsive and responsible reader of professional writing can teach you to respond helpfully to your composition classmates' essays and to improve your own.

PERSONAL REPORT

CHANG-RAE LEE

Coming Home Again

The Norton Reader, p. 1; Shorter Edition, p. 1

Korean American novelist Chang-Rae Lee graduated from Yale in 1988 and received his MFA in 1995 from the University of Oregon, where he taught writing. His first novel, *Native Speaker* (1995), won the PEN/Faulkner Award. He published a second novel, *A Gesture Life*, in 1999, which won the Anisfield-Wolf Literary Award and was a finalist for the *New Yorker* Book Award. He currently teaches creative writing at Princeton University.

In this essay, Lee describes his mother cooking for her family and trading cooking lessons with an American suburban mom: macaroni and cheese for *kimchi*. Lee is accepting of his own and his mother's desire to fit in, and is fond of the woman who was their friend. The center of the essay, however, describes how he cooked Korean dishes for his family when his mother was too ill with cancer to do so, and thus it focuses on the importance of his Korean heritage at a time of crisis. There is a lot to admire and discuss here: a version of multiculturalism that accepts (and embraces) it as fact, a story about the pain of leaving home for boarding school (Exeter), and a son who cooks, thus both satisfying his family's commitment to tradition and disappointing its ambitions for a *son*.

Students will immediately grasp the gentle irony of calling macaroni and cheese "exotic." This can be the springboard for a larger discussion of the symbolic importance of food—a central theme in Lee's essay. Food means one set of things within Lee's family and another when he compares his family to mainstream America (Mrs. Churchill, dorm food at boarding school). You might begin discussion by asking students to list the meanings of food in each context and compare them. Does food and cooking mean the same thing to each member of Lee's family? What role does it seem to play in his parents' marriage?

Questions from the NR 11

1. Chang-Rae Lee begins his essay *in medias res*—in the middle of things. How does his choice create drama, sympathy, and significance for the personal experience that he narrates?
2. Because Lee begins his account at a late stage of his mother's illness, he often flashes back to earlier points in their relationship. Mark the flashbacks in the text, and explain the purpose of each.
3. Details of food and cooking appear throughout the essay—for example, in paragraphs 8–9, 12–13, and 32–38. Besides giving us a flavor of Korean food, what function do these details serve?

4. Lee titles his essay "Coming Home Again," whereas Joan Didion titles hers "On Going Home" (see the next essay in "Personal Report"). What different connotations do "coming home" and "going home" suggest? How do these differences emerge in the personal accounts of each writer?
5. Write a personal essay about "coming home" or "going home."

Analytical Considerations

1. In paragraph 7, Lee offers an intensely detailed description of his mother making *kalbi*, Korean short ribs. Analyze and discuss the language here. Could you make the dish based on his description? How is it different from a recipe, and why is it different? What do we learn about Lee and his mother from this description?
2. This essay moves back and forth among many moments in Lee's life. It may help students understand Lee's themes—and discern the overall point—if you make a paragraph outline on the board, listing the topic of each successive paragraph. Show them the way he dances from his boyhood to his departure for boarding school to his return home during his mother's final illness and back. Once they see his timeline and structure on the board, discuss Lee's choices. Why is this recursive style appropriate to an essay called "Coming Home Again"? What does it tell us about his attitude to the revelation that his mother regrets sending him away for high school.
3. Ask students to identify what, for them, is the turning point of the essay. Then ask them to justify their choice in a few sentences. Discussing their different choices and the reasons for them will help them clarify what they see as the essay's core: the mother's death, her regret at sending him off to school, the lessons in Korean culture she offered through cooking, Lee's successful assimilation, or his reverence for his Korean heritage.

Suggested Writing Assignments

1. Write a short essay in which you pay tribute to a family member by describing the way she or he cooks. Aim for the kind of precise attention to method and ingredients that Lee exhibits here.
2. Read another essay about coming back to one's parents' house as an adult (Joan Didion's "On Going Home" [NR 9, SE 9] or Sonia Shah's "Tight Jeans and Chania Chorris" [NR 304, SE 210]) and write an essay comparing the attitudes in each essay.

JOAN DIDION

On Going Home

The Norton Reader, p. 9; Shorter Edition, p. 9

In this short essay (of six paragraphs) Joan Didion describes returning to her family's home to celebrate her daughter's first birthday. Her husband remains in Los Angeles, while she reenters the world of her father, mother, brother, and great-aunts. "On Going Home" proceeds by association: one experience reminds her of another, one question leads to another. What is "home"? Can you go home again? How does memory work to connect past and present, one home with another? Didion's essay links past and present by shifting incessantly back and forth between them. If you taught Chang-Rae Lee's "Coming Home Again" and discussed his use of a recursive style, you might also want to outline or construct a flow chart for Didion's essay, and discuss how and why Didion moves from one experience to another.

Questions from the NR11

1. Didion speaks of herself at home as "paralyzed by the neurotic lassitude engendered by meeting one's past at every turn" (paragraph 3). What about the essay helps explain these feelings?
2. What does Didion mean by "the ambushes of family life"? (Besides "ambushes" note Didion's other highly charged language: e.g., "betrayal" in paragraph 1 and "guerrilla war" in paragraph 3.)
3. In paragraph 6 Didion says she would like to give her daughter "home for her birthday, but we live differently now and I can promise her nothing like that." In an essay, explain whether or not you think parents today can give their children "home." Include examples.

Analytical Considerations

1. How does the "vital although troublesome distinction" (paragraph 1) between home as the place where Didion lives with her husband and baby in Los Angeles and home as the place where her family lives in the Central Valley of California thread through "On Going Home"?
2. Ask students to look closely at "On Going Home" as an essay developed by association and, in particular, at how Didion maintains the illusion of free association while behaving responsibly toward her readers. She is careful to do two things: to let us know where in time she is, particularly with respect to present and past, and to provide thematic coherence. For the first, you might ask students to look at transitions between paragraphs and then within them; for the second, ask them to elucidate the several concerns that run through the essay.
3. Look at Didion's "On Keeping a Notebook" (NR 90) in conjunction with "On Going Home" with respect to their development and rhetorical techniques. How do objects function in them? How do images function?
4. Consider the titles of both essays—"On Keeping a Notebook," "On Going Home." What does "on" followed by a participle serve to suggest about the kind of essay each will be?

Suggested Writing Assignments

1. Write a personal essay developed by associations radiating out from a return to a place. Give it a title beginning with "On" followed by a participle (a verb ending in "-ing").
2. One technique Didion uses is to organize her associations around objects. Write a personal essay in which you focus on objects. Attend to maintaining the illusion of free association while providing thematic coherence.

3. Read another essay about coming back to one's parents' house as an adult (Chang-Rae Lee's "Coming Home Again," M. Scott Momaday's "The Way to Rainy Mountain," or Sonia Shah's "Tight Jeans and Chania Chorris") and write an essay comparing the attitudes toward home expressed in each essay.

WAYSON CHOY

The Ten Thousand Things

The Norton Reader, p. 12; Shorter Edition, p. 12

Wayson Choy's essay—about discovering, at age fifty-seven, that he was adopted—proceeds by episodes. Each of the four sections can be divided into two parts: (1) the phone call with the impossible claim ("I saw your mother") and his initial assumption that the caller is "a crazy"; (2) the interview with Hazel, the caller, and his aunts' confirmation that he was adopted; (3) the historical climate in which he was adopted and his aunts' attitude toward having him in the family; (4) his father's death and a comparison between his adopted and biological fathers.

This episodic structure contributes to the overall feeling of peace and wonder at the discovery. Rather than expressing anger or betrayal, Choy presents his story as just one of "the ten thousand things," just another way of living and dying, one that makes his story more interesting than he'd imagined. Choy chooses to be grateful for the love of his adoptive parents and for "the blessing of a community that knew when to keep silent and when—at last—to speak up." Discuss with your students the factors that influence Choy's attitude and how he expresses it.

Questions from the NR11

1. How does the initial quotation—"I saw your mother last week"—set in motion Choy's search for his "real" parents? What are the stages of his search?
2. Choy's personal report takes the form of a quest: a mysterious phone call, a conversation with "a crazy," a history of Vancouver's Chinese during the Depression, memories of his adoptive parents, and a search for his birth parents. How does the quest end? How does Choy resolve the question of who his "real" parents are?
3. Why do you think Choy placed the photograph of Toy and Lily Choy at the end of his essay rather than at the beginning or in the middle?
4. By interviewing family members, looking at photos, or reading old family documents, write about your own quest to discover the facts about a deceased family member. You need not raise the issue of "adoptive" or "birth" relations; rather, define the question that you wish your quest to resolve in terms of its personal interest to you.

Analytical Considerations

1. Look at the paragraph in which Choy explains the meaning of the title phrase (in the fourth section). Ask students to do a timed in-class writing exercise on the title. Why is the saying such a comfort to Choy when he finds out he is adopted? What is its relevance to his discovery about himself? Why is it a good title for the essay?
2. In the third section of the essay, Choy places his birth in the context of Chinese immigration policies in the early decades of the twentieth century. Students may not be aware that similar immigration quotas existed — and still exist — in the United States. Ask students to research immigration quotas for a specific ethnic group — perhaps that of their ancestors. What were the quotas in the past, and how have they changed over the past century?
3. The essay concludes with the comment "Chinatown had been writing me." Discuss with your students what Choy might mean by this statement. In what sense is he a product of his environment? Why is this such an intense source of pride for him?
4. Think of one thing that you know to be true of your family — like Choy's faith in his father's steady confidence, or the fact that the man he called "father" was his adoptive father. What would change if you learned differently? If an admired trait had origins you hadn't considered or concealed a secret? How would you handle it?

Suggested Writing Assignments

1. The decisions not to tell Wayson he was adopted affected many people: both sets of parents, his aunts, and Hazel, the girl whose mother fostered him. Choose one of these people, and write a brief imaginative personal essay from their point of view about Choy's adoption. Be sure to consider their motive for keeping the secret, as well as the hopes and fears should Wayson find it out.
2. Write an essay in which you compare Choy's two fathers. What does Choy seem to have inherited from each? What is his attitude toward each man?

WALLACE STEGNER

The Town Dump

The Norton Reader, p. 18

In this recollection of childhood, Stegner seems able to remember absolutely everything that occurred to him in connection with his town's dump. This essay was published in 1959, and the events it records took place between 1913 and 1919, as Stegner helpfully tells us in the opening paragraph. In other words, the remembrance spans at least forty years, yet events are portrayed with extraordinary vividness: the particular sound a leech made when it let go (paragraph 8), the reply to a letter from a St. Louis junk house (paragraph 11), the fate of the family Shakespeare (paragraph 17), among others. Students ought to ponder the source of that incredible power of recall. Some will think that Stegner simply set himself to thinking hard about his adventures in the dump and then produced this account. More sophisticated readers will realize that Stegner has shaped his memories and removed extraneous images and recollections. (He never claims that this is everything he remembers.) The most sophisticated of all will speculate about how over time a novelist's imagination can build, shape, and produce an interesting memoir from just fragments of memory. (In this sense Stegner's piece has much in common with Angelou's remembrance of graduation [NR 32, SE 18]).

It is useful to show that Stegner was aware of the culturally impoverished life on the Canadian plains. When he says, "The dump was our poetry and our history" (paragraph 20), he means both that the dump contained a literal Shakespeare and the detritus of decades of settlement, and that the dump itself, at least to a young boy, stood for both the romance of faraway places and the history of his community.

The remembered details are what make this piece so appealing. The technique is simple. It opens with the site, near a river, and the items in the first eight paragraphs have to do with water, an appealing attraction for a young boy. Paragraph 10, beginning ". . . it contained relics of every individual who had ever lived there, and of every phase of the town's history," serves to organize paragraphs 11 to 19, which all have textbook-perfect topic sentences. It is only with paragraph 20 that Stegner reveals the true import of his piece: "The dump was our poetry and our history." There, in the refuse of civilization, was all a young boy needed to form his picture of life.

Questions from the NR11

1. Through what details does Stegner portray the dump as a record of his childhood? How is it also a record of the town's history? Is it also a record of the North American West? In what sense?
2. How seriously do you take Stegner's claim (paragraph 21) that "I learned more from the town dump than I learned from school"? He has been making allusions to Coleridge and Virgil; what kind of learning is he thinking of?
3. Describe a "treasure" someone found and held on to.

Analytical Considerations

1. The phrase "kitchen midden" (paragraph 19) was deliberately not glossed. Students who look it up in the dictionary will connect the dump to the work of archaeologists searching through middens of different civilizations. The last two paragraphs make all the case that is necessary for the study of dump sites, whether dating from prehistoric times, the classical world, or the nineteenth-century Canadian prairie.
2. Students may not know that Stegner was a strong environmentalist, the conscience of the West to many people. Ask students to speculate on Steg-

ner's attitude toward preservation of the environment, basing their thoughts on his ability to describe the natural and artificial world around him and his (implied) attitude toward humans' profligate use of resources.

Suggested Writing Assignments

1. Stegner says, "I think I learned more from the town dump than I learned from school: more about people, more about how life is lived, not elsewhere but here, not in other times but now" (paragraph 21). Write an essay about how you or someone you know learned more about life from something other than school. Or, expanding on sentiments Stegner expresses in this sentence, write a critique of school by showing how it does not adequately prepare students for the real world.
2. Using "The Town Dump" and Lars Eighner's "On Dumpster Diving" (NR 22, SE 27) as models, write an essay about a "treasure trove" you have found, making a larger point about a family, a community, or consumer society. Suggested locales: a closet, basement, or attic; a storeroom; a dump.

LARS EIGHNER

On Dumpster Diving

The Norton Reader, p. 22; Shorter Edition, p. 27

Originally written as a separate essay, "On Dumpster Diving" later appeared in Eighner's first book, *Travels with Lizbeth* (1993). It gives an account of the time he spent homeless, getting much of what he needed from what people threw away in Dumpsters. Eighner's essay has five parts: (1) a brief introduction (paragraphs 1 to 6) about words: the derivation of "Dumpster," the appropriateness of scavenging or foraging; (2) the inevitable question, as if posed by an imaginary interlocutor: "What is safe to eat?" (paragraphs 7 to 30); (3) a chronology of his own Dumpster diving, from beginning to scavenge to making the rounds of Dumpsters, with a concluding disquisition on what is wrong with can scroungers (paragraphs 31 to 48); (4) an examination of items found in Dumpsters (paragraphs 49 to 59); and (5) a philosophical conclusion that meditates on a throwaway society (paragraphs 60 to 68). Building on the first question in the NR, you might want to discuss why Eighner begins and ends where he does, and how he moves from description to social analysis.

Questions from the NR11

1. How does Eighner organize his essay? What does such an organization imply?
2. Eighner's simple, understated tone suggests that anyone can adapt to Dumpster diving with a little practice. Why do you think he uses such a tone?

3. Write about someone who does what Eighner deplores in his closing paragraphs, "invests objects with sentimental value." Let your description reveal whether or not you agree with Eighner.

Analytical Considerations

1. "On Dumpster Diving" and "The Town Dump" (NR 18) are natural companion pieces. Their structures are remarkably similar: a brief autobiographical introduction that places the writer in the setting; an extended list of the "treasures" to be found in a dump or Dumpster; and a concluding reflection on what the experience has taught the writer. These similar structures allow an opportunity for a compare-contrast discussion or writing exercise. One key difference is that Stegner recalls his dump over a forty-year gap, whereas Eighner's experience is much more recent. Another is that Eighner's essay has a kind of consumer-guide flavor, a sense that he's instructing us on how to scavenge if and when we need to. Stegner sees the poetry in refuse; Eighner does not. Instead, Eighner's matter-of-fact consumer-guide approach suggests that a Dumpster might well be in some of his readers' futures.
2. Ask students to speculate on why Eighner doesn't tell what made him homeless or what precisely made him begin raiding Dumpsters. How would mentioning the causes of his scavenging alter the essay?

Suggested Writing Assignments

1. Invent a name for something you do (as Eighner did for Dumpster diving) and describe its hazards and rewards.
2. Write three to five paragraphs (serious or humorous) defining and discussing the appropriate term for something you do, modeling them on Eighner's discussion of the proper term for his activities.
3. Eighner researched the term "Dumpster." Do your own research on a trade name or the correct term for a well-known product (examples: "boysenberry," "Polaroid Land Camera," "Oldsmobile," "Bostitch stapler," "Birds Eye" frozen foods, "shrapnel"). Explain how you went about your research as well as how you felt about what you found.

MAYA ANGELOU

Graduation

The Norton Reader, p. 32; Shorter Edition, p. 18

Maya Angelou's "Graduation," taken from the first volume of her autobiography, *I Know Why the Caged Bird Sings* (1970), focuses on a single, significant event: her graduation from eighth grade in Stamps, Arkansas, in 1940. The essay is organized chronologically. Angelou begins with the town's, her family's, and her own preparation for graduation; describes the excitement and anticipation of the event; and ends with the ceremony itself, particularly the speech of the white politician that deflates the expectations of young blacks in the audience. Chronology is a natural ordering for autobiographical narrative and, in Angelou's hands, an effective one. You might ask students to look at the "real" time and the "fictional" time in "Graduation"; the "real" time of events leading up to the ceremony is compressed in relation to the "real" time of the ceremony itself, or, conversely, the "fictional" time of the ceremony is extended with description, dialogue, and the young Angelou's own responses.

Chronological narrative is a form that students can handle well, provided they see that "real" time is malleable and in their control. This form also offers students opportunities for significant reflection on their experiences. The events of "Graduation" are told in the narrative voice that belongs to the mature Angelou looking back in 1969 at something that happened almost thirty years earlier. Like Alice Walker in "Beauty: When the Other Dancer Is the Self" (NR 68, SE 46), Angelou uses adult language but maintains the perspective of a twelve-year-old. Students may need to be reminded of events between 1940 and 1969, notably the Supreme Court's school desegregation decision of 1954 that abolished "separate but equal" black and white schools in places like Stamps. One argument against segregated education was that it disadvantaged black children. Although the mature Angelou's sense of being disadvantaged undoubtedly differs from that of the young Angelou, in "Graduation" she re-creates the sense of her young self.

Questions from the NR11

1. Presumably, all of Angelou's readers would have witnessed a graduation ceremony and brought their memories to her essay. How does she fulfill the reader's expectations for what graduation includes? How does she surprise us with details we don't expect?
2. In paragraph 43 Angelou writes that "the ancient tragedy was being replayed." What does she mean? How does her essay help to resist the tragic script?
3. Write a personal essay about an event you anticipated hopefully but that did not fulfill your expectations, incorporating an explanation of your disappointment into your account, as Angelou does.

Analytical Considerations

1. Ask students to examine the structure of "Graduation" and diagram the relation of "real" to "fictional" time. How can we measure "real" time? How can we measure "fictional" time?
2. Alternatively, ask students to examine the structure of the essay in terms of "anticipation" and "fulfillment" or "reality." How does Angelou build the readers' sense of anticipation? How does she convey the disappointment she and her fellow students felt?
3. What information does "Graduation" offer about the elementary-school education of black students in Stamps? To what extent was it vocational? To what extent were they "tracked"?

4. In paragraphs 33 through 49 Angelou recounts the speech that Edward Donleavy, a white man running for political office in Stamps, gave at her graduation ceremony. How does Angelou convey both the racist assumptions of the speech and her own better-informed sense of black history?
5. How does Angelou use the valedictory address of Henry Reed to rebut Donleavy's speech and to convey her own determination to be "a proud member of the wonderful, beautiful Negro race" (paragraph 61)?

Suggested Writing Assignments

1. Write a retrospective account of an important event that occurred when you were young. Use adult language but maintain the perspective of a child; manipulate "real" and "fictional" time.
2. Using the content of Angelou's narrative to illustrate and support your points, write an argumentative essay against tracking students who are different by virtue of race, gender, ethnicity, or national origin.

ZORA NEALE HURSTON

How It Feels to Be Colored me

The Norton Reader, p. 41

For many years Hurston was regarded by members of the African American literary community as someone whose works could not be taken seriously or even discussed. (And of course during that time she, like the vast majority of African American writers, was completely ignored by most white readers and critics.) In the past two decades Hurston's works have been revived, her biography written, and her status as a major American writer achieved. This essay provides an interesting insight into the ups and downs of Hurston's changing reputation. Perhaps she plays with the stereotypes too much; perhaps she makes "proper" or highly political people in the black community uncomfortable. At the same time, there's a spirit conveyed in the essay, a sense of life that shines as a beacon to writers so that they can feel comfortable in being different, and particularly to those proud of their African American identity. (A major force behind Hurston's revival was the African American writer Alice Walker, who became interested in Hurston's feminism and edited some of Hurston's out-of-print works.)

In paragraph 7 Hurston turns her back on the legacy of slavery—or at least claims to. In paragraph 14 she literally steps into the Harlem Renaissance, that outpouring of poetry, fiction, and music that influenced so much of both black and white America in the 1920s. Hurston is proud and defiant, exulting in the freedom she believes the times have granted her. As a black woman in 1920s America, she feels triumphant. One question for students might be, how much of this is genuine and how much is bravado, like whistling in a graveyard? It is useful to point out the extent to which Hurston's joy and anticipation are connected with place. She is happiest in Eatonville, the town of her African American family home in Florida, and in Harlem, surrounded by black Americans in a time of prosperity and the building of a genuine community. She feels most uncomfortable at Barnard, where she is overwhelmed by "the thousand white persons" (paragraph 10). (Note that Barnard is just less than a mile from Seventh Avenue and 125th Street, the center of Harlem.) A careful reading reveals that Hurston is fully aware that she can be herself only where other black Americans are free. She is quite aware of discrimination (paragraph 16) even if she says it doesn't bother her.

Questions from the NR11

1. From the beginning Hurston startles us: "I remember the very day that I became colored." Why does Hurston insist that one *becomes* colored? What happened on that day to make her so?
2. Each section of Hurston's essay explores a different possible identity, some based on skin color, others emphasizing history, culture, or gender. What does Hurston accomplish by such an approach?
3. The final paragraph introduces a key metaphor: "like a brown bag of miscellany propped against a wall." How does Hurston develop this metaphor? What does she mean by it?
4. Like other writers in "Personal Report," including Bruno Bettelheim in "A Victim" and Nancy Mairs in "On Being a Cripple," Hurston chooses a label, "colored me," to explore questions of personal identity. Compare Hurston's use of "colored" with either Bettelheim's use of "victim" or Mairs's use of "cripple."

Analytical Considerations

1. In what sense is Hurston's manifesto a product of the optimism that characterized the boom years of the 1920s? (President Hoover promised, for instance, "A chicken in every pot, two cars in every garage.")
2. Try to pin down Hurston's tone. What kind of persona does she convey in this essay? Students will need to know that she was an accomplished novelist and writer who knew very well how to achieve an effect. In other words, she was consciously aiming to present herself in a particular way. The question is, exactly what way is that?
3. How do metaphors help Hurston articulate her sense of self? See, e.g., paragraphs 10, 14, 15, 17.

Suggested Writing Assignments

1. Write an essay that connects Hurston's outlook in the 1920s with Alice Walker's in the 1980s (NR 68, SE 46) and Henry Louis Gates Jr.'s in the 1990s (NR 299). In what ways does Hurston's attitude toward race and participation in American society anticipate Walker and Gates? In what ways does she differ?
2. Walker and Gates are great admirers of Hurston and have been instrumental in reviving her reputation. Write an essay that explains what in Hurston's work might have made Gates and Walker such admirers, using their own accounts of African American life as evidence.

3. Write a Hurston-like essay, using a personal characteristic that some might view as a liability and treating it as an asset. Suggestions: short or tall, heavy or thin, from the "wrong" part of town (or the "wrong" state), Greek or independent, interested in a particular kind of art or music, or dressing in a way that stands out.

JOHN EDGAR WIDEMAN

Hoop Roots

The Norton Reader, p. 45

This essay has a complex structure that is worth identifying for your students: a narrative frame (watching playground hoop with a French woman friend) makes Wideman *imagine* explaining the phenomenon. (You might ask your students how the essay would be different if it described an actual conversation between them.) To explain playground hoop, Wideman contrasts street basketball with professional basketball. This contrast is interrupted by his friend's admiration for a particularly showy player, one who plays with the kind of ego he has just identified as typical of the NBA. The interruption leads Wideman to refine his sense of playground basketball through a reminiscence of his own youth. Discuss with your students the role that Catherine, the outside observer, plays in this essay. How does her outsider perspective (she is a white, French woman) aid Wideman's reflections? What difference does each of her differences—race, gender, nationality—make? Discuss, too, the placement of his own youthful experiences at the end of the essay: what does Wideman gain by violating chronology and deferring his most personal reflections until the end?

Much of the argument here depends on contrasts: Magic vs. Bird, playground vs. NBA, black vs. white vs. integrated, poor vs. rich, marginal vs. mainstream, showmanship vs. showboating. Yet one of the essay's strengths is that these contrasts do not all line up in a clear scheme. For instance, Wideman sees the rivalry between Magic Johnson and Larry Bird as a media invention that used racial and temperamental differences to create a false contrast between two otherwise similar players. After talking with your students about the role of these contrasts, you might want to address the larger question of Wideman's decision to break down oversimplified stereotypes through contrasts. What taboos about race and sport does it allow him to address? Are there other ways to accomplish this goal?

On several occasions, Wideman insists that pleasure is his point. Pleasure is a notoriously difficult subject to write about, but Wideman approaches it from many angles: he positively itches to get his hands on the ball in the opening section, he clearly delights in watching others play and in his own control of language, and he takes pleasure in his memories at the end. Most importantly, he wants us to see how basketball represents "outlaw pleasure" for young people, especially for many urban, black men. Discuss these approaches to the theme of pleasure with your students and ask them to think about the place of pleasure in the lives of these ball players and in their own lives. Is there a point to pleasure, or must it be an end in itself?

Questions from the NR11

1. In the opening paragraph Wideman tells his reader that he wants to explain the game of basketball to a French, female companion. In the next four paragraphs (2–5) what sorts of explanations does he imagine giving her? Why does he remain silent to her, but informative to us, his readers?
2. In paragraph 10 Wideman states that basketball is "not about race. Not about gender either," yet his subsequent discussion includes issues of race and gender. How does Wideman's discussion of Larry Bird and Magic Johnson help to explain this statement?
3. "Carnival" becomes an important event and symbol for Wideman's analysis. Explain what Carnival is and how Wideman uses it to analyze the significance of basketball.
4. What, finally, is basketball about—to Wideman personally and to African Americans more generally?
5. If you know a sport well, whether as player or spectator, discuss its significance to yourself or a specific group defined by race, gender, ethnicity, or some other relevant category.

Analytical Considerations

1. Discuss the role of race in Wideman's essay.
2. Pick a paragraph in which Wideman's shifts in diction are particularly pronounced (e.g., "His drive to the hoop . . ." or "You could call going to the hoop at the playground . . ."). Identify the different registers Wideman uses (not only levels of diction, but slang and curse words, African American vernacular English, and academic jargon), and discuss the effect of several of his transitions from one to another. Are there parallels between his style of writing and the style of basketball he admires?
3. Throughout the essay, Wideman refers to images of fences, prisons, and jail cells. Make a list of all the occurrences of such imagery of containment and confinement, and discuss the negative and positive connotations. What is at stake in the implicit comparison between the playground and a jail cell? How does that change when he compares it to the "pleasure dome" of the womb?

Suggested Writing Assignments

1. Wideman writes that "playground hoop is not about race," though his essay is very conscious of and interested in race. Defend or challenge his statement with reference to his essay and your own experience.
2. Rewrite the scene of watching playground hoop from Catherine's point of view.
3. Consider a group activity that you enjoy, and write an essay in which you analyze its symbolic importance to you individually and to a social group you belong to (racial, ethnic, religious, national, or other).

BRUNO BETTELHEIM

A Victim

The Norton Reader, p. 56

"A Victim" is an excerpt from Bruno Bettelheim's account of his experience in a German concentration camp during World War II, *The Informed Heart: Autonomy in a Mass Age* (1960). It is, explicitly, a flashback: Bettelheim, a psychologist, recollects an event that occurred more than twenty years earlier. Although recent biographers have challenged the facticity of Bettelheim's memories and some have even accused Bettelheim of inventing episodes of personal heroism, his writing nevertheless provides an excellent model for presenting personal experience and meditating on its significance. Students should notice that Bettelheim uses the event at the clinic to illustrate a point about relations between victims and their persecutors, and that he adopts a structure of point, illustration, and elaborated point. His narrative thus functions as both illustration and demonstration.

The excerpt is brief. Yet Bettelheim narrates the event at the clinic with enough density and specificity to win our assent, to convince us that, yes, it could indeed happen this way. He does not re-create the event with the intricate detail of other authors in this section who shape events for thematic and emotional resonance, but neither does he reduce it to "mere" illustration. Students need to see what Bettelheim does as relevant to their writing, to ask (of themselves) what is enough and what is too much in the re-creation of personal experience. Bettelheim's narrative engages us in its own right above and beyond the uses to which he puts it, and it is successful because it is well narrated.

Analytical Considerations

1. Ask students to consider Bettelheim's three-part structure of point, illustration, and elaborated point; also point out his simpler two-part structures of point-illustration and illustration-point. How does his announcing his point in advance of the illustration change our reading of it? How would we read the illustration if he withheld his point until later? How does the illustration permit and/or require him to elaborate (or qualify) his point?
2. Have students look at "A Victim" in connection with Maya Angelou's "Graduation" (NR 32, SE 18) or Alice Walker's "Beauty: When the Other Dancer Is the Self" (NR 68, SE 46). Two points of comparison might be made: first, between narrative as exploration and narrative as illustration; and second, between flashbacks from adulthood to childhood (Angelou) and from adulthood to adulthood (Bettelheim).
3. Bettelheim begins "A Victim" by making a large generalization about victims and persecutors. Can his illustration bear the weight of demonstrating it? Or does he, in his elaborated point, qualify his generalization? How can an individual case, or individual cases, demonstrate a generalization?

Suggested Writing Assignments

1. Write an essay using Bettelheim's three-part structure of point, illustration, and elaborated point. Take an experience and present it as an illustration and, insofar as possible, a demonstration of some larger point.
2. Write two variations on the same event, using Bettelheim's two-part structures: one of illustration followed by point, the other of point followed by illustration. Then write a paragraph commenting on the two structures and whether you shaped your illustration differently in each variation. (First drafts of these essays might profit from being discussed in small groups.)

NANCY MAIRS

On Being a Cripple

The Norton Reader, p. 58; Shorter Edition, p. 36

Mairs has written extensively about disability, using her own experience as a starting point. This essay directly confronts her multiple sclerosis, beginning with a comic reflection on the relation of writing and disability. Thinking about writing the essay makes her lose track of her disability, yet forgetting causes an accident that makes her think again about writing. There's a wry message here: writing may make one a more acute observer, but it can make one lose sight of the real situation as well. (There's a story about the Greek astronomer Thales who was so busy looking at the stars that he lost track of his way and fell into a ditch.) You may want to use this essay not only to discuss how people come to terms with disabilities (or fail to) but also how writing helps us understand the predicaments we find ourselves in, the experiences we must live through, and the pasts we carry with us.

Questions from the NR11

1. How does Mairs organize her essay? What connects the different parts to each other?
2. What stereotypes of "disabled" people does Mairs expect us to believe in? How does she set out to counter them?
3. Mairs deliberately chooses to call herself a "cripple." Select a person or group that deliberately chooses its own name or description and explain the rationale behind the choice.

Analytical Considerations

1. Why is Mairs so concerned with terminology? Discuss the importance of naming or identifying with a specific term.

2. In the 1990s many people or groups willingly accepted terms that in earlier decades might have incensed them. Mairs calls herself "cripple"; Gates titles his book *Colored People*; Eighner invents "Dumpster diving." Back in the 1920s Hurston playfully dealt with "Colored Me." Gays speak of "Queer theory." What do these acts of appropriation suggest? What is gained in taking a term once used in derision and proudly accepting or claiming it?

Suggested Writing Assignments

1. Use a collegiate dictionary to examine the differences among words like "cripple," "handicapped," and "disabled." Then have students ask three or four people what the terms mean to them. Ask students to use the results of their reading and the survey to write an essay about the nuances of such words.
2. Compare Mairs's attitude toward her impairment and Eighner's attitude toward Dumpster diving. Write an essay in which you discuss the ways their essays and attitudes are alike.

ALICE WALKER

Beauty: When the Other Dancer Is the Self

The Norton Reader, p. 68; Shorter Edition, p. 46

Walker writes about a wound she received in her eye when she was a child and its effect on her subsequent life. She chooses to write in the present, providing glimpses of separate moments from her life: before the accident, the years spent with a disfiguring white spot on her eye, after the spot was surgically removed. The perspective is extremely close up. We never see Walker's affliction in any way but through her understanding of it. In a sense this approach mimics Walker's actual attitude: she cannot get out of her own feelings, her own "take" on her wound. When her mother tells her that there was no difference in her behavior before or after the accident, she is shocked. For years what Walker thought of as the central event in her life—the "accident"—has made little impression on those closest to her.

The essay exists in a world where readers are expected to know certain words of wisdom: "Beauty is in the eye of the beholder" and "How can we know the dancer from the dance?" Significantly, it ends with Walker's persona dancing to the music of a blind musician, Stevie Wonder, and embracing "another bright-faced dancer"—herself. You might introduce these sayings in the course of discussion and ask students how Walker both illustrates and challenges them.

Questions from the NR11

1. Throughout her essay, Walker refers to the "accident." Why does she put the word in quotation marks? Has Walker made her peace with the "accident" and its consequences?

2. Walker writes her essay by selecting particular moments in her life. What does each moment show? How do these moments relate to Walker's theme?
3. What is the effect of ending the essay by recounting a dream? How does the dream relate to the essay's title?
4. Write an essay comparing and contrasting Walker's essay and Mairs's "On Being a Cripple." Consider especially their responses to injury or illness and their attitudes toward those subjects.

Analytical Considerations

1. What is the effect of using the present tense throughout?
2. How do the white spaces help shape our reading of the essay?
3. This essay is about Walker "making peace" with the accident. To what extent is it also about making peace with other things? Is the accident some kind of metaphor, or by calling it one, do we diminish the impact it had on her life?

Suggested Writing Assignments

1. Take an event that helped shape your life, a "defining moment," and tell about it and its influence as a series of moments narrated in the present tense.
2. Read Annie Dillard's "Sight into Insight" (NR 1180, SE 700) in connection with Walker's essay, and then write an essay of your own that addresses the way these two writers use different meanings of the word "see." You'll probably find yourself expanding on their notions, explaining what they're getting at, or agreeing or disagreeing with them.

LOREN EISELEY

The Brown Wasps

The Norton Reader, p. 74

Eiseley was an anthropologist, a historian of science, a nature writer, and a poet. "The Brown Wasps" gestures toward nature writing in its title, and wasps, field mice, and pigeons, along with human beings, appear in it. What humans share with such animals is a profound attachment to place. Eiseley develops "The Brown Wasps" by association of a particular sort—namely, analogy. By the time students have read the central vignettes—the field mouse, or mice, who burrowed in his flowerpot; the pigeons who hovered about the steelwork of the old El; and the man himself, who traveled two thousand miles to find the tree he and his father had planted—they should grasp how analogy links them.

The first section may seem somewhat puzzling: is Eiseley writing about the old men in the railroad station for whom the wasps are a metaphor or about the particular wasps for whom the old men are a metaphor? Neither, it turns out, but both. Humans and animals are related by their attachment to place and the support and consolation it affords them.

Eiseley's recourse to analogy leaves the meanings of "The Brown Wasps" to some extent open. Does analogy level humans and animals or open up differences between them? More specifically, does the analogy between the old men in the station and the brown wasps diminish the pathos of the humans or bestow pathos on the wasps? Is Eiseley's return to home as instinctive as that of the (faintly comic) mice digging in his flowerpot and the pigeons circling the deserted El? Or is it less instinctive than the return of the (somewhat pathetic) mice and pigeons because he understands what has happened in ways that they do not? Or is it both? Students, often impatient with ambiguity, may see some virtue in this essay of Eiseley's having it both ways.

Questions from the NR11

1. Eiseley writes of old men in train stations, brown wasps, a field mouse, pigeons near the El, and his own return to his boyhood home in Nebraska. What do these all have in common? State what you believe to be the essay's theme.
2. Some psychologists study animal behavior in order to learn about human behavior, but others write about animals in a very different fashion. Do you think that Eiseley's way of relating the behavior of animals to human behavior makes sense?
3. From close observation of an animal's behavior, write two brief descriptions, one using animal-human comparisons and one simply sticking to what you see.

Analytical Considerations

1. Students should take some time to analyze Eiseley's keen observations and his power to render what he sees in words. You might divide up the essay according to what Eiseley observes and have groups of students work on its various sections and report on them.
2. Ask students to assess anthropomorphic elements in the language that Eiseley uses to describe wasps, field mice, and pigeons. And the reverse: have them assess the language of animal observation that he uses to describe humans.
3. How are we to understand the sentence in Eiseley's final paragraph: "I spoke for myself, one field mouse, and several pigeons"?

Suggested Writing Assignments

1. On the basis of your observation of a particular animal or group of animals, write an essay involving an analogy to humans. Think carefully about how you want to use the analogy: to level humans with animals, to aggrandize animals, or to keep the two in an unstable relationship.
2. Write an essay about returning to a place that has disappeared or changed.
3. Write an essay in which you amplify Eiseley's remark: "It is the place that matters, the place at the heart of things" (paragraph 7). You may rely on personal experience alone or on experience, observation, and reading.

4. Write an essay in which you consider "The Brown Wasps" in conjunction with E. B. White's "Once More to the Lake" (NR 82, SE 52) as a meditation on death and its inevitability. You may want to make this essay a formal comparison and contrast.

GARY SOTO

The Guardian Angel

The Norton Reader, p. 80

This brief essay comes from Gary Soto's autobiographical book, *A Summer Life* (1990). Soto takes up the question, often difficult for autobiographers, of the "breaks" or special opportunities that he received versus the "tough luck" or lack of opportunities others around him (in this case, his brother) seem to have had. Other ethnic writers, most notably Brent Staples in *Parallel Time* (1994), have addressed this question of different fates using deep cultural analysis. Soto addresses it in a seemingly lighthearted way, invoking the old religious notion of a guardian angel. At the same time, it is worth considering with students how this notion allows Soto to take a more serious turn in the final three paragraphs of his essay, and how it allows him to include the possibility of "providence" in an analysis of human lives.

Questions from the NR11

1. What meanings of "guardian angel" did you bring to this essay? After reading Soto's personal account, how has your understanding of a "guardian angel" been revised or redefined?
2. Soto's essay turns on two contrasts: between his brother and himself and between his younger self and his older, present self. What does Soto accomplish with his double contrasts?
3. In the final paragraph Soto states, "Now I'm uncertain." About what? How do details convey and explain his uncertainty?
4. Do you believe in "guardian angels," or do you believe in other super-natural phenomena that others may doubt? If so, write a personal narrative that illustrates the basis for your belief. Think about the ways in which Soto's tone and evidence make his narrative appealing, even to those who don't believe in guardian angels.

Analytical Considerations

1. Soto's writing is spare: he often conveys a whole experience in a single sentence, an entire lifetime in a single paragraph. For contrast, ask students to compare a segment of Soto's essay, e.g., paragraphs 4–6, with a segment of Alice Walker's "Beauty: When the Other Dancer Is the Self" (NR 68, SE 46), e.g., paragraphs 8–14. What different effects do these writers achieve? How do their choices of details contribute to the effects?

2. How do writers' beliefs, whether political, philosophical, or religious, inform their writing? You might ask students to speculate about Soto's religious beliefs (he was raised in a Roman Catholic Chicano community in Fresno, California) and about how they inform his presentation and analysis. This topic is a complicated one, but important to students who hold firm beliefs but have difficulty expressing them in effective ways.

Suggested Writing Assignments

1. Write an essay in which you compare your experience—whether at home, in school, with friends, during a summer vacation, or in some other specific way—with that of a sibling or another family member, making it clear how you account for your different experiences.
2. Did Alice Walker have, in Soto's terms, a "guardian angel"? After reading her essay, "Beauty: When the Other Dancer Is the Self," explain why you think so, or why not.

E. B. WHITE

Once More to the Lake

The Norton Reader, p. 82; Shorter Edition, p. 52

"Once More to the Lake" is a classic essay on revisiting the past. With his son, E. B. White revisits the lake where he went as a child, and his account, by shifting between present and past, measures the passage of time. Generations blur: as White sees his younger self in his son, so he sees his father in his present self. The final sentence—"As he [White's son] buckled the swollen belt, suddenly my groin felt the chill of death"—may startle readers at first, but on reflection we realize that White prepares us for it. His narrative spans a natural cycle of life passing from one generation to the next; his rendering of natural landscape and pleasurable activity keeps the somber potential meanings of the cycle in the background until, at the very end, he foregrounds them.

In "Once More to the Lake" White combines particular and composite narrative. The particular narrative takes place in the present: White and his son return to the lake on a single occasion. The composite narrative takes place in the past: White recollects repeated episodes from the Augusts he vacationed at the lake. He moves easily but clearly back and forth in time. You might have students notice the shifts in the first paragraph: "One summer, along about 1904," "summer after summer," "A few weeks ago." These references mark transitions fluently, without emphatic breaks. You might ask students to continue to note how White marks them.

Questions from the NR11

1. What has guided White in his selection of the details he gives about the trip? Why, for example, does he talk about the road, the dragonfly, the boat's motor?
2. White speaks of the lake as a "holy spot." What about it was holy?
3. White's last sentence often surprises first-time readers. Go back through the essay and pick out sections or words or phrases that seem to prepare for the ending.
4. Write about revisiting a place that has a special meaning for you.

Analytical Considerations

1. How important is White's son to "Once More to the Lake"? How does his presence heighten the passage of time and the theme of mortality? Ask students to imagine the essay without him.
2. Comparison is an important device in this essay, as White again and again balances details from the past against details from the present. Sometimes things change, sometimes they don't. You might ask students which comparisons they remember and then ask them to reread the essay looking for additional ones.
3. Discuss what White reveals about himself (or his "persona," his created self) in "Once More to the Lake." Ask what in the text enables us to construct an image of the author.
4. "Once More to the Lake" reveals familiar aspects of E. B. White—see also "Progress and Change" (NR 562) and "Democracy" (NR 884, SE 520). Yet it differs from these other essays as well. You might ask students how they differ and whether they differ in expected or unexpected ways? How are the differences evidence of White's range and flexibility?

Suggested Writing Assignments

1. Write an essay about revisiting a place you cherished as a child. Where does "change" lie? In the place? In yourself? Did the experience lead you to sober reflection on big issues? If so, structure your essay so that you can include reflection as well as narrative and description.
2. Write an essay in which you move retrospectively from the present to the past, drawing specific comparisons between them. Make your thematic emphasis that of loss through the passage of time.

JOAN DIDION

On Keeping a Notebook

The Norton Reader, p. 90

Joan Didion is best known for her nonfiction reportage of contemporary cultural and political trends and for her novels *Play It as It Lays* (1971), *A Book of Common Prayer* (1977), and *Democracy* (1984). "On Keeping a Notebook," one of the most personal of Didion's essays, reflects on the relation of fact and fiction in personal life.

This essay provides either a provocative beginning to a unit on journal writing or a useful interlude to students' own writing of journals. "Why did I write it down?" Didion asks in paragraph 4 of the essay—and that question might provoke a discussion about why people keep diaries, journals, and personal notebooks. Perhaps even before students read Didion's essay, you might ask if they have ever kept a journal and what they hoped to gain (or if not, why they did not). Their initial answers might be compared with Didion's, whether to confirm their practices as writers or to offer possibilities for kinds of journal writing they haven't considered before.

If you use this essay as an interlude, you might want to discuss some of Didion's detailed reflections on her "facts" to show students how to analyze their own experiences. (Paragraphs 4 to 5 and 16 to 17 are useful on this score.) If you read the essay as a conclusion to a unit on journal writing, you might ask whether Didion accounts for all of the kinds of journals represented in this section. Didion concentrates, for example, on the personal and professional values of keeping a notebook: on persons afflicted with a sense of loss who for psychological reasons need to write things down, and on professionals who keep a writer's notebook for future use in constructing stories. She does not consider journals like Dorothy Wordsworth's, written to record facts of natural history, or commonplace books like Henry David Thoreau's, kept to record his own and others' words of wisdom.

Questions from the NR11

1. What distinction does Didion make between a diary and a notebook? What uses does a notebook have for Didion?
2. Didion says she uses her notebook to "tell what some would call lies" (paragraph 7). Why does she do this? Would some people call these things truths? Why?

3. Didion says, "*How it felt to me*: that is getting closer to the truth about a notebook." What writing strategies does she use to convey "how it felt"?
4. Try keeping a notebook for a week, jotting down the sort of things that Didion does. At the end of the week, take one or two of your entries and expand on them, as Didion does with the entries on Mrs. Minnie S. Brooks and Mrs. Lou Fox.

Analytical Considerations

1. This essay is loosely structured: it begins with an incident once recorded in a notebook now recalled and reflected on, followed by two sections on the motives for keeping a notebook. Ask students about the purpose of each section and what they think is the "heart" of each.
2. At what point does the reader realize that the woman in the plaid dress is Didion herself? Why does Didion describe herself in the third person? How does this objective form of description, used in her notebook, help Didion understand herself and her situation?
3. Didion is a master of observing and analyzing details. Ask students what details they remember best from the essay, why they remember them, and what purpose these details serve. The discussion might usefully connect with the students' own writing and their use of details.
4. In an essay titled "Why I Write" Joan Didion has noted: "I write entirely to find out what I'm thinking, what I'm looking at, what I see and what it means." In the same essay she reveals that for her "certain images shimmer" and that these images determine the "arrangement of words." Apply these comments to "On Keeping a Notebook" as well as to "On Going Home" (NR 9, SE 9).

Suggested Writing Assignments

1. Choose one of the journals in this section as a model for your own writing, and during the next week or two keep a journal in a similar style and form.
2. Choose an incident or a detail from a journal you have kept and expand it into a short story or nonfictional narrative. (Alternatively, let someone else read your journal and select the incident.) What extra details does such an expansion require?
3. Keep a notebook for a week or so; carry it with you and record whatever you like. At the end of the week review it, then write an analysis and commentary on your notebook. Do you share the same interests and motives in writing as Didion?
4. Write an essay in response to Didion's observation: "We are well advised to keep on nodding terms with the people we used to be whether we find them attractive company or not" (paragraph 16).

DOROTHY WORDSWORTH

The Alfoxden Journal 1798

The Norton Reader, p. 96; Shorter Edition, p. 352

Dorothy Wordsworth, sister of the poet William, kept a journal on and off for thirty years, from 1798 to 1828. Readers turn to Dorothy Wordsworth's journals for many reasons. Her first readers, her brother William and their friend Samuel Taylor Coleridge, turned to them for source material for their poems; scholars still find value in comparing Dorothy's accounts with those in William Wordsworth's and Coleridge's poetry. Some readers have argued that these journals, never intended for publication, exemplify a kind of purely un-self-conscious female (even feminine) writing, in contrast to the self-advertisements of Wordsworth and Coleridge or of their contemporary, the feminist Mary Wollstonecraft (author of A *Vindication of the Rights of Women* [NR 559, SE 337]). (Virginia Woolf's essay on the two women in *The Second Common Reader* [1932] makes this comparison.)

As these excerpts reveal, however, Dorothy Wordsworth's journals are worth studying in their own right. Her precise observation of plants, animals, people, and places make them a superb record of life in a small Somerset town in the late eighteenth century and an excellent model for any aspiring writer of natural history. In teaching these selections, you might want to assign each student a particular plant or animal to research and present to the class—e.g., the purple-starred hepatica and the snowdrop (January 20), the lark and the redbreast (January 31)—so that they gain a sense of what Wordsworth actually saw and how she recorded its features. You might also ask each student to keep a nature journal for a few days, whether in the mode of this one or May Sarton's (NR 107) or Henry David Thoreau's (NR 102). Even city dwellers can chart the changing course of the weather or the activities of birds and other animals.

The challenge in discussing this journal—and even more in keeping a nature journal—will lie in getting students to tie their impressions to specific textual moments. As the sky figures often in the entries, you might ask them to list every descriptive phrase for the sky in these selections and then to notice whether Wordsworth relies primarily on nouns, verbs, or adjectives, on similes or metaphors, for her descriptions. You might also ask them each to find a favorite phrase and explain to the class why it appeals to them.

Questions from the NR11

1. While living in the village of Alfoxden, Somerset, with her brother William, Dorothy Wordsworth kept a naturalist's journal. What aspects of nature does she record? Which seem most to interest or intrigue her?
2. In her *Journal of a Solitude* May Sarton also records aspects of nature. Compare her entries—and their uses—with Wordsworth's.

3. Keep your own naturalist's journal for a week or two, recording natural phenomena and describing the natural world around you, as Wordsworth did.

Analytical Considerations

1. Dorothy Wordsworth seldom mentions herself and rarely tells an anecdote with any explicit emotional content. What kind of person does she seem to have been? What clues in her reading lead you to that conclusion? What does her journal tell us about her?
2. Dorothy Wordsworth observes precisely—so much so that her brother could draw on her journals for his nature poetry. Ask students to analyze descriptions of plants, animals, and the weather—for example, the purple-starred hepatica and the snowdrop (January 20), the clouds at night (January 25), the lark and the redbreast (January 31)—to get a sense of how to rely on precise nouns and adjectives rather than flowery adverbs.
3. Many of the entries here begin with striking phrases. Have students choose one such opening and then, with their texts closed, write an entry to follow that opening. Share the results, comparing what they did to Wordsworth's original. What does the exercise tell you about Wordsworth's writing?
4. People appear infrequently in these entries, but when they do, they convey a sense of symbiosis between humankind and nature. Ask students to look at various entries where people appear (especially February 4) and explain how people fit into the natural landscape.

Suggested Writing Assignments

1. Choose an entry that particularly strikes you. Write a short essay analyzing Wordsworth's language. What writerly choices does she make that impress, move, or intrigue you?
2. Compare Dorothy Wordsworth's descriptions of nature with those of another nature writer, concentrating on what they describe, what words they choose, and what overall impression they convey. Some suggestions include Mary Austin, "The Land of Little Rain" (p. 186), Gretel Ehrlich, "Spring" (p. 575), or Edward Abbey, "The Serpents of Paradise" (p. 589).
3. Find a biography of Dorothy Wordsworth, her brother William, or of Coleridge. What was going on in their lives in January of 1798? Analyze the journal in light of this biographical information.
4. Read Wordsworth's "The Ruined Cottage," paying special attention to lines 330–36, or Coleridge's "The Rime of the Ancient Mariner," paying special attention to line 184. Find the parallel passage in Dorothy's journal. Write an essay in which you compare one of the poems to the corresponding journal entry.
5. Keep a journal of the natural world for a week. Leave your life out of it. Be sure to describe the same environment, as Dorothy Wordsworth does, in at least two different weathers or at two times of day. At the end of the week, write a brief essay in which you describe what was going on in your life that week. Discuss whether your descriptions of the natural world offer clues to the events in your life.

RALPH WALDO EMERSON

From Journals

The Norton Reader, p. 99

and

HENRY DAVID THOREAU

From Journal

The Norton Reader, p. 102

Emerson, one of America's most influential essayists, started a journal at age sixteen and kept it for over fifty years. Thoreau, his neighbor in Concord, Massachusetts, and an equally influential essayist, kept a journal for twenty-five years, from his late teens until his death at age forty-five. These entries represent what Didion calls in "On Keeping a Notebook" (NR 90), "a series of graceful pensées." More generally, the journals of Emerson and Thoreau could be called "commonplace books"—that is, collections of quotations and maxims from other authors along with their own original, memorable sayings and observations. Before or after students read the selections, you might discuss the motivations for collecting maxims and memorable sayings, and you might also discuss what makes a maxim or saying memorable.

Questions from the NR11

1. Thoreau writes that "Nothing goes by luck in composition. . . . The best you can write will be the best you are." In what sense are his journal entries examples of this belief?
2. Both Thoreau and Emerson write journal entries on the subject of education, both using metaphorical language. Compare their beliefs on education, in part by comparing the metaphors they use.
3. Choose one journal entry from either Emerson or Thoreau and write an essay by expanding, amplifying, or showing exceptions to it.

Analytical Considerations

1. These selections are not narratives of the sort one finds in other journals in this section, but rather pithy maxims, observations, and reflections. Ask students to describe an entry they recall well and then, in small groups or together as a class, analyze its language. More often than not, the parallel construction or metaphorical language has contributed to its memorability.
2. Both Emerson and Thoreau comment on similar topics: religion, education, truth, ethics. Ask students to compare these writers' beliefs on one or more such topics. Does the highly metaphorical language create distinctions between the writers or suggest similarities in their views?

3. If you have taught any selections from "Morals and Maxims," you might ask which of the entries are maxims and what other kinds of entries Emerson and Thoreau include. Emerson, for example, reflects on personal experience (as in the 1835 entry) and on his reading (as in the 1841 entries). Thoreau often writes definitions (as in the 1850 and 1859 definitions of education).

Suggested Writing Assignments

1. Keep a commonplace book for a week or two in which you record witty or wise sayings, your reflections on your reading, and your own, original maxims.
2. Choose two entries, one from each writer, that seem to address the same topic: education, friendship, good writing, etc. By closely analyzing the language and content of each entry, write a brief essay that compares and contrasts the writers' views on the topic.

WALT WHITMAN

Abraham Lincoln

The Norton Reader, p. 104

Whitman, the American poet who wrote *Leaves of Grass* (first ed., 1855), was also a journalist for much of his life. *Specimen Days* (1882), from which these entries derive, consists partly of diary material and partly of newspaper articles that Whitman wrote during the 1860s and 1870s. We can see the traces of the journalist's reportage in some of the entries—as, for example, in the opening sentence for April 16, 1865, where Whitman lets us know that he is copying from his notes.

In these four entries, Whitman observes and reflects on President Abraham Lincoln, first on his actions (1863), then on his death and his character (1865). As a form, the entries represent an important kind of journal writing that observes historical persons, facts, and events as they happen. You might ask students what value such immediate, red-hot records of the moment have over other kinds of history that re-create events.

Questions from the NR11

1. The first entries in Whitman's journal record his personal observances of Abraham Lincoln. Which details best give a sense of the president? Why?
2. The last entries in Whitman's journal give an assessment of Lincoln's character. How are these entries different from the first ones?
3. If you have an opportunity to observe a public figure up close, write a journal entry like the first of Whitman's, perhaps followed by an entry that reflects on the person's character.

Analytical Considerations

1. Before students read this selection or, alternatively, before you analyze it in class, you might ask what facts they know and what impressions they have of Abraham Lincoln. Then ask students to consider how Whitman either confirms or corrects such impressions, and how a public journal like his might be intended, almost by definition, to confirm impressions or set the record straight.

2. Questions 1 and 2 from NR11 (reprinted above) are meant to help students distinguish between journal entries that record and those that reflect. Although this distinction may ultimately break down, you might help clarify the difference by comparing specific sentences in the entry for August 12 with the entry for April 16, 1865. For example, the sentence on p. 104 describing Lincoln's appearance as he rides might be contrasted with the sentence on p. 106 beginning, "The tragic splendor of his death. . . ." What different versions of the president do these descriptions suggest? How does the language contribute to the differences?

3. Read Whitman's portrait of Lincoln in connection with Hawthorne's portrait of Lincoln (NR 119) and compare their accounts.

Suggested Writing Assignments

1. In the library, find another biography of Lincoln or an account of his presidency. Compare Whitman's impressions of Lincoln with the second author's description.

2. Find a portrait or photograph of Abraham Lincoln and describe the character of the man the portrait suggests. Do you think Whitman is right to suggest that "the current portraits are all failures—most of them caricatures"?

MAY SARTON

From Journal of a Solitude

The Norton Reader, p. 107

As one learns from this selection, May Sarton was a poet, novelist, and journal writer. During her eighty years, she wrote more than thirty volumes of poetry and fiction, plus a dozen volumes of nonfiction, most autobiographical. She began *Journal of a Solitude* just before she turned sixty, in part as an assessment of her life thus far, in part as an exercise in understanding and approaching the solitude of death. As she puts it in the entry for January 7, "I am proud of being fifty-eight, and still alive and kicking, in love, more creative, balanced, and potent than I have ever been" (paragraph 27).

This journal is a classic of modern spiritual introspection, a successor to the spiritual diaries of the Puritans and the journals of Transcendentalists like Emerson and Thoreau. Yet students may have difficulty "getting into" its ideas and concerns. To help them approach Sarton, you might begin by asking them what they hope to be like when they are old, what values they expect to have, and what issues they expect to confront. Such a discussion might provide an entrée not only into Sarton's journal but also into the uses of journal writing itself, especially the mode of the spiritual diary.

Analytical Considerations

1. Is there a pattern to Sarton's journal—or to these journal entries? Do we expect to find a pattern within a journal, as we do in a novel or autobiography? During the course of the year, Sarton moves from depression and despair to a reaffirmation of her life, yet it is worth discussing whether diaries and journals necessarily have such a pattern, whether positive or negative.
2. Throughout the journal, Sarton discusses her poetry and prose. Ask students to compare and contrast her views on these two genres: when she writes each, why she writes, and what values she attaches to them.
3. What function do friends serve during Sarton's solitude and in her record of it in her journal? Perhaps in small groups students might discuss the four friends mentioned in the entries: Perley Cole (paragraph 3), Arnold Miner (paragraph 9), Anne Woodson (paragraph 12), and Laurie Armstrong and others (paragraph 21). Does the unnamed neighbor (paragraph 27) serve a different function?

Suggested Writing Assignments

1. Choose one entry in which Sarton makes statements with which you disagree, and write your own account of an experience that explains why you have a different point of view.
2. Is May Sarton the kind of journal writer Joan Didion describes in "On Keeping a Notebook" (NR 90)? Using paragraph 4 of Didion's essay, write a brief analysis of Sarton's motives as a journal writer as they do or do not fit with Didion's description.

WOODY ALLEN

Selections from the Allen Notebooks

The Norton Reader, p. 113

Woody Allen's "Notebooks" are a parody of the journal form, as we can tell from his prefatory note to the text: "Following are excerpts from the hitherto secret, private journal of Woody Allen, which will be published posthumously or after his death, whichever comes first." Because they are parodic, the entries provide a humorous means of understanding the journal as a form: what writers tend to include in their journals, and why this might seem absurd or pretentious to an outside reader.

One way to conclude a unit on journals might be to ask each student to choose a favorite entry from Allen's "Notebooks," analyze what makes it funny and what kind of journal writing it parodies, and compare it with a serious version of the same kind of entry. Particularly good for such a discussion are entries that begin with a serious philosophical question, such as "Do I believe in God?" or "Should I marry W.?" or "What is it about death that bothers me so much?" These allow students to see how parody works by disappointing the reader's expectations and deflating the classic form. You might then want to consider what makes the classic form of the journal successful.

Questions from the NR11

1. Allen's "notebooks" are humorous parodies of various kinds of journals: the writer's notebook, the commonplace book, the personal diary, the religious or philosophical journal of meditation. Choose two or three entries you especially like and explain how the parody works.
2. Are Allen's notebook entries meant simply to be humorous, or do they have serious intentions? Argue your case using examples.
3. Write a parody of a serious journal included in this section. Share your parody with a small group or the entire class, and ask others to share theirs. Why do some parodies seem funny, while others fall flat? How fully must a writer understand the original form in order to write a parody?

Analytical Considerations

1. Analyze several of the entries to show how parody works by means of raising expectations and then deflating them. Then consider what changes might make the entry into a serious reflection, whether on God, death, love, or marriage.
2. Discuss the entries in which Allen parodies the notebook of creative writers. What attitudes or conceptions of the writer does Allen poke fun at?

Suggested Writing Assignments

1. Reuse the beginning sentence of an entry from Woody Allen's "Notebooks," but write a serious reflection on the topic.
2. Take a serious entry from the journal of another writer included in this section, and try instead to write a humorous entry as Woody Allen does. What are the difficulties in writing parody?

PEOPLE, PLACES

THOMAS JEFFERSON

George Washington

The Norton Reader, p. 116

The opening selections in "People, Places" give students a chance to read about famous men and to think about how one writes a character sketch or biographical portrait from a position of knowledge but not intimacy (an intimacy Virginia Woolf has, for example, in writing "My Father: Leslie Stephen," NR 136). Jefferson knew Washington quite well; indeed, he sums up their acquaintance in the last paragraph when he explains how they worked together in the Virginia legislature before and during the Revolutionary War and later when he served as secretary of state during Washington's presidency. Yet his account of Washington does not include personal anecdotes or familiar details. Instead, it is a "character sketch"—that is, an account of the physical, mental, and moral qualities that distinguish George Washington as a man.

You might want to recall that Jefferson wrote this account for a historian who wanted to gather firsthand information and know more about Washington's role in the Federalist-Republican controversy. You might also want students to know that, when Jefferson uses the word "character" in the first sentence, the term carries the older sense of "integrity," the moral and ethical qualities that a person possesses.

Questions from the NR11

1. What, in Jefferson's view, are Washington's outstanding virtues? What are Washington's greatest defects? From what he writes about Washington, can you infer those qualities of character that Jefferson most admires?
2. Do we learn anything from Jefferson's portrait about what Washington looked like? About his family life? About his hobbies? About his religion? If not, are these important omissions in the characterization of a person in public life?
3. Write in the manner of Jefferson a characterization of an important figure in public life today. Consider whether this manner enables you to present what you think is essential truth and whether the attempt brings to light any special problems concerning either the task itself or public life today.

Analytical Considerations

1. Before discussing Jefferson's portrait, you might ask students what they know about Washington and what qualities they associate with his character. What predictable details did they find in the portrait? What surprised them—either because it was a fact they hadn't encountered before or because they were surprised that Jefferson would mention it?

2. Look closely at the order in which Jefferson presents the details in paragraph 2: he moves from mental qualities and defects, to moral and ethical qualities, to physical features. Why might he have chosen this order?
3. Most modern writers would have broken paragraph 2 in the middle, after the description of Washington on horseback and before the account of Washington's behavior in private versus professional life. If we treat this second half as a unit, what contrast between Washington's public and private persona does Jefferson suggest? Does this make Washington seem more or less appealing as a person?
4. Why does Jefferson include the final paragraph explaining how long and in what capacities he knew Washington? It might help to know that Jefferson wrote this account in response to an inquiry from a historian fifteen years after Washington's death and five years after he completed his own term as president of the United States.

Suggested Writing Assignments

1. Find a modern character sketch or biographical portrait of a president, preferably one written by someone who knew the man. Compare and contrast the information included and the techniques used with Jefferson's portrait of Washington.
2. Read a brief biographical account of Washington from a modern source. What are the similarities and differences between its portrait and Jefferson's, and how do you account for them?

NATHANIEL HAWTHORNE

Abraham Lincoln

The Norton Reader, p. 119

Hawthorne wrote this sketch of Lincoln during the Civil War, when he visited the president as part of a delegation from Massachusetts. He published part of it in the *Atlantic Monthly*, although not paragraphs 3 through 7 included in *The Norton Reader* (and thus not the major portion of this selection). The editor of the *Atlantic* cut these paragraphs because, as he explained in the footnote to paragraph 3, "it lacks reverence." It might be useful and interesting to focus discussion on what is appropriate to include in a character sketch of an important person like the president of the United States, how attitudes have shifted during the past one hundred years, and what we now value in our reading of biography.

Questions from the NR11

1. In his final paragraph Hawthorne seeks to prevent misunderstanding by stressing his respect for and confidence in Lincoln. Is there anything in the paragraph that runs counter to that expression? To what effect?

2. In the footnote to the third paragraph the editor of the *Atlantic Monthly* explains his omission of the following four paragraphs. On the evidence of this statement, what sort of person does the editor seem to be? Is there anything in the omitted paragraphs that would tend to justify his decision as editor? Is the full description superior to the last paragraph printed alone? Explain.

3. What is the basic pattern of the opening sentence of the fifth paragraph? Find other examples of this pattern. What is their total impact on Hawthorne's description?

4. Write a paragraph of description of someone you know, using the same pattern for the entire paragraph that you discovered in the previous question.

Analytical Considerations

1. Jefferson's description of Washington unfolds as a sketch of his subject's character. Hawthorne's portrait of Lincoln unfolds as a narrative, as a story of what happened on the day he visited the White House. What different effects do these two approaches create?

2. Hawthorne calls Lincoln "the essential representative of all Yankees" (paragraph 4). What characteristics does he associate with Yankees? Why should he present the president as a stereotype or "pattern"?

3. Jefferson writes as a former president describing another president. Hawthorne writes as a New Englander observing and describing a "Western man" (paragraph 4). At what points does Hawthorne seem to distinguish himself from Lincoln? Does he seem to consider himself superior?

4. The editor of the *Atlantic Monthly* cut paragraphs 3 through 7 of this selection. Why? In the fifty years between 1814 when Jefferson wrote and 1862 when Hawthorne wrote, might there have been a shift in the way biography was written? The editor seems to think that Hawthorne's irreverence is partly a function of his age, that he is "falling into the characteristic and most ominous fault of Young America" (footnote to paragraph 3; Hawthorne was fifty-six at the time).

5. Look up the original article in the *Atlantic Monthly*. Might there have been other reasons for cutting five paragraphs out of Hawthorne's original submission?

Suggested Writing Assignments

1. Using some of the details from Hawthorne's sketch of Lincoln, write your own brief sketch but without the irony and irreverence of the original. In other words, write a "positive," "balanced" sketch of the president.

2. Using Jefferson and Hawthorne as examples, and perhaps including Whitman's account of Lincoln (NR 104), write an essay about your criteria for good biography. Try to answer the question, What should a good biography be and do?

3. If you have access to the original version of Hawthorne's article as published in the *Atlantic Monthly*, write an argument either for or against the editor's decision to cut five paragraphs from Hawthorne's original draft.

TOM WOLFE

Yeager

The Norton Reader, p. 123

Tom Wolfe's now-famous description of Chuck Yeager, the pilot who broke the sound barrier and helped teach some of the first American astronauts, comes from chapter 3 of *The Right Stuff* (1979). In vivid, often breathtaking prose, Wolfe gives an account of a popular American hero and an analysis of what makes such a man popular, what charisma or mystique appeals to the public and makes a superman of an ordinary man. As a form of biography, "Yeager" allows students to see how a writer moves from specific details and facts to larger claims about character and historical significance. As a form of history, Wolfe's book depends on the interweaving of the personal, private lives of early test pilots with the larger public history of the American space program. It provides a good model for writing projects that ask students to connect their own or their families' experiences with some aspect of the public history of the United States or Canada.

Questions from the NR11

1. Before recounting Yeager's personal history or the story of breaking the sound barrier, Wolfe begins with the voice of an airline pilot. Why does he begin this way? What connection does the first paragraph have with the rest of the essay?
2. Wolfe interweaves Yeager's personal history with a more public, official history of the space program. Make a flowchart or diagram to show how this interweaving works.
3. Write an essay that interweaves some part of your personal history with some larger, public story.

Analytical Considerations

1. The opening three paragraphs establish interest and significance. Ask students what made them interested in Yeager and what significance Wolfe establishes by showing the influence of Yeager's voice and personal style.
2. Perhaps in small groups, ask students to chart the interweaving of Yeager's personal history and the history of the space program: paragraphs 4 to 8, Yeager; 9 to 14, space program; 15, Pancho's Fly Inn; 16 to 18, space program; 19 to 21, Yeager; 22 to 40, October 14, 1947, the day Yeager broke the sound barrier. What advantages does Wolfe gain by combining personal details with official history?
3. How does Wolfe describe places, planes, and other details unfamiliar to most readers? Ask small groups of students to choose one such detail— whether the landscape at Muroc, Muroc air base, the X-1 plane, Pancho's Fly Inn, or some other detail—and figure out Wolfe's techniques.
4. Compare Wolfe's voice as an author with the voice he creates for Yeager. Ask students how they would describe Wolfe's voice (educated, ironic, intelligent, etc.) and why they think he chooses this voice for himself.

5. How does the ending echo—in style and content—the opening? After finishing the essay, what further significance do readers discover in the opening three paragraphs?

Suggested Writing Assignments

1. Write an account of another person important to the U.S. space program, using some of Wolfe's techniques for presenting a character.
2. View the movie version of *The Right Stuff* and write an account of how the movie adapts or uses Wolfe's account of Yeager's life and character.
3. Explain how some part of your personal history relates to or is an example of some larger, public story.

TONI MORRISON

Strangers

The Norton Reader, p. 132; Shorter Edition, p. 74

This essay serves as an introduction for a book of photographs by Robert Bergman, his first publication. It seems to work by indirection, and students can make some useful comparisons between it and the Updike pieces on art (NR 1085, 1087; SE 645, 647). The two writers take very different approaches: Updike, like Morrison, begins with personal recollection, but then proceeds to describe his objects in minute, impressionistic detail, relating them to his own history, not the history of art or their cultures. Morrison, on the other hand, tells a story that illustrates her point about others—one that will be familiar to readers of Morrison's novels and essays. The Other is always a key issue for her, and it appears here in two forms—the old woman she "meets" at the outset and these portraits, which she saves until the very end of her introduction.

Students might note the differences in outlook represented by these two ways of proceeding. Updike confidently relates the details of the art to his own musings, while Morrison is totally reticent about the photographs' details and technical qualities, but totally absorbing about what the encounter with them *means* to her. She doesn't write of the encounter with Bergman's people but with a person she may or may not have actually met and what that signifies to her. The images evoke a general mood, not accountable to any specific detail but by the overall presence of the people depicted in them. These are not static works of art demanding close inspection and commentary but images of the Other that must be met and understood.

Questions from the NR11

1. In his book, *A Kind of Rapture*, Robert Bergman included photographs of people he encountered on the streets of America. Why does Morrison not dwell on that fact?
2. In the opening paragraphs (1–3) Morrison relates a story about a woman she sees walking near her property; later in the essay she expresses regret,

even guilt, that her story "sentimentalized and appropriated" the woman (paragraphs 6–7). What does Morrison mean by this self-criticism? Do you agree that it may be ethically wrong to create stories about the strangers we see?

3. What do you see in these photographs? More than Morrison does? Different things? Can you read these images the way Updike reads paintings in "Little Lightnings" and "Moving Along" (NR 1085, 1087; SE 645, 647)?

Analytical Considerations

1. What changes in Morrison between the time she first tells the story of the woman and her next-to-last paragraph?
2. How did Morrison's initial reaction to the woman she met fit into Sartre's warning about "love as possession"?

Suggested Writing Assignments

1. In one or two sentences, explain how Bergman's portraits connect with Morrison's notion of strangers.
2. How would you describe common features of these Bergman photographs? What generalizations might you make based on this small sample?

VIRGINIA WOOLF

My Father: Leslie Stephen

The Norton Reader, p. 136

Virginia Woolf, one of the finest novelists and most sensitive literary critics of the twentieth century, was an acute reader and renderer of character. In this portrait of her father, a great scholar and essayist in his own right, Woolf brings the man to life. But we are certainly (and perhaps naturally) given a biased view of Leslie Stephen. Try as she might to leaven her praise with honest evaluation, the admiring daughter creates a glowing portrait of her father as a paragon of men. Perhaps Stephen was a paragon, a model scholar, father, and friend, but some students may feel that Woolf's portrait is a little *too* perfect. You might ask them to compare it with other portraits of family members in this section — say Annie Dillard's of her mother or Judith Ortiz Cofer's of her grandmother — to discuss the different purposes of these essays and to suggest how different purposes may lead writers to alternate approaches to biography.

Questions from the NR11

1. Would you like to have been Leslie Stephen's son or daughter? Why or why not?
2. Giving praise can be a difficult rhetorical and social undertaking. How does Woolf avoid the pitfalls or try to?

3. In some of her other work, Woolf shows a deep and sensitive concern for women's experience and awareness. Do you find a feminist awareness here? In what way?
4. Write a sketch about a father, real or fictional, adopting a tone similar to Woolf's in this sketch.

Analytical Considerations

1. As a class or in small groups, examine the essay for clues to Woolf's purpose in writing "My Father: Leslie Stephen." Direct attention to the original context of the essay—that of Woolf, the devoted daughter, writing her recollections for a general readership. In addition to Woolf's public purposes in writing, you might raise the idea that Woolf was writing for herself as a means of understanding her relationship with her father.
2. We know the audience for the original publication of this essay consisted of readers of *The Times* of London on November 28, 1932. (Leslie Stephen died in 1904, so this essay first appeared twenty-eight years after his death.) Ask students to look for textual clues that reveal Woolf's awareness of her audience, e.g., "Even today there may be parents . . ." (paragraph 10).
3. Analyze the design of the essay. Does it use chronology as an ordering mechanism? Does it organize details around abstract qualities that are taken up one by one? Or does it use some other principle of organization? Study and label what each paragraph contributes to the development of the essay. If you have read Dillard's essay, "Terwilliger Bunts One" (NR 151, SE 69), you might compare and contrast her mode of organization with Woolf's.
4. Good description often coalesces around a dominant impression. Discuss the dominant impression Woolf creates about her father and how she creates it. Ask about specific assertions and kinds of support (anecdote, quotation, memory, etc.). Distinguish between the use and value of "objective" information (the testimony of others; Stephen's remarks) and the use and value of "subjective" material (Woolf's own memories and opinions).
5. In paragraph 4, Woolf describes her father's habit of drawing beasts on the flyleaves of his books and scribbling pungent analyses in the margins; then she notes that these "brief comments" were the "germ of the more temperate statements of his essays." This aptly illustrates the process of composition for many of us. Encourage students to see that reading offers possibilities for establishing a dialogue between writer and reader, that careful reading involves annotation. You might devote some class discussion to fostering this sense of involvement with the text.
6. Woolf reveals, perhaps unconsciously, some rather unpleasant and dislikable aspects of her father. Do such elements belong in a biographical sketch? You might recall, if you have read Nathaniel Hawthorne's account of Abraham Lincoln (NR 119), the editor's remarks on "irreverence," quoted in the footnote to paragraph 3.
7. When Woolf says of Leslie Stephen, "The things that he did not say were always there in the background" (paragraph 5) and "Too much, perhaps, has been said of his silence" (paragraph 7), she directs our attention to an oft-neglected dimension of the text: silences and absences. Ask students to reconstruct the image of Leslie Stephen based on the information Woolf leaves out of her essay.

Suggested Writing Assignments

1. Write a character sketch of a parent or grandparent. Strive for the concreteness and balance that Woolf achieves in "My Father: Leslie Stephen."
2. Read two or three other biographical sketches in this section. Compare and contrast them with Woolf's on points of subject, purpose, content, and tone.
3. How does Woolf define fatherhood in her essay? Using examples from "My Father: Leslie Stephen," write an essay on Woolf's conception of fatherhood.

SCOTT RUSSELL SANDERS

Under the Influence

The Norton Reader, p. 140; Shorter Edition, p. 58

Scott Sanders's father was not, by most standards, an exemplary person: he drank too much, and his alcoholism did permanent harm to himself, his wife, and especially his children. Yet Sanders's essay is not a melodramatic account of the dangers of alcoholism or child abuse. It is an honest reminiscence and sensitive analysis of a father and his problem, and it contains thorough, relevant research on alcoholism as a disease and "public scourge" (paragraph 8). Sanders provides an excellent model for treating a difficult biographical subject with fairness and candor. If you are also reading (or have read) Sanders's essay "Looking at Women" (NR 244, SE 147), you might want to compare and contrast his techniques in writing on a personal, but somewhat more distanced, topic with this vividly autobiographical essay in "People, Places."

Questions from the NR11

1. Sanders frequently punctuates his memories of his father with information from other sources—dictionaries, medical encyclopedias, poems and short stories, the Bible. What function do these sources perform? How do they enlarge and enrich Sanders's essay?
2. Why does Sanders include the final three paragraphs (53–55)? What effect do they create that would be lost without them?
3. Drawing on your memories of a friend or family member, write an essay about some problem that person had and its effect on your life.

Analytical Considerations

1. Using the responses to question 1 (above), chart the structure of Sanders's essay, especially his placement of external, objective sources and their relation to personal experience and memory.
2. One source that Sanders gives prominence is the New Testament story of the madman possessed by demons and the Gadarene swine. Ask students to read an original version of the story (Matthew 8, Mark 5, or Luke 8) and compare it with Sanders's retelling. What does Sanders emphasize? How

does he apply the story? How does he later echo it (paragraph 51)?

3. Why does Greeley Ray Sanders drink? Consider those moments in the essay when Sanders seems ready to give an answer. Does he—or does he resist a final explanation?

4. Ask students what parallels Sanders sees between his own life as a "workaholic" and his father's as an "alcoholic." What are the differences between father and son? Why might Sanders want to draw parallels, even though the differences are significant?

Suggested Writing Assignments

1. Write a short sketch of a friend or family member who faced a serious problem, whether it was one he or she overcame or succumbed to.

2. Is alcoholism a "public scourge," as Sanders suggests in paragraph 8? Do research on this topic and write an "objective" report on your findings.

3. Is a "workaholic" really like an "alcoholic," as Sanders implies at the end of his essay? Write a brief essay comparing and contrasting the two types and pointing out differences as well as similarities.

ANNIE DILLARD

Terwilliger Bunts One

The Norton Reader, p. 151; Shorter Edition, p. 69

Taken from Dillard's autobiographical *An American Childhood* (1987), this selection might as readily have been titled "My Mother" as anything else, for in it Dillard attempts to characterize her mother—with all her amusing idiosyncrasies and annoying quirks, her remarkable strengths and forgivable weaknesses. Because Dillard depicts a person she knows well, her essay might be compared with Virginia Woolf's "My Father: Leslie Stephen" (NR 136) to raise questions about how a writer conveys a familiar subject to an audience unfamiliar with the person (through anecdotes rather than adjectives, through the subject's favorite phrases as much as the writer's own words). In contrast, you might use Tom Wolfe's "Yeager" (NR 123) to ask about the techniques needed to characterize someone famous whom the writer has never met.

Analytical Considerations

1. You might ask students what anecdotes they remember best about Dillard's mother, why they remember them, and what the anecdotes reveal about the mother's personality.

2. Dillard's mother has many personal qualities her daughter admires. What are those qualities? Does she have qualities about which Dillard is ambivalent? How does Dillard convey her attitude?

3. Dillard's mother lived during a time when the possibilities for women were more limited than they are now, yet Dillard never belabors this point.

She simply says, "Mother's energy and intelligence suited her for a greater role in a larger arena—mayor of New York, say—than the one she had" (paragraph 27). Why does Dillard work implicitly rather than explicitly? How does she make her point through examples and anecdotes?

4. This essay is constructed as a series of vignettes, each a page or two long. How does Dillard construct a single vignette? (You might compare the first with the last.) What organization does Dillard give to the series of vignettes— e.g., why does she begin as she does and end where she ends?

Suggested Writing Assignments

1. Write a character sketch about your mother or some other family member, using techniques from Dillard that you found particularly effective.
2. "Torpid conformity was a kind of sin; it was stupidity itself," according to Dillard's mother (paragraph 33). Write an essay in which you illustrate this thesis with examples from your own experience.
3. Take a phrase or common saying from your own family's history. Write a brief essay in which you convey what that phrase or saying means to you and your family.

JAMAICA KINCAID

Sowers and Reapers

The Norton Reader, p. 156

This essay leads us to wrestle with the question with which it begins: "Why must people insist that the garden is a place of rest and repose, a place to forget the cares of the world, a place to distance yourself from the painful responsibility that comes with being a human being?" Kincaid's passion for gardening is entwined with her fine sense of justice and ethics. This essay also makes us question the politicization of acts that typically do not appear inherently political. Alice Walker, in her essay "In Search of Our Mother's Gardens" (from a collection of the same title), also politicizes the act of gardening; it may be instructive to assign the Walker essay and ask students to compare the two in terms of the different ways in which they transform gardens and gardening into discussions of power and freedom.

Questions from the NR11

1. According to Kincaid, Frank Cabot, chairman of the Garden Conservancy, said she did the "unforgivable—I had introduced race and politics into the garden" (paragraph 2). Can you imagine how race and politics could ever have been left out? What might have led some garden people to ignore or suppress them?

2. The essay has two parts: the Charleston speech and the garden building project. What is the relationship between the two? Why does Kincaid spend so much time on her admiration for the workers?
3. Write an essay describing how you took on a task and completed it successfully. Or write about how someone you know did a good job on a difficult assignment. Go into the kind of detail Kincaid does about her wall.

Analytical Considerations

1. In the first part of her essay, Kincaid describes how the gardens at Middleton and Monticello were created. What are the characteristics or qualities she suggests are critical to making a good garden? Are these same qualities revisited in the second part of her essay, which focuses on her own garden? If so, how? If not, what other qualities or characteristics does she believe have gone into the making of her garden?
2. In October 2002, the memorial service for Minnesota Senator Paul Wellstone turned into a campaign pep rally, offending the sensibilities of some people who had come to pay their respects to the late senator. Similarly, some were offended by Kincaid's introduction of race and politics into her presentation at the South Carolina Garden Conservancy's tenth-anniversary celebration. What justifies Kincaid's inclusion? What might make it seem inappropriate?
3. Kincaid says that she had come originally prepared to talk about the Garden of Eden as being her favorite garden. But, on hearing one of the other speakers talk about the garden created by Jewish prisoners at Auschwitz, Kincaid felt that she would have to forgo her praise of the Garden of Eden. What rhetorical strategy does Kincaid employ by portraying her altered presentation as a response to another speaker's talk? How does it strengthen or weaken her own presentation?
4. How do race and politics figure in Kincaid's description of her garden and in the construction of the stone wall?

Suggested Writing Assignments

1. Write about the pleasures of gardening and what it might teach a person about matters beyond the garden. You may wish to interview a few avid gardeners and find out what makes them passionate about their pursuit.
2. When is an action political? How can a purely personal activity, pursued primarily for pleasure, be made or become political? Is politics tied up with the motivation of the person performing the action or with the perception of others interpreting the act? Ground your essay on a specific action or person you know.
3. Have you ever witnessed or participated in the introduction of a political message at an event or gathering that was organized for different reasons? Did you think that the politicization of the event was justified or appropriate? Why or why not?

FATEMA MERNISSI

The Harem Within

The Norton Reader, p. 162; Shorter Edition, p. 106

Mernissi is a Moroccan sociologist whose research and scholarship have focused on Islam and its impact on democracy and women's lives. Two of her books, *The Veil and The Male Elite* and *Beyond the Veil*, reveal the many complexities and nuanced significances of a garment that the West too hastily associates with Islam's oppression of women. This essay is taken from her 1994 memoir, *Dreams of Trespass: Tales of A Harem Girlhood*. Mernissi's exuberant and agile voice uncovers the energy that dwells in the female quarters of Islamic households and discloses the spirit of imagination and resistance that thrives there.

Questions from the NR11

1. As a professional writer and researcher, Mernissi is careful to define her terms and to translate foreign words and concepts. How successful is she? Are there any terms and concepts that are still unclear?
2. List some of the "invisible" rules that govern a particular domain you know about: a college class or dorm; a family; a workplace, a clique or group of friends. How do people learn the rules? How are they enforced?
3. Write about an occasion when you had things "explained" for you by a wiser or more knowledgeable friend or relative.

Analytical Considerations

1. Mernissi presents us with brief yet effective portraits of many different women in her family. How do these women variously respond to the physical and mental construct of the harem? What do their actions and attitudes tell you about independence, resistance, accommodation, and defiance? What do you think is the author's position on each of these women?
2. Who are the men in the essay? Read carefully the passages in which she describes their interactions with women and determine how she characterizes them.
3. "You'll miss out on happiness if you think too much about walls and rules. . . . The ultimate goal of a woman's life is happiness. So don't spend your time looking for walls to bang your head on": this is the advice the narrator, as a young girl, receives from Yasmina. What are the several lessons that Yasmina is attempting to give the young Fatima about freedom and opportunity and happiness? Would you say that she's advising the young narrator to accept her situation, or do you think she's actually couching a subversive message in language that appears to favor submission?
4. "Words are like onions. . . . The more skins you peel off, the more meanings you encounter. And when you start discovering multiplicities of meanings, then right and wrong becomes irrelevant." This is Yasmina's response to Fatima's question about the rightness or wrongness of the history of harems.

Moral relativism is not a sentiment with which many people are comfortable, and yet there are ideas that are best understood by withholding quick moral judgment. Take a word like "adultery," which has a definite moral judgment associated with it. How could peeling it for its multiple meanings undermine the clarity of right and wrong? Or take other controversial words like "abortion" and "cloning." Why does seeing the multiple meanings of words make it harder to hold a clear moral position on them? Or does it?

Suggested Writing Assignments

1. Yasmina tells the narrator, "[A]ny space you entered had its own invisible rules, and you needed to figure them out." Write about a space that you entered which confused you with invisible rules you had to figure out. How did you become aware of the existence of these rules and how did you learn what they were? How did you learn to make accommodations to the rules once you had determined what they were?
2. Using as a model Mernissi's definition of "harem," write your own definition of a term or word of significance to you. She provides historical background, dialogue, anecdote, event, and character examples to give us a substantial understanding of the many facets of the term. You could attempt a definition of "family" or "tradition" or "ritual," for example.

JUDITH ORTIZ COFER

More Room

The Norton Reader, p. 167

Born in Hormigueros, Puerto Rico, Cofer spent much of her childhood traveling between her Puerto Rican home and Paterson, New Jersey, where she also lived. This essay recalls her grandmother's bedroom: its sights, smells, symbols, and wonders. It also narrates the tale of a Puerto Rican woman who maintained control of her body and personal space. As such, it might be called a feminist parable, yet it is never so didactic that the message (made explicit in the final paragraph) intrudes upon the pleasure of the story. You might want students to use Cofer's essay as a model for their own exemplary tales: narratives and family stories that taught them a lesson about life.

Questions from the NR11

1. At the end of the essay, Cofer explains in fairly direct terms why her grandmother wanted "more room." Why do you think she uses narration as the primary mode in the rest of the essay? What does she gain by first narrating, then explaining?
2. Cofer uses many similes and metaphors—for example, in paragraph 1 she says that her grandmother's house was "like a chambered nautilus" and in paragraph 5 that grandmother's Bible was "her security system." Discuss the use of one or two such comparisons that you find particularly effective.

3. What are the possible meanings of the title?
4. Write about a favorite or mysterious place you remember from childhood.

Analytical Considerations

1. This is a short essay, only eleven paragraphs, similar in length to many essays students are asked to write. You might ask students to map out the "flow" of the essay: what happens in each paragraph, where Cofer allows herself more space (paragraphs 5 to 6), where she creates suspense and picks up the pace (paragraphs 10 to 11).
2. In preparing Question 2, above, students will have identified some of the key metaphors in this essay: "like a chambered nautilus" (paragraph 1), "like a great blue bird" (paragraph 2), "like a wise empress" (paragraph 3), the Bible as "her security system" (paragraph 5), etc. List their findings on the board and discuss the way each metaphor either clarifies or enriches Cofer's description of "la casa de Mamá."
3. Discuss the importance of the final paragraph, which explicitly states the reasons Cofer's grandmother needed her own room. If the students are writing essays similar to Cofer's, ask them to end with a similar explication of their story's meaning.

Suggested Writing Assignments

1. Retell a story often told within your family. Concentrate on a single person or place as Cofer does and suggest, either implicitly or explicitly, why this tale is so important to you or your family.
2. Write about a favorite place you remember from childhood, using details and metaphors as Cofer does to bring it alive.
3. Compare and contrast Cofer's depiction of her grandmother with N. Scott Momaday's of his grandmother in "The Way to Rainy Mountain" (NR 192, SE 78). Where they differ, suggest why their differences might reflect different backgrounds or intentions.

MARGARET ATWOOD

True North

The Norton Reader, p. 171; Shorter Edition, p. 90

Margaret Atwood is best known as a novelist, the author of such popular and award-winning works as *The Handmaid's Tale, Cat's Eye,* and *The Robber Bride*. Yet she also writes regularly as an essayist and has contributed to a Canadian magazine called *Saturday Night,* in which this piece first appeared. Whether Canadian or from the northern parts of the United States, many students will remember the song with which Atwood opens the essay: "Land of the silver birch, Home of the beaver."

If students recall the song, you might ask what emotions it evokes: do they think it corny? Or do they, like Atwood, find tears in their eyes? If they do not recall the song or if they think it is corny, then you might find another way to explain the nostalgia Atwood alludes to in the first paragraph. (Perhaps simply asking about the "wilderness" will do it.) Atwood means to explore our attitudes toward the wilderness, particularly Canadian attitudes. Indeed, comparing Atwood's piece with William Cronon's essay "The Trouble with Wilderness" (NR 617) provides a useful way to raise broad questions about North American attitudes toward nature and the environment—and whether or not there is a difference between Americans and Canadians on this score.

Questions from the NR11

1. What context does Atwood set for the opening section? How does her need to explain to American Southerners in a college classroom help her communicate with the readers of this essay?
2. Beginning in paragraph 18, Atwood reenacts a journey to the "north." What does this journey, re-created for the reader, help her achieve?
3. Why does Atwood include a section about "typical ways of dying" in a northern landscape? What qualities about northern Canada can she present through this unusual approach?
4. Write an essay about a geographical region that appeals to you but that may be unknown or unappealing to others. Using techniques learned from Atwood or other writers in this section, try to communicate the region's appeal as you write.

Analytical Considerations

1. Although this essay is a length common in sophisticated periodicals, it may seem slightly long to students accustomed to short pieces of 2,000 to 3,000 words. The questions (reprinted above) should help students begin to understand Atwood's approach and structure: the opening frame set in an Alabama classroom (paragraphs 1 to 7), the questions and definitions of "north" (paragraphs 9 to 13), the re-created journey (paragraphs 18 to 29), the discussion of acid rain (paragraphs 30 to 32), the comparison with Scotland (paragraphs 33 to 40), the imagined ways of dying in the Canadian wilderness (paragraphs 41 to 44), three scenes in the north "sitting around the table" or "on the dock" (paragraphs 45 to 56, 57 to 61, 62 to 64), the return to Toronto (paragraphs 65 to 67).
2. Atwood states that "everything in Canada, outside Toronto, begins with geography" (paragraph 3), and she shows a Canadian map to the American students she is teaching. It might help to show students a similar map, specifically to trace the route of the journey Atwood takes in paragraphs 18 to 27.
3. What happens in the essay after Atwood gets to "true north"? What do the three scenes "sitting around the table" (paragraphs 45 to 56, 57 to 61) or "sitting on the dock" (paragraphs 62 to 64) contribute?
4. When Atwood uses "us" and "we" in paragraph 10 and throughout the essay, to whom is she referring? Canadians only? Ask students whether Atwood's sense of the wilderness is similar to, say, William Cronon's in "The Trouble with Wilderness" (NR 617) or Edward Abbey's in "The Serpents of Paradise" (NR 589, SE 362), or whether she describes a uniquely Canadian attitude toward the northern wilderness.

Suggested Writing Assignments

1. Do all North Americans share Atwood's attitudes toward the "north"? Write an essay in which you either show how your views differ or confirm your basic agreement with Atwood.
2. Write about your own region and the values you see embodied in it; write your essay to an audience of readers unfamiliar with that region.
3. In the final paragraphs, as Atwood traces the journey south back to Toronto and its pollution, she asks, "we're going into that?" Write an essay in which you analyze why you (or other people) choose to live in cities, even those hit hard by pollution.

KATHLEEN NORRIS

The Holy Use of Gossip

The Norton Reader, p. 181; Shorter Edition, p. 101

In the wrong hands Norris's essay could be a dangerous example, since it operates through assertions rather than extended demonstrations. Norris will tell a story or two, assert a claim, and move on. Nowhere does she stop to provide careful, step-by-step support for her statements and claims. She doesn't even seem to be aware that they are in need of further explanation. For example, the essay opens and closes with anecdotes. In between come rather large claims about her topic, gossip: "Gossip done well can be a holy thing" (paragraph 10); "Gossip is theology translated into experience" (paragraph 22); "When we gossip we are also praying. . . ." (paragraph 22). Why doesn't Norris let on that these are huge, deliberately improbable claims?

Some composition teachers might be tempted to scorn Norris's approach as too superficial, too anecdotal. They will regard Norris as a bad example for college students, who need to learn how to handle a formal argument composed of claim and demonstration. To be sure, if all *Norton Reader* essays employed this type of example there would indeed be a problem. Fortunately, *The Norton Reader* is large and rich enough to encompass all kinds of essays, and this particularly nice example of anecdotal arguing can be opposed by many more orthodox examples of traditional arguments.

Ask students what they think of the anecdotal approach. Where wouldn't it work? What subject matter lends itself to this kind of anecdotal style? What kind of person would be convinced by this type of essay? Who would resist it? (A thought experiment: Imagine what kind of formal argument could ever support one of those three claims Norris makes about the religious nature of gossip. Can we see any of those claims being the subject of formal proof?) Interestingly, a professional theologian, one whose job it is to think about the divine, might find Norris's essay seriously wanting as theology but perfectly fine as an interesting kind of writing about ethics, spirituality, or small-town living.

Questions from the NR11

1. Exactly how is Norris using the word "gossip"? How do you use the word yourself? What range of meanings of "gossip" do you usually encounter? Check a collegiate dictionary to pin down the most common meanings.
2. Norris situates her essay in a small town in a rural part of the country where population is decreasing. Can you imagine her situating a similar essay in a suburb? In the heart of a large city? Would some of the strengths Norris discerns be lost in the translation to a different setting?
3. Norris sees the religious value of what is often regarded as human failing. In an essay of your own, take a similar "failing" and, like Norris, show its good side, though it doesn't have to be religious. (Some possible examples include: silence, nosiness, jealousy, pride.)

Analytical Considerations

1. Does Norris fall back on overused language at times? How else would you interpret sentences like "the town breathed a collective sigh of relief" (paragraph 20) and "the whole town rejoiced" (paragraph 23)? They both sound like clichés. Are they? Do they work in their settings?
2. What is theology? Look it up in an encyclopedia. (A dictionary entry would be too short.)
3. Students can consider why Norris chooses to end with a series of anecdotes. (Rachel Carson does something similar in her otherwise very different essay, "Tides" [NR 568].)
4. By connecting this essay to its epigraph by noted short-story writer Grace Paley, students can test the claim that gossip is "the way all storytellers learn about life." Is Norris, a storyteller herself, doing something like that in her essay?

Suggested Writing Assignments

1. Write about a situation in which many people were hoping a friend or neighbor or admired figure would "pull through."
2. Describe an incident of gossip, making it as vivid as you can through quotes and detailed descriptions of faces, tones of voice, and physical reactions.
3. Tell how the values of these small-town and ranch people seem to be similar to or different from those of the people where you live.

MARY AUSTIN

The Land of Little Rain

The Norton Reader, p. 186; Shorter Edition, p. 84

This essay can be appreciated on two levels: one, as a celebration of nature in general and the desert in particular, and, two, as a compelling use of language. One approach to Austin's essay would be to study her word choice, imagery, and creation of mood. Austin wants us to acknowledge both the brutal power of the desert and its surprising capacity to bear life—insect, plant, and human. Even the sounds of the words she uses suggest the abundance of vibrant energy in the desert.

To prepare students to be attentive to language one could have them study nature poetry by such Native American writers as Simon Ortiz, Ron Weldon, and Louise Erdrich. It may be useful to note as well how these poets celebrate the natural world and use this celebration as a backdrop to articulating an intimate personal relationship with a relative or with cultural traditions.

Questions from the NR11

1. In paragraph 13 Austin speaks of "the lotus charm" that overcomes visitors. Is she exempt from this charm? Do you see any signs that the narrator has become enraptured with the land and its wildlife?
2. Austin is a distinctive stylist. Choose three phrases or sentences that seem typical of her writing. Then try to make a generalization: What is a key characteristic of Austin's style?
3. Tom Wolfe's "Yeager" (NR 123) contains a vivid, highly stylized description of another uninhabited part of southern California, but from the perspective of someone repelled by the oddness and unfriendliness of the area. Compare the styles of Wolfe and Austin.
4. Take a flower or tree and write a close-up, Austin-like description of it, using her look at the yucca as a model.

Analytical Considerations

1. Austin sets out to personify the land, to make it a living, breathing character. Do a close reading of the first three or four paragraphs of the essay. Find the phrases that animate the land; look for the active verbs. What is the mood created by words such as "squeezed," "streaked," "intolerable"? Compare the mood or moods of these opening paragraphs with that created in the essay's closing paragraph.
2. "Nothing the desert produces expresses it better than the unhappy growth of the tree yuccas," writes Austin. What spirit of the desert is revealed in this passage? How does the last line of the paragraph—"In Death Valley, reputed the very core of desolation, are nearly two hundred identified species"—complicate and/or embellish the spirit of the desert as expressed by the tree yuccas?
3. Austin tells of her coming to the aid of two birds that are trying desperately to provide shade for their unhatched eggs in the fierce glare of the desert sun. What do we learn about Austin from her description of this incident? Why does she not help the birds immediately and why does she use the word "constrained" to describe how she felt when she finally decided to assist them?
4. Compare Austin's portrayal of Native American tribes and white settlers, including miners. What is her attitude toward these two groups of people? Comment on the complexity of her characterizations of them.

Suggested Writing Assignments

1. So much of the effect that Austin achieves is through her careful observation. She notices objects, creatures, and details in the landscape that typically escape one's vision. Spend a minimum of thirty minutes at a town green, a playing field, urban park, or even an alleyway and look closely at the plant and animal life and objects in the area. Once you've made your careful observations and taken notes, write a descriptive essay that conveys your attitude toward the place. Pay attention to diction and the creation of mood.

2. In the final paragraph of the essay, Austin writes that the stars in the desert sky "make the poor world-fret of no account." Recall an experience in which your encounter with the outdoors or with any aspect of nature made you feel that the problems of the world or your personal problems were somehow diminished.

N. SCOTT MOMADAY

The Way to Rainy Mountain

The Norton Reader, p. 192; Shorter Edition, p. 78

Momaday's description of his grandmother and his return to Rainy Mountain, a place sacred to the Kiowa Indians, employs a structure common to many cultures: the journey as an actual and metaphorical quest. You might ask students about their own journeys and journeys they have read about in literature—whether in Homer's *Odyssey* or Jack Kerouac's *On the Road* or some even more recent book of travel writing. Why do we travel? What do we expect to gain from travel? What did Momaday hope to discover by returning to his grandmother's house and retracing the traditional movements of the Kiowas? Such questions might help students to think about the journey structure as a possible one for their own personal reports or for their descriptions of a place of special interest to them. The journey Momaday describes in "Rainy Mountain" beautifully links realistic descriptions of the West, sacred myths of the Kiowas, and memories of his grandmother and her stories to evoke a sense of the importance of place in his own life.

Analytical Considerations

1. What is the structure of this essay? You might ask students to compare Momaday's actual journey (introduced in paragraph 2 and again in paragraph 5) with the historical journeys of his ancestors, the Kiowas. How are the two journeys linked?

2. Why does Momaday begin and end with descriptions of Rainy Mountain? How and why are the two descriptions different?

3. Where does Momaday include cultural myths, historical events, or his grandmother's stories in this essay? How do these enrich our understanding of the places Momaday revisits?

4. To what extent are "people" essential to our understanding of "place"? Discuss the ways in which Momaday describes his grandmother both as grandmother (i.e., a real person, a family member) and as Kiowa Indian (i.e., a representative of an older culture that no longer exists). Why do we need both views of his grandmother to understand the significance of Momaday's return to his ancestral home?

5. Look closely at sentences in which Momaday chooses words with metaphorical or symbolic significance—e.g., in paragraph 1, where he links Rainy Mountain to the place "where Creation was begun," or in paragraph 5, where he refers to his journey as a "pilgrimage," or in paragraph 9, where he refers to the soldiers' stopping of Indian rituals as "deicide." Discuss the connotations of such words and how they enrich the literal journey Momaday takes.

Suggested Writing Assignments

1. Write about a journey you took to an important place in your family's history—whether an ancestral home, the home of a relative, or a home you lived in as a child.

2. Write about a place with historical and cultural significance, combining your own observations with history, legend, and/or myth.

3. Write a descriptive essay about a person and place that seem intertwined. In doing so, think about why the person seems so essential to understanding the place.

DAVID GUTERSON

Enclosed. Encyclopedic. Endured: The Mall of America

The Norton Reader, p. 198; Shorter Edition, p. 111

Guterson's essay, published in *Harper's Magazine*, is a thorough report on—and devastating critique of—the Mall of America. It begins in classic journalistic form by establishing the interest and significance of its subject: the 4.2 million miles of floor space, the 12,750 parking spaces, the 10,000 employees, the 44 escalators and 17 elevators, and so on. Then (in paragraph 4) it poses the question: "What might it [the Mall] tell us about ourselves?" The answer is a chilling one about loss of community, a feature of ancient marketplaces like the Greek agora or the Persian bazaar but absent in modern America.

This essay might be read in conjunction with Anthony Burgess's "Is America Falling Apart?" (NR 286, SE 181).

Analytical Considerations

1. Ask students which details they remember from Guterson's essay and why those details are significant to them and/or the essay. If there is a difference in terms of significance, you might ask how Guterson wants his readers to interpret his facts and what obstacles their own impressions might create for him as writer.

2. It's helpful to create a diagram or outline of this essay and its parts: introduction (paragraphs 1 to 3), sense impressions (paragraphs 4 to 5), interviews with shoppers (paragraphs 6 to 14), a history of marketplaces in various cultures (paragraphs 15 to 19), an extended description of the stores and their contents (paragraphs 20 to 26), a history of the American shopping mall (paragraphs 27 to 33), a descent into the basement of the mall (paragraphs 34 to 40), upstairs in the "woods" (paragraphs 41 to 45), religious services (paragraph 46), concluding analysis (paragraphs 47 to 50). Ask students what Guterson hopes to achieve with any one of these sections.

3. Why does Guterson descend to the basement? What negative features and false facts does he expose? Why is his survey of Camp Snoopy linked to this section?

4. "Community" is a word that recurs in Guterson's analysis and takes prominence in his conclusion. Ask students what he means by "community" and why he thinks the mall doesn't have it.

Suggested Writing Assignments

1. Visit another place of commerce and write your own analysis of it, using some of Guterson's techniques.

2. If you have access to relevant periodicals or online data sources, report on the success of the Mall of America. Look especially at the projections in paragraphs 31 to 32.

3. Guterson argues that modern shopping malls do not create a sense of community. Do you agree or disagree? Why?

HUMAN NATURE

JACOB BRONOWSKI

The Reach of Imagination

The Norton Reader, p. 210

Jacob Bronowski wrote about both science and literature and was responsible for a television series that you (and perhaps some of your students) may have seen, "The Ascent of Man" (1973–74). He held that scientific and poetic thinking are essentially the same, both originating in the imagination and both tested by experience. "The Reach of Imagination" may be read in conjunction with his essay "The Nature of Scientific Reasoning" (NR 924, SE 535); although written for independent publication, that essay extends the concept of imagination that appears in this one. Here Bronowski defines the imagination by its nature and scope. His illustrations from science and from literature exemplify his general argument, affirm similarities between scientific and poetic thinking, and buttress his authority.

Students may (legitimately) recognize Bronowski's magisterial range of illustrations as beyond their resources. What kinds of authority, then, are available to them? Many kinds, it's important to emphasize, so long as they learn to moderate their claims to pronounce on large issues, stake out smaller ones, and deploy the authority of others in developing their own without at the same time losing a personal voice. You may wish to require Suggested Writing Assignment 2 and then use both successful and less successful student papers to illustrate problems of authority.

Questions from the NR11

1. *To imagine*, according to Bronowski, means "to make images and to move them about inside one's head in new arrangements" (paragraph 9). How do his illustrations support and expand this definition?
2. Bronowski argues that imagination works similarly in artists and in scientists. List his illustrations and references in two columns, one for science and one for literature. Why do you think he demonstrates the working of the imagination in science more fully than in art?
3. Read Bronowski's "The Nature of Scientific Reasoning" (NR 924, SE 535). Write an essay in which you describe his illustrations from the work of Newton in both "The Reach of Imagination" and "The Nature of Scientific Reasoning." Could he have interchanged them? Why or why not?

Analytical Considerations

1. Ask students to list Bronowski's illustrations and references in two columns, one labeled science, the other literature. What does the range of each list indicate about him?

2. Which illustrations does Bronowski explain, and which does he simply refer to? What does his handling of illustrations and references indicate about his intended audience?

3. "Indeed, the most important images for human beings," Bronowski claims, "are simply words, which are abstract symbols" (paragraph 11). Read Erich Fromm, "The Nature of Symbolic Language" (NR 534) and compare Fromm's and Bronowski's conceptions of language as symbolic representation.

4. "Animals do not have words," Bronowski observes (paragraph 11). Read Carl Sagan, "The Abstractions of Beasts" (NR 604, SE 373). How would Bronowski respond to Sagan's claims that animals are capable of abstract thought?

Suggested Writing Assignments

1. Write an essay in which you imitate, on a smaller scale, Bronowski's procedures. Take the simplest definition available (in a dictionary) of some abstract term of your own choosing: you may wish to try terms such as "harmony," "knowledge," "paradox," or "similarity." Extend this definition with at least three illustrations, one of which is drawn from experience, another from reading.

2. "Imagination," Bronowski claims, "is a specifically human gift" (paragraph 1). Argue against or qualify this claim. Draw your evidence from and buttress your own authority with other authorities by using one or both of the following: Alexander Petrunkevitch, "The Spider and the Wasp" (NR 595, SE 368), Carl Sagan, "The Abstractions of Beasts" (NR 604, SE 373), and/or Edward Abbey, "The Serpents of Paradise" (NR 589, SE 362). While you use the voices and authority of Petrunkevitch, Sagan, or Abbey through quotation and paraphrase, don't let their voices drown out yours or their authority inhibit you from claiming your own.

3. Writing in 1967, Bronowski predicted that "on the day when we land on the moon . . . [i]t will be not a technical but an imaginative triumph, that reaches back to the beginning of modern science and literature both" (paragraph 25). Read one of the works of fiction Bronowski mentions in paragraph 23 and a newspaper or magazine account of the first actual landing on the moon, and then argue for or against his assertion.

WILLIAM GOLDING

Thinking as a Hobby

The Norton Reader, p. 217; Shorter Edition, p. 124

In this essay, William Golding uses a three-part classificatory scheme, rather casually introduced, to shape an autobiographical account of his development from school to university in learning what it means to think. Although the essay proceeds in chronological order, his classificatory scheme—three kinds of thinking classified by value and presented in ascending order—overrides its narrative development. Yet because Golding illustrates "grade-three" and "grade-two" thinking with a couple of comic figures each and turns even his illustration of "grade-one" thinking, an encounter with Einstein, into comedy, his discussion of thinking is light and amusing. A serious discussion would require more analysis and different illustrations; it might also require a less easy and tidy classificatory scheme.

In addition to his three-part made scheme, Golding introduces a found scheme (at least according to what he tells us in the essay): the three statuettes on the cupboard behind his headmaster's desk. The found scheme is more arbitrary than the made scheme and contributes to the essay's comedy. Found schemes, in their arbitrariness, often make good writing exercises: students are likely to perform well—and be pleased with themselves—when challenged with difficult or impossible writing tasks that come with built-in excuses for failure. As a whole, however, "Thinking as a Hobby" may not be an easy model for students, inasmuch as many will be unable to reproduce Golding's wry perception and tonal subtlety.

Analytical Considerations

1. How does Golding's title, "Thinking as a Hobby," signal his comic intent? You may want to ask the same question about his categories: "grade-three thinking," "grade-two thinking," and "grade-one thinking."
2. How does Golding use his made classificatory scheme of three kinds of thinking and his found scheme of three statuettes on the cupboard? Consider other kinds of made and found categories. What are their differences?
3. Golding's made and found schemes both contain three categories. How frequent are classifications by three? How do they differ, say, from classifications by two or four? How many ways can three categories be arranged? ("Goldilocks and the Three Bears" will remind students of means and extremes.)

Suggested Writing Assignments

1. Write a satiric account of at least two individuals you know who exemplify Golding's "grade-three" and "grade-two" thinking.
2. Write a serious account of an individual you know or have read about who exemplifies Golding's "grade-one" thinking; you may want to give it another name. You may want to read the description of Einstein in Jacob Bronowski's "The Nature of Scientific Reasoning" (NR 924, SE 535) and use him.
3. Write an essay in which you use a found and arbitrary classificatory scheme. Find or invent one that challenges your ingenuity.

ISAAC ASIMOV

The Eureka Phenomenon

The Norton Reader, p. 223; Shorter Edition, p. 130

Discussion of "The Eureka Phenomenon" can begin with form or content. A formal approach may involve a transition from William Golding's "Thinking as a Hobby" (NR 217, SE 124). Like Golding, Asimov uses a classificatory scheme, though he uses his less emphatically than Golding does. Asimov's scheme contains two categories: voluntary and involuntary thinking, or reason and intuition, call them what you will. You may want students to mark the places in the essay where Asimov describes each and notice how often his descriptions involve contrast, both explicit and implicit. You may also ask the class to list as many of the pairs as they can and distinguish between these two kinds of thinking. You will want to point out their interdependence. First, the names are usually linked, often conventionally: we do not, for example, ordinarily pair voluntary thinking with intuition, or reason with involuntary thinking. Second, each term of the pair is ordinarily defined by what it is not as well as by what it is. Third, in most pairs, one term will be more or less approving, one term more or less pejorative. This exercise dramatizes binary thinking and, usefully, makes students aware of how conventional it is, how ingrained it is in our language and habits of thought. It also makes them aware of how it invariably involves value judgments. A formal approach shows Asimov, in "The Eureka Phenomenon," reclaiming and transvaluing involuntary thinking or intuition.

An approach focusing on content might begin with the hardest section of the essay, Kekule's discovery. You might read this section out loud with students and point out that Asimov includes it in order to show that Kekule, after seven years of trying to conceptualize the structure of a benzene molecule, came upon the model of a ring—rather than a chain—while sleeping. But you will also want students to see how Asimov's prose explanation of the structure of a benzene molecule is virtually unintelligible without diagrams—and thus to appreciate the power of images. (Instructors for whom his explanation is virtually unintelligible even with diagrams will usually find some students in the class who understand Kekule's theory and be able to turn to them for help; demonstrating a transition from incomprehension to comprehension can be a valuable lesson in reading.) You might then go back to an easier section of the essay, Archimedes' discovery, and ask students to generate and even to draw their own images. Experienced readers use imagery habitually but may not be aware that they do; inexperienced readers often need to learn consciously to make and deploy images as an aid to comprehension.

"The Eureka Phenomenon" might well have appeared in the section called "Science and Technology." It raises issues explored in that section about the increasing unintelligibility of science to nonscientists and the difficulties of writing about modern science for a popular audience. These issues are also raised in Jacob Bronowski's "The Reach of Imagination" (NR 210) and in another essay by Bronowski, "The Nature of Scientific Reasoning" (NR 924, SE 535) in "Science and Technology."

Questions from the NR11

1. Consider Asimov's narrative of Archimedes' and Kekule's discoveries. What elements does he heighten and how? How does he include the scientific information necessary to understand them? How does he make (or attempt to make) this information accessible to nonscientists?
2. Scientists, Asimov concludes, "are so devoted to their belief in conscious thought that they . . . consistently obscure the actual methods by which they obtain their results" (paragraph 81). Consider your own experiments in science courses and the way you have been taught to report them. Do you agree or disagree with Asimov? Why?
3. Have you ever had a "Eureka" experience? Does Asimov's account of the "Eureka phenomenon" help you to understand it? Write about your experience with reference to Asimov's essay.

Analytical Considerations

1. Consider the role of mathematics in both Archimedes' and Kekule's discoveries.
2. William Wordsworth, in the 1800 Preface to the second edition of *The Lyrical Ballads*, wrote: "The remotest discoveries of the Chemist, the Botanist, or Mineralogist will be as proper objects of the Poet's art as any upon which it can be employed, if the time should ever come when these things shall be familiar to us, and the relations under which they are contemplated by the followers of these respective sciences shall be manifestly and palpably material to us as enjoying and suffering human beings." Was Wordsworth's confidence misplaced? How was he wrong about the future of science? Thomas S. Kuhn's "The Route to Normal Science" (NR 928), in "Science and Technology" (paragraphs 16 to 18) provides a useful discussion. How was Wordsworth wrong about the future of poetry?
3. Read (at least the section on methodology in) Carl Cohen, "The Case for the Use of Animals in Biomedical Research" (NR 687); it was published in the *New England Journal of Medicine*. Consider the article's form and how it must, as Asimov puts it, "consistently obscure the actual methods by which they [i.e., scientists] obtain their results" (paragraph 81).

Suggested Writing Assignments

1. Choose a set of paired terms in Asimov's essay and identify the approving and pejorative term. Write an essay in which you reclaim and transvalue what the pejorative term refers to. Some suggestions: "reason and emotion," "mind and body," "order and disorder," "masculine and feminine," "sacred and secular."

2. Do library research on one or more of the scientists Asimov mentions in paragraphs 75 to 80. Construct an explanation of Asimov's decision not to feature their discoveries in this essay.

HENRY DAVID THOREAU

Observation

The Norton Reader, p. 57

This selection from Thoreau is part of a journal entry he made on May 6, 1854. (Other short excerpts from his journal—pithy maxims, observations, and reflections—appear on p. 102.) In his journals Thoreau wrote disjunctive segments rather than a sustained argument. More often than not, he used parallel construction and metaphorical language. You may want students to mark some memorable sentences in this selection that exhibit one or both of these stylistic features.

Many of Thoreau's statements in this entry are extravagant: he makes one sweeping generalization after another, each calling for qualification but of course not receiving it here. An effective critical-thinking exercise in qualifying them may be done collectively or in groups; it will help students to scrutinize their own sweeping generalizations. Of course, in a journal extravagance is often appropriate. It facilitates rapid thinking and, with luck, invites fresh and original ideas.

Rather like Isaac Asimov in "The Eureka Phenomenon" (NR 223, SE 130), Thoreau's journal entry reclaims and transvalues the more-or-less pejorative term "subjectivity." This journal entry usefully opens up discussion about the shifting and interdependent relations between objectivity and subjectivity. It will be useful to elicit from students some of the anecdotes that lead them to consider objectivity preferable to subjectivity; they invariably have some, if only the delivery of injunctions to avoid the pronoun "I." Whether they really believe that objectivity is preferable to subjectivity or merely recite the conventional wisdom may or may not emerge from this exercise. Students' belief that objectivity is the appropriate stance for a writer is apt to impoverish and conventionalize their writing. Thoreau provides a useful antidote.

Analytical Considerations

1. "Every important worker will report what life there is in him," Thoreau observes. In what ways might Asimov in "The Eureka Phenomenon" (NR 223, SE 130) or Bronowski in "The Reach of Imagination" (NR 210) be said to agree with him?
2. "Anything living," Thoreau observes, "is easily and naturally expressed in popular language." What does Thoreau mean by this statement? How many ways can it be interpreted? Do any of these interpretations contradict one another?

1. Write a brief essay in which you qualify one of Thoreau's extravagant generalizations.
2. Write some journal entries of your own in which you make sweeping generalizations, preferably extravagant generalizations about a controversial topic.
3. Write a brief essay in which you qualify one of your own extravagant generalizations.

PAUL THEROUX

Being a Man

The Norton Reader, p. 58

Paul Theroux is a novelist and essayist known for his writing on travel, particularly by train. "Being a Man" was published in a collection called *Sunrise with Seamonsters* (1985). Theroux takes a calculatedly strong and unqualified line that is both personal—"I have always disliked being a man" (paragraph 2)—and general—"Any objective study would find the quest for manliness essentially right-wing, puritanical, cowardly, neurotic and fueled largely by a fear of women" (paragraph 7). Midway through the essay he discloses an ax to grind, his desire to be a writer when in the United States to write, especially fiction, is considered unmanly. His personal involvement, however, does not lead him to qualify his assertion that the quest for manliness is bad for everybody. It is possible to argue that Theroux's strong line is subverted by his involvement. But is that necessarily the case? Academic writing, which minimizes personal involvement, is usually qualified writing, but it is only one kind of writing, and its rules are the rules of a specialized discourse.

Analytical Considerations

1. Ask students to mark Theroux's generalizations and consider how he makes them. You may also ask them to rewrite one or two as qualified generalizations.
2. Call attention to Theroux's illustrations. Ordinarily he uses one for each point he makes. The exception comes in paragraphs 10 and 11, where he surveys a number of writers. What are the uses of single and multiple illustrations?
3. Theroux asserts that men, at least in America, aren't expected to be writers; many feminists claim that women aren't expected to be scientists. What kind of thinking lies behind these expectations?

Suggested Writing Assignments

1. Both Theroux and Harvey Mansfield, in "The Partial Eclipse of Manliness" (NR 236, SE 139), look at the condition of being a man. Write an

essay in which you consider the advantages and disadvantages of each strategy.

2. Do library research on one or more of the writers Theroux mentions in paragraphs 10 and 11. Write an essay in which you test his assertion that the quest for manliness is particularly destructive for writers. In qualifying his generalization, be sure to qualify your own.
3. Write an essay called "Being a Student" in which you argue forcefully that being a student constitutes a hardship.

HARVEY MANSFIELD

The Partial Eclipse of Manliness

The Norton Reader, p. 236; Shorter Edition, p. 139

In this mostly dispassionate (but occasionally huffy) apologetic, Mansfield attempts to recuperate and rehabilitate a definition of "manliness" by examining its political, sociological, and intellectual meanings. In this way, his essay serves as a useful foil for feminist treatments of gender issues and patriarchy, which are found in print far more commonly.

Moreover, the text serves as a strong example of "classic," Montaignean essaying at work: the author is subversive, rejecting "common wisdom" and received opinion, calling into question what we think we know; the author takes a dismissed or overlooked phenomenon and goes to remarkable lengths to show that it is far more interesting and significant than it appears on the surface; the author explores the topic both deeply and broadly, bringing a variety of interpretive lenses to bear on it.

Since the text lacks an explicit, deductive organizational structure, and since the author circles back to some points several times, some care should be spent in delineating all of the qualities and characteristics that Mansfield eventually attributes to manliness. Moreover, given the possibly divisive subject matter, introducing the text with a discussion about the difference between *reacting* to a text (instantaneously, automatically, instinctually) and *responding* to a text (slowly, thoughtfully, deliberately) would probably be wise.

Questions from the NR11

1. How does Mansfield go about defining "Manliness"? Does he provide a single precise description, or is his definition to be found at a number of places throughout his essay?
2. What support does Mansfield provide for his major points about manliness? Does his concept of manliness fit with your concept of the term?
3. Paul Theroux writes about "being a man" (see the previous essay in this section), and Mansfield writes about "manliness." Do their essays have any concerns in common? What are their differences?

4. Choose a term or concept that seems to have gone out of style and write a Mansfield-type essay calling for a return to the traditional meaning. Some suggested terms: "manners," "courtesy," "discretion," "privacy."

Analytical Considerations

1. Looking over the entire text carefully, make a list of all of the different attributes, qualities, or characteristics that Mansfield eventually ascribes to manliness. Can you group them into categories? Which seem generally positive to you? Which strike you as problematic?
2. Rather than reinscribing the either/or logical fallacy (is manliness nature or is it nurture?), consider which of the aspects of manliness you delineated in number 1 above seem to come from nature and which seem to come from nurture. What patterns of meaning can you discern in the distribution? In what ways might these patterns be significant?
3. Mansfield writes that "Manly men are romantic about women; unmanly men are sensitive. Which is better? Which is better for women?" Indeed, from your perspective, in your experience, which is better: men being romantic about women or men being sensitive about women? Moreover, from your perspective, in your experience, which is better for women?
4. In discussing parenting, Mansfield suggests that "the authoritative father and the loving mother correspond to the public and private spheres as a whole, the one where aggression is paramount, the other where caring is the theme. Abolition of sexual roles might then be expected to produce a mixing of public (understood broadly as the wider world) and private (the realm of familiars). He then asks, "Is this possible and desirable?"
   a. Do you agree with Mansfield that authority and aggression are paramount in the public sphere, whereas love and caring are of foremost importance in the private sphere? Why or why not?
   b. In your opinion, is it possible to mix the public and the private? Authority and love? Aggression and caring? Father and mother? Why or why not?
   c. In each case, would such mixing be *desirable*, in your opinion? Why or why not?

Suggested Writing Assignments

1. Following Mansfield's example, write your own apologetic, your own defense of some person, place, thing, or idea. First, locate some phenomenon that is generally denigrated, disparaged, or belittled by many people in our contemporary society (for example, N'Sync, Barney, Wal-Mart, Taco Bell, cigarette smoking, communism, etc.). Then write an essay in which you demonstrate that this person, place, thing, or idea is actually far more valuable, significant, and worthy of respect than most people care to realize. An easy approach here is to be playful, if not sarcastic, and write a parody of an actual defense. More difficult, more interesting, and more intellectually useful is to write an actual and sincere apologetic that opens your readers' eyes to the value of something they have uncritically dismissed.
2. In this essay, the author spends considerable time and energy defining his key term, an abstract human quality or character trait. He does so by exca-

vating its meanings in a variety of different contexts (political, sociological, and intellectual, among others) and gathering them together. Try your hand at this kind of analysis: write your own essay in which you develop an elaborated definition of some abstract human quality. First, identify some human quality or trait you think worthy of extended, philosophical consideration (femininity, bravery, aspiration, compassion, duty, sympathy, sacrifice, etc.). Then, trace out its various layers or strands of meaning. As Mansfield does here, explore how the definition of the term changes from one context to another. Conclude your essay by trying to synthesize the various meanings of the term you have uncovered into a singular statement of definition.

SCOTT RUSSELL SANDERS

Looking at Women

The Norton Reader, p. 244; Shorter Edition, p. 147

Scott Russell Sanders tells us in the course of "Looking at Women" that he was eleven when he saw the girl in the pink shorts and that, thirty years later, he is married and the father of two. We even learn his wife's name: Ruth. If we are interested in him as an author as well as a looker at women, we can further learn that he is also a professor of English at Indiana University (which may explain his quoting the improbable Miss Indiana Persimmon Festival) and that he has published scholarly works, science fiction, and nonfiction. In an essay called "The Singular First Person," he talks about the rules for writing he was taught as a schoolboy and his impatience with them: among them, using linear development (that is, thesis sentences and transitions) and avoiding I, the "singular first person" of his title. He prefers what he calls "dodging and leaping," "the shimmer and play of mind on the surface and in the depths a strong current." He is also fond of metaphor, as when he likens his preferred essay form to a stream.

Much of "Looking at Women" is personal report and, if Sanders does not succeed in making his experiences and his perceptions interesting, readers will find it hard going. Students may find it repetitive; instructors will appreciate the way Sanders circles, thickens, and complicates his perceptions. Sanders's essay, however, is more than personal report. In it he treats a timely and loaded question: how the gaze, directed at women by men, by construction workers as well as by artists, can reduce them to objects of desire. Through his reminiscences and musings, Sanders looks at men's looking at women and women's being looked at. He wants to exempt himself (and other men like him) from reducing women to objects, to demonstrate that he views them not as "sexual playthings but as loved persons" (paragraph 31). Because the essay is wide-ranging, Sanders suggests the complexity of male gazes other than his and the complexity of female self-presentation. The responses of students, both male and female, to Sanders's essay should raise questions about making the personal representative, about using the I for analysis, both particular analysis—about Sanders himself—and general analysis—about men and women. This essay, with its focus on the personal and particular, gestures toward inclusiveness and generality. Sanders's success in combining the particular and the general is an open question, as is, indeed, what we mean when we say that a piece of writing is a success.

Questions from the NR11

1. Several sections of this essay are grounded in specific episodes from Sanders's life. Identify the episodes and explain how he uses them.
2. The five sections of this essay are separated by typographical space rather than connected by prose transitions. Determine the content of each section and explain its relation to the content of the section that precedes it. Describe Sanders's strategies of organization and development.
3. In paragraph 12 Sanders asks: "How should a man look at a woman?" What is his answer? Where does he provide it?
4. Write an essay in which you answer, in your own terms, Sanders's question, "How should a man look at a woman?"

Analytical Considerations

1. What kind of development does Sanders provide in place of linear development? You may direct students to his statement, "What I present here are a few images and reflections that cling, for me, to this one item" (paragraph 13).
2. What does the pronoun "I" entail for Sanders? How is self-presentation as he uses it both risk-taking and self-protective?
4. What kinds of metaphors does Sanders use? To what extent are they subsumed into the essay? To what extent are they showy, calling attention to themselves?

Suggested Writing Assignments

1. Write an essay with at least four sections developed by association in which you use, as Sanders puts it, "images and reflections that cling" (paragraph 13). Begin the first section with an incident and return to it in the fourth.
2. Locate and read the *Playboy* interview with Jimmy Carter that Sanders mentions (paragraph 20) and some of the responses to it. Write an essay in which you analyze the interview and the responses. Use "I" in a way that seems appropriate to you. Think about how much of your experience will go into your essay, and how you will include it.
3. Look at Sanders's definition of pornography: "making flesh into a commodity, flaunting it like any other merchandise, divorcing bodies from selves" (paragraph 37). Do library research on the Supreme Court's definition of pornography. Write an essay in which you contrast Sanders's definition with the Supreme Court's definition.

ANNA QUINDLEN

Between the Sexes, a Great Divide

The Norton Reader, p. 254; Shorter Edition, p. 158

Anna Quindlen begins this brief essay with a "perhaps"—"Perhaps we all have the same memory of the first boy-girl party we attended" (paragraph 1)—and expands it into an exploration of gender differences. If students haven't paused over the "perhaps," ask them about it. Is the memory shared, or is it gendered female? Is it gendered uniformly female? What would be a male memory—or male memories—of such a party? How might the entire essay be rewritten from a different memory of a similar event? Instructors may profitably move from this discussion to a discussion of the "great divide" of the waxed floor: how it originates as a real object of somewhat indeterminate meaning and then takes on complex meanings through Quindlen's embedding it within a context. Students like to say "this symbolizes that," as if to symbolize means to equal. This essay illustrates the making of a symbol, the loading of that "great divide" with more meanings than can simply be predicated of it. Quindlen makes much out of little; her essay, which contains approximately one thousand words, appeared as a "Hers" column in the *New York Times,* as did Gloria Naylor's "'Mommy, What Does "Nigger" Mean?'" in "Language and Communication" (NR 485, SE 290).

Anna Quindlen joined the *New York Times* in 1977 as a reporter. She became metropolitan editor, columnist, and writer for the Op-Ed page; in line to become an editor in the early 1990s, she resigned to have time to write fiction. As she explains in "Altogether Female," the introduction to a collection of her essays, *Thinking Out Loud* (1993), she benefited from affirmative action in both her hiring and promotion: six women brought a class-action suit against the *Times* in 1974 that was settled in 1978, and as a result the *Times* began to hire and promote women.

Questions from the NR11

1. Mark the places in this essay where Quindlen, after describing "the first boy-girl party we attended" (paragraph 1), returns to it. How does she turn an event into a symbol of male-female differences?
2. Consider Quindlen's statement, "I've spent a lot of time telling myself that men and women are fundamentally alike, mainly in the service of arguing that women should not only be permitted but be welcomed into a variety of positions and roles that only men occupied" (paragraph 4). Does her admission that they are not fundamentally alike mean that women should not be welcomed into male positions and roles? Why?
3. As Quindlen, in this essay, casts men as the Other, so Scott Russell Sanders, in "Looking at Women" (NR 244, SE 147), casts women as the Other. How do they present and try to decipher what they do not fully know or understand?
4. Write an essay in which you turn an event into a symbol.

Analytical Considerations

1. Ask students to look at the amaryllis in the bathroom (paragraph 8) as another example of Quindlen's symbol-making.
2. "I've always been a feminist," Quindlen writes (paragraph 4). How, in the course of this essay, does she define feminism? Are there other definitions of feminism? Where do they come from? Who uses them? Why is "feminism" a term whose meaning needs to be stipulated when it is used?
3. Does Quindlen lock herself into binary thinking about gender differences? See, for example, the discussion of binary thinking with respect to Isaac Asimov's "The Eureka Phenomenon" (NR 223, SE 130).

Suggested Writing Assignments

1. Everybody engages in binary thinking about gender differences: as Quindlen points out, they help children "classify the world" (paragraph 10). Catch yourself doing it or hearing someone else doing it until you locate an instance you interpret as damaging, another you interpret as innocuous. Write an essay in which you reflect on what each instance entails and the differences between them.
2. What does Quindlen mean by "linear thinking" (paragraph 9)? What would be its opposite? Write an essay in which you offer one or more examples of each and discuss their advantages and disadvantages. You may also wish to consider whether these two kinds of thinking are necessarily gendered.
3. Read four or five additional essays on gender issues by Quindlen—a number of them can be found in her collection *Thinking Out Loud: On the Personal, the Political, the Public, and the Private* (1993)—and write an essay in which you trace several concerns of Quindlen's that run through them.

ANDREW SULLIVAN

What Is a Homosexual?

The Norton Reader, p. 256; Shorter Edition, p. 165

This essay comes from Andrew Sullivan's autobiographical book about gay identity, *Virtually Normal* (1995); it represents his attempt to define for himself and others what it means to be homosexual in late twentieth-century society. Sullivan does not attempt a scientific or social-scientific definition (although he refers to such research in paragraph 10 with the phrases "in a string of DNA" and "in a conclusive psychological survey"). Instead, he analyzes his personal experience and its effects, beginning with the need for "self-concealment" (paragraph 1) and the sense of rejection, of being "forlorn" (paragraph 4). You might ask students why they think Sullivan does not turn to scholarly research, why his notion of "evidence" (paragraph 9) is insistently personal. If you wish to extend discussion beyond the bounds

Sullivan sets, you might ask them to gather "evidence" from scientific or social-scientific studies and consider why Sullivan might have chosen to exclude it from his essay.

Questions from the NR11

1. Throughout this essay Sullivan distinguishes between the "human experience" of all adolescents and experiences particular to or common among "homosexuals." Make a list of each. Were there features that you would have listed in the opposite column? What features did you expect Sullivan to mention that he did not?
2. Sullivan notes that it is currently unfashionable to think in terms of "stereotypes" of any group, whether based on race, gender, sexuality, or some other classification (paragraph 11). Even so, he has set himself the task of answering the question "What is a homosexual?" How does he define this key term without resorting to stereotypes?
3. Although Sullivan does not advance a political agenda or a set of social reforms, his essay implies actions that would be beneficial to homosexuals and, more generally, to American society. What are these?
4. Write an essay that attempts to define the characteristics of a particular group, using a variation of Sullivan's title, "What Is a ____?"

Analytical Expectations

1. Why does Sullivan begin with the example of the locker room? How does it serve both to rivet our attention and introduce a key concept?
2. How does Sullivan handle opposing views? For example, he raises the issue of choice in sexual orientation in paragraphs 9 and 10. What is his attitude toward others, including gays and lesbians, whose views differ from his own? What does Sullivan gain by his stance? What does he lose?
3. Why does Sullivan move to the issue of "diversity" and "stereotyping" in the final third of the essay (beginning with paragraph 11)? What argument about homosexuality does it allow him to make? You might ask students if members of minority groups that Sullivan names would all agree with his argument.

Suggested Writing Assignments

1. Do all homosexuals share the traits Sullivan treats as fundamental? Do some nonhomosexuals share them (for instance, self-concealment)? Write an essay in which you either take exception to one of Sullivan's fundamental traits or show that it applies to nonhomosexuals.
2. Do research in the sciences or social sciences on theories of homosexuality. What explanations do researchers give that are compatible with Sullivan's essay? What explanations do they offer that are different from, or even contradictory of, his views?
3. Discuss Sullivan's essay with a gay or lesbian friend or acquaintance and write about his or her views of it. You may wish, in particular, to discuss Sullivan's relative silence about lesbian relationships and consider whether homosexual women offer a different view.

AMY CUNNINGHAM

Why Women Smile

The Norton Reader, p. 261; Shorter Edition, p. 160

Cunningham's text is an accessible and effective model of an *exploratory* essay. Her essay is centered not on a thesis she is seeking to support, but rather revolves around a specific yet fecund question she is attempting to answer: "What is it in our culture that keeps [women's] smiles on automatic pilot?" Her essay does not endeavor to present a single, most convincing answer to this question; nor does it argue that one interpretive lens is more productive than others. Rather, it attempts to explore the topic, to offer as many *different* worthwhile answers to the question as it can muster.

The essay is also a useful example of the need for and value of interdisciplinary research when attempting to construct whole and complex answers to questions of human nature. In exploring her question, Cunningham ranges freely across disciplinary boundaries, weaving together information from wildlife biology, literary studies, medicine, developmental psychology, anthropology, feminist studies, anatomy, theology, art history, cultural studies, management science, sociology, and communication studies, among other fields.

Finally, this piece is quite effective in helping students understand the value of analytical thinking, of pursuing "small" topics, of attending to the significances of those things we typically overlook as unworthy of our interest. "Smiles," Cunningham writes, "are not the small and innocuous things they appear to be." In contrast to taking on massive, earth-shattering topics in an effort to manufacture authority and significance in their writing, students realize they can insert their own pet topics into her construction to launch personally meaningful research projects that still speak cogently to a wide audience: "Kisses [billiard balls, running shoes, fireflies, etc.] are not the small and innocuous things they appear to be."

Questions from the NR11

1. Were you or some people you know urged to smile or to smile more? How was the advice given? What do you think was the motive?
2. Collect some observational data on the way men and women interact with strangers and see if you can confirm any part of Cunningham's essay.
3. Write a comparison of the ideology behind this article and that behind Mansfield's essay on "manliness" (NR 236, SE 139).

Analytical Considerations

1. a. Cunningham's essay ranges freely across a variety of different academic disciplines as she develops her topic. How many different fields of study does she cite research from? Name them.
   b. Which of these fields of study did you find offered the most *surprising* explanation as to why women smile? Why? Which one offered the most

compelling explanation? Why? Which one offered the *weakest* account for the phenomenon?

    c. What is the effect on the reader of this kind of interdisciplinary development? How does it work to construct your sense of the subject matter? How does it work to construct your sense of the author?

    d. In sum, do you *like* Cunningham's approach here? Why or why not? In what ways do you find her interdisciplinary roaming and ever-widening lens engaging and effective? In what ways is her refusal to focus on a single analytical perspective or interpretive lens frustrating or disappointing?

2. Have students consider the exploratory nature of the text.

    a. Cunningham's text is decidedly unlike most of the short pieces of intellectual nonfiction. Rather than featuring a central claim or assertion that it attempts to support with evidence, her text features a central *question* which it attempts to answer in as many worthwhile ways as possible. What is your personal response to this *exploratory* form? Do you like this approach? Why or why not? Do you find its lack of straightforwardness, its meandering development, attractive or frustrating? Why?

    b. What sort of values does such a textual form imply? What does it suggest about the nature of truth? What does it suggest about the knowledge? What does it suggest about the value of certainty and uncertainty?

    c. How do you think your teachers would respond if your essays followed this kind of exploratory format, beginning not with a thesis that you supported with evidence, but rather with a question to which you provided multiple different answers? Why do you think they would respond this way?

Suggested Writing Assignments

1. Try your hand at Cunningham's approach to writing on questions of human nature. First, generate a list of those questions about human behavior that have always baffled you, but that you really don't know the answer to: "Why do people stay with abusive partners? Why do people still become Deadheads? Why do people become addicted to getting tattoos?" Then, select one that interests you enough to sustain your efforts over several weeks of research. Next, using interviews, field study, library work, and other kinds of investigation, write an exploratory essay like Cunningham's that attempts to present as many different answers to your question as possible, and attempts to address your question from as many different disciplinary perspectives as possible, melding answers from anthropology, psychology, biology, literary studies, physics, engineering, and so on.

2. Write an essay in which you emulate Cunningham's exploratory fascination with and analytical work on a "small" topic. Her essay does a great deal to demonstrate the significance of something we typically overlook as unworthy of our interest. "Smiles," she writes, "are not the small and innocuous things they appear to be." First, insert your own "small" topic into her construction: "Shoelaces [handshakes, guitar strings, hamburgers, etc.] are not the small and innocuous things they appear to be." Then, conduct wide-ranging research and render the evidence necessary to prove that your assertion is valid. Your goal here is to show that your topic is far

more complex and interesting than it first appears. In how many different ways is your topic significant and worthy of our time and interest? How many different fields of study can shed light on its hidden complexity and importance?

MALCOLM GLADWELL

The Sports Taboo

The Norton Reader, p. 68

If you have an opportunity to introduce this essay in class before your students read it, you might ask them if they believe that some racial or ethnic groups do better in some sports than others—and why. For example, do they think it's true that "white men can't jump"? Or how do they explain the relative dominance of white men and women in golf (Tiger Woods being the obvious recent exception)? Asking students to articulate their views, some based on biology, others on sociology, will prepare them for Gladwell's essay.

Gladwell takes on the biological question, arguing that "elite athletes are elite athletes because, in some sense, they are on the fringes of genetic variability. As it happens, African populations seem to create more of these genetic outliers than white populations do" (paragraph 13). But he also addresses the sociological, or "nurture," question, often referring to his own experience as a runner but more seriously considering this issue in terms of country of origin (beginning in paragraph 14). Students interested in this question of national influence might want to do further research, including reading biographies of athletes or histories of an individual sport.

Questions from the NR11

1. To discuss the "racial dimensions of sports" can be, Gladwell notes, "unseemly." What strategies does he use to introduce controversial issues? How does he minimize the tensions readers might feel? Does he always choose to minimize tensions?
2. What theories about the dominance of blacks in sports does Gladwell consider and reject? Why?
3. After Gladwell rejects inadequate explanations (paragraphs 1–7), he offers alternatives. What are they, and how are they developed?
4. Gladwell begins and ends with personal experience. What is the effect of his final story?
5. Write an essay on a topic that is "taboo," using some of the writerly strategies you have learned from Gladwell.

Analytical Considerations

1. The essay begins with personal experience. How does this introduction help Gladwell establish his credentials?
2. The essay is divided (by means of white space) into four sections, the first and last using personal experience. Ask students to identify the argument

and evidence in the second and third sections, one focusing on racial stereo-types and using genetic and anthropological research, the other focusing on national or regional influences. How does Gladwell's interpretation of this evidence further establish his credentials?

3. Why does Gladwell return in the last section to personal experience? Does it merely complete the essay as a literary piece? Does it introduce another factor not covered by the research in sections two and three?

Suggested Writing Assignments

1. Do your own research on an issue of race or ethnicity and sports by read-ing a biography of an athlete or a history of an individual sport (for instance, Roberto Gonzalez Echevarria's history of Cuban baseball, *The Pride of Havana*). What explanations, explicit or implicit, does the author give for the success of the individual or racial group in the particular sport?

2. In the penultimate paragraph of his essay, Gladwell states, "To be a great athlete, you have to *care*." Write an essay in which you agree or disagree with Gladwell about this criterion as the basic one for success in sports.

3. Use Gladwell's concept of "learned helplessness" (paragraphs 17–18) to explain the relative failure of some person or group in a sport or some other area of endeavor, such as academics, business, or politics.

ELISABETH KÜBLER-ROSS

On the Fear of Death

The Norton Reader, p. 274; Shorter Edition, p. 170

Two essays in this section of *The Norton Reader* discuss dying and death: Elisabeth Kübler-Ross's "On the Fear of Death" and Stephen Jay Gould's "Our Allotted Lifetimes" (NR 280, SE 176). Both are critical of the way we have made dying and death into medical problems instead of accepting them as natural occurrences, and they adopt various strategies to allay our fears. You may wish to assign these two essays together and ask students to assess the extent to which they think each succeeds and why.

Dr. Elisabeth Kübler-Ross, a Swiss psychologist, was a pioneer in examin-ing attitudes toward dying and death; her book *On Death and Dying*, from which this essay comes, was published in 1969. In it Kübler-Ross announces as her intended audience professionals who work with the dying, like chap-lains and social workers (paragraph 2), and her excursus on the communica-tions of the dying may be of particular interest to them. The book, however, was a best-seller that clearly transcended the particular audience she had in mind. In the selection reprinted here, Kübler-Ross presents and analyzes vari-ous kinds of material—experience, observation, and reading—to make a series of related points about patients and their needs and the often competing needs of those who take care of them and the families who arrange for their care. Her psychiatric orientation—what she claims as the unconscious motives that impel the behavior of the dying and the living—may need careful scrutiny.

Do students understand the claims she makes and the Freudian psychology that warrants them, which she takes for granted?

Since the publication of *On Death and Dying*, medical technology has made it possible to prolong life almost indefinitely, and court cases have complicated what Kübler-Ross regards as patients' rights. Students will probably have some familiarity with these issues; they may need prompting to discuss them with reference to the rights that Kübler-Ross articulates.

Questions from the NR11

1. Kübler-Ross incorporates various kinds of evidence: experience, observation, and reading. Mark the various kinds and describe how she incorporates them.
2. In this essay Kübler-Ross attends to the needs of the living and the rights of the dying. Describe where and how she attends to each and how she presents the conflicts, actual and potential, between them.
3. In paragraphs 24 to 27 Kübler-Ross describes the experience of the trip by ambulance, the emergency room, and the hospital from a patient's point of view. What does this shift in point of view contribute to the essay?
4. Imagine a situation in which a child or children are not isolated from death. What might be the consequences? Using this situation and its possible consequences, write an essay in which you agree or disagree with Kübler-Ross's views.

Analytical Considerations

1. You may ask students to reread paragraphs 15 to 17 and consider what Kübler-Ross's vignette—her personal report, so to speak—enables her to say and to imply about dying and death. The implication may be of two sorts: the texture and emotional resonance of the episode she recollects and its modern obverse. How would this farmer die today?
2. Consider what Kübler-Ross has to say about the mechanical prolongation of life. Ask students to gather other material—newspaper or magazine articles, scientific studies, etc.—about this issue and try to articulate the various different views that exist today.
3. Look at Kübler-Ross's discussion of avoidance techniques (paragraph 22). You may wish to ask students to discuss these and other techniques for avoiding unpleasant truths. What would be the consequences of speaking plainly and acting openly?

Suggested Writing Assignments

1. Write an essay in which you focus on your own experience of the death of someone you love. Frame it by considering Kübler-Ross's point that our treatment of the dying ordinarily reflects the needs of the living.
2. Do library research on one court case involving the mechanical prolongation of life. Look in particular at who is on each side and what arguments their lawyers make. Write an essay in which you describe and analyze the arguments of each side with respect to the rights of the dying and the needs of the living as Kübler-Ross conceives of them and as you conceive of them.

3. Read sections of Philippe Ariès's *The Hour of Our Death* (1981). Giving proper credit to both Ariès and Kübler-Ross, describe and analyze a set of customs that once surrounded death with reference to Kübler-Ross's scheme, that is, the rights of the dying and the needs of the living.
4. Kübler-Ross's attention to death and dying is repeated now in college courses on death and dying. If your institution offers one, get a copy of its syllabus, interview a couple of students who are taking or have taken it, and write an essay in which you describe the course and analyze what you understand to be Kübler-Ross's influence on it.

STEPHEN JAY GOULD

Our Allotted Lifetimes

The Norton Reader, p. 280; Shorter Edition, p. 176

Two essays in this section of *The Norton Reader* discuss dying and death: Elisabeth Kübler-Ross's "On the Fear of Death" (NR 274, SE 170) and Stephen Jay Gould's "Our Allotted Lifetimes." To different degrees, both are critical of the way we have made dying and death into medical problems instead of accepting them as natural occurrences, and they adopt various strategies to allay our fears. You may wish to assign these two essays together and ask students to assess the extent to which they think each succeeds and why.

Stephen Jay Gould was a biologist, an historian of science, and a superb popularizer; this essay, like others by him in *The Norton Reader*, was first published in the column he wrote for *Natural History* magazine. You will want to make sure that students understand his explanations of scaling theory and relative (and absolute) time. (Instructors for whom they are virtually unintelligible will usually find some students in the class who understand them and be able to turn to them for help; demonstrating a transition from incomprehension to comprehension can be a valuable lesson in reading.) You may also want to consider Gould's presentation of mathematical information through both equations and words. But it's Gould's larger strategy that deserves the most attention. Considering humans under the category "mammal," he reframes and provokes us to rethink death: "We live," he observes in an arresting parenthesis, "far longer than a mammal of our body size should" (paragraph 7).

Gould may be said to draw reductive parallels between humans and mammals, emphasizing similarities and neglecting differences. He neglects our feelings with respect to our own deaths; when he alludes to our feelings, it is with respect to the death of a pet mouse or gerbil, and he writes them off in a parenthesis: "our personal grief, of course, is quite another matter; with this, science does not deal" (paragraph 8). Nevertheless, his conclusion that we distort the way we interpret events measured on a large-scale geologic clock, trying "to bend an ancient world to our purposes," indicates that he is aware of tension between accepting the natural order of things and experiencing it as alien to us.

Questions from the NR11

1. In paragraph 7 Gould observes: "We live far longer than a mammal of our body size should." Describe, first, how he leads up to this statement, and, second, what consequences he draws from it.
2. Explain, first in Gould's words and then in your own, Galileo's example (paragraph 3), the scaling of brain weight versus body weight (paragraph 4), the scaling of heart rate versus body weight (paragraph 5), the scaling of metabolic rate versus body weight (paragraph 6), the scaling of mammalian lifetime versus body weight (paragraph 7), the equations for mammalian breath time and heartbeat time versus body weight (paragraphs 13 to 14), and the deviance of human lifetimes (paragraph 15).
3. In this essay Gould describes three kinds of time: Newtonian time, metabolic time, and geologic time. Consider how you experience each one. Then write an essay in which you describe your experience of all three and their relative importance to you.

Analytical Considerations

1. Have students, probably in groups, take one another's pulse and measure one another's breathing rate. Are they in accord with Gould's ratios of four to one? Have them explain the ratios; also have them explain how many heartbeats and breaths they can anticipate in their allotted lifetimes.
2. Have students mark Gould's arresting formulations and look at his use of words, sentence structure, and analogies. You may also have students experiment with rewriting them to diminish their force.
3. Direct students to locate Gould's parenthetical remarks. What characterizes all of them? Does he use parentheses conventionally both to interrupt and to subordinate?

Suggested Writing Assignments

1. Locate and read the essay on "neoteny" that Gould refers to in paragraph 7. Write an essay in which you explain it with reference to "Our Allotted Lifetimes." You should also add a paragraph of conjecture about why he skirts the subject in "Our Allotted Lifetimes."
2. Describe what you take to be Gould's views on the mechanical prolongation of life. Write an essay in which you use (and credit) evidence of his views in "Our Allotted Lifetimes."
3. Read Gould's other essays in *The Norton Reader*: "The Terrifying Normalcy of AIDS" (NR 720, SE 433) and "Darwin's Middle Road" (NR 1011, SE 600). Describe some of his strategies in writing about science.
4. Read Gould's other essays in *The Norton Reader*: "The Terrifying Normalcy of AIDS" (NR 720, SE 433) and "Darwin's Middle Road" (NR 1011, SE 600). Write an essay in which you consider what he thinks science includes, what he thinks it excludes, and the consequences of his views.

CULTURAL CRITIQUE

ANTHONY BURGESS

Is America Falling Apart?

The Norton Reader, p. 286; Shorter Edition, p. 181

Anthony Burgess, an Englishman (as he makes clear in the course of his essay), offers an outsider's response to the title question, "Is America Falling Apart?" You might ask students how they think Burgess acquired the authority (in 1971, when he spent his year in America) to estimate that nearly 50 percent "of the entire American population" think that their country is "coming apart at the seams" (paragraph 21): to whom did he talk, and what did they tell him? Research and documentation are not among the personal experiences that serve as evidence for his strictures on America. He situates himself, vaguely, in New Jersey. Where in New Jersey? Newark? Princeton? Ho-Ho-Kus? It makes a difference. Students can try to reconstruct Burgess's year in America from the evidence he provides in the essay.

The paragraphs in Burgess's essay are loosely connected. Although individual paragraphs are coherent and speak to his title question, the connections between them are as often associative as consecutive. He divides the essay into five sections through the use of blank space: paragraphs 1 through 5, 6 through 8, 9 through 13, 14 through 18, and 19 through 21. These spatial divisions mark units within the essay only in the most impressionistic of ways. What, then, is their function? Ask students to speculate. Also call their attention to Burgess's reversal at the end of the essay (paragraph 21), in which he owns that he finds America "more stimulating than depressing" and expects to return. Does he prepare us for this reversal in the course of the essay, or is it somewhat of a surprise?

Students will probably need to be encouraged to pull apart an essay by a professional writer and see how many of the principles of "good" writing can be, and at times should be, violated. Most likely, they will have been engaged by Burgess's essay; if they haven't been, or won't admit to having been, then you'll have to dramatize your own engagement. You might turn the discussion to the differences between having an opinion and being opinionated. Opinionated writers can be boring and tedious; for most people, Burgess isn't, and that's why they think him worth reading.

Questions from the NR11

1. This essay appeared in 1971. What might Burgess leave out, add, or modify if he were to write it today?
2. Burgess says that in his son's school there was "no readiness to engage the individual child's mind as anything other than raw material for statistical reductions" (paragraph 10). Precisely what is he referring to? Does your own experience support or counter Burgess's claim?

3. Visitors like Burgess can sometimes see things natives miss; they can also overlook the obvious. Write a response to Burgess, pointing out where he is on target and what he has missed.

Analytical Considerations

1. Burgess's exaggerations, such as his assured estimate of the percentage of Americans who agree with him, fall under a technique called "hyperbole." You might ask students to identify other hyperbole in the essay and consider their effect. How does the frequent hyperbole characterize Burgess's style as a writer? What kind (or kinds) of responses do they elicit from readers? In what kinds of writing is it legitimate to use hyperbole, in what kinds illegitimate?
2. Ask students to identify some of Burgess's criticisms of America that they find valid. Do they find them valid in Burgess's own terms or by toning down his hyperbole? You might ask them, perhaps in small groups, to rewrite some of Burgess's claims in more moderate language.

Suggested Writing Assignments

1. Write an opinionated essay of your own in answer to a provocative question.
2. Burgess describes Americans as guilty and masochistic, eager to confess their national faults and accept blame for them (paragraph 13). Write an essay in which you play this kind of American. (You might, in a coda, discuss whether this kind of role-playing is easy or difficult for you.)
3. Burgess calls America "a revolutionary republic based on a romantic view of human nature" (paragraph 20) and refers to the "dangerous naiveté of the Declaration of Independence" (paragraph 12). Read the final version of "The Declaration of Independence" (NR 874, SE 513) in conjunction with these statements; try to reconstruct his reading of the document and respond with your own.

ADAM GOODHEART

9.11.01: The Skyscraper and the Airplane

The Norton Reader, p. 292; Shorter Edition, p. 187

In this essay about September 11, 2001, Adam Goodheart focuses on the ironic mutual destruction of two great nineteenth-century American inventions, both born in the big skies of the Midwest. Offering brief histories of the invention of both, Goodheart works to remind us how unnatural tall buildings and flying once—and perhaps still—seem. Central to his essay is a distinction between how we live with these two inventions. Whereas people were once terrified by skyscrapers and predicted that airplanes would soon become ordinary, until September 11, we accepted skyscrapers as quite ordinary while continuing to find flight odd (if not downright scary).

Goodheart's is a strikingly unpopulated essay: Osama bin Laden is only alluded to briefly; there are no profiles of victims, heroes, or hijackers. This fact offers an opportunity to discuss the events of 9/11 in light of the philosophical issues of modernity. Ask your students if the essay—and the events of 9/11 themselves—caused them to question any of their values, any of what they had previously taken for granted. Then focus their attention on the assumptions of progress—especially technological progress—and what it says about American success that Goodheart takes as his theme. In paragraph 5, he asks questions ("What keeps it up? What, that is to say, keeps us up?") that seem to be about engineering and the physical world but are also meant metaphysically. Ask your students how these questions are related (if they are). What is Goodheart's approach to answering them?

Eventually, you will probably want to point out to them that the essay is depopulated and discuss with them the implications of that choice. Does depopulated mean depoliticized? What comes to the fore with this approach and what is neglected?

Questions from the NR11

1. After the destruction of the World Trade Center towers on September 11, 2001, many writers attempted to analyze and comprehend the event. What is Goodheart's approach? As you (re)read the essay, mark sentences that articulate or summarize his key points.
2. Goodheart chooses an epigraph from Thomas Hardy's poem "The Convergence of the Twain," originally subtitled "Lines on the Loss of the *Titanic*," to introduce his analysis. To what extent is the tragedy of the *Titanic* like or unlike the tragedy of September 11?
3. Throughout his analysis, Goodheart quotes other writers, thinkers, and inventors. Choose one quotation that you think is particularly effective and explain why.
4. Goodheart's essay is, in a sense, an analysis of a visual image from September 11; he calls it "an image that will stand for as long as any tower" (paragraph 24). Choose another image from that day or the aftermath and, like Goodheart, write an essay in which you analyze its meaning and significance.

Analytical Considerations

1. Bring (or ask students to bring) definitions from an historical dictionary (such as the *Oxford English Dictionary*) of the words Goodheart highlights: "skyscraper," "airplane," "rocket," "computer," and "network." Look at Goodheart's discussion of the shifting meaning of "skyscraper" and construct your own history of one of the other words. What do the various meanings suggest about the role of this object in our society?
2. Ask students to explain what the relationship is between Goodheart's argument and the example from *Anna Karenina* at the end of the essay? Is it a good analogy?

Suggested Writing Assignments

1. Write an essay in which you discuss how your attitude to either skyscrapers or airplanes has changed since September 11.

2. Goodheart's essay looks at the mutual destruction of two human inventions—airplane and skyscraper—on September 11 as a way of thinking about the role of modern technology in that event. Most of us heard about the events in New York and Washington via other modern inventions: television (with images brought to us via satellite), cell phones, pdas, e-mail, and the Internet. Choose one of these inventions and write an essay in which you discuss both its history and what role it played on September 11. Did the inventors of the technology imagine the use to which people put it on that day? Have people's attitudes toward the technology changed in light of September 11?

HENRY LOUIS GATES JR.

In the Kitchen

The Norton Reader, p. 76

Gates, a literary critic and professor of African American studies at Harvard University, published his memories of growing up in *Colored People*; this section of that memoir appeared in the *New Yorker*, not usually an outlet for university professors but one appropriate for this personal reminiscence.

Gates's subject is hair in the African American community during the 1950s and 1960s. Students should note that he does not discuss the well-known reactions to these hairstyles, the Afros of the late 1960s and 1970s, as worn by such cultural icons as Jimi Hendrix and the young Michael Jackson. Instead, his essay can be seen as an act of recovery. The cultural practices he celebrates have mostly fallen into disuse. During the 1970s they were vigorously opposed by activists who denounced the "process" as too imitative of white styles. Gates's essay is not a refutation of such denunciations but an attempt to pin down exactly what styles existed, set in the context of his family life in West Virginia of the 1950s, and why they were popular. Interestingly, though he starts out with an extensive portrait of his mother's hair preparation, his real subject is men's hair, especially his own in relation to the figures he admired.

Analytical Considerations

1. Note the colloquial air to paragraph 2, the back-and-forth movement of "I liked that smell. Not the smell so much, I guess, as what the smell meant for the shape of my day." Ask students what reactions they have to this movement. What kind of mental operation is suggested by it? What kind of relationship to the reader does Gates assume by writing this way?
2. Students might consider whether Gates's obvious admiration for hair like Nat King Cole's "magnificent sleek black tiara" (last paragraph) indicates that he favors such hair for himself today or, on the contrary, that he regards it as an impressive achievement for the 1950s but not to be imitated.
3. Analyze the elements that make the concluding paragraph so effective. Include Nat King Cole, the African setting (Zanzibar is off the east coast

of Tanzania), the hair itself. (Some students will not know what Cole looked like; they might need to see a photo.)

Suggested Writing Assignments

1. How were hair and hairstyles regarded in your family? Write about hair-care incidents, pleasant or unpleasant, you remember from growing up. Connect them to the kind of family you had or the type of person you were then.
2. Report on hairstyles and practices among identifiable communities and/or subgroups. Suggestions: nursing homes, military bases, punk rockers, farmers, teenage Latina girls, sports figures. (Just make sure the group you pick is well defined.)

SONIA SHAH

Tight Jeans and Chania Chorris

The Norton Reader, p. 304; Shorter Edition, p. 210

Sonia Shah's writing on Asian American and feminist topics has appeared in *Ms. Magazine, Sojourner, In These Times, Listen Up!: Voices from the Next Feminist Generation* (where this essay appeared), and elsewhere. Her essay offers an unusual take on the "I was a slut and then I got wise" personal essay. Shah writes about her sister's sexuality and about her own and her parent's disapproval. The twist here is that when the sister returns from a visit to relatives in India, she's dressing in sexy *Indian* clothes rather than tight jeans. Looking like "one of Krishna's cow-girls," the young sister wins her parents approval. This leads her shocked feminist sister to think about white feminist ideals and Asian cultural values in very vivid terms. Shah is both righteous and honest about her own confusion here.

Students will probably be most interested in discussing the relationship between the two sisters. Some may see Shah as just jealous that her sister is having better luck with boys than she herself did. Help them see where Shah herself considers this possibility. Why does she ultimately see this as only a partial explanation? Her experience leads her to rethink her college-acquired commitment to feminism. In the end, she is able to arrive at a new feminism that acknowledges her Asian American heritage and values while still standing up for herself as a woman. Discuss this process with your students. What has Shah learned? Where does it leave her in regards to her sister's sexy clothes?

Questions from the NR11

1. The two phrases of the title—tight jeans and chania chorris—refer to two objects of clothing, one from American culture, the other from Indian. In Shah's analysis, how do these two objects represent a split in her sister's cultural identity? Do they also represent a split in her sister's sexual identity?

2. Shah incorporates her parents' biographies into her account. What relationship does she assume between their personal histories and their present-day actions? Can—or should—writers always assume such a relationship between a person's past and present?
3. At the end of her essay Shah wonders if she should have encouraged her younger sister to wear a chorri with her tight jeans. Do you think this combination would have resolved the problem of her dual cultural identities?
4. If you have read Henry Louis Gates Jr.'s essay "In the Kitchen" (in this section), compare the ways the two writers respond to and resolve the question of dual cultural identities—Indian and American, black and white.
5. Recall a family conflict that involved cultural (or ethnic, religious, sexual, or political) difference. Write about that conflict, both analyzing the cause of the difference and imagining how it might have been resolved.

Analytical Considerations

1. What, in Shah's experience, is the price of a young woman expressing her sexuality, of being flirtatious? How does that experience compare to that of her mother? Her sister?
2. Much of this essay hinges on clothing. Perhaps before discussing the essay itself, discuss the messages that clothing sends to your students. What role do status, self-expression, fidelity to their culture(s), flirtation, and rebellion play in their choices of what to wear? How do other people's clothing affect their impressions of them? If there are clothing battles in their family, ask them to share what is at stake in those disagreements. Ask, then, how Shah uses such battles to explore the larger topic of cultural identity.
3. Shah's essay concludes with her thoughts on how best to make a persuasive case for her feminism to her parents. This essay was first published in a collection of essays by young feminists. Given this context, ask your students what they think is the purpose of these concluding thoughts. You might discuss the way that Shah constructs a dual audience here—her parents and other women of her generation.
4. Ask students if they've had the experience of changing an opinion at college. What happens when they go home?

Suggested Writing Assignments

1. At the end of her essay, Shah briefly sketches a new way to explain her feminism to her parents. Write an essay using Shah's proposed method in which you explain, in terms they would understand, your opinion to a skeptical elder.
2. Central to the essay is Shah's disagreement with her sister about the meaning of dressing sexily. Write an essay in which you defend where you stand in this debate.
3 Shah's experience at a predominantly white college and in an Asian American home leads her to be critical of assumptions in both places. Think of a cultural divide that you have crossed—be it of race, social class, religion, or something more subtle. (It could be something as strongly marked as Shah's or simply the difference between a menial summer job and your

life as a college student.) Write an essay in which you discuss what this movement taught you about your beliefs.

JOHN McMURTRY

Kill 'Em! Crush 'Em! Eat 'Em Raw!

The Norton Reader, p. 309; Shorter Edition, p. 200

John McMurtry, a Canadian professor of philosophy, writes in this essay about his experiences as a professional football player. He moves smoothly from personal report to impersonal generalization. He starts in the present, with the flaring up of an old injury, and moves back to his love of athletics, the increasing professionalization of his participation in sports, and the injuries that finally led him to quit the game. He then broadens his scope to consider the social role of professional sports, particularly violent and damaging ones like football.

Although his arguments for and against professional sports may seem familiar, indeed overrehearsed, McMurtry derives his authority from his unusual career as both player and philosopher. He condemns professional football, but judiciously. Perhaps what is most engaging about his essay is his depiction of himself as a player caught up in the ethos of the sport, accepting its rules and hazards with some sense of disquiet but without much questioning.

Questions from the NR11

1. What similarities does McMurtry see between football and war? How persuasive do you find the linkage?
2. Is McMurtry's essay mainly about his personal experiences in football, or is it about some larger point, with his experiences used as examples?
3. Draw connections between "real life" and some kind of game or play familiar to you. Does this illuminate any social arrangements or help you to see them in a new light? How far can one generalize?

Analytical Considerations

1. Ask students to consider the various dimensions of McMurtry's overarching analogy between football and war. What claims about football does the analogy make? And, conversely, what claims about war? Are both these sets of claims acceptable to them?
2. In "The Battle of the Ants" (in the "History" section), Henry David Thoreau describes a natural phenomenon in terms derived from human warfare. To what extent does he—and McMurtry 150 years later—assume that war is "natural" to the male species. Ask students whether they agree or disagree.

Suggested Writing Assignments

1. Perhaps you have found yourself in a situation similar to McMurtry's, participating in an activity that you later decided you should not have

participated in or did not want to participate in. Write an essay in which you reconstruct your state of mind during your participation and the process that led you to change your mind about participation and/or to give it up.

2. Critics from a number of spheres are calling into question the professionalization of sports on college campuses. What is the status of sports on your campus? Write an essay in which you argue for their lesser or greater professionalization.

3. Write an essay in which you consider why becoming a professional athlete is so attractive to some men and women. You can develop your essay through experience or research. If your own experience or the experience of a friend is relevant, use it, or do library research, either on a particular athlete or on the general topic, to expand your range of examples.

JESSICA MITFORD

Behind the Formaldehyde Curtain

The Norton Reader, p. 314; Shorter Edition, p. 194

Mitford's essay is drawn from her brilliant book, *The American Way of Death* (1963), a biting analysis of American funeral practices. Mitford revised and updated her book for a new edition just before her own death in 1996; it was published in 1998.

The masterful opening warrants attention. The metaphor of stage presentation governs the entire essay (as the title suggests), so the *Hamlet* quote is apposite. The object of the behind-the-scenes drama is to prepare the body for "public display," the ultimate objective a "Beautiful Memory Picture" (paragraph 1). Contrasted with this use of metaphor is her litany of verbs: "sprayed, sliced, pierced, pickled, trussed, trimmed, creamed, waxed, painted, rouged. . . ." (paragraph 1). (Otto von Bismarck's remark that it is better not to see sausages and laws being made might usefully be extended to "memory pictures.")

Mitford's British background gives her the distance that is needed to survey American funeral practices with a traveler's eye; what seems normal to us seems quite odd to her. Interestingly, this was not the only British send-up of America's funeral industry. Evelyn Waugh's *The Loved One* (1948) focused on pet cemeteries and extravagances such as Los Angeles's famous Forest Lawn Memorial Park. (It was made into a movie starring Robert Morse and Jonathan Winters.)

Questions from the NR11

1. Mitford's description might be called a "process essay"—that is, it describes the process by which a corpse becomes a "Beautiful Memory Picture." What are the stages of the process? Mark them in the margins of the essay, and think about how Mitford treats each one.

2. Mitford objects to the American funeral industry and its manipulation of death, yet she never directly says so. How do we as readers know her attitude? Cite words, phrases, or sentences that reveal her position.
3. Describe a process that you object to, letting your choice of words reveal your attitude.

Analytical Considerations

1. As a follow-up to question 2 (reprinted above), you might look closely at paragraph 4 as a typical expression of Mitford's attitude. Some students might find it disagreeably superior; others, appropriately sarcastic. Students can look closely at how her word choice denigrates the people who pay so much money for embalming. One might usefully ask why she omits any mention of the survivors' state of mind at the time they decide such matters.
2. A close look at names reveals Mitford's scornful delight in incongruities. The "Vari-Pose Head Rest" (paragraph 8), the Eckels College of Mortuary Science (paragraph 9), Flextone (paragraph 11), and "Lyf-Lyk tint" (paragraph 11) are only a few of the odd names Mitford mentions in her deadpan style. Ask students to list more from the essay. The next step would be to come up with some odd-sounding names for commonly used American products and ask about the source of amusement in them. (Examples: Dr Pepper; Oil of Olay; Oldsmobile; Pepsodent; fancy British-sounding cigarettes, such as Sir Walter Raleigh, Parliament, Marlboro [its crest reads "veni, vidi, vici"], Philip Morris, Herbert Tareyton, Pall Mall [its crest reads "in hoc signo vinces"], Chesterfield, etc.) With Mitford's sardonic eye for incongruity, such slightly odd names turn up everywhere.

Suggested Writing Assignments

1. Take a common American practice and describe it from the perspective of someone from a distant country who doesn't automatically get it. Suggestions: engagement rings, football pep rallies, cheerleading, hanging out in malls, school newspapers.
2. Write an account of a procedure in the Mitford style, going step by step and providing both the main actions as well as suggesting alternatives.

WITOLD RYBCZYNSKI

Weekend

The Norton Reader, p. 321

In looking at the "weekend" as a concept, this essay also interrogates our basic assumptions about leisure. Besides giving a useful history of how the weekend came to be, Rybczynski records the changes in the activities that have come to occupy this space of time external to the formal work week. He not only probes the concept of leisure, but also examines the relationship between hard work and hard play and wonders whether we are ever really free from the demands of both. We all know what it is to be enslaved to work. Rybczynksi makes us consider the ways in which we might become enslaved to planned recreation.

Questions from the NR11

1. Before you read Rybczynski's essay, what did the term "weekend" mean to you? What other meanings or nuances did the essay add?
2. Rybczynski describes (and redescribes) other terms in the course of his essay—e.g., "leisure" (paragraph 7), "free time" and "freedom" (paragraph 10), "play" and "work" (paragraph 13). Choose examples from your own experience to explain what his (re)descriptions mean in practice.
3. Write an essay in which you agree or disagree with G. K. Chesterton's conception of leisure, as described by Rybczynski in the last paragraph: "the opportunity for personal, even idiosyncratic pursuits, not for ordered recreation, for private reverie rather than for public spectacles."

Analytical Considerations

1. The author argues that weekend leisure activity has become increasingly structured and strenuous over time. To what factors does he attribute such a change in weekend activity from idle recreation to planned activity? To what do you attribute the change?
2. How would you define "leisure"? What is the relationship between sport and leisure? How would you characterize rock-climbing or bicycling? Who decides what is leisure and what is a sport? What is a common leisure activity in your community? Does this activity require much training or preparation? Can it be enjoyed if done badly? Is an activity no longer leisure if it involves an outlay of effort?
3. Discuss the similarities and differences among leisure, hobby, and sport.
4. Rybczynski believes that the substitution of the long two-or-three-week vacation with several three-or-four-day long weekends has led to the intensification of weekend leisure activity. Why would a long vacation discourage the type of heightened "leisure" activity that characterizes the long weekend?

Suggested Writing Assignments

1. What do you do for weekend leisure? Does your leisure activity have the quality of Chesterton's activities, or is it something that requires much effort? Write about your weekend activity, and why you consider it leisure.
2. A Marxist reading of the modern weekend would see it as serving the needs of the capitalist economy—i.e., requiring the purchase and consumption of expensive equipment, products, and services, and facilitating the continuation of enslavement to labor. Rybczynski appears to rue the loss of the "'noble habit of doing nothing.'" Discuss the ways in which such an idle weekend would either benefit or work against the individual. Consider what would happen if everyone decided to indulge in the habit of doing nothing over the weekend. How would your family be transformed? How would your immediate community change? How would your extended community change?

ROLAND BARTHES

Toys

The Norton Reader, p. 325

Roland Barthes, French philosopher, literary and cultural critic, and social commentator of the mid-twentieth century, has written some of the most provocative analyses of how individuals encounter and react to the printed word and to visual images. Barthes holds that the manner in which people read text or view images is conditioned by social and cultural forces. Interpretation is culturally conditioned. In this essay, he argues that play is also socially and culturally informed. He "reads" French toys as one would read a literary text—analyzing the toys' forms and functions and drawing conclusions from these elements about French society and the expectations placed on French children. The point he makes is that social norms structure all aspects of life, even the games that children are encouraged to play.

Analytical Considerations

1. What appears to be the purpose of play in French society, according to Barthes? What, in your opinion, ought to be the function of play?
2. Many psychologists see playing with toys as critical to a child's experimenting with the adult world. Why does Barthes object to such preparation for the adult world? What arguments could you use to counter his objections?
3. What kinds of toys would enable a child to engage in play that does not have as its primary objective an introduction to the roles the child would have to assume as an adult?
4. Barthes celebrates wood as a substance that, unlike the plastics and metals with which most toys are made, connects the child with life—with the energy of the tree and the person who crafted the toy. But plastic has its own advantages. What are some of the reasons that plastic toys might be preferable to wooden toys?
5. Legos are a popular plastic toy in many parts of the industrialized world. How do they foster creativity? How are they better or worse than wooden blocks?

Suggested Writing Assignments

1. Write about your favorite toy when you were a child. Keep in mind Barthes's distinction between toys that make the child a user and those that make the child a creator. What did your favorite toy enable you to do?
2. Many household items make wonderful toys—for example, lids of cans make wonderful spinning tops. Think of other common objects around the house that are or could be used as toys. What kinds of qualities do these toys foster in the child?
3. Interview a few adults about their favorite childhood toys. Use their responses to write an essay that discusses the characteristics that people seek

in toys. If possible, make connections between the choice of favorite toy of your respondents and the kinds of adults they have become.

DANIEL HARRIS

Light-Bulb Jokes: Charting an Era

The Norton Reader, p. 327

Harris's essay, which appeared as a brief article in the *New York Times Magazine*, represents a common but important genre of contemporary American writing: the analysis of a seemingly trivial cultural phenomenon that, under scrutiny, becomes deeply revealing. Other examples in this section show variations on this form: Jessica Mitford's more extended analysis of American funeral practices in "Behind the Formaldehyde Curtain" (NR 314, SE 194) and John Tierney's account "Playing the Dozens" in "Language and Communication" (NR 516).

Virtually all students have heard light-bulb jokes; indeed, they can probably add several more to the list printed at the head of the essay. You might ask students to consider how some of Harris's analysis works by extracting a single feature of the joke (the words "how many" in paragraph 2, the use of contrasting groups in paragraph 6), and how some of it proceeds under a general rubric (the age of consumerism in paragraph 3, "our aging democracy" in paragraph 5, "social unrest" in paragraph 9). You might then ask them if Harris's opening statement—that light-bulb jokes are "uniquely political" in contrast to knock-knock, dead-baby, and dumb-blonde jokes—holds true. Could one analyze these other types of jokes in similar terms?

Analytical Considerations

1. Ask students to note the various categories in which Harris "reads" the light-bulb joke: for example, within the age of consumerism in paragraph 3, within "our aging democracy" in paragraph 5, within the computer age in paragraph 8, and as "social unrest" in paragraph 9. Can students suggest other categories? What might these additional categories add to Harris's analysis?
2. Ask students to engage with Harris's argument (paragraphs 6–7) that the light-bulb joke is "an equal-opportunity leveler" that belittles minorities and the intelligensia alike. Are there other ways to interpret such belittlement?
3. If students know other light-bulb jokes, ask them to analyze the jokes either in Harris's terms or in their own.

Suggested Writing Assignments

1. What does another type of joke reveal about American culture? Choose a category that Harris doesn't consider (knock-knock, dead-baby, dumb-blonde jokes, etc.) and show its meaning(s).

2. Choose something ordinary in American culture and write a Harris-like essay showing what it really expresses. Suggestions: bread, sneakers, backpacks, CDs, MTV, gourmet takeout.

FRED STREBEIGH

The Wheels of Freedom: Bicycles in China

The Norton Reader, p. 330; Shorter Edition, p. 215

An experienced journalist goes to China to report for a magazine on how bicycles are omnipresent. While there, Strebeigh witnesses the start of the 1989 Tiananmen Square uprising—the outpouring of democratic spirit that would end with brutal government repression. So Strebeigh has a problem: how to fulfill the original intent of his trip, to produce a report on bicycles in China for his audience of cycling enthusiasts, while remaining true to his own instincts as a reporter witnessing history being made in a student revolt. He solves it brilliantly by regarding the bicycle as a cultural symbol of China. It represents a way to gain independence and, paradoxically, freedom to meet people in a time of troubles.

The opening is a model for students to examine and borrow techniques from. Strebeigh places us in the midst of the flow of cyclists in Beijing, meeting a stranger who feels empowered to talk, knowing she will be free from suspicious eyes. The simple quotation at the opening and the ominous "as we rode together we broke the law" frame a paragraph that introduces readers to Strebeigh's two themes: the ubiquity of bicycles and their key presence in the lives of participants in the uprising.

It would be helpful to a class to have some understanding of bicycle technology; perhaps a class member knows enough to serve as a guide. Strebeigh was writing for a highly knowledgeable audience who ride sleek chromoly road bikes with lightweight Shimano components that make the clunky, heavy Chinese bicycles look like they're from another century, hopelessly outclassed by the modern machines found in American bike shops. How is Strebeigh to make those bikes interesting to his readers? He finds a simple way: connect them to the lives of the people who ride them and focus on their cultural significance. For, the Chinese have something hard-core American cyclists can only dream of: a society in which the bicycle is the central mode of transportation. The actual kind of bike doesn't matter; its role is what counts.

Questions from the NR11

1. Strebeigh's magazine assignment was to depict and analyze the role of bicycles in modern-day China. What important roles does the bicycle play? Which do you think are most important—to Strebeigh? To the Chinese people he interviewed?

2. The article is titled "The Wheels of Freedom." Why? What relationship between bicycles and freedom does the essay suggest?
3. Write about an important product or artifact in American culture, analyzing its significance to its users and, if relevant, to yourself.

Analytical Considerations

1. Ask students to study the illustrations to Strebeigh's essay. What do they illustrate, and what do they add to the story? Given that Strebeigh went to China as a photojournalist, how might his photographs have triggered memories of what he saw and heard, and how might they have triggered segments of his essay?
2. Have students bring in similar "lifestyle" magazines with their complement of ads for the appropriate, expensive implements: skis, snowboards, stereos, sports cars, boats. Ask them, What's the context in which Strebeigh's essay would have been seen? What function do the ads play in such magazines? How does Strebeigh's essay fit with — but also challenge — the context in which it appeared?
3. Fang Hui's story is of triumph over discrimination, inexperience, and great physical obstacles. Ask students if they think Strebeigh might be making a subtle point about American reliance on fancy machinery and expertise.

Suggested Writing Assignments

1. Describe the significance to your own life of a form of transportation. Ask, as Strebeigh does, what the bike, bus, car, plane, or train does to human interaction.
2. Write about someone who excelled at a physical activity against great odds. (It doesn't have to be as dramatic as Fang Hui's story.)
3. Take a seemingly utilitarian implement, appliance, or tool and describe it to show the meaning it has for the people who proudly use it.

BETTY ROLLIN

Motherhood: Who Needs It?

The Norton Reader, p. 341

Although Betty Rollin never says so, the answer to her question "Who needs motherhood?" is "Nobody." This essay, written in 1970 for *Look*, a mass-circulation magazine now defunct, still generates strong responses. Virtually all students disagree with her argument and object to the tough way she argues; very few admit even to enjoying the essay. It's hard for students to imagine anyone taking her uncompromising position and calculatedly choosing to antagonize readers.

What students need to see is that Rollin makes her case against motherhood like a debater: she illustrates her argument with clear-cut evidence—no one she quotes has anything good to say about motherhood—and apparently she is out to win. If she brings up counterarguments, she dismisses them as propaganda and brainwashing. But does she really expect us to agree with her position? Think of a debate. The case for motherhood has been made often enough, as strongly and with as little qualification as Rollin makes the case against it. In place of all the "goo" that has been spread on the subject, Rollin throws acid. Somewhere between goo and acid must lie a reasonable viewpoint.

Questions from the NR11

1. Why does Rollin use the term "myth" to describe what she believes is the common attitude toward motherhood?
2. Arguing against motherhood is likely to cause problems in persuading an audience. How does Rollin go about dealing with those problems?
3. Rollin allows that "nothing could be worse or more unlikely" than "a world without children" (paragraph 30). Does this contradict her previous argument?
4. Choose a common "myth" in contemporary society and argue against it.

Analytical Considerations

1. Ask students, individually or in groups, to look at Rollin's language, particularly at her exaggerated, frequently outrageous statements (or hyperboles). Can they hear her as quotable and appreciate the wit of her formulations?
2. You might ask students to consider their antagonistic response to Rollin as gender based. Do they identify argument and debate as a masculine form, persuasion as feminine? Is a tough style legitimate for men, illegitimate for women?
3. Direct students to paragraphs 30 through 32, the last three paragraphs of Rollin's essay. How are they different from the rest of the essay? Why did she include them?

Suggested Writing Assignments

1. Write a debater's argument against some generally revered custom or institution. You might try "Fatherhood: Who Needs It?"
2. Try thinking of "Motherhood: Who Needs It?" as an example of sustained irony. Write an essay in which you compare it to Swift's "A Modest Proposal" (NR 857, SE 499). Consider how both Swift and Rollin may be seen as creating a putative author who offers proposals that violate feeling.

MAGGIE HELWIG

Hunger

The Norton Reader, p. 350; Shorter Edition, p. 225

Helwig writes of a problem afflicting not just individuals but a whole category of people, in this case well-off women in their teens and twenties: anorexia and bulimia. She herself has been a victim, as paragraph 26 makes clear ("I nearly died"). But Helwig writes less as a survivor than as a committed observer—that is, she does not make use of her own experience in anything like the way that, say, Nancy Mairs does in "On Being a Cripple" (NR 58, SE 36). A comparison of opening paragraphs—Mairs's versus Helwig's—displays two very different ways of treating material one has experienced personally. Helwig has just as much right to do an "engaged" or "you are there" opening, but she chooses instead to be a more distant narrator. Students might speculate on the gains and losses from each approach.

Helwig regards anorexia as a form of communication: the desire to be thin, though it has some connection to the world of fashion, is more spiritually based, a criticism of the existing order. It is, for Helwig, "the nightmare of consumerism acted out in women's bodies" (paragraph 4), and thus her long, admiring portrait of Simone Weil's self-abnegation. For Helwig, anorexia is both a life-threatening condition and an anguished cry about the nature of life in the present.

Questions from the NR11

1. Psychologists, social workers, or medical doctors would describe eating disorders according to their own professional criteria and in their own style. What particular language, style, and tone does Helwig use?
2. Helwig says that anorexia and bulimia are particularly feminine statements about consumption and consumerism. What evidence does she offer for this claim?
3. Helwig says that "women's magazines" claimed that anorexia was "understandable, almost safe really, it was just fashion gone out of control" (paragraph 23), while it was really something deeply symbolic of what is wrong in the culture. Write about something else that people are often told is simply a matter of lack of proportion.

Analytical Considerations

1. Paragraph 23 contains a critique of feminist understandings of anorexia. Have students refer to ads and illustrations of the type the feminists were relying on, and then explain why Helwig is not satisfied with such explanations.
2. Students should ask what more they'd need to know in order to agree totally with Helwig's main point. What ultimately would convince them that anorexia is communication?

Suggested Writing Assignments

1. People often treat eating and drinking disorders as trivial. Describe examples of serious disorders that are, or were, laughed at or scorned rather than addressed as the problems they in fact represent.

2. Based on a comparative examination of reference sources (general purpose dictionaries and encyclopedias are best) from the 1960s and the present, write an account of the growing awareness or changing notions of eating disorders.

GLORIA STEINEM

The Good News Is: These Are Not the Best Years of Your Life

The Norton Reader, p. 354

This essay appeared in 1979 in *Ms.* magazine, of which Steinem was a founder. Steinem asks a question she is now ready to answer: why are younger women, college-age women in particular, not actively feminist? The genre of her essay is persuasion, and of a particular sort: she wants readers not only to understand her position but also to understand why she once believed something else and then changed her mind. By taking a second look, she not only questions her mistaken beliefs but also looks at the false expectations and assumptions that underlie them.

The structure of the essay is well marked. After describing her former beliefs, she turns to what she believes now. "Consider a few of the reasons," she concludes in paragraph 3; in paragraphs 4 through 15 she considers the contemporary scene; in paragraphs 16 through 18, the first and second women's movements, throughout regularly devoting one paragraph to developing and explaining each reason. Then she concludes with the inverse of what her present position implies: if college-age women are not actively feminist, older women are.

Women students, both younger and older, may or may not accept Steinem's view of their lives. They may need to be reminded that Steinem, rather than criticizing them, explains and excuses them. Moreover, the developmental scheme she traces in their lives she sees as also present in her own (paragraph 3). Students may or may not be willing to talk about this developmental scheme, although older women are usually more willing to talk about such things than are younger women. Men students may be only too willing to talk about the pressures on them. At some point, you will probably want to turn the discussion back to the false assumptions that Steinem sees underlying her former views: single-sex models of cultural patterns, including, in this essay, human development and revolution.

Analytical Considerations

1. Steinem creates four categories to describe college-age women's responses to feminism (paragraph 15). Discuss the adequacy of her classificatory

scheme. You might also ask students to imagine this scheme, which appears in only a minor way in Steinem's essay, as the organizing scheme of another essay. What kind of essay would it be?

2. Ask students to read Anne Fadiman's "The His'er Problem" (NR 518, SE 308) for a discussion of how language creates many of our concepts. Does this essay shed light on differing responses to the word *feminist* or on why some women embrace the label readily, while others do not?

Suggested Writing Assignments

1. Taking a second look: Write an essay in which you look at something you've changed your mind about, accounting for what you used to believe, what you believe now, and how you changed your mind.
2. Steinem claims a "depth of feminist change" on campus that observers often miss (paragraph 26). Assemble what evidence of change you can, through your own experience and by interviewing at least one woman of another generation. Depending on whom you interview, you can compare the present with the past of ten, twenty, thirty, or even more years ago.
3. Carol Gilligan's *In a Different Voice* (1982) is an extended study of a single-sex model of moral development. Read it and write a brief essay in which you explain Gilligan's theory of how single-sex cultural patterns affect women.

JAMES BALDWIN

Stranger in the Village

The Norton Reader, p. 360

This classic essay is a product of James Baldwin's stay in a Swiss village, where he went to live in a friend's family chalet to get some writing done. Baldwin's experiences with the Swiss villagers' reaction to a black man in their midst causes him to see a paradox. In the normal course of things, the relationship of Europeans to Americans is straightforward: Europeans came first; Americans are of the New World; therefore, Europeans are more worldly, more sophisticated, more complex. But in matters of race, Baldwin argues, it is the Europeans who are naive, simple, and somewhat foolish. They have a few unsophisticated attitudes toward a black visitor in their village: fear and wonder, or at most a grudging acceptance. In fact, it turns out that these Swiss are much like the stereotypical Africans who first encountered white-skinned Europeans (though Baldwin knows there is a difference between an American black in Europe and whites in nineteenth-century Africa).

For Baldwin, America, more than anyplace else, is where black and white citizens have had the most interaction, the most to do with one another. Difficult as that relationship has been, Baldwin sees America as the only place where racial interactions are likely to continue to make progress.

Questions from the NR11

1. Baldwin begins with the narration of his experience in a Swiss village. At what point do you become aware that he has a larger point? What purpose does he make his experience serve?
2. Baldwin relates the white man's language and legends about black people to the "laws" of the white man's personality. What conviction about the source and the nature of language does this reveal?
3. Describe some particular experience that raises a large social question or shows the working of large social forces. Does Baldwin offer any help in the problem of connecting the particular and the general?

Analytical Considerations

1. For Baldwin, America is unique: "no other people has ever been so deeply involved in the lives of black men, and vice versa" (paragraph 26). Ask African American studies students if contemporary scholars of African American history might dispute Baldwin's claim, perhaps citing the long history of multiracial relations in Brazil or the Sudan or in Spain under the Moors.
2. Baldwin's picture of Africa is drawn from what he knew in the 1950s, just about half a century ago. Recent developments in recapturing the past might have given him a somewhat different attitude toward African history, though without altering his main point. What knowledge about the African past is missing from Baldwin's picture?

Suggested Writing Assignments

1. Describe the experience of being an outsider in a community.
2. In an essay, show whether or to what extent American attitudes have changed since 1955, when Baldwin published his essay. Is his basic point still valid, or have conditions altered so much that this essay has more value as history and literature than as contemporary commentary?

BRENT STAPLES

Black Men and Public Space

The Norton Reader, p. 369; Shorter Edition, p. 229

In this essay Brent Staples writes about himself as an individual and as a universal — that is, as a well-educated and nonviolent black man who, by virtue of his gender and race, is perceived as belonging to a class: violent black men. He is not unsympathetic to women who avoid him on the streets at night: "the danger they perceive is not a hallucination" (paragraph 5). The essay provides an account of his initiation into awareness and his attempts to distinguish himself from other members of his putative class.

"Black Men and Public Space" is an episodic narrative with commentary. You might call students' attention to the four times and places of the essay— childhood in Pennsylvania, graduate school in Chicago, Chicago of the late 1970s and early 1980s, and New York City now—and how Staples manipulates chronology. You can also have them note how the particularized narrative of the opening (his first encounter with a "victim" as a graduate student in Chicago) reverberates against his more generalized narrative of other times and places.

Questions from the NR11

1. Staples writes of situations rightly perceived as threatening and of situations misperceived as threatening. Give specific instances of each and tell how they are related.
2. Staples's essay contains a mixture of rage and humor. Does this mix detract from or contribute to the seriousness of the matter?
3. Write about a situation in which someone was wrongly perceived as threatening.

Analytical Considerations

1. Ask students to distinguish between narrative and commentary in this essay— and to notice how Staples combines them. It is more than a personal report; it calls attention to larger problems.
2. The pressure of the unspoken in this essay generates irony. Students might consider verbal irony, such as Staples's describing the woman he encountered in Chicago as his "victim," and dramatic irony, such as his whistling Vivaldi and Beethoven when he walks the streets late at night. Another irony would be Staples's "solution": his precautions against being taken for a mugger and a rapist. Are they a solution? How does the unspoken exert pressure? What are the advantages and disadvantages of irony in this essay?

Suggested Writing Assignments

1. Analyze Staples's essay as an unironic indictment of America as a racist society.
2. Write a personal essay about your experience of reading (and discussing) "Black Men and Public Space."
3. A longer version of this essay appeared in the September 1986 issue of *Ms.* magazine as "Just Walk on By." Find it in the library, read it, and write an analysis in which you focus on two things: the relation of "Black Men and Public Space" (excerpted for *Harper's* magazine) to the longer "Just Walk on By" (published in *Ms.*) and the question of audience in both essays. Why might *Harper's* have printed the shorter version? What is omitted, and what is the effect?

SHELBY STEELE

The Recoloring of Campus Life

The Norton Reader, p. 372

In "The Recoloring of Campus Life" Shelby Steele, a professor of English at San Jose State College in California, addresses a volatile and controversial subject: race relations and affirmative action on college campuses. Whether or not you decide to have students read and discuss it may depend on the situation on your campus and the dynamics of your class. The essay was published in *Harper's* magazine in 1989; in other words, it wasn't written with student readers in mind. Nevertheless, it is exemplary in Steele's judicious evenhandedness and careful assumption of authority. If you do assign this essay, you will probably notice its tight structure: Steele presents his credentials, explains how he gathered his evidence, and then divides his presentation of it—black students speak, then white students speak—before presenting his own proposal for a politics of commonality rather than a politics of difference. Although he has a proposal, the essay is not primarily an argument for it. Steele devotes more attention to analyzing the social and psychological dynamics of campus unrest than to advancing his solution.

Students will probably begin discussion in their own terms: after all, when someone generalizes about a group of which you are a member, your first response is, Is this true of me? The question of constructing universals has surfaced in other essays in this section—for instance, in Gloria Steinem's "The Good News Is: These Are Not the Best Years of Your Life" (NR 354). You might consider this concept again as you discuss Steele's essay. Has Steele constructed false universals—black students, white students? How might he construct true universals? How much qualification would be necessary? Is the entire enterprise of constructing universals doomed to fail? You will probably need to remind students that talk about groups rather than individuals is characteristic of academic disciplines other than literature: it is something they can expect to hear a lot of and do a lot of in college. Perhaps, then, universals are most problematic when we write about contemporary issues, when we read as individuals, when we look for signs of the times.

Questions from the NR11

1. What are the differences Steele cites between black-white campus relations in the 1960s and 1980s? Do you see other differences today?
2. What leads Steele to say that today's campus is given over to "politics of difference"? What are the "politics of difference"?
3. Using the same kind of interviewing approach that Steele does, write about the extent to which his conclusions apply to your own campus today.

Analytic Considerations

1. Steele tends to highlight what he sees as paradoxes: for example, "I think racial tension on campus is the result more of racial equality than inequality" (paragraph 6). You might ask students to consider his evidence and his formulation of this paradox by the use of antitheses: equality versus inequality. They should be able to locate other instances of paradoxical formulations in the essay.

2. How does Steele incorporate personal experience in his analysis and to what ends? Would he argue for its importance as strongly as Paul Fussell does in "Thank God for the Atom Bomb" (NR 724, SE 437)?

Suggested Writing Assignments

1. Ask yourself: Is this true of me—i.e., is Steele's construction of a group to which I belong by virtue of my race accurate? Write a private journal entry (for yourself), a semi-private journal entry (to be shared with the class), and a public essay (to be read to an audience that does not know you) in response to this question.

2. In a footnote Steele refers to an earlier essay of his also published in *Harper's* magazine: "I'm Black, You're White, Who's Innocent? Race and Power in an Era of Blame" (footnote 2). The title suggests that he treats at greater length the theme of innocence that appears in "The Recoloring of Campus Life." Read this earlier essay and write an analysis of its relationship to the later essay. Does Steele demonstrate similar evenhandedness and careful assumption of authority in both? How?

DEBRA DICKERSON

Who Shot Johnny?

The Norton Reader, p. 383; Shorter Edition, p. 232

Debra Dickerson defines herself in the opening paragraph: she is black, single, middle-class, feminist, Harvard-educated, and well-read in contemporary American politics. What happens to her nephew is not what she (or we) would expect: he is shot and paralyzed in a random and still unexplained attack by another black man.

Given her background, students might expect Dickerson to write a certain kind of essay, especially to write in a certain kind of style. In a sense, she gives us what we expect in the first two-thirds of her essay: a careful narrative of the episode and her frustrated attempt to make sense of it. Yet the final four paragraphs startle the reader. Dickerson shifts to the language of the streets, a language of rage and a style of derisory parody. Students will inevitably want to discuss the shift; it will be important for them to see the relation of both styles, the effectiveness of the shift, and the use of the "colloquial" in the face of the limitations of the "academic."

Questions from the NR11

1. Why did the *New Republic* include the first paragraph? Do you think the essay would be more or less effective if it began simply with the sentence "On July 27, 1995, my sixteen-year-old nephew was shot and paralyzed"?
2. Dickerson feels—and expresses—anger throughout this essay. How? Against what or whom?
3. Why does Dickerson use the term "brother" in the final paragraphs? How does this composite characterization work? How does it answer the question "Who shot Johnny?"

Analytical Considerations

1. Why is it important for Dickerson to describe her immediate reaction to the shooting as well as the routine in its aftermath? That is, how does she gain pathos and establish ethos?
2. Is Dickerson's use of the category "brother" in the final four paragraphs a "false universal"? Ask students why Dickerson might choose to universalize at this point.
3. Dickerson does not conclude with a sociological analysis, with a discussion of the economic, social, or historical sources of violent crime. Yet her enraged commentary shows that she is aware of such sources. Ask students to discuss sentences that show her awareness.

Suggested Writing Assignments

1. Who shot Johnny? Ask students to write a sociological analysis of the causes of the crime that Dickerson describes.
2. Read Molly Ivins's "Get a Knife, Get a Dog, but Get Rid of Guns" (NR 389, SE 206). Write a brief essay in which you explain how the proposal might have prevented the crime Dickerson describes—or why it might not.

MOLLY IVINS

Get a Knife, Get a Dog, but Get Rid of Guns

The Norton Reader, p. 389; Shorter Edition, p. 206

If Op-Eds range from dull and earnest to witty and smart-alecky, Ivins is firmly in the latter camp. Agree or disagree with her, everyone is pretty clear about exactly where she stands. Here her title says it all. You don't need to read on to find out what she thinks of guns. But when you do read on, you find out why.

For many readers, Ivins provides a short, sharply argued "take" on a subject. Here she sets out to skewer Second Amendment traditionalists by quoting them the entire amendment and telling exactly what she thinks it means by glossing it with statements such as "Fourteen-year-old boys are not part of a well-regulated militia" (paragraph 5).

This is not subtle writing. It's not meant to be. In fact, some can argue that Ivins is simplifying a difficult and complex subject, one that was until recently considered closed but now seems to have some life in it. That is, the Second Amendment was considered to govern group rights, not the rights of single individuals. (Courts almost always rule that the government can regulate firearm possession and use.) Now, however, legal scholars are having another look at the amendment, and even liberals are agreeing that there seems to be some room in it for the rights of individuals to possess guns.

By taking a complex issue and simplifying and condensing it to the length of a short newspaper column, Ivins (and her newspaper opponents as well) seems intent on arguing the case in sound bites, which is what tends to happen in television ads at election time. Her column and Anna Quindlen's "Evan's Two Moms" (NR 392) stand in contrast to the longer, less clever, and perhaps less lively think pieces by Henry Wechsler et al. (NR 397) and Kenneth A. Bruffee (NR 404).

Questions from the NR11

1. What do you think of Ivins's examination of the Constitution? What kind of evidence would make you be convinced even more? Why doesn't Ivins provide more evidence?
2. Characterize Ivins's language. What words, phrases, or structures seem typical of her style?
3. Examine the analogy between guns and cars. How does it hold up? Where does it break down?

Analytical Considerations

1. Ask students to examine the Second Amendment, which Ivins quotes (paragraph 5). Does the second clause depend on the first? What is the link

between "militia" and "the people"? How do we decide precisely what the amendment means? Whose interpretation gets to "count"?

2. Ivins says that the Second Amendment is clear. Many disagree with her. What arguments do her opponents give? Many students in the class, no matter what their beliefs, should be able to lay out the two sides of the argument.

3. Examine Ivins's diction to pick out the words that make her writing seem sharp and down-to-earth.

4. Ivins lives in Texas, where guns have historically been highly popular and readily available. Are there any signs of her Texas roots in this essay?

Suggested Writing Assignments

1. Answer Ivins in a debate-style piece of your own, trying for a similarly brisk, no-nonsense style.

2. Rewrite Ivins's Op-Ed in a more reflective, less combative style—for example, in the style of Kenneth A. Bruffee's "Binge Drinking as a Substitute for a 'Community of Learning'" (NR 404) or Henry Wechsler et al.'s "Too Many Colleges Are Still in Denial about Alcohol Abuse" (NR 397, SE 566).

3. Research some of the material supplied by pro-gun and gun-control advocacy groups and explain how their approaches are different from or similar to the way Ivins argues.

BRENT STAPLES

Why Colleges Shower Their Students with A's

The Norton Reader, p. 390; Shorter Edition, p. 287

With its strong opinions about the deterioration of American colleges, Staples's editorial can provoke some sharp reaction among students, who will not always see things the way he does. A teacher can turn that student reaction into valuable writing assignments.

The first issue is getting to Staples's real point: that the rules of economics force colleges to keep the customers satisfied by raising grades. The experience of a class of first-year students might not extend to grade inflation, but they can do some research on their own. It is not difficult to find out which departments and programs on campus are hard and which are easy. It's the kind of research students will be doing on their own anyway, so it's relatively simple to channel it into composition assignments.

Staples's essay also lets students examine some of the rhetorical strategies good writers employ. One is the generalization. Staples employs the terms "colleges," "departments," "students," and "teachers" but is rather short on specific examples, on individual cases. Is that permissible? Don't generalizations need support? What constitutes sufficient support? (Short opinion essays often don't supply much support, as Staples and the *New York Times* demonstrate here, and as Molly Ivins does in her Op-Ed column on gun control [NR 389, SE 206].)

Another useful term is analogy. For Staples, the college is a "product" and the students are the "customers." Class members can trace this commodity analogy throughout the essay and then decide how accurate it is. Do they think of themselves as customers? Just what happens when we think of college as a product? Is the market analogy a sign of the rising prominence of business in American life?

Questions from the NR11

1. What is the grade situation on your campus? Have you been showered with A's recently? Have you noticed professors inflating grades?
2. Staples writes, "An Ivy League professor said recently that if tenure disappeared, universities would be 'free to sell diplomas outright.'" Analyze this statement. What are its implications? Why does the professor think tenured faculty serve as protection against the "selling" of diplomas? What level of confidence does this professor have in the administration?
3. A Duke University statistics professor proposed "recalculating the grade point average to give rigorously graded courses greater weight." He was opposed by humanities professors. What might have been the source of their opposition? What do you think is meant by "rigorously graded"? What is the situation on your campus: do math profs grade more "rigorously" than English profs? Who are the hardest graders?
4. How broad is Staples's range of examples? Would he need to adjust his position if he considered other colleges? Write an analysis of the situation at your college either to confirm or to contest Staples's argument.

Analytical Considerations

1. Staples's market analogy does not include the notion of college as a brand name. Do some students regard colleges like designer labels? Are these students making an informed judgment about the value of different colleges? What can go wrong in such thinking? This train of thought can lead to excellent discussion, since students are likely to have their own college searches fresh in their minds.
2. Are there any traces of elitism in Staples's essay? The University of Phoenix, a for-profit school with a job-focused, "superficial" curriculum, is his first example of a "less rigorous" college. On what evidence does he brand Phoenix as watered-down? Does Staples supply any evidence that Phoenix gives higher grades? His other examples are strictly Ivy League, which often but inaccurately serves as a convenient stand-in for "college." (For instance, Staples's essay doesn't reflect the fact that most first-year students begin at a community college, and that the large majority of students attend public universities.)

Suggested Writing Assignments

1. Write about the college searches conducted by people you know, including yourself if you wish. What kind of information did prospective students find or receive? How did they make up their minds?

2. Describe a campus tour you took while considering a particular college. Was that tour helpful in making up your mind? In light of Staples's essay, what information could you have used in making your decision?
3. Conduct a survey of the grading practices among some departments in your college. Which have the highest percentages of A and B grades? Which mark on curves? Which have the highest dropout rates? (If departments discourage marginal students early on, they don't have to give so many low grades.)
4. Write a response to Staples's depiction of college as product and student as customer based on your own experience.

ANNA QUINDLEN

Evan's Two Moms

The Norton Reader, p. 392

Famous for her witty, engaging newspaper columns and her popular novels, Anna Quindlen has championed liberal issues by making them seem like commonsense notions, much the way the more flippant Molly Ivins does in her piece on gun control (NR 389, SE 206). Reasoned argument is not part of Quindlen's technique here. Clever positioning and a strong emphasis on the down-to-earth verities of love, fairness, and plain dealing characterize this essay.

Quindlen's essay consistently places love and devotion ahead of a narrow, rigid interpretation of the law, making it seem that there is no contest: a couple's love and devotion are far more important than narrow rules, she claims, and she quite cleverly assumes that no one thinks differently. In other words, Quindlen proceeds on the assumption that her "answer" to the issue of gay marriage is sensible, down-to-earth, and shared by all right-thinking people. The only disquieting moment comes with her sharply written sentence: "Gay marriage is a radical notion for straight people and a conservative notion for gay ones" (paragraph 4). This well-crafted sentence admits what everyone has known all along: that Quindlen's position is the minority one, that the fifty states have consistently ruled against gay marriage, that gay Americans do not share the right to marry the person they choose. As the sentence acknowledges, Quindlen is arguing for a right that most Americans oppose as too radical.

Thus the brief column is a nice example of making the "radical" seem sensible, commonplace, rooted in traditional values. And Quindlen does a fine job in foregrounding the positive aspects of her case: having two moms, rooting marriage in love and commitment, fostering the conservative desire to formalize a bond that already exists. When you want to argue for something radical, it is often a good strategy to make it seem safe and traditional.

Questions from the NR11

1. What is the precise subject matter of Quindlen's column? How far afield does she stray from that subject matter?

2. What do you think of the personality that lies behind this piece? What seem to be Quindlen's values? Compare them to the values espoused by Brent Staples, her fellow *New York Times* writer, in his Op-Ed in this section.
3. Compare Quindlen to Molly Ivins in "Get a Knife, Get a Dog, but Get Rid of Guns," both journalists writing columns. How does Quindlen begin? What is her hook? Why doesn't Ivins provide a similar hook to an event in the news?

Analytical Considerations

1. Why doesn't Quindlen put the argument in terms of partisan politics?
2. What's the effect of the closing comparison with interracial marriage? Spell out each aspect of the comparison Quindlen is making.
3. Is there anything underhanded in trying to make a "radical" notion seem safe and ordinary? Or is Quindlen confident her readers will understand that she is simply positioning her subject in a new, more favorable light?

Suggested Writing Assignments

1. Write a comparison of the two pieces by liberal women columnists, Anna Quindlen and Molly Ivins. Both make commonsense arguments in favor of very large shifts in public policy. How do they both treat the central issue?
2. Research and write an essay explaining why almost all governments have traditionally banned same-sex marriages.
3. Taking Quindlen's approach for a model, write an essay making something "radical" seem safe and ordinary.

RUSSELL BAKER

American Fat

The Norton Reader, p. 394

This is a light, witty update on the same general subject as Orwell's "Politics and the English Language" (NR 540, SE 319), though here the evil is depicted in terms of obesity and poor style rather than political manipulation. Could it be that Baker, a World War II veteran writing in the 1980s, is forty years away from Orwell's close-up familiarity with the Stalin and Hitler period? For historically minded students, it's worth reflecting on the change in language of criticism from Orwell to Baker. Both of them have devoted a good deal of thought to how in the twentieth century those in power used the media in an attempt to manipulate popular opinion. Orwell imagined it in sinister ways, Baker comically.

If the political angle is played down, except for the presence of one of Baker's heroes, Truman, the style angle is played up. Orwell and Baker both locate the source of fat, evasive language in the bureaucracy—and heap particular scorn on professionals who aim to make everything seem grander or more diffuse than it is. Baker's key example is the doctor. Students can no doubt find similar examples all around them, in the world of education, where searching for examples of overblown language is always fun and revealing. A college catalog or Web site are usually good places to start: names of departments and programs are a fertile ground; so too are the pompous mission statements that often precede course descriptions or describe the university's overall philosophy. Other good hunting grounds are law enforcement, the funeral industry, and psychology.

Questions from the NR11

1. Examine Baker's first paragraph closely. Do you find any examples of "lard" in his own writing, if only added for humorous effect?
2. Examine the way Baker alternates short and long sentences. What is the ratio? Can you discern a method in Baker's style?
3. Baker cites the Truman campaign of 1948 as the last example of plain talk. What do you think has happened since then to account for our supposed love of fancy, overdone language?
4. Compare Baker's essay with Orwell's "Politics and the English Language" (NR 540, SE 319). On what points do they agree? Do they cover the same ground?

Analytical Considerations

1. Use "facilitate" in a sentence, seeing if you can get it to sound appropriate. What are the problems involved in making it work?
2. To what extent is Baker's a serious attack? Do you think this essay works to make people change, or only to make them a bit more worried?
3. Besides doctors, what kinds of professionals use words like "facilitate"? Why might they use such Latinate words? What uses do you think are legitimate?
4. Many students will have their own lists of words that they find repellent. A good class discussion can ensue from students asking each other what is wrong with some words on their own lists. Some will be quite surprised to see what their classmates dislike.

Suggested Writing Assignments

1. Write a column-length essay (500–800 words) telling what would happen if everyone followed Baker's advice and removed the lard. What would prose be like? Would life be better?
2. How worried are people you know about their use of English? Outside of English classes, are people terrorized by the language police? Write about this subject, basing your essay on interviews.
3. Using a collegiate dictionary, check the current status of the word "presently" (paragraph 14). Then ask people you know what the word means. Make sure you keep track of their responses when you explain what the dictionary says. Write up the result of this little experiment.
4. Interview five similar people (all students, all from comparable occupations, all from the same neighborhood) about the overused, empty words they come across. Write up your results.

HENRY WECHSLER, CHARLES DEUTSCH, AND GEORGE DOWDALL

Too Many Colleges Are Still in Denial about Alcohol Abuse

The Norton Reader, p. 397; Shorter Edition, p. 566

This Op-Ed derives from research that Wechsler, Dowdall, and their colleagues at the Harvard School of Public Health conducted on binge drinking in 140 U.S. colleges and universities. (See also "Health and Behavioral Consequences of Binge Drinking in College" in the "Science and Technology" section.) Instructors may want to emphasize the rhetorical changes that researchers must make when they translate their work from a scholarly to a general audience, or they may want to treat this Op-Ed in the context of an ongoing debate about binge drinking and what should be done about it. In this article for the *Chronicle of Higher Education*, Wechsler, Deutsch, and Dowdall lay out the problem (which for them is not only binge drinking, but college administrators' denial of the problem) and suggest ways of correcting this health and behavioral problem.

Questions from the NR11

1. This article, written for college administrators, is a heavily revised version of a scientific study (see the authors' research article in "Science and Technology" [NR 948, SE 551]). Note the changes you see between the original study and this version. Are they changes in style? In audience? In format? In details? Which changes matter most to the overall impact of the essays?
2. What does the term "in denial" mean? Where does it come from? Do authorities on your campus act as if they were "in denial" about alcohol abuse?
3. Take the "weekend tour" the authors recommend on your own campus or a campus you know. Write up your results as a newspaper article.

Analytical Considerations

1. In their conclusion, the writers switch from discussing their research to calling for change by directly addressing college administrators. The transition is handled deftly and subtly: note the invocation of "administrators" in paragraph 15 and "college officials" in paragraph 19; by paragraphs 21 and 22 the authors are using imperatives and, finally, explicit second-person direct address in the last paragraph (paragraph 24).
2. Find parts of the essay that are not supported by the data in the scientific study. (See "Health and Behavioral Consequences of Binge Drinking in College" in the "Science and Technology" section [NR 948, SE 551]).
3. Ask students which article—the scientific report or the Op-Ed piece—has more redundancy, and whether it seems to be intentional. Is a certain amount of redundancy helpful in some kinds of writing? Which types benefit from redundancy? Which types lose impact?

Suggested Writing Assignments

1. Interview a sample of people on your campus about their drinking habits, and write a piece aimed at authorities about whether they are in denial about drinking on their own campus.
2. Explain what would have to change at your college if college officials acted on the warnings in this article. How would campus life be different?
3. Write an essay explaining why college officials have every incentive to keep alcohol-related problems covered up.
4. Write a description of a "problem" caused by drinking. Choose the problem from the list in Table 2 of the scientific article.
5. Take the Saturday night campus tour that Wechsler and his colleagues urge administrators to take. Record what you observe and write a descriptive or narrative essay about it.

JACK HITT

The Battle of the Binge

The Norton Reader, p. 401; Shorter Edition, p. 207

Over the past decade the research of Henry Wechsler and his colleagues in the Harvard School of Public Health has provoked a national debate about the binge drinking of college students: what causes it, what effects it has on students' academic lives, what measures might stop or, at least, reduce it. The seminal research report by Wechsler et al., "Health and Behavioral Consequences of Binge Drinking in College," is included in the "Science and Technology" section (NR 948, SE 551). Updates on the research may be found at the Harvard Web site: www.hsph.harvard.edu/cas.

Jack Hitt's opinion piece, published in the *New York Times Magazine* after a follow-up study by the Harvard research team, addresses the problem of binge drinking first by drawing on his personal experience at Sewanee in the 1970s, and then by asking a current student (his nephew) about binge drinking there today. You might want to use the opening paragraphs (1–2) and the account his nephew gives (6) as a starting point for discussing the kinds of evidence that Op-Eds allow. Personal experience is one means of challenging public policies or of imagining solutions to current problems.

Although Op-Eds represent personal opinion, it is important for students to see that Hitt links personal experience to public history and political agendas. His goal is to make a public point. Hitt's experience leads him to argue that the problem of binging increased when the drinking age was raised to twenty-one (paragraph 4). His nephew's experience further leads him to advance an argument about the responsibility of colleges and universities to educate the whole person, not just the mind. Using Hitt's allusion to "a kind of wild child"—a reference to an eighteenth-century child found in the woods and thought to be deaf and mute because it could not speak—might provide a way to underscore Hitt's critique of college policies that force students to drink off campus; in effect, Hitt argues, colleges that don't teach appropriate drinking behavior produce half-educated, "feral" children.

Questions from the NR11

1. The research by Wechsler and his colleagues at the Harvard School of Public Health has provoked a national debate about the drinking habits of college students. To what extent does Jack Hitt engage the scientific research? To what extent does he engage the public opinions expressed by Wechsler and his colleagues about actions that should be taken to stop binge drinking?
2. Is Hitt's Op-Ed focused more on the problem of binge drinking or on its solution? Does Hitt propose a solution?
3. Enter the public debate by writing your own Op-Ed on this topic, perhaps for your college or hometown newspaper. Consider your personal experience or other evidence you can add to public knowledge, and use it, as well as existing research, to make your argument.

Analytical Considerations

1. Ask students to list the kinds of evidence that Hitt employs in this Op-Ed: personal experience, a conversation with a current college student, historical observations, a survey of measures taken at college campuses to curb binge drinking, etc. Discuss why and how Hitt uses each kind of evidence to advance a case about how colleges should respond to binge drinking.
2. In paragraph 4, Hitt suggests that binge drinking became a "problem" when the drinking age was raised from 18 to 21. What evidence does he give for this claim? What evidence might students find by looking at the Harvard studies, as well as newspaper and magazine accounts from the 1980s and 1990s?
3. In paragraph 6 Hitt asks his nephew, a current student at Sewanee, why all of the students he took to a pub "sheepishly ordered cider." What answer does his nephew give? Ask students what answers they might give for similar behavior on their campus.
4. In the final paragraph Hitt alludes to a famous "wild child" found in eighteenth-century France who had never been taught to speak. The historical case was made into a 1970 film L'Enfant Sauvage (The Wild Child) by François Truffaut. Based on the 1806 memoirs of the French physician Jean Itard, the story begins in 1798, when a child is found living in the forest like an animal. Dr. Itard sets out to educate this child, who is totally alien to civilization. Give students an account of the historical case, and ask them to show connections with points Hitt makes throughout his essay.

Suggested Writing Assignments

1. Refer to the Harvard School of Public Health Web site for the most recent studies of binge drinking. What new findings has the Wechsler team reported since their 1991 study (NR 948)? Give a summary of one article.

2. Find Op-Eds about binge drinking in local newspapers, in national magazines, or on public Web sites. Write an essay explaining what you consider to be the best solutions that colleges have applied to the problem.
3. Interview administrators and health professionals at your college about the problem of binge drinking. Write an account of the current state of affairs.

KENNETH A. BRUFFEE

Binge Drinking as a Substitute for a "Community of Learning"

The Norton Reader, p. 404

Like Jack Hitt, Kenneth Bruffee responds to the research of Henry Wechsler and his Harvard colleagues on the problem of binge drinking. The seminal research report by Wechsler et al., "Health and Behavioral Consequences of Binge Drinking in College," is included in the "Science and Technology" section (NR 397, SE 566). Updates on the research may be found at the Harvard Web site: www.hsph.harvard.edu/cas.

For Bruffee, a college English professor, the "problem" is not so much binge drinking as the loneliness, fear, and isolation that lead new students to join sororities and fraternities to find companionship, and thus to enter a social realm in which binge drinking becomes a regular ritual. Bruffee advocates changes in college education—collaborative learning instead of individualistic, competitive classes. A life-long advocate of peer groups and collaborative writing, Bruffee argues that "collaborative learning can give entering college students a chance to experience a refreshingly new kind of social intimacy with their peers" (paragraph 20).

Questions from the NR11

1. The research by Wechsler and his colleagues at the Harvard School of Public Health has provoked a national debate about the drinking habits of college students. To what extent does Ken Bruffee engage the scientific research? To what extent does he engage the public opinions expressed by Wechsler and his colleagues about actions that should be taken to stop binge drinking?
2. Is Bruffee's Op-Ed focused more on the causes of binge drinking or on its solution? Does Bruffee propose a solution? How is a "community of learning" a solution?
3. Enter the public debate by writing your own Op-Ed on this topic, perhaps for your college or hometown newspaper. Consider your personal experience or other evidence you can add to public knowledge, and use it, as well as existing research, to make your argument.

Analytical Considerations

1. Bruffee uses personal experience to enter the debate about binge drinking. What facts about himself as a college student does he reveal? How do these facts advance his case about the causes of binge drinking?
2. Beyond personal experience, what kind of evidence does Bruffee introduce to advance his case? Students might mention the 1987 study conducted at Brooklyn College.
3. Ask students if they agree with Bruffee's assessment that first-year college students join fraternities and sororities because they feel "green, scared, lonely, and small-town." What other reasons might students give? Would Bruffee's concept of collaborative learning address these reasons? What other measures might address the feelings that lead to binge drinking?
4. Like Hitt, Bruffee sees a link between the "academic" and "social" in the lives of college students (paragraph 10). Are his connections similar to or different from Hitt's? How does each writer define the academic and the social to aid the cause of his argument?

Suggested Writing Assignments

1. Interview administrators and health professionals at your college about the problem of binge drinking. What solutions have they tried? Do any of them address the academic issues that Bruffee raises? Write an account of the current state of affairs.
2. Find Op-Eds about binge drinking in local newspapers, in national magazines, or on public Web sites. Write an essay explaining what you consider to be the best solutions that colleges have applied to the problem.
3. Refer to the Harvard School of Public Health Web site for the most recent studies on binge drinking. What new findings has the Wechsler research team reported since their 1991 study (NR 397, SE 566)? Give a summary of one article.
4. Read a chapter of Bruffee's book, *Collaborative Learning: Higher Education, Interdependence, and the Authority of Knowledge* (1983), and show how his ideas as a scholar inform his thinking in this Op-Ed.

Questions from the NR11 on Op-Eds

1. What characteristics do the Op-Ed pieces in this secton have in common? Consider technique, argument, and attitude.
2. Examine the four column-length Op-Ed pieces: those by Ivins, Staples, Quindlen, and Baker. What features do they have in common? What kind of arguments do they tend to make? How would you characterize their language? From your reading of these four, discuss the range available to the writer of a newspaper Op-Ed column.
3. Look for three other essays in other sections of *The Norton Reader* that also fit into the category "Op-Ed." Do they have features similar to or different from those you identified in question 2?

EDUCATION

FREDERICK DOUGLASS

Learning to Read

The Norton Reader, p. 408; Shorter Edition, p. 236

This essay is chapter 7 of the *Narrative of the Life of Frederick Douglass, An American Slave, Written by Himself,* published in 1845. "Written by Himself" is important: as Douglass tells us, it was "almost an unpardonable offence to teach slaves to read in this Christian country" (paragraph 4). He was taught, as we discover elsewhere in the *Narrative*, by Sophia Auld, until her husband put a stop to lessons. There were obvious practical reasons for keeping slaves illiterate: reading and writing made information accessible to them and multiplied their opportunities to escape. But there were also symbolic reasons: the ability to read and write was evidence of their rationality and humanity. Douglass escaped to the North when he was eighteen. His powerful *Narrative of the Life of Frederick Douglass* gave powerful support to the Abolitionists in their campaign to end slavery. He wrote two additional autobiographies, one, *My Bondage and My Freedom,* before the Civil War, and another, *The Life and Times of Frederick Douglass,* after.

In this selection Douglass tells how he learned to write as well as read. Like Eudora Welty (in "Clamorous to Learn" [NR 413, SE 244]), Douglass, after his introduction to literacy, virtually taught himself to read. But, unlike Welty, he was actively discouraged from reading, indeed forbidden to read. His account, dignified in presentation, has moments of high drama, sharply rendered. It also contains passages of impressively subtle analysis that students should be asked to look at with some care.

Questions from the NR11

1. Douglass's story might today be called a "literacy narrative"—an account of how someone gains the skills of reading and writing. What are the key features of this narrative? What obstacles did Douglass face? How did he overcome them?
2. Many literacy narratives include an enabling figure, someone who helps the young learner along his or her way. is there such a figure in Douglass's narrative? Why or why not?
3. At the end of this narrative Douglass mentions that he wrote "in the spaces left in Master Thomas's copy-book, copying what he had written" (paragraph 8). To what extent is imitation (copying) part of learning? To what extent does this narrative show originality?
4. Write your own literacy narrative—an account of how you learned to read and write.

Analytical Considerations

1. Slavery, according to Douglass, gave Sophia Auld "irresponsible power" (paragraph 1). Ask students to look carefully at Douglass's analysis of the corruption that accompanies such power.
2. Look at the selections from *The Columbian Orator* Douglass names (paragraphs 5–6). Why were they important to him?
3. Ask students to look carefully at Douglass's analysis of why learning to read "had been a curse rather than a blessing" (paragraph 6).

Suggested Writing Assignments

1. A number of people helped Douglass in his attempts to read and write. Who were they? Why do you think they helped him? Locate all the evidence that appears in Douglass's narrative and write an essay in which you answer this question.
2. Look in either *My Bondage and My Freedom* or *The Life and Times of Frederick Douglass* to see what Douglass says about learning to read. Write an essay in which you consider how and why these accounts differ from the account in the *Narrative of the Life of Frederick Douglass, An American Slave, Written by Himself*.
3. Write a literacy narrative, an account of how someone else learned to read. If suitable, include details about the specific book or books remembered as important.

EUDORA WELTY

Clamorous to Learn

The Norton Reader, p. 413; Shorter Edition, p. 244

"Clamorous to Learn" and "One Writer's Beginnings" (NR 1019, SE 607) both come from Eudora Welty's best-selling memoir *One Writer's Beginnings* (1985). Taken together, they comprise an account of her curricular and extracurricular education and may well be read together. Welty was fortunate to grow up in a family of readers, in a house rich with books and music. While her formal schooling was rich in books as well, she was not dependent on it for her acquisition of literacy. Rather, she was permitted to enroll in school at age five (when, today, a child would be enrolled in kindergarten) because she already knew how to read.

"Clamorous to Learn" is memorable for its portrait of Welty's elementary-school principal, Miss Duling. The other adults Welty talks about are minor characters: Mrs. McWillie, the stern fourth-grade teacher; other teachers; and her parents. Miss Louella Varnado, her own fourth-grade teacher, gets short shrift. Welty depicts Miss Duling from a significant distance. She remembers her as a figure of power and authority, much larger than life. Miss Duling tells the governor how his daughter will be named, and she calls on old grads when she wants to right some obvious wrong. It's clear that Welty admires Miss Duling's exercise of authority in a good cause, educating the children of Jackson. In retrospect, she sees Miss Duling's life as one of denial; as a child, "this possibility was the last that could have occurred to us" (paragraph 4). From the perspective of a child, authority figures are all-powerful and complete in themselves.

Questions from the NR11

1. Like Frederick Douglass's narrative (see previous essay), Welty's essay might be called a "literacy narrative"—an account of how someone gains the skills of reading and writing. What are the key features of this narrative?
2. If you have read Douglass's narrative, compare the similarities and differences. Might both learners have been described as "clamorous to learn"?
3. Write your own literacy narrative—an account of how you learned to read and write.

Analytical Considerations

1. Welty does not mention that the schools in Jackson were segregated, that the Jefferson Davis School was for whites only. The black school was, no doubt, considerably less impressive; see Maya Angelou's "Graduation" (NR 32, SE 18) for a description of a black school in a small southern town. Ask students what effect this omission has on their understanding of Welty's account.
2. Why does Welty describe Miss Duling's physical characteristics and clothing so thoroughly?
3. According to Welty, "I did nothing but fear her [Miss Duling's] bearing-down authority, and did not connect this (as of course we were meant to) with our own need or desire to learn, perhaps because I already had this wish, and did not need to be driven" (paragraph 7). This complex statement needs unpacking: Welty makes some connections between fear and learning and implies others. Ask students what they believe about the relation between fear and learning, what they think most people believe, and what beliefs were embedded in their own educations.
4. Welty's left-handedness was "broken" when she entered the Jefferson Davis School, though her parents were not in agreement (paragraphs 14–15). Why are children no longer forced to write right-handed? What does it signify about schooling that they once were?
5. Both Edward Rivera, in "First Communion" (NR 1127, SE 658) and Welty, in this essay, mention "deportment." Ask students if the word has any resonance for them. Some will never have heard it, while others are likely to have had it engraved on their consciousness. Ask them if they know the word "conduct." Then ask them if they see any significance in different schools naming concepts differently.

Suggested Writing Assignments

1. Write a Welty-like piece on memorable teachers, coaches, or authority figures you have known, keeping an eye out for the telling detail or quotation.

2. Write an essay in which you compare Welty's description of her teachers with Adrienne Rich's description of hers, in "Taking Women Students Seriously" (NR 448). Pay particular attention to questions of gender stereotyping.
3. According to Welty, the people of Jackson, Mississippi, believed in "the value of doing well in school"; see paragraph 16 for details. Write an essay in which you consider how much emphasis your own community puts on doing well or, alternatively, compare your own community and Jackson, Mississippi, in this respect.
4. Write an essay in which you analyze the role of fear in one or more particular episodes in your own education; see Analytical Consideration 3 (above).

DIONNE BRAND

Arriving at Desire

The Norton Reader, p. 418; Shorter Edition, p. 241

This essay records the coming into being of a postcolonial consciousness. Postcolonial writing comprises a formidable body of work by authors who record both creatively and analytically the experiences of once-colonized nations and peoples that have liberated themselves from colonial rulers and engage in the process of reimagining their nations and identities in the aftermath. Postcolonial nations that have produced powerful writing of this type include India, Algeria, Nigeria, Trinidad, Jamaica, and South Africa. Well-known postcolonial writers include Salman Rushdie, Jamaica Kincaid, Chinua Achebe, and Ngugi wa Thiong'o. In this essay, Brand, who was born in Trinidad and now lives in Canada, tells how she stumbles upon a book in a drawer in her grandmother's kitchen, a book about the Haitian revolution of 1971 in which Toussaint L'Ouverture led an uprising against the French colonizers.

Questions from the NR11

1. Brand's first sentence states, "recalling is all art." Point to examples of the "art" she uses in her recalling. How would you characterize the way she writes about her memories?
2. Why doesn't it matter who wrote the book Brand describes? Brand could easily look up the author, but she doesn't. Why not?
3. We later find out that Brand's discovery of the book occurred at about age eight. Can you remember things that happened to you at that age with such specificity? What do you think happens when you try to remember details from so far back? Or has "art" begun to do its work in the act of recalling?
4. Write about an experience of discovery that happened to you at a young age, using details the way Brand does or choosing an "art" of your own to do the telling.

Analytical Considerations

1. What does Brand mean by the phrase "recalling is all art" in her opening sentence?
2. What function do food and the sensuality of food fill in the essay?
3. Brand does talk about her discovering the book while trying to steal a taste of her grandmother's cakes or sweetbreads. How does Brand's description of the food items in her grandmother's kitchen shape our understanding of how *The Black Napoleon* affects Brand?
4. Brand finds three books in the kitchen drawer—*The Black Napoleon*, a book on geometry, and the Bible. What conclusions can we draw about the household from these books? Why do you think Brand devotes considerable attention to the Bible and what it meant to her grandmother? What does the geometry book symbolize for Brand?
5. Brand, born in an independent Trinidad, tells us that she "did not know about slavery" and had "never felt pain over it." Why, then, is the discovery of *The Black Napoleon* so important to her? Explain what she means by "The book was a mirror and an ocean."
6. When she was done reading *The Black Napoleon*, Brand "lost innocence and acquired knowledge," in a clear reference to Adam and Eve. She tells us that she "lost the idea that desire was plain." What desire is she talking about? And what does she mean by "plain"?

Suggested Writing Assignments

1. If you're in the habit of reading while you eat, the next time you do so, recall how you felt while you were engaged in those simultaneous activities. How did eating enrich or distract from your reading? And, conversely, how did reading increase or diminish the pleasure of reading?
2. Write about some aspect of your family's history of which you've only recently become aware; in particular, discuss your responses both at the time of your knowledge and later, when you had a chance to think about the revealed history.
3. Write about a book that transformed your understanding of yourself; or write about a person, real or fictional, who deepened your knowledge of yourself and the world.

JOHN HOLT

How Teachers Make Children Hate Reading

The Norton Reader, p. 420; Shorter Edition, p. 249

John Holt, after ten years as a teacher, wrote *How Children Fail* (1964), a critical analysis of American education, followed by *How Children Learn* (1967). "How Teachers Make Children Hate Reading," which appeared in *Redbook*, a general-circulation women's magazine in 1967, is a compendium of both: how children fail to learn and yet succeed in learning that complex of subjects referred to in elementary school as "language arts" (Holt's editorial comment on that term, in paragraph 33, is "ugh!"). Holt writes for a general rather than a professional audience: in paragraphs 44–45, for example, he addresses parents. He includes a lot of information about what works and what doesn't through vignettes, a few of them about particular students, most of them about particular classes. His essay disperses itself into a set of precepts, how-not-to and how-to. You may want to ask students to trace Holt's assumptions about learning, about children as learners, and about the value of reading and writing through these precepts.

Running through Holt's essay is another theme: the education of John Holt, the teacher. Most revealing, probably, is the opening vignette, in which Holt's professional wisdom is challenged by his sister's experiential wisdom. As the essay proceeds, Holt again and again invents new and more successful modes of teaching that run counter to professionally sanctioned modes; only after he invents the writing derby, for example, does he find that S. I. Hayakawa has invented Non-Stop writing (paragraphs 28–29). Holt's inventions always succeed. Ask students to consider his antiprofessional bent. Is it possible to codify his wisdom as professional wisdom? Some twenty-five years after Holt published "How Teachers Make Children Hate Reading," has any of his wisdom become professional wisdom?

Questions from the NR11

1. Mark the anecdotes that Holt uses and describe how he orders them in time and by theme. Consider the advantages and disadvantages of his organizing this essay to reflect his own learning.
2. "[F]or most children," Holt observes, "school was a place of danger, and their main business in school was staying out of danger as much as possible" (paragraph 12). Locate instances in which he makes this point explicit and instances in which he implies it.
3. Holt's "Composition Derby" and Hayakawa's "Non-Stop" are now usually called free writing. Have your teachers used free writing? In what grades? In your experience, how much has the teaching of writing changed since 1967, when Holt wrote this essay?
4. Holt begins this essay by describing the "game of wits" played by teachers and students alike: teachers ask students what teachers want students to know and students ask teachers for clues about what teachers want (paragraph 1). Do you recognize this game? Do you remember learning to play it? Do you think you play it well? Do you like playing it? Write an essay that answers these questions. Be sure to include anecdotes from your own experience.

Analytical Considerations

1. Ask students to look at Holt's advice to parents (paragraphs 44–45). What assumptions does he make about parents' circumstances and their involvement with their children's education? Are these assumptions legitimate? What kind of families does he take for granted?
2. Ask students about their own education in reading and writing, particularly with respect to how much of Holt's experiential wisdom has become

professional wisdom since 1967, when "How Teachers Make Children Hate Reading" was published. The results are hard to predict. In general, since Holt's essay appeared, the teaching of writing has changed more than the teaching of reading, but not uniformly.

3. Follow up Analytical Consideration 2 (above) with students' responses to Holt's methods of teaching reading and writing. What force does their experience have, individually and collectively?
4. What do students think about Holt's advice on reading: "Find something, dive into it, take the good parts, skip the bad parts, get what you can out of it, go on to something else" (paragraph 21)?
5. If a high school English course ran on Holt's principles, what would it be like? Describe a typical week in such a course: assignments, teaching style, classroom arrangements, discussion of reading, work on writing, homework.

Suggested Writing Assignments

1. Two antitheses are often used with respect to pedagogy: teaching versus learning, teacher-centered versus student-centered. Write an essay in which you define these antitheses using Holt's essay and amplifying them with your own experience. Is Holt firmly on one side or the other? Are you?
2. According to Holt, "we make books and reading a constant source of possible failure and public humiliation" (paragraph 13). Write an essay based on your experience, observation, and reading in which you discuss education as failure and humiliation. Are failure and humiliation chiefly associated with reading?
3. Imagine yourself sending Holt's "How Teachers Make Children Hate Reading" to one of your elementary school or high school English teachers. Write a letter to accompany the essay.
4. Locate two or three instances in your own education when your experiential wisdom ran counter to the apparently professional wisdom of your teachers. Use them in an essay in which you evaluate the nature and importance of personal experience, at least of the instances you choose, versus professional wisdom.
5. Do research on Whole Language teaching, which involves many of Holt's precepts (such as invented spelling). Has education in your state or locality moved toward Whole Language? Write an essay in which you discuss Whole Language and some of the controversies associated with it.

CAROLINE BIRD

College Is a Waste of Time and Money

The Norton Reader, p. 429; Shorter Edition, p. 268

In *The Case Against College* (1975), Caroline Bird argues that the college experience, good though it may be for many young people, is not good for all of them. In this chapter, also published as an essay, Bird argues that while providing a college education to all high school graduates is "a noble American ideal" (paragraph 3), many students don't want to be there, and college itself is a bad investment for them and their parents. Her evidence? Plenty of anecdotes from faculty and students.

Your students may share her bleak outlook; asking them what they think of Bird's essay may lead to lively discussion. Although it was written over twenty years ago, Bird's arguments are still relevant. Indeed, today there seems to be a kind of disenchantment with college—and certainly resistance on the part of parents and taxpayers to assume its costs.

Analytical Considerations

1. Ask students to list Bird's bad reasons for attending college. How many of them do they take seriously? This exercise may well be done in groups.
2. Bird frankly admits that she addresses the issue as a journalist, not as a scholar or policy analyst. Ask students to point to examples of what Bird calls "the journalistic tools of my trade" (paragraph 11).
3. Bird relies heavily on anecdotes to support her generalizations. Ask students if they have anecdotes of their own that confirm or contradict Bird's. How do we weigh the evidence of anecdotes when agreeing or disagreeing with arguments?

Suggested Writing Assignments

1. Interview students, teachers, and college officials you know and write an essay that updates Bird's. Are conditions the same as they were twenty years ago? Is the outlook for someone without a college degree still the same?
2. Some regard a college degree as a necessary kind of license, a union card, a piece of paper they have to have. Write about people who believe this, showing how such a belief colors their attitude toward learning, classes, and interaction with other students.
3. According to Bird, in 1970 colleges were spending more than thirty billion dollars annually to educate half of America's high school graduates. Do research to ascertain the comparable figures today, or figures for as recent a time as they are available. Write an essay in which you consider how economists justify such an expenditure. Are there other economists who regard it as a bad investment?

JAMES THURBER

University Days

The Norton Reader, p. 437; Shorter Edition, p. 257

James Thurber is known for his stories, fables, and cartoons. "University Days," published in 1933, is an example of deadpan humor. Thurber creates himself literally and metaphorically as a near-blind innocent who stumbles through the strange world of the university, trying to understand its odd customs without much success. The essay is a series of vignettes: botany lab, economics, gym, journalism, and ROTC. The other undergraduates who figure in it are even dimmer than Thurber. You might, for example, look at Bolenciecwcz's adventures in economics class as a stripped-down sequence from a comic book (paragraphs 5–12).

"University Days" is a comic essay, not a critique of higher education, and few students will take it as seriously critical. Considering how we know how to take it can be a useful exercise. You might take it as a critique yourself and let students argue against your view. They should be able to point to Thurber's exaggerations, his use of idiosyncratic and extreme examples as representative; they will be less likely to point to his verbal wit, to the comic precision of his language.

Questions from the NR11

1. Analyze how Thurber creates a comic persona by using his literal and metaphoric blindness. What, in the various anecdotes that constitute the essay, does Thurber not see?
2. In an essay called "Some Remarks on Humor," E. B. White says: "Humorists fatten on trouble. . . . You find them wrestling with foreign languages, fighting folding ironing boards and swollen drainpipes, suffering the terrible discomfort of tight boots. They pour out their sorrows profitably, in a form that is not quite fiction nor quite fact either. Beneath the sparkling surface of these dilemmas flows the strong tide of human woe." Discuss the relevance of this quotation to Thurber's essay.
3. Ethnic stereotypes are often a staple of humor: in this essay, Bolenciecwcz, the dumb football player, is Polish American. Is the anecdote offensive? Would it be more or less offensive if he were African American? Why?
4. Find some incident that will yield to a Thurberesque treatment, that is, that can be told from the point of view of a "blind" narrator, and write about it.

Analytical Considerations

1. What do the incidents Thurber writes about have in common?
2. Is it possible to determine, on the basis of this essay, what Thurber might have thought an ideal liberal arts education to be?
3. Look also at the comedy in Thurber's fable, "The Owl Who Was God" (NR 1140). Can students generalize about Thurber's comic techniques?
4. Students need help apprehending Thurber's verbal wit. Probably they read with such attention to content that sentences like "He would wander around the laboratory pleased with the progress all the students were making in drawing the involved and, so I am told, interesting structure of flower cells, until he came to me" (paragraph 1) slip by them. Try the sentence without "so I am told"; try putting "so I am told" in other places in the sentence. Ask students to find additional carefully modulated sentences in "University Days"; ask them to "spoil" Thurber's verbal wit by rewriting them. This exercise can be done successfully in groups.
5. Compare Professor Bassum with John Holt's portrait of himself in "How Teachers Make Children Hate Reading" (NR 420, SE 249). Is Bassum an example of "How Teachers Make Students Hate Economics"?

6. Many students will know by heart some of the scenes from the 1986 movie *Ferris Bueller's Day Off* that probably were based on "University Days." It's worth showing clips from the film and comparing them to Thurber's particular brand of verbal humor.

Suggested Writing Assignments

1. Rewrite Thurber's essay as a serious critique of some elements of higher education. Use his material and add to it, using idiosyncratic and extreme examples as representative makes for comedy, not critique. You may find Caroline Bird's "College Is a Waste of Time and Money" (NR 429, SE 268) helpful.
2. Find one incident from your university days that will yield to a Thurber-like treatment and write about it.
3. Do research on Thurber's university days at Ohio State University; a recent biography—*James Thurber: His Life and Times* (1995) by Harrison Kinney—has information about them. Write an essay in which you consider this question: were they a waste of time and money?

WILLIAM ZINSSER

College Pressures

The Norton Reader, p. 442; Shorter Edition, p. 262

William Zinsser, a writer and journalist, taught at Yale University from 1971 to 1979 and served, he explains, as master of Branford College. "College Pressures" was published in 1979; students will probably notice that room, board, and tuition in most private colleges then cost as much as $7,000 and that students might leave college with a debt of as much as $5,000. What are room, board, and tuition now?

Zinsser introduces "College Pressures" with notes from students and then, in an odd maneuver, first generalizes and then limits their relevance: "students like the ones who wrote those notes can also be found on campuses from coast to coast—especially in New England and at many other private colleges across the country that have high academic standards and highly motivated students" (paragraph 2). Does Zinsser restrict the relevance of this essay to elite colleges? Are most/many/some students still harried, driven by the same external and internal pressures he describes? Which students, and where are they to be found? Among the pressures Zinsser does not mention are work and family. How do these exert pressure on students, and on which students?

"College Pressures" appeared in a little-known magazine, *Blair and Ketchum's Country Journal.* Who does Zinsser think his audience is? What evidence is there in the essay? Is it written to students, to professors, to parents, to outsiders? Which elements of it seem directed to each of these groups?

Zinsser uses a four-part classificatory scheme in characterizing the pressures on students as economic, parental, peer, and self-induced. His scheme does not provide structure for his entire essay. It is, however, elaborately framed, and the divisions according to kinds of pressure are not only weighted with illustrations but also cross-referenced (see, for example, paragraphs 15–19 and 24). Zinsser apparently sees his classificatory scheme as rhetorically useful in ordering his material but distorting in compartmentalizing it. You may want to discuss the value of using classification within an essay rather than as the framework for an entire essay.

Questions from the NR11

1. What are the four kinds of pressure Zinsser describes for the 1970s? Are they the same kinds of pressure that trouble students today? Or have new ones taken their place?
2. Some people believe that students perform best when subjected to pressure, others that they perform best when relatively free of pressure. How do you respond to pressure? How much pressure is enough? How much is too much?
3. Write an essay in which you compare your expectations of college pressures with the reality as you have experienced it to date.

Analytical Considerations

1. Zinsser combines personal experience with description, analysis, and both explicit and implied prescription. Ask students to locate personal passages and discuss their contribution to the essay. What is Zinsser's authority to describe, analyze, and advise, and how does he claim it in this essay?
2. Ask students to imagine Zinsser's four-part classificatory scheme as organizing this entire essay. What parts of "College Pressures" would remain, what parts would go? What would be the effect of these omissions?
3. "Where's the payoff on the humanities?" Zinsser inquires (paragraph 20). Ask students to define the payoff Zinsser illustrates.
4. Pressures, according to Zinsser, lead students to do more than asked (paragraphs 27–29). Do you think this is still true at Yale? Is it true at other institutions?

Suggested Writing Assignments

1. What are the pressures on college students today? Write an essay in which you describe and analyze them, perhaps using evidence from Zinsser's essay to suggest that some pressures remain the same.
2. "Where's the payoff on the humanities?" Zinsser asks (paragraph 20). Write your own answer to this question, drawing on experience, observation, and reading.

ADRIENNE RICH

Taking Women Students Seriously

The Norton Reader, p. 448

Adrienne Rich is a poet as well as an essayist. Born in 1929, she graduated from Radcliffe College in 1951, the year her first book of poems was published;

her early poetry antedates the women's movement. In "Taking Women Students Seriously," an address given to teachers of women, Rich professes her intention not to lecture but to "create a context, delineate a background" for discussion (paragraph 1). She begins with her own education and her experience teaching minority students as well as her own women students. "The personal is political"—this is a maxim of the women's movement and an enabling principle of consciousness raising. It is also a strategy of feminist writing.

Rich sets in parallel form the questions discussed by instructors of minority students and the questions she came to ask about teaching women. Both minorities and women are disadvantaged, she believes, and the pedagogy appropriate to one has parallels with the pedagogy appropriate to the other. Note Rich's emphasis on activity versus passivity, questioning rather than accepting. Her discussion of women as students leads to a discussion of women in society: the academy mirrors society at large in putting women down or not taking them seriously.

Analytical Considerations

1. Ask students to review the personal elements in Rich's essay and their political meanings. "The personal is political"—political in what sense or senses?
2. Rich discusses what she calls "the precariously budgeted, much-condescended-to area of women's studies" (paragraphs 8–9). What does women's studies teach, and why, according to Rich, do women need to learn these things?
5. Rich speaks of women (and men) as if gender unites them more than other circumstances—large circumstances of social and economic class, of race and ethnicity, or small circumstances of infinite variety—divide them. She creates universals that may well be false. Consider the following: "Men in general think badly; in disjuncture from their personal lives, claiming objectivity where the most irrational passions seethe" (paragraph 16). Does Rich's generalization suggest a counter-generalization about how women think? Are there familiar generalizations about how women think?
6. "Feminists are depicted in the media," Rich says, "as 'shrill,' 'strident,' 'puritanical,' or 'humorless,' and the lesbian choice—the choice of the woman-identified woman—as pathological or sinister" (paragraph 12). The last became Rich's choice. Does she run the risk of such labels in this essay? Does she care? Who is her audience, and what assumptions does she make about them?

Suggested Writing Assignments

1. From your experience and observation (of high school or college or both), are women students taken seriously? Do teachers and faculty members treat them the same way as male students? Do male students regard them as equals? Write an essay addressing these questions. You might also consider differences between male and female teachers and between fields of study, for example, between education and engineering, or English and physics.
2. He: "Women take everything personally." She: "The personal is political." Write an essay in which you make a case for or against the personal.
3. Write an essay on a larger issue in which you focus on your own experience as evidence and illustration.

4. Read Gloria Steinem's "The Good News Is: These Are Not the Best Years of Your Life" (NR 354). On the face of things, Steinem and Rich take opposing views of women's college experience. Write an essay in which you discuss how you think their views are opposed, why you think they are opposed, and the extent to which you can reconcile them.

5. If you have a women's studies program at your institution, find out more about it. What are its aims, what courses does it teach, and who teaches them? Interview some students, some faculty, and/or both who are active in women's studies. Write an essay in which you discuss women's studies at your institution. Enunciate your own position with respect to women's studies as part of your discussion.

WAYNE C. BOOTH

Boring from Within: The Art of the Freshman Essay

The Norton Reader, p. 454; Shorter Edition, p. 276

Although Booth focuses on how to teach students to write well, his ultimate objective is to guide students to think for themselves. Booth views his two aims—good writing and cogent thinking—as complementary; only "thinking boys and girls" (paragraph 16) will write papers that aren't boring or in other ways frustrating to teachers. As he elucidates the problem of boring essays and potential remedies for them, Booth himself attempts to be not only organized and clear but also interesting and controversial.

Questions from the NR11

1. What is the occasion for Booth's address? How does it shape his language, structure, and evidence?
2. Divide the essay into sections and explain what Booth does in each and how each functions as part of the whole.
3. Select three essays from other sections of *The Norton Reader* that you think would engage Booth. Explain his criteria and how the essays meet them.
4. When you write, do you consciously attempt not to bore your reader? If so, list your strategies. Or, if the obligation not to bore your reader is a new idea to you, think of some strategies you might employ and list them. Use the list to develop an essay on strategies for generating interest and the circumstances in which they are appropriate.

Analytical Considerations

1. The occasion for Booth's address is a conference of college teachers of English; students in your class are overhearing him talk about their writing to other teachers. How much blame for boredom does Booth assign to teachers? How much to students?
2. How do paragraphs 5 and 6 set up the rest of his essay?

3. Are Booth's attacks on the *Reader's Digest, Time,* and *Newsweek* still justified? Bring in recent issues (or ask your students to) in order to test the
legitimacy of Booth's remarks for the present (paragraph 8).
4. Extract three principles for good writing from "Boring from Within." Then
compare Booth's philosophy of composition with George Orwell's in "Politics and the English Language" (NR 540, SE 319). Would Orwell agree
with Booth's principles?
5. Point out examples of exaggeration and satiric humor in Booth's essay. Is the
tone that these elements create geared to Booth's audience and thesis?
Explain.
6. In light of some of his comments, would you call Booth an elitist? If so,
what statements make him seem so?

Suggested Writing Assignments

1. Read the Op-Ed page in the *New York Times* or another major newspaper
for a week and select a column that isn't boring. (You may want to look at
the "Op-Eds" section in *The Norton Reader* to see Op-Ed pieces the editors
thought weren't boring, but you are responsible for finding your own.)
Analyze it and write an essay that explains why and how the writer avoids
the pitfalls of "boring from within."
2. Test the validity and accuracy of Booth's criticism of popular magazine journalism by reading several issues of the *Reader's Digest, Time,* or *Newsweek,*
choosing representative articles and writing an analytic essay.
3. Select and write about a model of "genuine narration, with the sharp
observation and penetrating critical judgment that underlies all good story
telling. . . ." (paragraph 28).
4. Booth does not soft-pedal his criticism of typical freshman writing. Does
this essay offend you? Does it contain a fair assessment of students' abilities
and productivity? Does it offer ideas that may help you to write better, more
interesting essays? Write a closely argued response to Booth's assessment
of student writing in "Boring from Within."
5. Booth seems to believe that topics concerning "social problems and forces,
political controversy, and the processes of everyday living around them"
can personally engage most college students (paragraph 19). Make up a
list of topics that engage you and topics that don't; this can best be done
in groups. Then write as essay that isn't boring on one of the topics the
group agrees on as engaging and share it with the group.

WILLIAM G. PERRY JR.

Examsmanship and the Liberal Arts:
A Study in Educational Epistemology

The Norton Reader, p. 465

William G. Perry Jr.'s urbane and erudite discussion of examsmanship, while
it contains much of interest to students, is not addressed to or written for them;

it was published in *Examining in Harvard College: A Collection of Essays* (1964), a volume written by members of the Harvard faculty and addressed to college instructors. Perry approaches "educational epistemology"—ask students, after they have read his essay, to define it—through a story that, were it told simply, is comic: "the picture of a bright student attempting to outwit his professor while his professor takes pride in not being outwitted," Perry observes, "is certainly ridiculous" (paragraph 4). Perry's elaborate irony and extended explanations defuse its comedy. What students will understand are the surprising uses to which Perry puts the story of Metzger's prank: he not only defends it as harmless but also, and more importantly, defends the section man's grade of A on Metzger's examination. A less complicated telling might have turned the story into a trickster tale.

Perry's educational epistemology involves framing, in which a fact becomes "'an observation or operation performed in a frame of reference'" (paragraph 40). With this statement in mind, direct students back to Perry's account of Metzger's examination: he wrote exclusively about framing because he had no facts to frame. Be sure students can discriminate between Perry's educational epistemology and their own cruder one, which Perry describes as finding "the right mean" between particulars and generalizations. They are not the same: "The problem is not quantitative," Perry writes, "nor does its solution lie on a continuum between the particular and the general" (paragraph 25).

Perry calls framing "bull" and facts "cow." The first comes from "bull session": shooting the breeze, talking loudly and authoritatively. "Cow" is Perry's invented opposite, and the genders of the pair are unfortunate, inasmuch as thought becomes male, facts female. Perry, again surprisingly, defends "bull," redeeming it in an academic context from its pejorative sense. While framed facts are best, if it comes to choosing between them, framing is better—even though students who present unframed facts are seldom given grades as low as they deserve. Perry also analyzes the mistaken educational epistemology of elementary and high schools: students are given high grades for remembering facts and graded down for misremembering them.

Questions from the NR11

1. Perry divides this essay into four sections, an introduction and sections numbered I, II, and III. Identify the focus of each and its relation to what precedes and what follows.
2. Perry makes the point that "bull" and "cow" are not the equivalent of generalizations and particulars, not "poles of a single dimension" (paragraph 25). Explain how, according to Perry, they differ from generalizations and particulars.
3. Perry's essay appeared in a volume on examinations, written by members of the Harvard University faculty and presumably addressed to them and to others like them. How does Perry address his audience? What kind of persona does he construct? Point to evidence for it.
4. Have you found the grading practices of your teachers mysterious or confusing? Write an essay in which you describe the practices of two or three of your teachers and try to discern the theories of knowledge that account for them.

5. Perry proposes that his colleagues "award no more C's for cow" (paragraph 52). Write an essay in which you argue for or against his proposal.

Analytical Considerations

1. What does Perry mean by *bull* and *cow*? How does he oppose them to each other? Ask students first to locate Perry's definitions and then to write their own. Is it necessary to provide examples to define terms? This exercise can profitably be done in groups.
2. How necessary are Perry's terms "bull" and "cow"? Can students find gender-neutral terms to fit Perry's and their definitions? See Analytical Consideration 1 (above).
3. Ask students to look at paragraph 44, the "productive wedding" of "bull" and "cow." How do Perry's gendered terms lend themselves to metaphoric expansion? What are the consequences?
4. How might the audience of Perry's essay have determined its shape and tone? What changes might Perry make if he were writing for a group of high school teachers? A group of educators from developing nations? First-year college students?
5. Perry, confronting the moral issues that "bull" raises, asserts: "Too early a moral judgment is precisely what stands between many able students and a liberal education" (paragraph 5); education of the right sort leads "not away from, but through the arts of gamesmanship to a new trust" (paragraph 40). Ask students to discuss these assertions with reference to the essay as a whole.
6. See Perry's account of the history examination that entering students at Harvard and Radcliffe are asked to grade (paragraphs 48–49). How do the results warrant his generalization that "better students in the better high schools and preparatory schools are being allowed to inquire"? Is this a demonstrated generalization or an elitist one?

Suggested Writing Assignments

1. Write an essay addressed to college freshmen in which you pass on what is important in Perry's essay. You may of course include what Perry says as advice about getting good grades. But grades, Perry observes, reflect an educational epistemology (paragraph 2). Do not slight epistemological issues.
2. Write an essay in which you describe and analyze the educational epistemology underlying your high school education. Introduce the essay with a fully developed incident.
3. Perry suggests that educational epistemologies differ according to field of study, with English teachers privileging "bull" and science teachers "cow" (paragraph 38). Is this true of your experience? Write an essay in which you contrast your experience of "bullish" and "cowish" fields of study.

ALFRED NORTH WHITEHEAD

The Rhythmic Claims of Freedom and Discipline

The Norton Reader, p. 475

This essay, drawn from Whitehead's *The Aims of Education* (1929), calls for revitalized educational practices: scrapping the modern notion of studying subjects and returning to the ancients' quest for wisdom. It bears some of the marks of its original appearance in a lecture series, as well as its British origins. (The spelling and some of the punctuation remain in British form, as in the original.)

Whitehead's prose is seldom lively. He writes like an elderly sage—which, in 1929, he was: sixty-eight years old, with a record of major contributions to the study of both mathematics and philosophy. Nor are the terms of his argument immediately engaging. But the issues he discusses are vital to any consideration of education, and the practices he suggests are in fact attractive to many students. The stage of romance, where Whitehead says education must begin, particularly interests them; you may find yourself hard-pressed to get equal time for precision and generalization.

Questions from the NR11

1. Whitehead addresses his audience as "you." Mark the instances where he does so and make what inferences you can concerning his imagined audience. Who, collectively, do you think they are?
2. Whitehead often uses the language of biology to describe education, as in "the natural mode by which living organisms are excited towards suitable self-development is enjoyment" (paragraph 5). Locate other examples of this language. How does it define his conception of education? Do you find such language helpful or surprising?
3. Although Whitehead constructs a sequence—the stage of romance, the stage of precision, the stage of generalization—he describes education as cyclical. His essay is also organized circularly rather than linearly. Identify repetitive passages.
4. Look carefully at Whitehead's concluding paragraphs (18–21). What does he see as the values of education in art? Do you accept his arguments?
5. Both Whitehead and Perry, in "Examsmanship and the Liberal Arts: A Study in Educational Epistemology" (NR 465), regard the goal of education as more than the acquisition of facts, though they describe the process in different terms. Write an essay in which you consider the extent to which they agree about the goal of education. You will have to consider the terms each uses, especially the different meaning each gives to "generalization."

Analytical Considerations

1. Compare Whitehead's definition of "wisdom" with William J. Perry Jr.'s definition of "framing" ("Examsmanship and the Liberal Arts" [NR 465]). How close to each other are they?
2. Define in your own words what Whitehead calls the "stage of Romance," the "stage of Precision," and the "stage of Generalisation."
3. Ask students if and when they have had ideas and subjects presented "romantically"? At what stage of their education? What do you remember about these presentations?
4. Whitehead says that schoolmasters "are apt to forget that we are only sub-ordinate elements in the education of a grown man; and that, in their own good time, in later life our pupils will learn for themselves" (paragraph 9). Do you agree? If so, what is the role of a teacher?
5. At a rough estimate, according to Whitehead, the years till age thirteen or fourteen are for romance, fourteen to eighteen for precision, and eighteen to twenty-two for generalization (paragraph 16). Why do you think he came up with these years? Do you agree with his calculations?
6. Whitehead confidently pronounces that "you can never greatly increase average incomes" (paragraph 20). He was wrong. What are the consequences for his argument that art, drama, and music should be included in the curriculum? Are there other reasons for studying them?

Suggested Writing Assignments

1. Whitehead writes of the "evil" of "barren knowledge" (paragraph 6). Write an essay in which you describe what you consider "barren knowledge" in your own education, using Whitehead's discussion to help you think through what the term means to you. Is Whitehead's term "evil" too strong?
2. Wisdom is the end of education for Whitehead, as it was for the ancient philosophers. Write about someone you know who you think has wisdom. Describe this wisdom in action and explain how this person developed it.
3. Choose a subject and describe what it would be like if it were presented according to Whitehead's concept of romance. Or tell how you or some-one you know became excited about a subject through something like Whitehead's concept of romance.
4. "To speak the truth" Whitehead writes, "except in the rare case of genius in the teacher, I do not think that it is possible to take a whole class very far along the road of precision without some dulling of the interest" (para-graph 11). Write an essay in which you agree or disagree, using evidence from your experience and observation.

LANGUAGE AND COMMUNICATION

GLORIA NAYLOR

"Mommy, What Does 'Nigger' Mean?"

The Norton Reader, p. 485; Shorter Edition, p. 290

A graduate of Brooklyn College and Yale University, now a novelist, Gloria Naylor takes up the question of racially loaded language in this essay reprinted from the "Hers" column of the *New York Times*. For Naylor the term "nigger" can, when used by whites, be an insulting, destructive epithet; yet, when used within black communities, it can become a term of endearment, even pride. Analyzing the examples Naylor gives from her childhood will help students to draw out the principles by which she makes this distinction and the position against which she argues.

If it seems relevant, you can discuss the problem of racially biased language on campuses today. Many colleges and universities have adopted—or are considering adopting—a "code" that would prohibit insulting language based on race, class, gender, sexual orientation, or ethnicity; others have given them up or are considering giving them up. If your campus has (or had) such a code, analyze it to determine whether it is consonant with the principles underlying Naylor's argument or whether it takes the oppositional position to which she alludes at the end of her essay (paragraph 14). If your campus has faced any alleged violations of the code, or if students can cite incidents that might violate such a code, ask them to imagine what Naylor's analysis of the incident(s) might be.

Analytical Considerations

1. Like other pieces written for the "Hers" column, Naylor's essay uses a combination of personal experience and impersonal generalization. Why does Naylor choose to begin with two paragraphs of generalization rather than with her third-grade experience?
2. What makes Naylor's narrative of her third-grade experience so powerful? Help students analyze the concise, objective style, the effect of words such as "nymphomaniac" and "necrophiliac," as well as the unstated assumptions about black students that Naylor writes against.
3. The bulk of Naylor's essay recounts memories in which "nigger" occurs in nonderogatory contexts. What are the possible connotations of the term as used by blacks? Why does Naylor wish to show the richness of this term within the black community? How does this richness contrast with the starkness of the white third-grader's language?
4. In paragraph 14, Naylor summarizes a position against which she is arguing: "the use of the word nigger at this social stratum of the black community [is] . . . an internalization of racism." Ask students what evidence they

might bring to support the opposing argument—and why Naylor treats it only briefly when and where she does.

5. Naylor never tells us how her mother answered the question, "What does 'nigger' mean?" Instead, she simply concludes: "And since she [her mother] knew that I had to grow up in America, she took me in her lap and explained." Why does Naylor end this way?

6. What persona does Naylor create in this essay—and how? What kind of person do we imagine her to be? Why is this persona important to her argument?

Suggested Writing Assignments

1. Write an essay about the use of the term "nigger" in which you disagree with Naylor and take the opposing position that she alludes to: "the use of the word nigger at this social stratum of the black community [is] . . . an internalization of racism" (paragraph 14).

2. If you come from a racial or ethnic minority, write an analysis of a term that can have negative or positive meaning, depending on the context in which it is used.

3. Write an essay about your own experiences with a word that someone used to insult or denigrate you. As you analyze your experience, try to draw out the various connotations of the word used, as Naylor does.

MAXINE HONG KINGSTON

Tongue-Tied

The Norton Reader, p. 487; Shorter Edition, p. 293

Maxine Hong Kingston's *The Woman Warrior* (1976) combines autobiography with family history, cultural myth, and fictional tale to capture the meaning of growing up female and Chinese American. As in other sections of her autobiography, Kingston here retells a story originally told by her mother to probe the problem of silence and speech. Though painful, even cruel as Kingston retells it, the story prepares for the complexity of Kingston's linguistic responses, a paradoxical combination of refusing speech and speaking out, depending on the context.

If students have read Gloria Anzaldúa's "How to Tame a Wild Tongue" (NR 510, SE 303), you might ask them whether her position that language is a form of political dominance and social control applies to Kingston's situation: why can't Kingston speak in English school, for example, when she can speak, shout, even scream in Chinese school? If students have read Richard Rodriguez's "Aria" (NR 492, SE 297) or Maria Laurino's "Words" (NR 498), you might compare the essays to explore the complex patterns of gender, ethnicity, and class that affect students' ability to speak. Such discussion will prevent students from assuming that only one factor creates a condition of silence. Both Kingston and Rodriguez, female and male, suffer from an inability to speak in school; yet Kingston can speak at home and in Chinese school, whereas Rodriguez notes the growing silences at the family dinner table. In addition, learning a new language affects family members in different ways: the mothers in these two families learn to speak out in English, whereas Rodriguez's father (Kingston does not mention hers) becomes quiet, almost shy as his family learns its second language. Anzaldúa talks different "home tongues" with different members of her dispersed family.

Questions from the NR11

1. Like Gloria Anzaldúa in "How to Tame a Wild Tongue" (NR 510, SE 303), Kingston uses the tongue as both a physical body part and a metaphor for speech. Locate examples of these uses of "tongue" and explain them.
2. Why does Kingston call non-Asians "ghosts"? Are these the only ghosts Kingston confronts? Discuss her usage of this term in the essay and in the subtitle of her autobiography, *Memoirs of a Girlhood Among Ghosts*.
3. If you have had difficulty speaking up or if you have faced a language problem in your past, write about it in an essay that explains your experience in terms of a family or social context.

Analytical Considerations

1. As Kingston tells it, her mother cut her frenum to loosen her tongue. Nevertheless, her essay includes a Chinese proverb to the effect that "a ready tongue is an evil" (paragraph 2). Gloria Anzaldúa's "How to Tame a Wild Tongue" (NR 510, SE 303) contains additional proverbs about tongues. As a follow-up to the first question in the NR11, ask students if they know of similar proverbs from other cultures. Why is the tongue a universal metaphor for speech? Why are loose tongues attributed to women, and why are women chastised for them?
2. Encourage students to interpret the story that Kingston's mother tells. What meanings do they see? What meanings does Kingston emphasize?
3. How does Kingston convey the differences between being a person, an "I," in English versus being one in Chinese? What other strategies does she use to explain the differences between Chinese and Americans?
4. Compare Kingston's experiences in grade school with Rodriguez's ("Aria" [NR 492, SE 297])? How and why are they similar or different?

Suggested Writing Assignments

1. Retell a story that your mother, father, or grandparent told to communicate appropriate (or inappropriate) behavior within your ethnic community. Try to capture the richness of the story, as well as your responses to it.
2. Is silence always a mark of social control? Can it also be a form of resistance? Analyze Kingston's, Rodriguez's, or Anzaldúa's account to suggest ways in which they are both being controlled and resisting control.

RICHARD RODRIGUEZ

Aria

The Norton Reader, p. 492; Shorter Edition, p. 297

"Aria" comes from the first chapter of an autobiography, *Hunger of Memory: The Education of Richard Rodriguez* (1982). This selection is its opening, in which Rodriguez draws on the memories he has narrated and makes a case, explicitly and forcefully, against bilingual education. When *Hunger of Memory* was first published, it provoked heated controversy among Spanish-speaking Americans. Rodriguez opposes bilingual education not only because he believes that it delays the acquisition of English crucial to American citizenship but also, more importantly, because he believes that all education requires the assumption of a "public" voice and the loss of "private" language. To avoid the process of loss and gain is, for Rodriguez, to undermine or sentimentalize education.

If you have students whose first, "public" language is not English, this essay provides an occasion for allowing them to speak for—or against—bilingual education. If they agree with Rodriguez, you might ask them to narrate incidents that support his views and the analysis he provides. If they disagree, you might help them find alternate modes of analysis or counterarguments to define their own positions. Even with classes of students whose only language is English, the issue of the "private" language of home versus the "public" language required at school can provoke an excellent discussion of education.

Questions from the NR11

1. What, according to Rodriguez, did he lose because he attended an English-speaking (Catholic) school without a bilingual program? What did he gain?
2. Rodriguez frames this section of his autobiography with an argument against bilingual education. How convincing is his evidence? Does he claim that all nonnative speakers of English educated in English would have the same losses and gains as he did?
3. According to Rodriguez, what are the differences between private and public languages, private and public individuality? Can both exist when the family language and the school language are English? How might a native speaker of English describe the differences?
4. Make a case, in writing, for or against bilingual education using material from Gloria Naylor's "Mommy, What Does 'Nigger' Mean?", Maxine Hong Kingston's "Tongue-Tied," and Gloria Anzaldúa's "How to Tame a Wild Tongue"—as well as your own experience, observation, and reading.

Analytical Considerations

1. What is Rodriguez's thesis? How does he use the arguments of opponents to define and support his own view? After the opening paragraphs, at what other points does he introduce the arguments of his opponents in order to refute them?

2. How does this essay incorporate personal narrative within an argumentative structure? To get at this question, try analyzing the opening sentences of paragraphs 1 through 4, in which Rodriguez articulates his position on bilingual education, and the opening sentences of paragraphs 5 through 10, in which he condenses his educational experiences.
3. Rodriguez's account shows both Spanish and English to be "rich" languages. How—and why—does he accomplish this?
4. Have students read Gloria Anzaldúa's "How to Tame a Wild Tongue" (NR 510, SE 303). Compare the ways in which Rodriguez and Anzaldúa show Spanish and Chicano Spanish, respectively, to be "rich" languages.
5. Rodriguez's autobiographical account of his education might be subtitled "Loss and Gain." What are the gains Rodriguez discusses? What are the losses? Are there some losses or gains that Rodriguez might have avoided mentioning? Why? What are they?
6. What persona does Rodriguez create in this essay—that is, what kind of person do we as readers imagine him to be? In classical rhetoric "persona" involves the issue of "ethos," argument the issue of "logos." How do the two interact in this essay?

Suggested Writing Assignments

1. Is the transition from the private language of the home to the public language of the school a necessary part of education? Write an essay, based on your experience, observation, and reading, in which you address this question.
2. If your native language is something other than English, recount your own experience(s) of learning English in school, either implicitly or explicitly agreeing or disagreeing with Rodriguez's position on bilingual education.

MARIA LAURINO

Words

The Norton Reader, p. 498

Laurino's often humorous memoir focuses on her efforts to both understand the meanings and validate the worth of the Americanized southern Italian dialect she learned from her mother as a child in suburban New Jersey. Several sections are deeply confessional, with the author grappling with the shame we often feel toward our heritages, our families, and the gross, childish missteps we make that continue to haunt us throughout our adult lives.

Many students will identify strongly with Laurino's story of the difficulties of assimilation and with her lament that her "closest cultural links to [her] past . . . collided with everyday life." Coming to college involves a similar negotiation for students between who they were and who they need to become, a struggle that may leave them, like the author, "deeply uncertain about [their] place in the world."

Laurino eventually finds vindication as a linguist uncovers Tuscan Italian roots for her family's jargon, but her enthusiasm is quickly tempered as she realizes the patterns of meaning in her family's distinctive lexicon and what these patterns reveal about her family: all were "funny, bitter, expressive words of criticism or emotional release." The essay concludes with a consideration of how language binds individuals to communities and keeps communities together, even over vast separations of time and space.

Questions from the NR11

1. Laurino associates English and her family's southern Italian dialect with different spheres and different values. Mark the words and phrases that she attaches to each, and explain the values that these words suggest.
2. Laurino's essay takes the form of a quest. For what is Laurino searching? What does she find?
3. Like many Americans who speak English in public and another language or dialect at home, Laurino reports that she felt "shame" and kept her "'ethnic' details, the keys to our identity, under lock and key" (paragraph 2). Other writers in this section, including Maxine Hong Kingston, Richard Rodriguez, and Gloria Anzaldúa, also discuss their bilingualism. Write an essay in which you compare and contrast Laurino's conflict and resolution with one of theirs.
4. Choose a word with special meaning within your family (ideally, from another language or dialect), and in a brief essay explain its meanings to you and your family.

Analytical Considerations

1. Laurino writes of the intimacy and privilege of keeping her family dialect a secret, noting that "as with any secret, there were pleasures in knowing and tensions in keeping it." Think of some particular secret you have kept. How many *different* kinds of pleasure were there in knowing that secret? How many *different* kinds of tension were there in keeping that secret?
2. This essay portrays the struggle of trying to honor one's home culture while trying to assimilate to new circumstances. At one point, for instance, Laurino laments how "southern Italian food and dialect words, my closest cultural links to our past, collided with everyday life in our suburban cul-de-sac." What are your closest cultural links to your past? In what ways do these collide with your everyday life here in college?
3. In discussing the vast variety of dialects that once flourished in Italy, Laurino notes that this historical diversity "doesn't stop northerners and southerners from making judgments about the worth of each other's words." Ask students:
   a. What judgments do *you* make about the worth of other people's words based on their dialect or accent, vocabulary or diction, speed of delivery, gestures or lack of gestures when speaking, eye contact or lack of eye contact?
   b. What judgments do *you* make about the worth of the speaker himself or herself, based on his or her dialect or accent, vocabulary or diction, speed of delivery, gestures or lack of gestures when speaking, eye contact or lack of eye contact?

Suggested Writing Assignment

1. "As I decipher the meanings of my childhood language, I'm bombarded with relentless negativity, notes of jealousy belittling quips . . . expressions that let judgment and envy free . . . and yet [are] filled with a belief in the ultimate value of human beings." As Laurino does here, do a study of your own family's distinctive vocabulary, analyzing that lexicon to discover what it reveals about your family's character or worldview. First, search your own memory and interview family members to gather and list as many family-specific utterances as you can. What words, phrases, sayings, nonsense sounds, etc., are particular to your family? What are the "secret passwords" by which you can instantly recognize members of your particular "tribe"? Next, analyze what that set of words might mean collectively. How can these words be grouped together? What do they have in common? What patterns seem to reveal themselves across the field of words you have gathered? What ideas, values, emotions, etc., seem to link these words together? Finally, interpret what this family-specific vocabulary seems to manifest about your family's distinctive character or worldview. What does this lexicon reveal about your family's perceptions and conceptions of life, of other people, of the world?

GLORIA ANZALDÚA

How to Tame a Wild Tongue

The Norton Reader, p. 510; Shorter Edition, p. 303

Gloria Anzaldúa is a Chicana, that is, an American of Mexican descent, born in south Texas; she is also a Latina, the more general term for Spanish-speaking Americans. She is a writer, a poet, a lesbian feminist, and a social activist. This essay, "How to Tame a Wild Tongue," comes from a collection whose title, *Borderlands/La Frontera* (1987), is bilingual, like the essay itself. Anzaldúa mixes English and various forms of Spanish, often without translating the Spanish. Call students' attention to her statement near the end of the essay: "Until I am free to write bilingually and to switch codes without having always to translate, while I still have to speak English or Spanish when I would rather speak Spanglish, and as long as I have to accommodate the English speakers rather than having them accommodate me, my tongue will be illegitimate" (paragraph 24). In this essay she claims that freedom for herself.

Readers without Spanish are likely to be put off and see Anzaldúa's use of untranslated Spanish as an act of linguistic terrorism—which it probably is: she compels them to accommodate her. Much of the essay, however, can be understood without translating the Spanish. Anzaldúa defies the convention that, in writing, one translates from a subaltern language to the dominant language, and by doing so, she registers her protest against Anglo dominance. (Indeed, she insists that editors who collect her work leave the Spanish untranslated.)

In this essay Anzaldúa explains—and celebrates—varieties of Chicano Spanish, the five "home" tongues on the list of eight that Chicanos speak (paragraph 11). However, she begins this essay by complaining about the Chicano culture that silences women and even, grammatically, excludes their bonding. The word she didn't know existed, *nosotras*, is the female form of "we"; in Chicano Spanish the masculine form, *nosotros*, is used by women and men alike (paragraph 15). Yet the gendered inflections of Chicano Spanish allow her to make distinctions that English does not: have students note when she uses the masculine singular *Chicano* and *Tejano*, the feminine singular *Chicana* and *Tejana*, and the gendered plurals *Chicanos* and *Chicanas*.

Questions from the NR11

1. Anzaldúa includes many Spanish words and phrases, some of which she explains, others which she leaves untranslated. Why? What different responses might bilingual versus English-only readers have to her writing?
2. The essay begins with an example of Anzaldúa's "untamed tongue." What meanings, many metaphoric, does Anzaldúa give for "tongue" or "wild tongue"? How does the essay develop these meanings?
3. Anzaldúa speaks of Chicano Spanish as a "living language" (paragraph 8). What does she mean? What is her evidence for this point? What other languages do you know that are living, and how do you know they are living?
4. If you speak or write more than one language, or if you come from a linguistic community that has expressions specific to itself, write an essay in which you incorporate that language and/or alternate it with English. Think about the ways that Anzaldúa uses both English and Spanish.

Analytical Considerations

1. Anzaldúa refers to Chicano Spanish as a "patois," a term that can connote a regional dialect considered substandard by those who do not speak it. Why does she use this term? Ask students what "patois"—or, less pointedly, regional or ethnic language varieties—they have encountered or know of.
2. Ask students how many of them think they speak with an accent. What does it mean, in the United States, to speak with an accent? Do some accents have a higher status than others? Have any students been told to get rid of their accents? Have any tried to get rid of their accents? Why?
3. According to Anzaldúa, Chicano Spanish is necessary "for a people who live in a country in which English is the reigning tongue but who are not Anglo" (paragraph 9). Why?
4. Richard Rodriguez, in "Aria" (NR 492, SE 297), apparently agrees with many of Anzaldúa's points about "home" languages. Nevertheless, he argues that children must give them up as soon as possible to learn the "reigning tongue." Why? Do you think Anzaldúa would agree?
5. "By the end of this century," according to Anzaldúa, "English, and not Spanish, will be the mother tongue of most Chicanos and Latinos" (paragraph 23). What do you think this development will mean for Chicano Spanish and other "home" languages?
6. Those who grew up speaking Chicano Spanish "have internalized the belief that we speak poor Spanish" (paragraph 19), Anzaldúa writes. How

widespread is mistrust of one's ability to speak "good English"? How many people feel uncomfortable about their English? What are some of the reasons?

Suggested Writing Assignments

1. "Language is a male discourse" (paragraph 5). Use Anzaldúa's piece in conjunction with Anne Fadiman's "The His'er Problem" (NR 518, SE 308) to write an essay in which you explore features of speech and the gendered power relations they reflect. Or, alternatively, take issue with Anzaldúa and argue against her statement.
2. Do research on the French language spoken in Canada, particularly its incorporation of anglicisms, and write an essay in which you discuss parallels between the Spanish in the United States as Anzaldúa describes it and French in Canada. Or do research on the "Singlish" spoken in Singapore, and write an essay about the controversy over "Singlish" versus "pure" English.
3. Write a personal essay in which you describe one or more occasions when your "incorrect" speech made you uncomfortable, or one or more occasions when you heard someone else's "incorrect" speech. You may use Anzaldúa's "How to Tame a Wild Tongue" as a model, but you need not.

JOHN TIERNEY

Playing the Dozens

The Norton Reader, p. 516

John Tierney is a reporter for the *New York Times* who frequently writes the column called "The Big City," from which this essay comes. Students may notice the journalistic "hook" of the opening: Tierney plunges right in with a person (Alfred Wright, 19), a place (Longwood Avenue in the South Bronx), an incident, and a "snap," an exchange of insults also called "playing the dozens." In the course of his essay Tierney includes a number of snaps. He also names his informants: Monteria Ivey, 35, and Stephen Dweck, 33; Ivey first developed a nightclub act based on playing the dozens, and then the two turned to collecting the dozens and produced a book.

Tierney describes playing the dozens as "an African-American oral tradition that developed among slaves and evolved in urban ghettos" (paragraph 6). The insults exchanged are not formulaic profanities but imaginative inventions, competitive hyperboles, each one, if the game is played skillfully, more outrageous than its predecessor. They are also, among the younger generation "astonishingly crude" (paragraph 12); Tierney manages to convey an idea of their crudity while still conforming to the rules of what the *New York Times* will print. In his brief essay Tierney manages to suggest regional as well as generational differences in playing the dozens.

Analytical Considerations

1. Ask students if they have heard snaps among African Americans. Does their culture or their family have a tradition of insults? Or some other oral tradition? What is it? Who participates?
2. Snapping, Tierney writes, is "more egalitarian than status competitions based on money or clothes or sports ability" (paragraph 12). Do you think verbal ability is more equally distributed than athletic ability? Or is it just easier to acquire through practice?
3. Tierney half-jokingly attributes the fact that playing the dozens is a male pastime to testosterone (paragraph 12). Do women have their own verbal games? See, for example, Gloria Naylor's "'Mommy, What Does "Nigger" Mean?'" (NR 485, SE 290). Write an essay either about "playing the dozens" as a males-only linguistic game or about an equivalent among female speakers.

Suggested Writing Assignments

1. Write some snaps. This assignment may profitably be done in groups. (Afterward, ask the women in the class if they participated and if they enjoyed their participation.)
2. Look at Ivey and Dweck's book *Snaps*. Choose a couple of snaps you find particularly successful and analyze what makes them work.
3. In Chicago, according to Tierney, playing the dozens is still called "signifying" (paragraph 11). Do research and write a paper on signifying in black culture.

ANNE FADIMAN

The His'er Problem

The Norton Reader, p. 518; Shorter Edition, p. 308

Fadiman's piece offers a tempered, thoughtful treatment of both the political and aesthetic stakes involved in making the English language more inclusive. While too many of the texts on this subject shrilly or myopically propound one of two extreme, mutually exclusive positions on the issue (revising language to alleviate its gender bias is imperative—revising language to alleviate its gender bias is silly), Fadiman's position here is deeply ambivalent: "I find my peace as a reader and writer rent by a war between two opposing semantic selves, one feminist and one reactionary. . . . Am I the only one who feels torn?"

Pulled between her politics and her aesthetics, Fadiman argues that "The end is estimable; it's the means that chafe." In the end, she both mourns "the loss of our heedless grace" and acknowledges that "High prices are attached to many things that are on the whole worth doing." Her essay thus serves as a useful model of the need for and value of complex, nuanced perspectives on matters of public, social policy.

Questions from the NR11

1. Why does Fadiman begin with an incident from her personal history, in which she struggles with the pronunciation of *Ms.?* What facts about herself and about linguistic history does the incident allow her to convey?
2. In Fadiman's estimate, the use of gender-neutral language has both pros and cons. List some of each, and decide on which side she ends up—pro or con.
3. If you are using a handbook in your writing course or if your college has an official style sheet, consult its section on gender-neutral language. What recommendations does it have for the usage problems that Fadiman raises? With which do you side—Fadiman or the handbook? Write an essay in which you explain the differences and your stance on the issues.

Analytical Considerations

1. Living languages like English (in contrast to dead ones like Latin) are always growing and changing. Fadiman exemplifies the kind of ambivalence that many feel toward the endless evolution of language. Make a list of the ways in which the English language has changed in your lifetime. Which of these changes do you like, embrace, or find valuable? Why? Which of these changes do you not like, reject, or find objectionable? Why?
2. As Fadiman suggests, the use of the third-person singular, masculine possessive pronoun in generic contexts (using "his" to mean "his or her") reflects both the need for, and the problems with, our efforts to make English less gender biased and more inclusive. Discuss with students which of the following solutions to the problem most appeals to them and why:
   a. continuing to use the traditional generic "his" to mean both "his or her"
   b. modifying each use of the generic "his" to explicitly read "his or her"
   c. transforming each instance of the singular generic "his" to the plural "their"
   d. substituting some newly coined word (such as "his'er," "hyr," or "hes") for the generic "his"
   e. alternating between the using "his" to mean both "his and her" and "her" to mean "both his and her" (using "his" in one sentence or paragraph and "her" in the next, for instance)
3. Fadiman's text brings up the problem of "unintentional bias." When she confronts Salisbury about his sexist omission of her mother's work on *Thunder Out of China,* his response is "Oh, oh, oh. You are totally right. I am completely guilty. . . . What can I say? It is just one of the totally dumb things which I do sometimes." Fadiman's response is that she believes that he "was motivated by neither malice nor premeditated sexism." Ask students:
   a. For you, does Salisbury's lack of intent make his sexism less objectionable? Does the fact that he didn't *mean* to be biased make his prejudice less problematic? Why or why not?
   b. For you, does Salisbury's lack of awareness and intent make his bias even more objectionable than if he was *trying* to be offensive? Why or why not?

c. Think about examples from your own experience. Have you found that someone's lack of awareness or intent has made his or her prejudice (sexism, racism, ageism, classism, homophobia) less objectionable or more objectionable? Why?

Suggested Writing Assignments

1. Fadiman's essay is a useful example of the need for and value of complex, nuanced perspectives on issues of public, social policy. Fadiman represents herself as deeply divided over one such issue. Whereas, she notes, most people belong to "one camp or the other," she feels "rent by a war between two opposing . . . selves." This contrast compels her to ask, "Am I the only one who feels torn?" Write an essay in which you explore and express your ambivalent feelings toward some important issue of public policy. Rather than generating the typical argument for or against some plan, rule, law, or policy, your task here is to locate some issue about which you are as yet undecided or at least conflicted. Try to render the full range of your thoughts and feelings on the issue, to show how and why you are both for and against.

2. In her conclusion, Fadiman contends that "High prices are attached to many things that are on the whole worth doing." Write an essay in which you use Fadiman's contention as your working thesis. Mine your own experience to provide supporting evidence for this claim. Perhaps tell a story of one specific time you or someone you know paid a high price in order to accomplish something important. Be sure to develop your essay in enough specific detail for readers to appreciate clearly both the significance of the sacrifice made and the significance of what was gained in the process.

GARRISON KEILLOR

How to Write a Letter

The Norton Reader, p. 522; Shorter Edition, p. 312

and

Postcards

The Norton Reader, p. 525; Shorter Edition, p. 315

Garrison Keillor offers sound advice about writing in these two easy, seemingly off-the-cuff essays. He is an accomplished monologuist, as listeners to *A Prairie Home Companion*, his long-running show on National Public Radio, will know. You may want students to listen to a broadcast; you may want to tape part of one to play in class. Students should be able to hear Keillor's diffident, breathy voice behind these essays, as in "We shy persons need to write a letter now and then, or else we'll dry up and blow away" (paragraph 1).

Keillor's instructions for writing letters are applicable to writing in general, freewriting and first drafts in particular, and they may make more of an impression coming from the sage of Lake Woebegone than from a writing instructor. You may assign this essay early in the semester so students can get instructions from Keillor first. If you assign it later in the semester, ask them which instructions have been working for them and which haven't; you (or Keillor) may even persuade them to try again instructions that haven't been working. With "Postcards," you may want to ask students to try their hand at writing short, fifty-word, informative descriptions or narrations of what they have done each day within a single week. These short pieces of writing can be valuable on their own or as possible starting points for longer essays.

Analytic Considerations

1. Mark Garrison Keillor's self-deprecating statements. What is their effect? What does he gain and what does he lose by making them? Is being self-deprecating in a piece of writing ordinarily risky?
2. What are Keillor's reasons for writing letters rather than telephoning? How many of these reasons also apply to using e-mail rather than telephoning?
3. "The telephone is to shyness what Hawaii is to February," Keillor observes (paragraph 1). His riddling comparison provokes suspense—until he resolves it, wittily and somewhat enigmatically: "it's a way out of the woods." Ask students to mark Keillor's metaphors in both essays and to look at the ways he handles them. (This exercise can be done in small groups.)
4. Are women more likely to write letters than men? Why? Is the same true for postcards?

Suggested Writing Assignments

1. Try handing out small, postcard-size pieces of paper at the beginning of the semester and assigning students five other students to whom they will write a postcard in the first two weeks of class. According to Keillor, letters are saved, reread, and "improve with age" (paragraph 15). You can follow up this exercise by asking if the same holds true for postcards.
2. "Writing is a means of discovery, always," Keillor writes (paragraph 14). Write an essay in which you discuss Keillor's observation in relation to something you have written this semester.
3. Read around in the collected letters of some nineteenth- or twentieth-century figure who interests you. Choose a couple of letters you would have enjoyed receiving and analyze what makes them good letters. Use Keillor's instructions for writing letters if they help your analysis.

LEWIS THOMAS

Notes on Punctuation

The Norton Reader, p. 527; Shorter Edition, p. 317

"Notes on Punctuation" provides a lighthearted and witty supplement to classwork on punctuation. Thomas's conversational tone and obvious delight in learning give life to the arguably dry topic of punctuation. His "rules" are likely to be remembered longer than those in any grammar handbook, for they are simple, nontechnical, personal, and wittily illustrated. Students may be interested to know that Thomas was a medical doctor and researcher as well as a science writer, not an English teacher.

Questions from the NR11

1. The title of this piece begins with the word "notes." Is that the right word? Is this a series of notes or something else?
2. How long did it take you to realize that Thomas is playing a kind of game with his readers? (For instance, paragraph 1 is a single sentence.) Is punctuation the kind of thing people usually play games with?
3. Choose one or two writers from the next section, "An Album of Styles," and describe how they employ commas, colons, and semicolons. Do any of the semicolons serve as "a wooden bench just at a bend in the road ahead" (paragraph 9)?
4. Compare Thomas's technique of illustrating his points as he explains them with Garrison Keillor's similar technique in "Postcards" (NR 525, SE 315). What other forms of writing might be treated this way? Find other examples that, like Thomas's "Notes" or Keillor's "Postcards," merges form and content.

Analytical Considerations

1. What is the difference between the comma, semicolon, and period, on the one hand, and the question mark and exclamation point, on the other? How does Thomas communicate this difference?
2. In one sentence, summarize Thomas's sense of the purpose and value of punctuation. Why is his essay more effective in making this point than a single sentence can be?
3. Thomas's first and last paragraphs are one sentence each. Ask students to sort out the twelve parentheses that close the first paragraph and the structure of the last paragraph. What goes on in each sentence?
4. Thomas writes paragraphs that conform to traditional principles of unity, coherence, and emphasis. Ask students to analyze, for example, paragraphs 2 or 5.
5. Thomas's tone is particularly important because his topic is potentially dry. Locate some passages in which his wit and personality come through (e.g., paragraphs 2, 5, and 9) and use these to work toward a description of his persona. In the end what makes "Notes on Punctuation" an interesting and engaging essay on a potentially dull subject?
6. Does Thomas really believe there are "no precise rules about punctuation" (paragraph 1)?

Suggested Writing Assignments

1. Select an essay you like in *The Norton Reader* and analyze its author's use of commas, semicolons, and exclamation points according to Thomas's guidelines. Turn your analysis into an essay on punctuation.
2. Test Thomas's principles of punctuation on several poems. Write an essay on your discoveries.

3. Do you agree with Lewis Thomas that "the essential flavor of language . . . is its wonderful ambiguity" (paragraph 1)? Write an essay in which you elaborate on or disagree with this point.

ELLEN LUPTON AND J. ABBOTT MILLER

Period Styles: A Punctuated History

The Norton Reader, p. 529

This entertaining and performative piece explicitly demonstrates how typography and punctuation have evolved from manuscript through print to digital culture, beginning with Roman inscriptions and concluding with e-mail emoticons. It also traces the history of how writing has been slowly distanced from speech: thus, in explaining the oratorical origins of punctuation marks (the virgule, for instance, was originally a cue for a rising inflection in reading aloud), the authors call into question the whole concept of "correctness" and repeatedly insist that "punctuation remains a largely intuitive art."

Lupton and Miller's piece works very well to heighten students' awareness of and attention to the difference between visually informative and visually noninformative textuality. It serves as an excellent springboard into rhetorical analyses of texts from contemporary popular culture and how they work typographically to secure emphasis and direct readers' attention. Last, but not least, this is a fun piece, one which encourages students to be playful with written language.

Questions from the NR11

1. Throughout their essay Lupton and Miller explain by illustrating. What do their illustrations teach the reader about paragraphs, punctuation marks, and print typefaces?
2. In "Notes on Punctuation" (NR 527, SE 317) Lewis Thomas also illustrates punctuation usage. How is Thomas's approach similar to, yet different from, Lupton and Miller's? What usage issues does Thomas cover that they do not?
3. Choose one or two writers from the next section, "An Album of Styles," especially writers from an earlier century, and describe how they use commas, colons, semicolons, and other punctuation marks. If there are variations, what do you think explains them?

Analytical Considerations

1. Lupton and Miller write that "ALTHOUGH PARAGRAPHS ARE ANCIENT THEY ARE NOT GRAMMATICALLY ESSENTIAL THE CORRECTNESS IS A MATTER OF STYLE HAVING NO STRICT RULES." Compare and contrast this assertion with what you have been *taught* about paragraphing in school. Then, compare and contrast this assertion with how you actually *do* paragraphing when you write.

2. Lupton and Miller discuss the invention of many punctuation marks, some of which no longer are in use, such as the inverted semicolon and the horizontal question mark. If you could be like Aristophanes of Alexandria, what punctuation mark(s) would you invent? What kind(s) of punctuation marks do we need that we don't yet have? Be playful. Be creative.
3. This text explains how writing has slowly moved away from speech and oral delivery. Nonetheless, we still often assume a close relationship between speaking and writing (discussing a writer's *voice* or the *tone* of an essay, for instance). Discuss with students:
   a. In what ways are your speaking and writing related? In what ways are your speaking and writing decidedly unlike?
   b. In what ways is effective writing like speaking, in your opinion? In what ways is effective writing decidedly unlike speaking, in your opinion?
4. Have students locate and analyze visually informative texts from popular culture (*USA Today*, magazines, professionally designed Web pages, etc.).
   a. How does this text use space to separate and organize information?
   b. How does this text use differing fonts and other typographic techniques to secure emphasis and direct your attention as a reader?
5. Brainstorm a list of all of the typographic techniques you employ when writing in digital domains, such as e-mail and instant messaging.

Suggested Writing Assignment

1. Write a visually informative, typographically adventurous, experimentally punctuated essay on a topic of your choice. Produce a text that uses a variety of visual and typographic techniques to secure emphasis and direct readers' attention. As Lupton and Miller do, try to make your printed page actually *perform* the meaning of your piece. For instance, how might your prose embody/perform your looking at your subject from different perspectives? Your being confused? Your losing control over your subject matter? Have fun with this assignment, but remember not to play games just because you can: every unusual thing you do with your text should be *purposeful*, calculated to secure some specific effect.

ERICH FROMM

The Nature of Symbolic Language

The Norton Reader, p. 534

Erich Fromm's many books and articles made him a popular interpreter of twentieth-century psychology. His career began in Germany and then continued in America after Hitler's accession to power.

What characterizes Fromm's writing is a touch for the clear explanation, as this essay makes plain. He takes on a notoriously difficult subject, symbolic language, and explains it simply and effectively, breaking the subject into three distinct parts, then applying the newly explained distinctions to an interpretation of a story everyone has heard, Jonah and the Whale. It's an impressive performance that students should understand as a fine case of exposition.

Questions from the NR11

1. Fromm begins his essay by classifying symbols. Identify each class, the name he gives to it, and his definition of it. List his examples and add one of your own to each.
2. In paragraph 16 Fromm speaks of "the universal character of symbols"; in paragraph 17 he acknowledges that the "foregoing statement needs qualification." Identify other instances of statement followed by qualification in his essay. How do you as a reader respond to this strategy? Is it one that you as a writer would use?
3. The "accidental symbol cannot be shared by anyone else except as we relate the events connected with the symbol," Fromm observes (paragraph 11). Write an essay in which you share the events that made some object, person, or scene powerfully symbolic to you.

Analytical Considerations

1. Examine Fromm's notion of "dialects" in paragraph 18. Some might claim that calling the sun the life-giver in one culture and the destroyer in another means that the sun is not at all a universal symbol. Ask the students how Fromm attempts to get around this difficulty.
2. Does Fromm seem consistent in his notion of universal symbols and the particular meaning they may take on, "in terms of the predominant experiences of the person using the symbol" (paragraph 19)? What problems is he trying to overcome?

Suggested Writing Assignments

1. Fromm's essay interprets a well-known story, Jonah and the Whale. Interview people of different backgrounds about what they think of this story's accuracy. Is it literally true, as many people believe? Is it true to human nature? Is it true to "the way things are"? Is Fromm's interpretation the one people believe? Write up the results of your survey in a report to the class.
2. For group work: Take a well-known story and examine it, the way Fromm does, for its symbolic content. Then ask how plausible the interpretation is to other class members who have read Fromm's essay and are interpreting their own stories.

GEORGE ORWELL

Politics and the English Language

The Norton Reader, p. 540; Shorter Edition, p. 319

This essay on language and meaning from one of the twentieth century's best English prose stylists is justifiably famous. Most of us share a belief that "language is a natural growth and not an instrument which we shape for our own purposes" (paragraph 1). Orwell, on the other hand, refuses to take a passive stance; rather, he actively seeks to purge the English language of errors, obfuscation, cant, and corruption. He does more than diagnose its illnesses; he offers prescriptions that are practical—though not painless. Implicit in his proposals for the reform of the English language is the need to reform political systems as well, for, as Orwell sees the matter, corruption in the use of language and corruption in politics are interrelated.

Questions from the NR11

1. State Orwell's main point as precisely as possible.
2. What kinds of prose does Orwell analyze in this essay? Look, in particular, at the passages he quotes in paragraph 3. Where would you find their contemporary equivalents?
3. Apply Orwell's rule iv, "Never use the passive where you can use the active" (paragraph 19), to paragraph 14 of his essay. What happens when you change his passive constructions to active? Has Orwell forgotten rule iv or is he covered by rule vi, "Break any of these rules sooner than say anything outright barbarous"?
4. Orwell wrote this essay in 1946. Choose at least two examples of political discourse from current media and discuss, in an essay, whether Orwell's analysis of the language of politics is still valid. If it is, which features that he singles out for criticism appear most frequently in your examples?

Analytical Considerations

1. Describe Orwell's goals and methods in "Politics and the English Language." Which methods do you find most effective?
2. Orwell turns a passage from Ecclesiastes into "modern English of the worst sort" (paragraphs 9–11)? Why do you think Orwell uses the Bible to illustrate his point?
3. Does Orwell seem to lose his way in the first half of this essay, particularly after paragraphs 1 and 2, in which he discusses politics and language? Is his deliberate postponement of his analysis of the five writing samples an effective device?
4. Orwell writes, "In our time, political speech and writing are largely the defence of the indefensible" (paragraph 14): he names as indefensible British rule in India, Russian purges and deportations, and dropping atom bombs on Japan. Did his readers agree? What contemporary equivalents can students name? Do they agree?
5. Ask students to find and evaluate some of Orwell's metaphors. Are they fresh and lively? Are they dated or drawn from a cultural context too far removed from those of the students? Ask students which metaphors they find most powerful—and why.
6. Ask each student to summarize Orwell's essay by extracting six statements that best represent the spirit and intention of the writer. Then ask students to compare their choices of the six statements. What does it mean that we, as readers, make so many of the same choices?
7. Ask students to bring in examples of the problems discussed by Orwell and to rewrite at least one passage for consideration in class.

Suggested Writing Assignments

1. Revise an essay written for this course by following Orwell's six rules.
2. Locate a speech made by a politician on an issue you consider indefensible; the *New York Times* is a good place to look, since it is a newspaper of record. Write an analysis of the speech based on Orwell's ideas in "Politics and the English Language."
3. Give the speech and your analysis of it (see Analytical Consideration 4, above) to a classmate who finds the issue defensible. Have the classmate write his/her own analysis, either taking issue with or not taking issue with yours.
4. Select another essay by Orwell and analyze it according to his principles and standards.

AN ALBUM OF STYLES

The Norton Reader, p. 551; Shorter Edition, p. 330

What is style? The question eludes easy answers. *"Le style est l'homme même,"* the Count de Buffon observed in 1753, in an address on his admission to the French Academy. His words, translated into English, have become proverbial: "The style is the man." (To avoid the false generic "man," we might translate his statement as "The style is the person.")

Buffon's words suggest that we can gain insight into a person's character by considering his or her self-presentation, whether in action or in words. A writer's style is a recognizable expression of self that permeates a text, the clear, distinct, and individual voice that readers "hear when they read an essay." We can work toward an understanding of a writer's style by examining the elements that create it—words, metaphors, syntax, rhetorical techniques and maneuvers.

There are different types of prose style: for example, Renaissance or Augustan, Baroque or plain. As students read the older selections in "An Album of Styles," they may mistake the conventions of a period for a writer's individual voice. It can be difficult to distinguish convention from invention (and perhaps it's not always necessary to do so). The selections from more recent writers tend to be strongly, even idiosyncratically, voiced—even though some, like White or Updike, are following a strong modern preference for clean, spare prose.

The purpose of this section, in spite of its chronological organization, is not to provide students with a brief history of English prose but rather to give them examples that focus attention on, even force attention to, their stylistic features. Those who read for content tend to extract meanings and discard the texts themselves. Those who read as writers must notice and hold on to texts, for self-conscious attention to others' texts will help these students be self-conscious readers of their own work.

When we ask students to notice writers' styles, we need to provide them with ways of identifying and talking about stylistic features. You may want to add questions to the list below. You may also want to encourage students, individually, in groups, or as a class, to develop their own style checklists.

1. What kinds of words does the writer use? From what sources (Anglo-Saxon, Latin, French, Greek, etc.)? How does a dictionary, even a collegiate dictionary, enable us to trace the derivation of words? What more can be learned from an unabridged dictionary, and from the *OED*?
2. What types of sentences does the writer prefer? Long or short? Loose or periodic? Exercises that ask students to turn their own loose sentences into periodic ones provide a useful introduction to types of sentences.
3. What kinds of sentence patterns does the writer employ? Do the sentences have rhythm and balance, or not? What kinds of parallel constructions provide rhythm and balance? How do repetition, variation, and contrast contribute to rhythm and balance?
4. What features of sound are evident in the writer's prose? Are alliteration and assonance important? Are there noticeable differences between prose designed for oral delivery and prose designed for silent reading?

5. What conventions of punctuation does the writer follow? What commas appear in the prose of older writers that modern writers would eliminate?
6. What conventions of paragraphing does the writer follow? To what extent are paragraphs determined by meaning, to what extent by sight? Can paragraphs that seem long be split? To what effect?
7. What is the writer's characteristic voice or tone? How does the writer use voice or tone to create a persona? What kinds of personae are there? How do we as readers respond to them? How do we talk about them?
8. How do writers create readers? What strategies do they use to address them? Are some strategies preferable to others?
9. What adjectives are available for describing styles? Are any self-explanatory? Which need to be defined, stipulatively, with examples?

The classical tradition of imitating stylistic models may be helpful for some students. (An alternative exercise is to ask students to obliterate the stylistic features of others' prose—to mess it up, so to speak.) Imitation is an exercise that has fallen somewhat out of fashion, yet you may want to read to students Ben Jonson's advice on imitation (from *Timber*) or Benjamin Franklin's account of reading and imitating the essays of Addison and Steele (in his *Autobiography*). Both writers advocate imitation not as an end in itself but as a means to discovering a style of one's own. Students will learn to write cleaner, crisper, clearer styles than the ones they bring from high school in the course of a semester of college writing; that in itself will give them an individual voice. Learning to revise prose is a slow and difficult process. As usual, Samuel Johnson's reflection on revision speaks volumes: "What is written without effort is in general read without pleasure."

The following exercises are appropriate to all of the selections in "An Album of Styles." They may be completed in class or assigned as homework.

1. Write a paragraph or two in deliberate imitation of this selection.
2. Take a paragraph or two from this selection and alter it so that it sounds different. What stylistic features have you obliterated?
3. Enter this selection into a computer program designed to revise and improve texts. Compare the original and the new text. What has been gained, what lost? What can be learned from this experiment in style?

FRANCIS BACON

Of Youth and Age

The Norton Reader, p. 552; Shorter Edition, p. 331

Francis Bacon's essays appeared in 1597, 1612, and 1625. The 1597 edition contained ten essays, the 1612 edition thirty-eight (twenty-nine new essays and nine of the original ten, altered and enlarged), and the 1625 edition fifty-eight (twenty new essays and the earlier thirty-eight, altered and enlarged). This essay, "Of Youth and Age," appeared in the 1612 edition and again, altered and enlarged, in the 1625 edition; we reprint the 1625 version in its entirety. You may want to reproduce the 1612 version from Edward Arber's parallel texts in *A Harmony of the Essays* (1871 and 1895) in order to consider what Bacon added to enlarge what is still a remarkably brief essay.

Bacon's essays are thought to derive from his commonplace book in which, as his schoolmasters would have recommended, he took notes on his reading and copied down, in particular, wise sayings (or *sententiae*). The 1597 essays are the briefest: pithy, discontinuous, and sparing in illustrative material. In all versions he uses parallel constructions and figurative language. In this version of "Of Youth and Age" he also develops contrasts through antitheses.

BEN JONSON

From Timber, or Discoveries

The Norton Reader, p. 146; Shorter Edition, p. 333

Ben Jonson, a poet, playwright, and essayist, kept a commonplace book in which he recorded notes and reflections on his reading. These reflections were posthumously published in the 1640–41 edition of his *Works* under the title of *Timber, or Discoveries Made Upon Men and Matter As They Have Flowed Out of His Daily Readings or Had Their Reflux to His Peculiar Notion of the Times*. The passage we have selected considers what it takes to write well. Jonson insists on three things: reading the best authors, listening to the best speakers, and "exercising" one's own style. The first two involve imitation—a practice that students might not expect. To help them understand that imitation does not mean slavishly copying but rather creatively emulating, you might ask them what it takes to master a sport or learn a musical instrument, then ask what they think it takes to become a good writer. The comparison will bring out the role that observing and emulating others—whether a good basketball player, a fine pianist, or a skillful writer—plays in most learning. It will also underscore the role of "exercise" or practice in learning to write. Indeed, Jonson himself makes the comparison with sports in his analogies to the jumper and the javelin thrower.

JOHN DONNE

No Man Is an Island

The Norton Reader, p. 555; Shorter Edition, p. 334

John Donne, a preacher as well as a poet, was notably attentive to oral delivery in his prose. While this selection comes from a series of meditations in which he traced the course of an illness, its cadences give evidence of Donne's close attention to sound, well known to those who have read his sermons. You will certainly want to read this passage aloud or have students read it aloud. It is sonorous, melodic, and demands slow, emphatic reading; it concludes, memorably, with "and therefore never send to know for whom the bell tolls; it tolls for thee." Donne develops the idea of human interconnectedness through a single metaphor: man as a continent rather than an island. You will probably want to ask students how many of Donne's phrases and sentences they have heard before. Their familiarity reminds us that some styles are more memorable and quotable than others.

SAMUEL JOHNSON

The Pyramids

The Norton Reader, p. 555; Shorter Edition, p. 334

Samuel Johnson's *The History of Rasselas, Prince of Abyssinia* (1759) is a philosophical fiction in which Rasselas, his sister Nekayah, and her maid, Pekuah, travel in the company of a guide, Imlac, to see the world and make what Rasselas calls "a choice of life." In Egypt they wonder at the pyramids; this selection is Imlac's answer to their questions about them. Imlac, like Johnson himself, makes general statements: he speaks of "that hunger of the imagination" that belongs to everyone; of the pyramids as "a monument of the insufficiency of human enjoyments"; and concludes by applying his remarks generally to "Whoever thou art." You will want to draw students' attention to Johnson's frequent use of parallel structure (as in the clauses that modify "Barbarians" in paragraph 1 or those that qualify "king" in paragraph 3); to his use of "King James" English ("imaginest" and "dreamest" in the final sentence); and to his use of dual nouns ("the satiety of dominion and tastelessness of pleasures") and verbs ("survey the pyramids, and confess thy folly").

ADAM SMITH

The Watch and the Watch-Maker

The Norton Reader, p. 556

Most students know Adam Smith, if they know him at all, as a political economist and the author of *The Wealth of Nations* (1776). Smith, a Scotsman educated at Glasgow University, in fact began his career with an appointment to lecture in rhetoric and belles-lettres in Edinburgh. Before the age of thirty, he had moved back to Glasgow, where he was appointed professor of logic in 1751 and of moral philosophy in 1752. His revolutionary work in economic theory came much later in his career in the 1770s.

This selection from *The Theory of Moral Sentiments* (1759) gives a nice example of workmanlike eighteenth-century prose. Its subject—the watch and the watchmaker, or how to read the creator in the creation—was a familiar one, though Smith's treatment is original. Students may need to know the difference between "efficient" and "final" causes: the "efficient" being the force, instrument, or agency by which a thing is produced; the "final" being the purpose or end for which it is produced. The other two "causes," as defined by Aristotle, are the "formal" (the form or essence of the thing caused) and the "material" (the elements or matter from which it is produced). See the *OED*, s.v. cause, n. 5. This example raises the question of specialized vocabulary and its advantages (or disadvantages) in writing for a knowledgeable audience.

LADY MARY WORTLEY MONTAGU

Letter to the Countess of Bute, Lady Montagu's Daughter

The Norton Reader, p. 557; Shorter Edition, p. 335

Lady Mary was a well-educated, ambitious, and bold woman. She secretly taught herself Latin, she pioneered in introducing smallpox vaccination to England, she married for love, and when her husband was appointed ambassador to Turkey, she studied the language, traveled through the country, and visited harems. Today she is best known for her letters, both the familial letters she regularly sent to her sister, husband, and daughter and the more public letters issued in 1763 as her Turkish Embassy correspondence. The letter we have included comes from her private correspondence with her daughter. It contains advice on educating Lady Mary, her granddaughter. Lady Mary Wortley Montagu advocates education for the pleasure and contentment it will bring to a young woman "desirous of learning," but also because of the modest prospect, perhaps even spinster life, that her granddaughter faces. You might ask students what motives they—or their parents—have for obtaining an education, and how their motives compare and contrast with Lady Mary's. You might also ask whether they think young women still implicitly take the advice in paragraph 4: "to conceal whatever learning she attains" so as not to draw the envy or hatred of "all her acquaintance."

MARY WOLLSTONECRAFT

From A Vindication of the Rights of Women

The Norton Reader, p. 559; Shorter Edition, p. 337

Wollstonecraft's *Vindication* (1792) represents the first fully elaborated feminist analysis of patriarchal culture and its deleterious effects on women's lives. It includes a critique of the frivolous education given young girls in the eighteenth century and an impassioned plea for a rightly conceived, *rational* program of education for all women. The passage we have included can be compared to the letter by Lady Mary Wortley Montagu to her daughter— both in terms of style and of content. Most readers find Lady Mary's writing more subtle, gentle, and conciliatory and Wollstonecraft's more forceful, emphatic, and impassioned. If your students share this response, you might ask them why. Some of the difference arises from context (Lady Mary offers private advice, whereas Wollstonecraft engages in public debate); some derives from sentence construction (Lady Mary uses a loose sentence style, whereas Wollstonecraft prefers forceful periodic sentences); and some reflects choice of metaphor (Lady Mary advises that her granddaughter hide her learning as she would "crookedness or lameness," whereas Wollstonecraft derides the current system of education as making women "only fit for a seraglio"). You might also ask students what Wollstonecraft means by the adjective "masculine" and whether they think Lady Mary would advocate a "masculine" education for her granddaughter.

JOHN HENRY NEWMAN

Knowledge and Virtue

The Norton Reader, p. 561

This selection comes from a series of lectures delivered in Dublin in 1852 and published the same year. Newman converted to Roman Catholicism in 1845; he was not elevated to cardinal until 1879. The lectures were delivered after he had been named rector-elect of what was to become a Catholic university in Dublin. Newman's *Idea of a University* is a classic statement of the nature and value of a liberal arts education. In this paragraph, however, he deprecates "human knowledge and human reason" by paraphrasing what he sees as overblown claims made for them and by discriminating between knowledge and virtue.

Selections like this from *Idea of a University* may be difficult for students who see education primarily as a way to a better job and a better life defined in economic terms. It takes careful explication to persuade them that Newman, contrasting knowledge and virtue, nevertheless thinks highly of knowledge; they apprehend his antithetic structures better than his conceptual oppositions. You might begin by disentangling overblown claims from the real claims that Newman himself makes and the values he attributes to gentlemanliness. You might also explain, briefly, the kind of university education young men (not young women) received in the nineteenth century and how it was thought to embody the classical tradition that knowledge makes good men. Ask students what courses in the present curriculum resemble those Newman took for granted and whether we still think of them as embodying his values—albeit values that we subsume under terms other than *gentlemanliness*.

In addition to his use of antithesis, Newman was a master of parallelism, of metaphor, and of catalogs that define or elaborate a term (as in his sentence on the "gentleman," which includes a list of gentlemanly features from "a cultivated intellect" to "a noble and courteous bearing in the conduct of life").

ABRAHAM LINCOLN

The Gettysburg Address

The Norton Reader, p. 561; Shorter Edition, p. 339

As legend has it, Abraham Lincoln's brief, moving address was scribbled on the back of an envelope. In fact, it was the result of considerable revision, not just sudden inspiration. Moreover, Lincoln was widely read in the classics of English prose and steeped in principles of oral delivery. He knew the power of repetition, variation, and parallel structure and brought all these devices to bear in crafting a brief and memorable address. You will certainly want to read it aloud and, perhaps, set it beside John Donne's "No Man Is an Island" (NR 555, SE 334) in this section or John F. Kennedy's "Inaugural Address" in "Spoken Words" (NR 906). Donne, like Lincoln, was a master of oral composition, and both created memorable prose, literally memorable because it is quoted so often. Kennedy clearly had Lincoln's prose in mind when he composed his inaugural address.

ERNEST HEMINGWAY

From A Farewell to Arms

The Norton Reader, p. 562; Shorter Edition, p. 339

Ernest Hemingway's style may be the most easily recognized in English prose, and this passage is typical of it: crisp, conversational, dominated by nouns standing free of adjectives, and developed by accumulation. Hemingway's preferred conjunction is *and*. This selection also provides a rationale for Hemingway's style, that things are themselves and the resonances we project on them through language are fraudulent. Name—that's all; don't try to invoke phony feelings.

E. B. WHITE

Progress and Change

The Norton Reader, p. 562

This selection, one of E. B. White's columns for *Harper's* magazine, was written over sixty years ago. White makes sharp and witty observations about reactionaries and sentimentalists who resist change, among whom he includes himself. After his opening generalizations, he moves from one homely, matter-of-fact particular to another. Is he for or against progress and change? The answer probably is "against . . . but . . . ." or perhaps "for . . . but. . . ." This selection invites comparison with White's "Democracy" (NR 884, SE 520) in its use of massed particulars and with his "Once More to the Lake" (NR 82, SE 52) in its reflection on past and present.

WILLIAM FAULKNER

Nobel Prize Award Speech

The Norton Reader, p. 563; Shorter Edition, p. 340

In this speech William Faulkner describes himself as on "a pinnacle" (paragraph 1). On the one hand, he deprecates himself: the award is not for him but for his novels. On the other hand, he aggrandizes himself: as a writer he works "in the agony and sweat of the human spirit" (paragraph 1, partially repeated in paragraph 2). The speech, written in what most of us would consider a ponderous and self-important tone, was written for an important international occasion, the awarding of the Nobel Prize for literature. Speaking in 1949, just after World War II, Faulkner characterized "our" tragedy as the fear of annihilation, ostensibly through atomic warfare. Nevertheless, the greater subject he recommends to young writers—and offers as his own—is "the problems of the human heart in conflict with itself" (paragraph 2).

JOHN UPDIKE

Beer Can

The Norton Reader, p. 564

Apparently John Updike was not the first person unhappy with the new "improved" beer can; we are now on the second "improved" can. How much of what he says of the plastic tab can be said of the metal tab? How much of this selection needs to be rewritten? Can students update Updike's essay while matching his disdain for progress, or rather for "Progress"? Are there other objects that make them yearn, as Updike does, for "Progress with an escape hatch"?

Updike's reflection on a beer can is not the lighthearted selection it first seems; rather it is a serious reflection on social and cultural change, cleverly focused on a mundane object. It invites comparison with E. B. White's "Progress and Change" (NR 562) in the simplicity of its focus and the complexity of its development.

JAMAICA KINCAID

The Ugly Tourist

The Norton Reader, p. 565; Shorter Edition, p. 341

Jamaica Kincaid was born in the West Indies and lives in the United States. Her ugly tourist is an American (an "ugly American," as Graham Greene called him) who vacations in a tropical "paradise." Kincaid reports from both sides: how the American (you) sees the natives and how the natives see the American. She is not kind to either; but she is more unkind to the American. Moreover, her direct address to the reader turns the selection into a challenge and a taunt: I am going to tell you some unpleasant truths about yourself.

Kincaid begins with a generalization: "The thing you have always suspected about yourself the minute you became a tourist is true: A tourist is an ugly human being." She follows it with a torrent of particulars, a heap of inclusive details. Her sentences are less emphatically parallel than those of other writers in this section, her particulars more disjunctive. Kincaid uses repetitions in blocks and frequently interrupts the patterns she sets up with parentheses. Her prose is easy to get lost in, and her heaping up of details concerning "your" ugliness becomes vindictive. You might ask students why she writes this sort of harangue, rather than a more moderate prose.

Questions from the NR11 on an Album of Styles

1. For any selection: What kinds of words does the writer use? From what sources (Anglo-Saxon, Latin, Greek, French, and so on)? (Most good collegiate dictionaries list word origins.) What effects are created by the writer's choice of words?
2. For any selection: What types of sentences does the writer prefer? Long or short? Loose or carefully balanced? What effects does the writer achieve with sentence form and length?
3. For any selection: What metaphors or similes does the writer use? Are they fundamental to the argument or primarily ornamental?
4. For any selection: What is the writer's characteristic voice or tone? What kind of person do you imagine this writer to be?
5. Which selection do you like best? Why? Identify and analyze those aspects of style that create this positive impression.

NATURE AND THE ENVIRONMENT

RACHEL CARSON

Tides

The Norton Reader, p. 568

Carson's essay was written and published in the middle of the twentieth century, but it will very likely seem old-fashioned to many students of the early twenty-first. Some of the questions below aim to get at the sources of Carson's powerful, classical-sounding style, a style very different from that of her contemporaries George Orwell, Wallace Stegner, and Arthur C. Clarke.

One source of Carson's style is her use of sweeping assertions, the large claims she makes with practically every sentence. She's explaining complex events in nature to an unspecialized audience. As the title of her book, *The Sea Around Us* (1951), suggests, she is looking at something that is familiar, yet upon close examination is really quite amazing. (This has been a tried-and-true approach to science writing for centuries; see Alexander Petrunkevitch's "The Spider and the Wasp" [NR 595, SE 368], for another example.)

Carson ends her essay with a series of illustrations of "the influence of the tide over the affairs of sea creatures" (paragraph 17). She provides a little story about many of these sea creatures, including oysters, palolo worms, grunion, all leading toward her striking conclusion on the Convoluta. A very different writer, Kathleen Norris, concludes her essay the same way Carson does, with a series of striking illustrations. No wrap-up, no finales: both state their points at the beginning, expand upon them, and conclude with illustrations that make their points. It's a narrative technique worth exploring in other essays as well.

Questions from the NR11

1. No one would call Carson's prose style lively. (Look closely, for example, at her verbs.) How, then, does this piece work? What accounts for its overall impact?
2. *The Sea Around Us* was translated into over thirty languages. Do you think it was easy or difficult to translate? On what characteristics of Carson's writing do you base your opinion?
3. Write about a common natural phenomenon like tides, using research or personal knowledge or both.

Analytical Considerations

To get a good sense of Carson's style, it might help to take apart the first few sentences. Her opening reads: "There is no drop of water in the ocean, not even in the deepest parts of the abyss, that does not know and respond to the mysterious forces that create the tide." This is a periodic sentence, with the main action ("know and respond") deliberately placed later, in the second half. With this sentence structure, Carson links herself to classical stylists, especially the masters of the English sentence such as Johnson in the eighteenth century and Macaulay and Stevenson in the nineteenth.

Carson's third sentence is equally interesting: "Compared with the tide the wind-created waves are surface movements felt, at most, no more than a hundred fathoms below the surface." The movement here is notable: there is no comma after "tide," where most classical and modern writers would place one. The interpolated phrase "at most" is inserted to slow down the motion so carefully built up in the first half of the sentence, where the pace is hastened by the absent comma after "tide," which forces us to read the first half in one breath.

These two sentences alone demonstrate the presence of a carefully crafted style operating in conjunction with a subject matter—the ebb and flow of the tides in the ocean—that has always given inspiration to poets and stylists. It is somehow fitting that the naturalist Carson deliberately crafts her sentences to depict the complex, ever-changing world of the sea.

Suggested Writing Assignments

1. Try rewriting the first sentence in a way that conveys the most information in the fewest words. Retain all of Carson's ideas, but shorten the sentence. What is gained? What is lost?
2. Follow the instructions in Suggested Writing Assignment 1 (above) for another two sentences in Carson's essay. Then use all three rewrites to make some tentative conclusions about the resources of Carson's prose style compared with a purely information-based style.
3. Write about the role that mystery, the unknown, plays in Carson's essay. Think of this question in light of the fact that Carson is dealing with super-human forces—the influence of the sun and the moon on the behavior of what she calls "sea creatures."

GRETEL EHRLICH

Spring

The Norton Reader, p. 575; Shorter Edition, p. 344

Three selections in "Nature and the Environment" represent the work of contemporary nature writers from different regions of North America: Gretel Ehrlich from the Northwest, Edward Abbey from the Southwest, and Farley Mowatt from Canada. Ehrlich is a much-admired writer from Wyoming, the author of essays (*The Solace of Open Spaces* [1985]), poetry (*To Touch the Water* [1981]), and fiction (*Heart Mountain* [1988] and *Drinking Dry Clouds* [1991]). "Spring," perhaps the most lyrical but also the most difficult essay in this section, is an attempt to come to terms with what spring means—to Ehrlich personally and more universally to the human race.

Students may find it easiest to discuss the personal narratives Ehrlich embeds within the essay: her bout with pneumonia and her use of spring as a metaphor for recovery; her discovery of an injured eagle and the personal significance she attaches to its survival; the proposal of marriage from Joel, his death in a pickup accident, and her spring-inspired dream of his riding across the range on "a black studhorse." In each of these episodes Ehrlich sees the restorative power of the natural cycle, of spring following winter. It is also important to ask, however, why Ehrlich includes allusions to time in Julius Caesar's reign and discussions with physicists about the illusoriness of human concepts: what is the significance of an Einsteinian concept of time in which past, present, and future become meaningless notions? You might ask whether Ehrlich successfully blends these different concepts of time, whether they stand in opposition to each other, or whether she finally privileges one over another.

Analytical Considerations

1. In paragraph 3, Gretel Ehrlich writes, "It's spring again and I wasn't finished with winter." How does the opening of her essay reflect this reluctance to come to terms with spring?
2. What does spring mean to Ehrlich? You might ask students to find places where Ehrlich uses metaphoric language to get at its significance. Why does Ehrlich rely on metaphors? Does any single metaphor capture spring's essence?
3. Why does Ehrlich include discussions of time—time in Julius Caesar's reign, Einsteinian time, cyclical time?
4. This essay works by association as much as by logical progression. Ask students to plot out the movement of the essay, trying to explain what each section achieves.
5. How does Ehrlich create a sense of unity? You might ask students to look for details—such as the conversation with the physicist or the injured eagle—that keep recurring and that give a sense of unity to the essay.
6. What is the significance of Ehrlich's ending—the dream of Joel riding a black horse north across the range? Does it successfully bring together the various strands of "Spring"?

Suggested Writing Assignments

1. Write your own essay about spring and its significance to you.
2. Write about another season—summer, fall, or winter—by blending your own experiences with meanings that human beings have traditionally attached to the season.

JOHN MUIR

A Wind-Storm in the Forests

The Norton Reader, p. 583; Shorter Edition, p. 356

In this lushly descriptive essay, America's seminal naturalist tells his tale of climbing a hundred-foot spruce "rocking and swirling in wild ecstasy" during a winter windstorm in California. Muir's treatment is archly Romantic: the windstorm is a "grand anthem"; the trees respond to it with "invincible gladness"; the sunset at the end of the storm is construed as an explicit communion between the trees and their "Creator."

Students will be challenged by Muir's prose style, which is marked by long, labyrinthine sentence structures, by complex accumulations of clauses joined by semicolons. In addition, these lengthy, flowing passages are frequently interrupted by complicating parenthetical remarks set off by dashes. The result is that the reader is forced to keep a great many related ideas or images in suspension while waiting for the final punctuation. A primer on the flora mentioned in the piece would be helpful as well so that students are not caught off-guard by the references to the *librocedrus*, *manzanita*, and the *madroños* when they appear, for instance.

Questions from the NR11

1. What preconceptions did you bring to Muir's title, "A Wind-Storm in the Forests"? How does the opening sentence—indeed, the entire opening paragraph—suggest a different perspective?
2. The central adventure in this essay occurs when Muir climbs a Douglas Spruce (paragraph 9). Why does Muir undertake this climb? What does he wish to experience?
3. Write about an experience you have had in nature, whether dramatic (as in Muir's essay) or more quiet (as in Aldo Leopold's, also in this section).

Analytical Considerations

1. Muir's prose style was recognized even in his day for its eccentricities: his editors often tried to revise away his "gloriouses." Locate one of his particularly long and complex sentences (fine examples end each of his first two paragraphs, for instance) and consider the significance of his style.
   a. What does Muir's style suggest about the author himself? What does it suggest about the workings of his mind? What does it suggest about his personality?
   b. What does his style suggest about the subject matter at hand? In what ways might his style be related to the meaning of the essay? In what ways might his style be *performing* the meaning of the essay?

c. What is the effect of Muir's style on you as a reader? Do you like it? Why or why not? What lesson can you draw from your response to Muir's style that you might apply to your own writing?

2. Consider Muir's overall treatment of his subject matter in this essay.

a. How would you describe his artistic relationship to nature? How would you characterize his philosophical relationship to nature? Locate specific passages in this text in which the artistic or philosophical relationship you have discerned is clearly in evidence. Explain how, exactly, these passages manifest that particular artistic or philosophical stance.

b. Do you like Muir's artistic/philosophical treatment of nature in this essay? Why or why not? What about his treatment speaks to you, personally? What about it does not ring true for you? If you were to write an essay on nature, would you adopt Muir's general stance toward the subject? Why or why not?

Suggested Writing Assignments

1. Muir twice acknowledges a close cause-and-effect relationship between violent forces and beauty. Early in the essay he writes, "we are compelled to believe that [these forests] are the most beautiful on the face of the earth, however we may regard the agents [hurricanes, avalanches, etc.] that have made them so." Likewise, in his conclusion, he notes that as he "gazed upon the impressive scene, all the so-called ruin of the storm was forgotten, and never before did these noble woods appear so fresh, so joyous, so immortal." Shifting the context away from the effects of weather on the natural landscape, write an essay in which you argue for or against Muir's position that violence can lead to beauty. Consider the possible relationships between violence and beauty in art, sports, physics, contemporary fashion, for instance. Consider the possible relationships between violence and beauty in your major or your hobbies. Be sure to make your argument within a singular, narrowly defined context and to address the ethics of your position at some point in your essay.

2. Muir describes the trees' "strong and comfortable" enjoyment of the storm, their response to its "most enthusiastic greetings":

> "We hear much nowadays concerning the universal struggle for existence, but no struggle in the common meaning of the word was manifest here; no recognition of danger . . . ; no deprecation; but rather an invincible gladness as remote from exultation as from fear."

In human terms, another, simpler way to describe this state might be "contentment." Have you ever had the good fortune to experience such "an invincible gladness as remote from exultation as from fear"? If so, write an essay in which you tell the story of one particular time in your life when you felt content. Be sure to explore and explain both the causes of your contentment and its effects on you and those around you. What conclusions can you draw from your experience about the nature of contentment?

EDWARD ABBEY

The Serpents of Paradise

The Norton Reader, p. 589; Shorter Edition, p. 362

Edward Abbey served for fifteen years as a fire lookout and park ranger in the American Southwest, much of the time at Arches National Monument, where he wrote this section of *Desert Solitaire* (1968). His later novel, *The Monkey Wrench Gang* (1975), which portrays a group of environmental guerrillas, became so famous that it inspired the formation of the radical environmental group *Earth First!* Abbey's love of the desert and his respect for the natural world emerge in this essay—as does, to some extent, his anger with human institutions that despoil nature. This essay provides a good springboard for discussing our fascination with nature and the current popularity of the environmental movement.

Questions from the NR11

1. Why is the word "paradise" included in the title? What does it reveal about Abbey's attitude toward the desert in which he lives?
2. "I'd rather kill a *man* than a snake," writes Abbey in paragraph 12; yet three paragraphs later he threatens, "if I catch you around the trailer again I'll chop your head off" (paragraph 16). What are the rhetorical purposes of these statements? How do they articulate the thematic concerns of the essay?
3. Write an essay in which you use your own experience in nature to defend an ecological or environmental cause.
4. Write about your own encounter with an animal, whether domesticated or wild.

Analytical Considerations

1. How do nature writers portray nature? Discuss the first four paragraphs of Abbey's essay, perhaps in comparison with the opening section (paragraphs 1–8) of Ehrlich's "Spring" (NR 575, SE 344) to discover the combination of specific detail, generalization, and metaphorical language. Why include specific detail? Why turn to metaphor?
2. Does Abbey anthropomorphize—that is, does he interpret and value animals in human terms? Consider different parts of the essay, including his introduction of the morning doves (paragraphs 5–8), his domestication of the gopher snake (paragraphs 20–22), and the final discussion of anthropomorphism (paragraphs 29–30).
3. Ask students to check the various definitions of "sentimental" in a good dictionary. Can any sentimentality be applied to Abbey's essay? This question might lead to a discussion of why writers wish (or do not wish) to arouse emotions via their writing.

Suggested Writing Assignments

1. Write about your own encounter with an animal, whether domesticated or wild.
2. Compare and contrast the views of Edward Abbey and Rachel Carson toward anthropomorphism, taking into account their stated views and their actual practice in writing about nature.

ALEXANDER PETRUNKEVITCH

The Spider and the Wasp

The Norton Reader, p. 595; Shorter Edition, p. 368

Two fascinating, if repellent, creatures allow Petrunkevitch to discuss animal instinct versus intelligence, the same issue that excites Carl Sagan in this section. The structure of Petrunkevitch's essay differs, however, from that of Sagan's. Whereas Sagan mounts a formal argument using chimpanzees and other primates to illustrate his points, "The Spider and the Wasp" begins with a detailed description of the physiological makeup of the tarantula, continues with an account of what happens when it encounters the digger wasp Pepsis, and concludes with deductions about animal reasoning versus instinctive behavior. You might discuss these different organizations that writers choose— and suggest that students, too, consider a range of options in their own work.

Questions from the NR11

1. Why is Petrunkevitch's initial description of the tarantula longer than his initial description of the wasp?
2. What are the major points of contrast between the spider and the wasp? Why does Petrunkevitch emphasize these particular points rather than others?
3. Petrunkevitch suggests more than one hypothesis for the behavior of the tarantula; indeed, he says that "no clear, simple answer is available." How does he test the possible explanations? Which one do you think he prefers?
4. What evidence is there that Petrunkevitch sees the tarantula and the wasp at least partly in human terms? In a brief essay explain why you think this is or is not a legitimate perspective for a scientist.

Analytical Considerations

1. Ask students to describe Petrunkevitch's opening paragraph, perhaps comparing it to other opening paragraphs in this section. What advantages do they see in his straightforward, workmanlike statement of purpose?
2. Plot the organization of this essay. Where do descriptive paragraphs tend to occur? Argumentative paragraphs? Why?

3. What details about the tarantula or the digger wasp were the most fascinating? How does Petrunkevitch's style contribute to the effect?
4. Is there any evidence that tarantulas behave intelligently? How does Petrunkevitch treat possible evidence against his case?

Suggested Writing Assignments

1. Write an essay about the spider or the wasp, using facts from Petrunkevitch's article but also including more information on human responses to the animal (whether personal, historical, or mythological). In other words, write an essay that is closer in style to Edward Abbey's "The Serpents of Paradise" (NR 589, SE 362).
2. Rewrite some of the material from Carl Sagan's "The Abstractions of Beasts" (NR 604, SE 373) or Edward Abbey's "The Serpents of Paradise" (NR 589, SE 362) so that it follows the form of Petrunkevitch's essay: description of animal, narration of its behavior in a specific situation, conclusions about its "instinctive" or "reasoning" ability.

FARLEY MOWAT

The Watcher Watched

The Norton Reader, p. 600

In this humorous excerpt from his book *Never Cry Wolf*, Mowat tells the story of his being repeatedly humbled through his initial interactions with a family of wolves in the wild. Along the way, his self-deprecating narrative critiques several strains of human arrogance. He punctures our faith in our "ascendancy" over "brute beasts," our pretensions about the supremacy of scientific observation and method, our sense of danger and high adventure when dealing with the wilderness, and our misplaced pride in our tools and machines as a source of power. Similarly, he likens our debilitating reliance on "accepted concepts" to our reluctance to let go of myth.

Despite his endearing self-critique, Mowat retains some prideful blind-spots right up to the very end; students really enjoy pouncing upon these. When he notes, for instance, that he was unwilling to accept the fact that he "had been made to look like a blithering idiot—not by my fellow man, but by mere brute beasts," students happily point out that he made *himself* look like an idiot, that the wolves had nothing to do with it, really.

Lastly, it would be wise to provide students with a quick gloss of the unusual terms found in the piece before they read so that they don't trip on words like *esker, prurient, virulence, scats, wadi, muskegs, skeins,* and *lupine* when they appear.

Questions from the NR11

1. How do you interpret Mowat's phrase "using consummate fieldcraft," in the second paragraph? Does your interpretation change upon rereading the entire essay?
2. To what extent is Mowat telling on himself? Does it help to think of two Mowats in this essay, the Mowat in the field and the Mowat telling the story? How can we tell them apart?
3. Write about the way the essay operates by a series of reversals, large and small, starting with Mowat's initial aim to understand the predatory, dangerous wolf.

Analytical Considerations

1. Consider the rhetorical significance of Mowat's self-deprecating humor.
   a. Locate one instance in the text where Mowat is clearly laughing at himself. What effect does this passage have on you as a reader? What does it do to your sense of the author? Does it make you like him? Why or why not? Respect him? Why or why not? Trust him? Why or why not?
   b. What do you think would happen if you used such self-deprecating humor in one of your academic papers? How would it affect your authority as the writer? How do you think your teachers would respond to it?
2. Examine Mowat's portrayal of the wolves in this piece.
   a. How would you characterize his treatment of the wolves? How, exactly, does he describe them? What do the various descriptions have in common?
   b. What are the implications, the positive and negative effects, of describing the wolves in this way? Why do you think Mowat chose to portray the wolves in this fashion?

Suggested Writing Assignment

In this essay, nature teaches the author some hard lessons about his overweening egotism and sense of human superiority. Following Mowat's lead, tell your own story of a time when nature taught you something significant. The key to success in such an essay is to focus on a very specific aspect of the natural world and what you learned as a result of a particular experience with that thing. You might write about your experience with one kind of weather, for instance (or one kind of landscape, one kind of body of water, one kind of plant, one kind of animal, etc.) and what you learned as a result of your experience with that specific thing. Render your story in enough sensory detail for readers to "see" the nature involved clearly. Be sure to discuss what you learned as a result of this interaction (about yourself as a person, about some other person, about human nature, about your preconceived ideas of the wilderness, etc.) and the value of that lesson.

CARL SAGAN

The Abstractions of Beasts

The Norton Reader, p. 604; Shorter Edition, p. 373

A professor of astronomy and space science, Carl Sagan (1934–1996) earned a reputation as a controversial and imaginative thinker whose ideas challenged the anthropocentrism underlying traditional scientific and philosophical thought. Sagan was perhaps best known as a scientist with solid academic credentials who publicly aired his belief in extraterrestrial life.

In this essay, taken from *The Dragons of Eden* (1977), Sagan argues that the distinction humans rely on to set themselves apart from and above other animals—the ability to reason and imagine—is false. He bases his assertion on evidence that at least some beasts, notably primates, seem to have abstracting powers. Though less extensive than in humans, primates' ability to "reason" demands that we reevaluate ourselves and our ethical views. Perhaps threatening, certainly controversial, Sagan's essay is lively and forceful in its skillful interweaving of theory, anecdote, and illustration.

Questions from the NR11

1. Instead of a traditional thesis statement, Sagan uses two rhetorical questions in his opening paragraph. What advantages—and disadvantages—does this technique have? Try writing a thesis statement to replace Sagan's questions.
2. Sagan's essay divides into two parts: paragraphs 1 to 14 and paragraphs 15 to 26. Why does he choose this arrangement? What is the function of each part?
3. At the end of his essay Sagan raises questions about the legal rights of apes. Respond to those questions in a journal, a brief essay, or class discussion.
4. Sagan begins with quotations from three philosophers: John Locke, Bishop George Berkeley, and Michel de Montaigne. Choose one of the three quotations and write an essay in which you agree with, disagree with, or correct the philosopher. Use evidence from Sagan's essay as well as from your own experience or research.

Analytical Considerations

1. Who said of animals, "The defect that hinders communication betwixt them and us, why may it not be on our part as well as theirs?" Why does Sagan quote this philosopher early in his essay?
2. Consider spending some class time on a careful analysis of the introduction. Is there a thesis statement? Does it predict the scope of the essay?
3. Analyze the ways in which Sagan develops his argument, leading students to recognize the function of the two parts (paragraphs 1–14 and 15–26).
4. Ask students about Sagan's tone. Is he belligerent or provocative? For reasons of conviction or rhetoric?
5. What paragraphs constitute the conclusion? Is it expected? Do students find it effective?

6. Sagan's essay provides a good opportunity to teach the technique of the rhetorical question. Ask students to note where they occur (paragraphs 1, 2, 5, 14, 23, 25, 26) and how they function.
7. Although this essay is included in the "Nature and the Environment" section, some readers might feel that it represents "scientific reporting" rather than "nature writing." Ask students if they think this essay is different in approach, style, or tone from others in the section—and whether they think it is closer to "science" than to "nature" writing.

Suggested Writing Assignments

1. Two abilities—abstract thinking and language use—seem to be the most important factors in intelligence. Define "abstraction" and "language," and explain their relationship to each other. Why do these elements seem crucial in a consideration of the value of species?
2. Write an essay in response to either of Sagan's questions (paragraph 23):
   a. "How smart does a chimpanzee have to be before killing him constitutes murder?"
   b. "If chimpanzees have consciousness, if they are capable of abstractions, do they not have what until now has been described as 'human rights'?"

CHIEF SEATTLE

Letter to President Pierce, 1855

The Norton Reader, p. 611; Shorter Edition, p. 380

Chief Seattle's "Letter," like the essays by William Cronon (NR 617) and Joseph Wood Krutch (NR 628) that follow, argues for the interdependence of man and the natural world—in Seattle's words, that "All things are connected" (paragraph 3). Yet these three writers argue their case in quite different ways, using different styles and rhetorical strategies. Seattle's "Letter," for example, abounds in maxims: "Continue to contaminate your bed, and you will one night suffocate in your own waste" (paragraph 5) or "Whatever befalls the earth befalls the sons of earth" (paragraph 3). Krutch's article, in contrast, draws heavily on scientific and historical data; indeed, his term for interdependence, cybernetics, comes from modern science: a "self-regulating mechanism."

You might also use Seattle's "Letter," and the essays that follow, to discuss how a writer gains authority to speak out on an issue of public importance. Today, we might assume that Seattle, chief of the Dwamish, Suquamish, and allied Indian tribes, would be respected for the wisdom about the natural world he and his people had accumulated; but, speaking in 1855, Seattle knew that many Americans considered the Indian to be only "a savage." Seattle takes this common view and recasts it ironically—repeating the phrase "the red man is a savage and does not understand" in somewhat different variations at moments when the white man's behavior seems most foolish and destructive. His speech, transcribed and edited by a white man, shows the way that a minority point of view can become an effective and necessary counterpoint to majority opinion.

Questions from the NR11

1. Chief Seattle repeatedly refers to the red man as "a savage" who "does not understand," yet in the course of this letter he gives evidence of a great deal of understanding. What is the purpose of such ironic comments and apparently self-disparaging remarks?
2. Scholars have recently suggested that Chief Seattle's "Letter" is in fact the creation of a white man, based on Seattle's public oratory. If so, what rhetorical techniques does the white editor associate with Indian speech? Why might he have done so?
3. A surprisingly modern note of ecological awareness resounds in the statement "[W]hatever happens to the beasts also happens to man. All things are connected." Locate two or three similar observations, and explain their effectiveness.
4. Chief Seattle says that the red man might understand the white man better "if we knew what it was that the white man dreams, what he describes to his children on the long winter nights, what visions he burns into their minds, so they will wish for tomorrow." Write a short essay explaining, either straightforwardly or ironically, how "the white man" might reply. If you prefer, write the reply itself.

Analytical Considerations

1. Listeners who heard Chief Seattle speak said that he was an impressive public orator. What elements of his style would contribute to this effect?
2. Ask students to compare/contrast Chief Seattle's ironic style with Terry Tempest Williams's attempt to blend traditions of feminine, western American, and Indian rhetoric (NR 636, SE 386).

Suggested Writing Assignments

1. Choose a maxim from Chief Seattle's "Letter" as the thesis for an argument you wish to make about a topic of environmental importance. Examples: "Continue to contaminate your bed, and you will one night suffocate in your own waste" (paragraph 5) or "[A]ll things share the same breath—the beasts, the trees, the man" (paragraph 2). Add your own evidence and experience to support the argument.
2. Write a letter to the President on an environmental issue of relevance today, or recast the material from another essay in this section into the form of a letter to the President.
3. In many essays on environmental topics, a member of a minority group (or a person holding a minority opinion) must persuade the majority to alter its course. Write an argument on an environmental topic that concerns you deeply, using your position as a minority writer as part of your strategy for persuading the majority to change its view.

ALDO LEOPOLD

Marshland Elegy

The Norton Reader, p. 613; Shorter Edition, p. 382

Leopold's song of lament is a classic piece of American nature writing. It is at once a lyrical description of the Wisconsin marsh, a short course in its geologic history, an attack on the short-sighted utilitarianism that often undergirds ideas of "progress," and a philosophical analysis of the paradox of trying to conserve the wilderness. Its spare and often simple syntax is combined with exquisitely varied diction to offer a strong model of lucidity for students to imitate.

In portraying the cranes as "wildness incarnate," Leopold insists upon the need for a thoughtful appreciation of the grand sweep of geologic time if humans are to truly understand the natural world they encounter today. It is a short move from here to helping students appreciate the need to understand the full history and evolution of *anything* in their contemporary experience if they care to really understand it and their relationship to it. His indictment of the "high priests of progress" and their single-mindedly pragmatic approach to the natural world is a tad heavy-handed, perhaps, but it is useful in prompting discussion of the ethics of engineering, architecture, medicine, and scientific/technical advancements, generally speaking. It is also a useful springboard into discussion of the common, nearly religious faith in progress as an idea and to what that faith commits us and blinds us. Students may need some help in negotiating the final section of the text, in which the author presents a complex perspective on governmental intervention in wilderness areas: a quick lesson on the history and purposes of Roosevelt's New Deal and the CCC (Civilian Conservation Corps) will be necessary, for instance, and significant time and attention should be paid to unpacking Leopold's final paradox that "all conservation of wildness is self-defeating."

Questions from the NR11

1. Why does Leopold connect cranes with significant historical figures and epochs?
2. Leopold employs white spaces in addition to normal paragraph divisions. Can you explain how these white spaces work in his essay?
3. Is the last paragraph a kind of warning about increased hunting? Fifty years after Leopold's essay, have other dangers to marshlands become more worrisome?
4. Write your own account of a natural phenomenon that has disappeared in your lifetime—or that is in the process of disappearing.

Analytical Considerations

1. Leopold's text is divided into five distinct sections, the separations clearly indicated by lines of asterisks across the page.

a. Ask students to describe the development in each section. What is happening in each? What is the author trying to accomplish? Describe the movement from one section to the next. How do they work together? Why are they in this particular order?

b. Ask students to consider the effectiveness of this structure. Why did Leopold arrange the piece in this manner? Would it be more effective or less effective as a singular movement without the separations? Why?

2. Look closely at Leopold's prose style to discuss the effects of his simple syntax and careful and varied diction.

a. Have students examine the syntax of the third to last paragraph ("For a decade or two crops grew poorer, fires deeper . . ."), for instance. How are the sentence structures themselves related to the larger meaning of the paragraph? In what ways do they *perform* the meaning?

b. Have students examine the diction in the first three paragraphs, for example. What is the effect on the reader of words like "morass," "phalanxes," "clamor," "blast," "pandemonium," "whence," "echelon," and "clangorous"? How do they work to construct our sense of the scene? How do they work to construct our sense of the writer?

Suggested Writing Assignments

1. Using Leopold's first three paragraphs as an example, write an essay fully and carefully describing some specific place, whether natural or man-made, trying hard to capture the wordless essence of that place in your prose and communicate that mood/sensation/ambience to someone who has never been there. Render the sights, sounds, smells, and textures of this place as vividly as you can. Pay close attention to the shapes and movements in this place, especially the smaller and less noticeable ones. Think about what is *not* there. Like Leopold, you can use chronological order to structure your description. You can also organize the details spatially (left to right, top to bottom) and/or by order of obviousness (the most striking thing about the place, the next most obvious thing, etc.).

2. Leopold deeply loves/respects the crane, and in trying to impart that love/respect to his readers insists that "our appreciation of the crane grows out of the slow unraveling of earthly history." Let us posit that our full appreciation of *anything* we love/respect grows out of an unraveling of its history. Write an essay in which you first identify something specific that you love/respect in your contemporary experience (a particular place, Labrador retrievers, soccer, Ethiopian cooking, whatever) and then trace its history. Your final text should combine your personal, subjective thoughts and feelings about your topic with external, objective research on its history to offer a rich account of how and why this thing is worthy of our love/respect.

3. Leopold argues that the "overlords" of progress did not understand mutuality, balance, or modesty, that "the high priests of progress knew nothing of cranes, and cared less." He asks, sardonically, "What is a species more or less among engineers? What good is an undrained marsh anyhow?" Write an essay in which you explore the idea of progress in terms of your particular career plans. In what ways is your prospective field of endeavor driven by our collective, nearly religious faith in the idea of progress? In what ways is this emphasis on progress in your field detrimental? In what

ways is this emphasis on progress in your field empowering? Think carefully and philosophically; try to develop a nuanced and complex position on the issue; beware of creating a shrill, one-sided argument for or against "progress" in your field.

WILLIAM CRONON

The Trouble with Wilderness

The Norton Reader, p. 617

This essay, particularly the first part, will seem oddly contrarian to many students; Cronon himself says his argument seems at first glance to be "perverse." He argues that we should understand the concept of "wilderness" as a human creation, and as soon as he makes this claim, some readers will get it, and many will scratch their heads in puzzlement. This is not to say that Cronon in any way disparages or denounces wilderness, only the quick assumptions that allow humans to easily demarcate such a concept from their everyday lives. As he reminds us, those who helped create the concept were often city folks with little or no understanding of what it is like to work the land.

If your class contains a good mix of rural and urban students, have them compare their own notions of wilderness with both the strict definition and the looser one Cronon seems to be employing throughout, a definition that encompasses Great Plains ranches as well as trackless forests in the Sierras. Rural students will usually have a much more familiar, more comfortable, and less mystical view of wilderness. (That doesn't mean they won't love it more, of course. Just that their love might be less misty-eyed.)

The last three paragraphs witness a turn toward a lesson. This is where Cronon tells us what we ought to do about wilderness, how we ought to react. Some will find the tone a bit preachy, but a careful reading will demonstrate that this tone has been carefully prepared for earlier on. In fact, the entire essay has the form of a classic sermon, one that examines a single word, in this case wilderness, and derives a moral lesson from its conclusions.

Questions from the NR11

1. In paragraph 12 Cronon writes: "We live in an urban-industrial civilization, but too often pretend to ourselves that our real home is in the wilderness." Cronon gives no examples. What examples might back up Cronon's statement? Can you think of counterexamples as well?
2. Who is Cronon's "we" throughout this essay? Why does he use "we" so frequently?
3. Paragraph 2 raises the issue of whether wilderness provides us with a "mirror." Look through the essay for similar visual imagery; then explain the role that such imagery plays.
4. If you found significant counterexamples in response to Question 1, write a letter to the editor in which you question or object to one aspect of Cronon's argument.

Analytical Considerations

1. This essay is taken from a book entitled *Uncommon Ground: Toward Reinventing Nature*. Show how this essay's subject matter and approach are appropriate for a book with such a title.
2. Cronon talks of "a natural landscape that is also cultural" (paragraph 14). Explain what he means.
3. Does Cronon show much awareness that his readers might have a very different view of the word "wilderness"? How does he meet his readers' expectations?
4. If wilderness is a construct, mainly mental, what are the rules for deciding what is wilderness and what is not? Who gets to decide?

Suggested Writing Assignments

1. Write about a place that would fit Cronon's notion of wilderness so your readers can decide if his main point is accurate.
2. There are many specifically designated "wilderness areas" in national parks and national forests. Is it contrary to the spirit of the term "wilderness" to have foot trails through these areas? Bicycle trails? Horse trails? Snowmobile trails?
3. Interview people about what the term "wilderness" means to them. Write up your findings.

JOYCE CAROL OATES

Against Nature

The Norton Reader, p. 621

Oates's essay is a challenging text in a number of ways, which makes it an excellent teaching tool.

First, it argues tenaciously against all of the romantic notions, theological exaggerations, and comforting personifications of "Nature" that we all have residing in our heads, which we all use without thinking, and are all committed to and dependent on in innumerable ways. It is a far less polite, more far-reaching version of the kind of critique that Cronon offers in "The Trouble with Wilderness."

Second, Oates's text is difficult, requiring students to stretch out as readers, to go beyond their known strategies and comfort zones as interpreters. It is discontinuous and fragmentary; its diction level and register are higher than average; its allusions are frequent.

Finally, students are frequently troubled by the fact that they admire Oates's writing ability, are persuaded by her arguments, and still don't like *her* very much. The writing is engaging and lively, but she comes off as mean-spirited: students are especially disturbed by her cold-heartedness in killing the ants in the conclusion. Her persona is abrasive and confrontational in ways that students are unfamiliar with and disconcerted by, which forces them to address the question "Do you have to be likable in your prose to be an effective writer?" Students want so much for their readers (including writing instructors) to like them that they never consider other possible relationships with their audiences.

Questions from the NR11

1. Oates is not afraid to picture herself as angry, abrasive, and mean, especially at the end of the essay, where she kills ants as she creates art, writing her poem. What are the dangers of such an approach? Are there gains?
2. Read the essays in this section by Carson, Muir, and Leopold, or the essay by Thoreau in "Philosophy and Religion" (NR 1155), and decide if Oates's critique of nature writing applies to them.
3. What might be the purpose of all the allusions Oates makes to classic nineteenth- and twentieth-century writers?
4. Oates's essay seems deliberately fragmented and disjointed, with plenty of jumps from one time to another and from point to point. Is there a method to her approach? Write an essay answering this question: Does Oates present a coherent argument against a certain point of view about nature?

Analytical Considerations

1. Ask students to analyze Oates's voice or persona in this text.
   a. How would they describe the writer's character or personality? What textual evidence can they provide to support their interpretation?
   b. What are the effects of the voice/persona on readers? Do they leave the piece liking the author? Why or why not?
   c. Given her subject matter and purpose in writing, is the author's voice/persona an effective one? Why or why not? Why do they think she chose to present herself this way? In what ways might her tone be related to the meaning of the essay?
2. Ask students to consider the disjointed structure of the essay, its lack of coherence and transitions between paragraphs.
   a. How would they describe the structure of the text? What textual evidence can they provide to support that interpretation?
   b. What are the effects of this structure on readers? What does this structure require of readers?
   c. Given her subject matter and purpose in writing, is the author's choice of a disjointed organization an effective one? Why or why not? In what ways might the disjointed organization be related to the meaning of the essay?
3. Ask students to examine one of Oates's strategic uses of repetition. For instance, the essay has nine consecutive sentences in the introduction beginning with "It." Likewise, near the end Oates begins five consecutive sentences with "My body" in describing her "waking dream of uncanny lucidity."
   a. What is their subjective response to such repetition. Do they like it? Why or why not? What do they see happening? What stays the same from one iteration to the next? What changes?
   b. What are the effects of this repetition on readers? In what ways does it affect your attention? In what ways does it affect your sense of the author?

c. Given her subject matter and purpose in writing, is the repetition effective? Why or why not? In what ways might her conscious use of such repetition be related to the meaning of the essay?
4. Ask students to consider Oates's extensive use of quotations and literary allusions.
   a. Make a list of the authors/texts Oates alludes to and cites in her essay. Which figures and texts do you recognize? Which are unfamiliar?
   b. What are the effects of all of these citations and allusions on readers? Do you like them? Why or why not? How do you feel when you "get" her allusions? How do you feel when you don't?
   c. Why do you think Oates makes all of these citations and allusions? In how many different ways do they function in the essay? What are their purpose(s)? How would the essay be different without them? In the final analysis, are they effective? Why or why not?

Suggested Writing Assignments

1. Write an essay in which you emulate Oates's approach and tone. Have some fun and spear a sacred cow. As Oates does, think of some person, place, thing, or idea that everyone you know admires, even reveres (Katie Couric, Disney World, a college education, or democracy, for instance) and argue aggressively, even abrasively, that this person, place, thing, or idea is really not at all what she or it seems to be, not nearly as good as everyone thinks he or it is. Feel free to emulate other characteristics of Oates's essay as well, including its disjointed organization, frequent use of allusion and quotation, and stylistic devices. (Cronon's "The Trouble with Wilderness," in this section, might be helpful here.)
2. Oates relates a series of disturbing and formative "Early Nature memories"— of leeches, a decaying pet, and a rabid raccoon—noting "it's best not to suppress" them. Moreover, she says that the self-mutilating raccoon is "a sight I seem to remember though in fact I did not see. I've been told I did not see." Write an essay in which you excavate and render in careful detail your earliest memories of some place, activity, or object that is important to you now (such as New York City, reading or doing mathematics, the piano, or a computer). Discuss how those initial experiences, whether positive, negative, or mixed, affected you then and continue to affect you today. (Please do not write about your earliest memories of or initial experiences with a *person* for this essay; our memories of our initial contact with people tend to be highly charged for us as individuals, but making that experience meaningful for *other* people, worthwhile for our *readers*, is very difficult, indeed. Places, activities, and objects are far more generalizable.)

   In developing your essay, you might want to interview people who were there with you during these earliest experiences with your subject, like your parents, siblings, teachers, or friends, perhaps. How do *their* memories of your initial experiences compare and contrast with *your* memories? In what ways are these similarities and/or differences significant? In what ways do these similarities and/or differences modify your sense of the importance of initial experiences and memory in determining your current relationship with your subject?

JOSEPH WOOD KRUTCH

The Most Dangerous Predator

The Norton Reader, p. 628

What is "the most dangerous predator"? The title leads us to expect a large ferocious animal, perhaps a lion, tiger, or jaguar, or even a small deadly insect we have heard little about. But the answer, we soon discover, is Homo sapiens, the human being. This essay, based on facts about the Baja Peninsula of Mexico, which stretches 760 miles south of California, is an early example of environmentally conscious nature writing and writing for environmental advocacy.

Joseph Wood Krutch began as a drama critic and professor of literature in New York; during a midlife crisis of conscience, he reread his Thoreau, moved to the southwestern desert, and began to write about nature and natural history. It might be interesting to ask students whether things have changed since Krutch wrote forty years ago—and, if so, whether for better or for worse.

Questions from the NR11

1. What is the distinction Krutch makes between predation within the non-human world of nature and predation on the creatures of that world by man?
2. Krutch obviously feels disdain for those who shoot and kill wild animals. Locate sentences in which he expresses disdain, and analyze how they work.
3. Krutch wrote this essay over forty years ago. Have any of the facts changed? If he were writing today, would he need to modify any of the conclusions he draws in paragraph 27?
4. Taking the gulls and terns as a kind of model, explore the similarities and differences between their relationship and some other relationship of predation—for instance, birds and mosquitoes, mosquitoes and people, hunters and deer—and write a brief account of how the relationship works.

Analytical Considerations

1. Like many other writers on science and natural history, Krutch must simplify. Using students' responses to Question 1 (above) you might ask them to suggest why Krutch creates simple dichotomies (this versus that).
2. Krutch calls the story of the gulls and terns of Rasa Island "absurd" and adds, "How decisively it gives the lie to what the earliest idealizers of nature called her 'social union'" (paragraph 17). Ask students to explain the concept of "nature's social union" and the point Krutch makes here.
3. Analyze the rhetorical effectiveness of the opening sentence of paragraph 3: "Someday—probably a little too late—the promoters of Baja as a resort area will wake up to the fact that wildlife is a tourist attraction and that though any bird or beast can be observed or photographed an unlimited number of times it can be shot only once." Find and analyze two or three similar examples of Krutch's style.

4. Near the end of the essay, Krutch explicitly states "three truths" he derives from the example of Guadalupe (paragraph 27). Discuss with students why he makes his points so directly and obviously, perhaps in comparison with other writers in this section who are more implicit or suggestive (e.g., Ehrlich or Carson).

Suggested Writing Assignments

1. Write an essay in which you consider whether things have changed since Krutch wrote his essay—for example, whether the tourist industry now recognizes the importance of preserving wildlife or whether the "three truths" mentioned in paragraph 27 still hold.
2. If you have access to information about some ecological problem or issue in your region, write an essay in which you, like Krutch, advocate a position on that issue.

TERRY TEMPEST WILLIAMS

The Clan of One-Breasted Women

The Norton Reader, p. 636; Shorter Edition, p. 386

Terry Tempest Williams explains the literal meaning of her title in the first paragraph: the women in her family suffer from breast cancer, and mastectomies are a frequent, devastating result. Students may also want to know about the mythological tribe of women warriors, the Amazons, who according to some legends cut off their right breasts in order to wield their bows and arrows more freely. This allusion prepares for Williams's discussion, later in the essay, of her dilemma about whether or not she, as a Mormon woman, should fight governmental authorities and risk imprisonment. Should she, like other Mormons, passively accept the risks that threaten her, or should she, like the Amazons, actively fight against them?

Williams served as naturalist-in-residence at the Utah Museum of Natural History and published several books of nature writing: *Pieces of White Shell: A Journey to Navajoland* (1984), *Coyote's Canyon* (1989), and *Refuge* (1992). This essay combines powerful personal experiences with research into historical and environmental issues to argue against nuclear testing in the desert. Students may find the combination of personal experience and research data rhetorically useful if they choose to write essays that take a stand on environmental issues. You might suggest that they use Williams's essay as a model for structure and for argument.

Questions from the NR11

1. Williams uses a variety of evidence in this essay, including personal memory, family history, government documents, and other sources. List the evi-

dence and the order in which she uses it. Why does Williams present her material in this order?

2. The essay begins with a description of what Williams calls a "family nightmare" and ends with a dream vision. What is the rhetorical effect of this interactive opening and closing?

3. What does Williams mean by the statement "I must question everything" (paragraph 36)?

4. Do some research on an environmental issue that affects you or your family and, using Williams as a model, write an essay that combines your personal experience and your research.

Analytical Considerations

1. The first section of Williams's essay narrates family history and personal memory. How does Williams shape her narration to build to a startling revelation?

2. How—and why—does a writer incorporate factual evidence into what is essentially a personal essay? In the second section (paragraphs 20–29), Williams condenses facts from several historical and governmental studies (see footnotes 1–10). You might ask students to look up these sources and explain how Williams uses evidence from her research, especially the quoted phrases. You might also discuss why Williams does not quote her research materials in certain places, whether because she can assume knowledge on the part of her readers or because her personal rendition of the material is more compelling.

3. What influence does Mormon culture and religion have on Williams's personal behavior? How does she convey her attitude toward her religious background, especially in the third section?

4. Williams's rhetorical strategies include many that might be called "feminist": naming her mother and grandmothers (paragraph 34), recounting her "dream" and the song of the Shoshoni women (paragraphs 38–39), metaphorically comparing the pangs of women giving birth with the death pangs of the desert (paragraph 42), referring to her memory of the Joshua trees (paragraph 57), and, more generally, as in her title, alluding to women's history and myth. Instructors interested in the possibilities of feminist rhetoric might want to consider the use of women's history and myth as an alternative to more traditionally "masculine" modes of argument in pieces of environmental writing, such as Abbey's.

Suggested Writing Assignments

1. Choose an environmental issue for which you have personal experience and factual data to draw on. (If you don't have factual data when you start, do research to collect the relevant evidence.) Write an essay about that issue in which you, like Williams, combine personal experience and objective facts.

2. Use an incident or story in your family's history as the starting point for an essay that makes an argument (explicit or implicit) about some important public issue.

3. Consult one of the sources Williams cites in her footnotes to learn more about nuclear testing in Utah and other western states. Instead of a personal essay, write a historical summary of the events that lie behind Williams's family experience. What purpose might your version of the events have that Williams's does not?

MICHEL DE MONTAIGNE

That One Man's Profit Is Another's Loss

The Norton Reader, p. 643; Shorter Edition, p. 394

This short essay by one of the founders of the genre reveals the essay's origins as a means for contemplating the pragmatic implications of philosophical ideas. It may help students to understand this essay—and the point of the genre overall—if they know that the word "essay" comes from the French verb *essayer*, "to try." Ask them how this essay represents an "assay," or an attempt or try. What is Montaigne trying to do here? In what sense is his thinking—and his essay—still in process? From these questions, you might take the opportunity to discuss the genre of the essay with your students: how is an essay different from an article? An Op-Ed? The papers they write for their courses?

Montaigne's essay is an unusual meditation on ethics in that it is descriptive rather than prescriptive. Discuss this difference with your students, and ask them if they can discern his perspective.

Questions from the NR11

1. In each paragraph Montaigne uses a quotation or paraphrase from a classical authority. Why does he use each—to disagree with, to support, or otherwise to amplify his argument?
2. In paragraph 2 Montaigne writes "let anyone search his heart and he will find that our inward wishes are for the most part born and nourished at the expense of others." Do you agree? Cite evidence from your own experience to defend your view.
3. Write an essay in which you agree or disagree with a common maxim, whether one from Montaigne or one from the section "Maxims and Morals." Use evidence from your own experience to defend your view.

Analytical Considerations

1. The final paragraph naturalizes a cash economy: Montaigne switches from financial profit in the human realm to the lifecycle itself. Discuss the aptness of the analogy with your students. Are there differences between the gains and losses of nature and those of the business world?
2. Compare the proverbs that begin and end the essay. What is the difference between them? What does that difference reveal about where Montaigne stands at the essay's conclusion?

Suggested Writing Assignments

1. Montaigne says "no profit can be made except at another's expense." Write a short essay in which you agree or disagree with this statement. Following Montaigne, draw from everyday life for examples to support your argument.
2. Choose a line of work in which a person stands to gain from someone else's loss—either one from Montaigne's list (funeral director, physician, etc.) or one of your own devising. Write a short essay exploring the ethics of that line of work. What challenges does a person holding this kind of job face? How should he or she balance the ethical issues with the need to make a profit?

LORD CHESTERFIELD

Letter to His Son

The Norton Reader, p. 644

Lord Chesterfield, in a "Letter to His Son," attempts to do what most parents wish they could do: pass on to their children the wisdom they have accumulated by experience. Students should be able to identify what Chesterfield takes for granted, that his son needs to acquire the "art of pleasing" (paragraph 1) in order to flourish in the station that is his by birth, the "great society of the world" (paragraph 10). They are likely to lack information about Chesterfield's social class and historical era and to need help in understanding how his wisdom reflects both. Chesterfield's advice is hardly stuffy and moralistic. It might be described as urbane, provided the word is stipulatively defined in relation to Chesterfield's urbs: eighteenth-century London.

Chesterfield's "Letter to His Son" has what the New Critics called "tonal complexity." You might want to work on paragraph 9 to illustrate it. How did Chesterfield expect his son to hear his remark about "that degree of pride and self-love, which is inseparable from human nature"? When he writes of "those whom we would gain," whom and what does he have in mind? Chesterfield passes over questions of morality and immorality, except to enjoin his son to distinguish between vices and crimes, weaknesses and vanities (paragraph 8). This selection may, of course, be paired with Mark Twain's more humorous "Advice to Youth" (NR 647, SE 395), and it is worth noting how both Chesterfield and Twain depend on a sense of what is socially acceptable behavior rather than what is intrinsically right or moral.

Questions from the NR11

1. Chesterfield recommends to his son the rule "Do as you would be done by" (paragraph 1). What kind of behavior does Chesterfield suggest? How does his injunction differ from Jesus' injunction "Therefore all things whatsoever ye would that men should do to you, do ye even so unto them" (Matthew 7.12; see also Luke 6.31)?

2. Chesterfield does not recommend "abject and criminal flattery" of vices and crimes but rather "complaisant indulgence for people's weaknesses, and innocent, though ridiculous vanities" (paragraph 8). Make a short list of what you consider vices and crimes and another of what you consider weaknesses and vanities. Be prepared to defend your distinctions.
3. Rewrite Chesterfield's "Letter to His Son" for a modern reader.

Analytical Considerations

1. You may want to encourage a free response from the class to see how students' reactions differ: some students will be censorious of Chesterfield, others approving. I've played devil's advocate on both sides.
2. What does Chesterfield take for granted about women?
3. Ask students to supply, from their experience, applications of the golden rule that are self-serving and applications that are self-denying. Is it possible to discover a consistent pattern of differences between the two?

Suggested Writing Assignments

1. Write a letter of advice to yourself from your father or your mother. Think carefully in advance about their assumptions. Can they take your understanding of and concurrence with their assumptions for granted? Or will they need to spell them out or argue for their views? Append a paragraph in which you explain your decisions and how they are reflected in the letter.
2. In the mode of Chesterton's "Letter," write a letter to a younger sister or brother, offering advice about the next stage of life—perhaps finishing high school, going to college, and taking a job.

MARK TWAIN

Advice to Youth

The Norton Reader, p. 647; Shorter Edition, p. 395

Mark Twain—or Samuel L. Clemens—is nineteenth-century America's best (and best-known) comic author and satirist. "Advice to Youth," a lecture Twain gave in 1882, was not published until 1923; we do not know the circumstances under which he gave it or who was in the audience. He says he was asked for something "suitable to youth . . . didactic, instructive, or . . . good advice" (paragraph 1). He then proceeds to mimic a conventional form of precepts for behavior delivered by age to youth. Those in the audience who expected comedy from him would probably have taken his "serious" beginning ironically—that is, as saying one thing and meaning another. Those who did not would have been startled by—or perhaps even missed—the comic turn he gives his first precept, "Always obey your parents" by adding "when they are present" (paragraph 2). The pattern of precept subverted by irony persists throughout the lecture. Eventually, we imagine, most of the audience would have apprehended Twain's mode of speaking as ironic. Students should be able to identify his two modes, the ironic and the comic.

Irony is an unstable mode whose success presupposes ideal auditors (and readers)—in this instance, adults who would be amused by Twain's satirizing the pompous advice age delivers to youth. Ironists contribute to its success by evoking an ideal audience. But irony can go wrong. Have students imagine a range of responses from the adults in Twain's audience, from enjoyment to indignation. Then raise the question of children in the audience who, in the nineteenth century, attended lectures. How might they have responded? How might their presence have complicated the adults' responses?

Satire can be for as well as against. However, in "Advice to Youth" we can identify what Twain is satirizing (what he is against) more surely than we can identify what he is commending (what he is for). Students who have read Jonathan Swift's "A Modest Proposal" (NR 857, SE 499), in "Politics and Government," should look again at paragraphs 30 to 31, where Swift lists "other expedients," that is, what he is for. Is it possible to make a similar list of what Twain is for?

Questions from the NR11

1. Underline the various pieces of "serious" advice that Twain offers and notice where and how he begins to turn each one upside down.
2. Mark Twain was already known as a comic author when he delivered "Advice to Youth" as a lecture in 1882; it was not published until 1923. We do not know the circumstances under which he delivered it or to whom. Using evidence from the text, imagine both the circumstances and the audience.
3. Rewrite "Advice to Youth" for a modern audience, perhaps as a lecture for a school assembly or a commencement address.

Analytical Considerations

1. Have students, as a class or in groups, imagine a range of responses from adults in Twain's audience. What evidence in the text would have triggered these responses?
2. What is Twain for? Ask students, as a class or in groups, to list or describe the values implicit in his lecture.

Suggested Writing Assignments

1. Imagine yourself an auditor offended by Twain's talk and write a letter to its sponsors berating them for inviting him to give it. Or imagine yourself an adult amused by Twain's talk and write a letter to its sponsors commending them for inviting him to give it. Or write both letters.
2. Take Polonius's precept-filled speech to his son Laertes (*Hamlet* 1.3) and use it as the skeleton of a talk in which you alternate irony and comedy in the manner of Twain.
3. Invent a series of precepts for youth to deliver to age, and write a talk in which you alternate irony and comedy in the manner of Twain.

4. Write a letter of advice to an adult invited to give a high school commencement address about what kind of serious advice to give and how to give it without sounding pompous.

ANNETTE BAIER

Trust and Its Vulnerabilities

The Norton Reader, p. 650

Baier is a professor of philosophy in Pittsburgh. She is a scholar of the philosopher David Hume and a feminist. This beautiful, sharp essay on trust is a fine example of how moral philosophy draws on ordinary experiences (of sexual harassment, for example) and literature (Updike's "Trust Me") to reach its conclusion. Baier's feminism is very sophisticated and of a type few will have encountered: she is totally committed to it—that is, her feminism is in her pores. But this essay is primarily one on trust. She demolishes Scanlon's attempt to codify trust through her examples (mostly about women) and then asks, quite directly, if these problems apply only to women. She refutes arguments point by point (one good model), then stops and asks if the grounds of her refutation are too narrow (another good model). In doing so, Baier abstracts from her examples the fact of unequal power relations and posits this situation as a central problem for anyone thinking about trust.

Although her anecdotes are vivid, Baier never tells us who the protagonist is. Ask your students about this choice: what would change if they knew that these things happened to Baier herself? To a friend of hers? Her daughter? Her student? What would change if she presented them as Scanlon might, in more algebraic terms (Tenant, T, sees Landlord, L, weekly for ten weeks at the end of which time L attempts assault on T.) Baier's anecdotes are deliberately ordinary and ambiguous; they do not recount grave or criminal betrayals, but the more bewildering everyday ones. Give your students the chance to discuss all of the issues of ethics and judgments raised by the story, and then refocus the conversation on trust. How do they feel trust should have worked in these situations? Do their conclusions accord with Baier's?

Questions from the NR11

1. In paragraph 4 Baier suggests that trust, as a mental phenomenon, cannot be easily classified within the standard categories of "cognitive," "affective," and "conative," but that it includes all three. Explains what she means by these three categories, using an example from her essay or your own experience.
2. In paragraph 8 Baier introduces moral principles set forth by Thomas Scanlon that should govern the conduct of anyone who says "Trust me." Explain Principles M, D, L, and F, again using an example from Baier's essay or your own experience.
3. Baier believes that Scanlon's principles are useful but not fully adequate for understanding relationships of trust. Why not? Why and how does

she shift attention from the person trusted to the person trusting in the remainder of the essay—as, for example, in paragraphs 13–15?

4. Like other philosophers and ethicists, Baier relies on examples to illustrate and analyze her own arguments and those of others. Choose one example—perhaps the story told by John Updike or one of the anecdotes in paragraphs 18 and 20—and explain how it functions as illustration and/or analysis.

5. Write about a personal experience that involved a relationship of trust, and use some part of Baier's analysis to illuminate this relationship.

Analytical Considerations

1. Help students see how Baier rebuts Scanlon not in debating style, point-by-point, but by questioning his fundamental assumption that it is possible to codify rules for trusting. You might find it helpful to put Scanlon's principles up on the board and then discuss how she demolishes them and why they don't apply in the case of the anecdotes she presents. Discuss the questions with which she ends her essay: if it's not possible to make rules for how to trust, then, how do we teach people when trusting is wise?

2. Have students think of moments in their own lives when trust was betrayed. Where and why did things go wrong?

Suggested Writing Assignments

1. Read Updike's "Trust Me" (available in the collection by that name). Write an analysis of how trust works in one of the other episodes of trust and betrayal that make up the story. What is Updike suggesting about trust? What does his character seem to have learned about trust in the story's final moment? How do the later episodes of trusting connect with Baier's argument?

2. Baier develops her argument about trust through anecdotes. Think of a moment in your own life when trust was betrayed (you may have been the wrongdoer, the wronged, or a bystander). Write a short essay modeled on one of her anecdotes in which you tell the story and analyze where trust went wrong. Does your anecdote suggest a new vulnerability for trust that Baier doesn't discuss? Does it confirm or challenge one of those she presents?

3. Write an essay on trust in which you take Baier's concluding questions as your starting point.

JONATHAN RAUCH

In Defense of Prejudice

Norton Reader, p. 666; Shorter Edition, p. 398

Most students assume that prejudice is a bad thing. Rauch's essay does not attempt to resuscitate prejudice as an ethical good; rather, he examines the negative consequences of trying to eradicate prejudice by forbidding "hate speech" or by prosecuting racial bias, whether on campus, in politics, or in the workplace. In essence, Rauch argues that policing people's speech won't work; he makes the case for "intellectual pluralism, which permits the expression of various forms of bigotry" (paragraph 3). He believes that such pluralism will get the negative ideas and attitudes out in the open, where they can be discussed and countered. As you will want students to observe, Rauch's argument depends on close analysis of contemporary events, theoretical statements about the values of intellectual pluralism, and practical arguments about how best to achieve a just society.

Questions from the NR11

1. Rauch advances a controversial argument: that we should allow prejudice to be expressed rather than seek to repress or eradicate it. How, in the opening paragraphs, does he establish himself as a reasonable, even likable person whose views should be heard? Where else in the essay does he create this persona? Why is persona (or ethos) important in ethical argument?
2. What does Rauch mean by "intellectual pluralism"? Where does he come closest to giving a definition? How does he use examples to imply a definition?
3. In the third section of the essay (paragraphs 12–20), Rauch defines the position antithetical to his own as "purism." Why does he choose this term rather than another? What does it mean?
4. What are some counterarguments to Rauch's position? How many of these arguments does Rauch himself raise and refute? How effective is he at refuting them?
5. Rauch ends with quotations from Toni Morrison and Salman Rushdie. Why? What do their experiences as writers add to his argument?

Analytical Considerations

1. As a follow-up to Question 1 (above) ask students to trace the places in Rauch's essay where he uses "I" or describes a personal experience. You might ask them what they know about him after the introduction (paragraphs 1–5) and what else they know about him by the end. Why, for example, does he mention that he is a "homosexual" and a "dissident" only near the end of the essay?
2. As a follow-up to Questions 2 and 3 (above) discuss the ways that binaries or opposing terms help a writer advance an argument. "Intellectual pluralism" versus "purism" is one binary Rauch uses. Are there others? What about enlightened versus authoritarian regimes (paragraphs 6–11)? Does Rauch introduce opposing terms for "multiculturalism" or "political correctness"?

Suggested Writing Assignments

1. If students formulate good counterarguments in response to Question 4 (above) ask them to write a letter to the editor of *Harper's* magazine, where this essay was published, to point out the flaws or omissions in Rauch's argument.
2. Use an incident of prejudice from your campus or community, along with Rauch's concept of "intellectual pluralism," to describe how you think it should be (or should have been) handled.

MICHAEL LEVIN

The Case for Torture

The Norton Reader, p. 675; Shorter Edition, p. 407

Michael Levin is a professor of philosophy at the City College of the City University of New York. He writes for nonprofessional readers as well as for professional philosophers. This essay originally appeared in the "My Turn" column of *Newsweek*.

Levin is calculatedly aware that, in making a case for torture, he is making an unpopular, even shocking case: "It is generally assumed that torture is impermissible," he begins, "a throwback to a more brutal age" (paragraph 1). Although he clarifies the circumstances under which torture is permissible, his position that it is justified in extreme and in less extreme cases is controversial. The use of torture by regimes we condemn makes even more shocking his argument that we must, as he puts it, "choose to inflict pain as one way of preserving order" (paragraph 12).

This essay may profitably be read along with Paul Fussell's "Thank God for the Atom Bomb" in this section. Fussell, like Levin, makes a controversial case. His essay is of course longer than Levin's: he lets readers hear the voices of those who disagree with him, even though he denies their counterarguments. Because his essay is more inclusive than Levin's, his case for the bombing of Hiroshima and Nagasaki is neither simple nor clear-cut. The genre of his essay is persuasion; he wants readers to understand his position even if they do not agree with it. Some students, as readers and as writers, will prefer Fussell's persuasive strategies.

Levin makes a case for torture like a debater, and like a debater, he is out to win. He illustrates his argument with hypothetical and clear-cut cases rather than complexly contextualized ones. For example, he does not consider whether or not we have found the right terrorist to torture or whether or not the bomb is really there. He brings up the counterarguments of those who disagree with him—as in a debate, they are his opponents—in order to rebut them rather than to acknowledge that they make his case less clear-cut, more hedged with uncertainty. His mode of writing is argument; he stakes out a position that we must agree or disagree with. Some students, as readers and as writers, will prefer such argumentative strategies.

Analytical Considerations

1. In paragraph 12 Levin poses as the alternative to "inflict[ing] pain as one way of preserving order" becoming paralyzed "in the face of evil." Ask students if this is a fair statement of alternatives. Can they produce fairer statements? Do fairer statements yield less clear-cut alternatives?

2. Have students look at Levin's hypothetical cases and ask them to invent hypothetical countercases. Does context complicate Levin's argument? What are the advantages and disadvantages of arguing from hypothetical and decontextualized cases?

3. You can use this essay as a springboard to ask students to consider what constitutes an ethical decision. Must it be absolute? Could a decision to torture and a decision not to torture, in the same instance, both be ethical? What are students' criteria for ethical decisions?

4. You may want to ask students to consider what leads them to prefer either persuasion or argument, both as writers and as readers. Do they, as writers, self-consciously make choices as to which mode they use? Should they?

Suggested Writing Assignments

1. Write an essay in which you argue against torture with debater's strategies: using clear-cut hypothetical cases and rebuttal rather than incorporating counterarguments.

2. Write an essay in which you make a persuasive case either for or against torture in a particular context, with the aim of having readers understand your position whether or not they agree with it.

3. Read Ursula LeGuin's story "Those Who Walk Away from Omelas"; it appears in her collection *The Wind's Twelve Quarters* (1975) and is frequently anthologized. Write an essay in which you consider how the context she creates complicates Levin's position that we must "choose to inflict pain as one way of preserving order" (paragraph 12).

TOM REGAN

The Case for Animal Rights

The Norton Reader, p. 677; Shorter Edition, p. 409

Tom Regan is a philosopher who writes about theoretical and applied ethics; this essay, contributed to a collection of essays edited by Peter Singer, *In Defense of Animals* (1985), is an abridgment of his book by the same name, *The Case for Animal Rights* (1983). Regan's contribution to the defense of animals, he believes, is "asking and answering deep, foundational moral questions about what morality is, how it should be understood and what is the best moral theory, all considered" (paragraph 6). He has strong feelings about animals, he claims, and he concludes this essay with some expression of them (paragraph 38).

The circumstances of publication may account for his emphasis on both argument and argumentative procedures, which he enunciates along with his case. They may also account for the density of his argument as he lays out four positions—indirect duty, contractarianism, cruelty-kindness, and utilitarianism—and argues against them before advancing his own rights case.

According to Regan, his rights case is rationally the soundest. It also eliminates complexity: the human use of animals as a resource is either right or wrong and, if wrong, no compromises (such as he describes in paragraphs 1–4 and paragraphs 35–36) are possible. But what if Regan had been unable to make a rationally sound case for animal rights? Would a flawed case have altered his experience of what he regards as the abuse of animals? (You will want to call attention to what he says in paragraph 37.) Regan's essay deserves reading in conjunction with experiential essays such as Sallie Tisdale's "We Do Abortions Here: A Nurse's Story" (NR 713, SE 426). His emphasis on argument and argumentative procedures and Tisdale's emphasis on context raise important questions about the relation of principle to experience in ethics.

Questions from the NR11

1. Regan argues against four views that deny rights to animals: indirect duty, contractarianism, cruelty-kindness, and utilitarianism. Locate his account of each and explain his objections to it.
2. Regan then argues for what he calls a "rights view," which is, he claims, "rationally the most satisfactory moral theory" (paragraph 28). Explain both his view and his claim.
3. What are the advantages of arguing for views that conflict with one's own before arguing for one's own? What are the disadvantages?
4. Regan includes among his goals "the total dissolution of commercial animal agriculture" and "the total elimination of commercial and sport hunting and trapping" (paragraph 1). Do these goals include vegetarianism? If so, why does he not use the word "vegetarian"?
5. Write an essay in which you take a position on an issue about which you have strong feelings. Following Regan's example, focus on argument while both acknowledging and excluding your feelings.

Analytical Considerations

1. You may want to divide Questions 1 and 2 (above) into five parts and have students work in groups on one part each. You may also want to identify students who have encountered these views in philosophy or ethics courses and assign them to different groups. At the end of this exercise, try asking the various groups to describe their experiences of following and comprehending a philosophical argument.
2. What assertions does Regan make about political and social change? Do your students accept them? How important are they to his argument?
3. Carl Cohen, in "The Case for the Use of Animals in Biomedical Research" in this section, finds Regan's argument for a rights view flawed. After students grasp it, you may want to refer them to Cohen's argument against it.

Suggested Writing Assignments

1. Of the relation of this essay to his book *The Case for Animal Rights* (1983), Regan writes: "Most of the details of the supporting argument are missing. They are to be found in the book to which I alluded earlier" (paragraph 33). Follow, in his book, one of the four views he argues against in his essay or the view he argues for, with attention to its detail. Then write an essay in which you describe the detail he includes and evaluate the difference it makes to his argument.
2. Write an essay in which you imagine and describe, for your own life, the consequences of assenting to and acting on Regan's argument.

3. Look at the collection of essays edited by Peter Singer, *In Defense of Animals* (1985), and survey the other approaches to animal rights. Write an essay in which you choose one approach, describe it, and evaluate it in comparison with Regan's approach.

4. Read Sallie Tisdale's "We Do Abortions Here: A Nurse's Story" in this section. Regan alludes to "the terribly difficult question of the morality of abortion" (paragraph 16) and speaks of settling it. What does he mean by "settle"? Does Tisdale attempt to "settle" the question? Write an essay in which you discuss the relative merits and problems of their two approaches to difficult ethical questions.

CARL COHEN

The Case for the Use of Animals in Biomedical Research

The Norton Reader, p. 687

Carl Cohen's "The Case for the Use of Animals in Biomedical Research" is something of an oddity. Although it appeared in the *New England Journal of Medicine*, it is a philosophical argument rather than a scientific report, written by a philosopher rather than a medical researcher and by a single person rather than a team. Because Cohen does not report on or analyze data, he does not follow the form prescribed for scientific reports or present information in tables and figures. Nevertheless, like other scientific researchers, including Henry Wechsler et al. (in "Science and Technology" [NR 948, SE 551]), he emphatically segments his argument, heads the segments with titles, and divides his conclusion into three parts: Substitution, Reduction, and Consistency (paragraphs 28–38).

Cohen also follows the *New England Journal of Medicine*'s system of annotation, which does not identify the authors of quotations in the text or refer to them by name. Consequently, stationing Cohen's essay in relation to Tom Regan's "The Case for Animal Rights" (NR 677, SE 409) requires careful reading of Cohen's notes. He rebuts (or attempts to rebut) two arguments against the use of animals in biomedical research, the rights argument (in Tom Regan's version) and the antispeciesist argument (in Peter Singer's version). Cohen, who published his article in 1986, cites Regan's 1983 book, *The Case for Animal Rights*, in note 1 (he does not cite the article in this section of *The Norton Reader*, which appeared in Peter Singer's *In Defense of Animals* [1985]), Singer's 1975 *Animal Liberation* in note 2, and a 1985 essay Singer wrote for the *New York Review of Books* in note 13. (An injunction to students writing nonscientific papers with quotations and documentation: Never use quotations in your text without identifying, in the text, who said them, and never force readers to consult your notes in order to make sense of your text.)

Questions from the NR11

1. Cohen limits his argument to the use of animals in biomedical research. What are the advantages of this limitation? What are the disadvantages?

2 Cohen defends speciesism; Tom Regan, in "The Case for Animal Rights" (NR 677, SE 409), condemns it. What are the issues at stake between them?

3. "Neither of these arguments is sound," Cohen opines. "The first relies on a mistaken understanding of rights; the second relies on a mistaken calculation of consequences" (paragraph 1). Find other examples of the language Cohen uses to dismiss arguments in opposition to his own. How do you respond to it? Is it the kind of language you would use in your own writing? Explain.

4. Write an essay in which you argue for or against speciesism. Be sure to define it. You may use Regan's and Cohen's arguments (with proper credit) in support of your own, but you need not.

Analytical Considerations

1. Cohen limits his argument to justifying the use of animals in biomedical research. You may want to ask students what other uses of animals his argument justifies and why they think he limited it to biomedical research.

2. Tom Regan, in "The Case for Animal Rights" (NR 677, SE 409), asserts: "Inherent value, then, belongs equally to those who are the experiencing subjects of a life" (paragraph 32). Ask students first to explore the full meaning of this assertion and, second, to consider the adequacy of Cohen's rebuttal.

3. Cohen, in paragraphs 37 to 38, extends Regan's (and Singer's) position and calls such extension a "reductio ad absurdum." Regan hedges on such an extension. Is it consistent with his argument? Ought he to have made it? Is it, as Cohen alleges, absurd?

4. Ask students to identify the no-holds-barred argumentative strategies of Cohen and Michael Levin, in "The Case for Torture" in this section. You may want to begin by having them mark, in their texts, examples of what they take to be Cohen's and Levin's argumentative strategies. Levin dares us to confront unpleasant truths; Cohen, unpleasant truths and shoddy arguments. As readers, how do we respond to these strategies? As writers, how likely are we to use them? What other strategies are available?

Suggested Writing Assignments

1. Recast Cohen's arguments in a persuasive mode. Probably you will have to abandon the form of a scientific report as well; append a paragraph to your essay explaining the form you use and how you found it.

2. "Medical investigators are seldom insensitive to the distress their work may cause animal subjects," Cohen states (paragraph 273). What kind of evidence could rebut this statement? How much of it would you need? Do library research to find some, and write an essay in which you consider the function of experiential evidence in arguing with Cohen. If you can prove that medical investigators are sometimes or frequently insensitive, does Cohen's argument fail?

NORA EPHRON

The Boston Photographs

The Norton Reader, p. 696

Many students will know (or know of) Nora Ephron as the novelist who wrote *When Harry Met Sally* and *Heartburn*, both turned into popular movies. But Ephron began her writing career as a serious essayist. As she told a group of aspiring writers, "In college all I could think about was going off to New York and becoming a journalist. If you want to go into screenwriting, become a journalist first, especially if you're like me, and have no area of expertise."

This essay, which explores the ethics of photojournalism, comes from a collection of Ephron's serious journalism, *Scribble, Scribble* (1978). It documents and analyzes the controversy that erupted when the *Boston Herald American* published three dramatic photos by Stanley Forman: a series taken on July 22, 1975, in which a firefighter attempts to rescue a mother and child from a burning apartment building, only to watch them fall from an unstable fire escape. Forman won the Pulitzer Prize in 1976 for these photographs, but for well over a year the controversy raged.

There are several ways to approach this essay and the accompanying photographs. You might ask students to describe what they see in the photographs and to respond to the images before discussing Ephron's essay. Or you might ask students to recall the responses of newspaper readers in 1975 to the photos and ask students why they think viewers responded so vehemently. Or, if you have a local newspaper that prints photographs of fires or other such sensational events, you might ask students to compare these images with Forman's photos and then consider why Forman's caused such a controversy. Ultimately, students should compare their conclusions with Ephron's, that the photos "deserve to be printed because they are great pictures, breathtaking pictures of something that happened" (last paragraph).

Questions from the NR11

1. Why does Ephron begin with the words of the photographer Stanley Forman? What information—as well as perspective—does her opening paragraph convey?
2. What was public reaction to the publication of the Boston photographs? What reasons did newspeople give for printing the photographs? How does Ephron arrange these responses?
3. What conclusions does Ephron reach about the ethics of publishing sensational photographs? Does she offer ethical guidelines?
4. Find a startling photograph recently printed in a newspaper or magazine, and argue for or against its publication, using Ephron's terms and your own.
5. Examine the Vietcong assassination photo in H. Bruce Franklin's "From Realism to Virtual Reality" (NR 792). Were the issues about publishing

this photo the same as those for the Boston photographs Ephron discusses? Were they different? Or different enough? Write an essay about he issues surrounding the two photo publications.

Analytical Considerations

1. Throughout this essay, Ephron quotes extensively, both the negative viewers' reactions and the defending editor's responses. Ask students to mark these quotations and discuss why Ephron uses them.
2. How much of Ephron's essay is recounting the facts? recounting the viewers' reactions and the editor's defense? giving her own analysis? Ask students to note these parts of the essay and discuss the balance among them.

Suggested Writing Assignments

1. Choose one of the three Boston photographs and describe, in detail, what you see and what response the image elicits.
2. Find a photograph in your local newspaper or a fire or other human disaster. Compare this image—what it shows, what response it elicits—with Forman's photographs.
3. Imagine yourself to be the editor-in-chief of a newspaper. Write a "code of ethics" for what visual images your newspaper will—and will not—print. Present your policy in a letter to the newspaper staff.

LEIGH TURNER

The Media and the Ethics of Cloning

The Norton Reader, p. 702

Leigh Turner comments not so much on the cloning debate, at its peak late in 1997, as on the way it has been treated in the media. Although she seems to exonerate journalists and news commentators in the second paragraph by acknowledging the haste with which they are usually forced to write, she nonetheless blames them for falling into hyperbole, depending on sound bites, and oversimplifying views. In her essay, originally a column in the *Chronicle of Higher Education* (September 26, 1997) and thus much like the Op-Ed form she criticizes, Turner tries to avoid such oversimplification; she does so not by offering a thorough analysis of the debate but by presenting a list of suggestions for improving the discussion (paragraphs 11–18). You might call students' attention to Turner's three-part structure, often a strategy used by writers and speakers who need to get their message heard.

Questions from the NR11

1. This essay begins with a journalistic "hook," a paragraph about the artist Andy Warhol and how his work anticipates some issues of cloning. For

what purposes does Turner use Warhol? Does the reader need to have seen Andy Warhol's art to understand the argument Turner makes?

2. Like several selections in the "Ethics" section, this essay first lays out the problems, then proposes some solutions. What problems does Turner blame on the media? What solutions does Turner propose that address the media? Why are some of the solutions focused less on the media than on scientists and ethicists?

3. Take an issue of local or national relevance, and study how it is treated in the media. (You may want to limit your analysis to a group of newspapers or make it a comparison of newspaper and television coverage.) Which aspects of the media's coverage are good? Which are inadequate? What might be done to correct the problems?

Analytical Considerations

1. Ask students to outline or diagram Turner's essay: introduction with statement of the problem, analysis of the problem, suggestions for improving the debate. Why must Turner use this relatively simple structure for the column she is writing? What are its advantages and disadvantages?

2. How many of the issues about cloning does Turner manage to convey, despite her emphasis on the media? Ask students to list the issues and then add any she omitted.

Suggested Writing Assignments

1. What has happened to the debate about cloning? Do library research to find recent examples of articles and Op-Eds on cloning, and write a brief account of what the current issues are.

2. Turner argues (paragraph 16) that university researchers and scholars should "write for newspapers, popular magazines, and even community newsletters" so that the issues they study are clearly presented to the general public. Choose an essay in which a faculty member has done so—for example, Henry Wechsler or Kenneth Bruffee on binge drinking (in the "Op-Eds" section), Tom Regan on animal rights (in the "Ethics" section), William Cronon on conceptions of nature (in the section "Nature and the Environment"), or an Op-Ed by a faculty member in your campus newspaper—and discuss whether the writer has met the standards Turner discusses in the final paragraphs (15–18).

ALDO LEOPOLD

The Land Ethic

The Norton Reader, p. 707; Shorter Edition, p. 420

This excerpt from A *Sand County Almanac* presents the concept of the "land ethic," a seminal concept in environmental studies. Leopold argues that ethics must include not just relationships among human beings but also between humans and the land. For Leopold, incorporating the land into our ethical vision is the next step in the evolution of ethical thinking. If we think about the land as a part of our community, then our sense of obligation to that land emerges, changing the way we use the land.

Leopold uses two contrasting examples: Kentucky, where the bluegrass thrives, and New Mexico, where the grazing of animals led to massive soil erosion. The different results, according to Leopold, are entirely owing to differences in plant succession; in New Mexico, "the pioneers were equally brave, resourceful, and persevering." You may want to show your students that what is important here is the contrast. While a human-centered account might emphasize the difference between success and failure, a land-ethicist's account such as Leopold's uses contrast to demonstrate the major role that the land itself plays in human history.

Leopold's style is both passionate and methodical. Collaboratively outlining his argument may help students see how he builds from one premise to another. His belief in evolution clearly shapes the step-by-step logic of the argument. Leopold uses clear signal phrases at the beginning of paragraphs ("In short," "To sum up," "A parallel situation exists"). Listing these shows students their use both as orientation aids in their reading and as tools to deploy in their own writing.

For all that is logical here, the essay advocates a specific point of view. Students may have trouble understanding the possibility of being a logical advocate, as Leopold is. They may be interested to know that an early version of this book was rejected for not being personal enough. Ask them to find moments of advocacy in the essay, moments where Leopold permits his passion to show (as in the parenthetical "In human history we have learned [I hope] that the conqueror role is eventually self-defeating.")

Questions from the NR11

1. Leopold begins with a story of the Greek hero Odysseus returning from the Trojan War and executing "a dozen slave-girls of his household." What relevance does this story have to his argument about progress in human ethics?
2. What is the "ethical sequence"? What three aspects or stages of ethical development does Leopold include?
3. How does the concept of a biotic community alter the relationship of humans to the land? Why does Leopold use the Latin designation *Homo sapiens* in paragraph 13 as he redefines this relationship?
4. What problems does Leopold anticipate in putting a land ethic into effect? Do environmentalists face the same or different problems today?
5. How far have Americans come since 1949, when Leopold's essay was published? If your course includes a research paper, consider writing on contemporary responses to problems that Leopold enumerated in his day.

Analytical Considerations

1. Bring examples of moral codes to class (e.g. the ten commandments, the Code of Hammurabi, the Bill of Rights). Then, as a class, generate an ethical code for land use.

2. Leopold points out that in ancient Greece, the ethical structure "that covered wives . . . had not yet been extended to human chattels." Discuss the historical development of some current ethical principles with your class. How did people come to extend civil rights to women and minorities? What is the status of the pursuit of rights for noncitizens or homosexuals? Do the failures and successes of these movements provide a lesson for the environment?
3. Leopold wrote his essay in 1949. In the half-century since then, scientists have discovered economic uses for all sorts of organisms that were never before imagined as potential cash crops. Ask your class to discuss whether the extension of the economic argument works to the advantage or disadvantage of the environment.

Suggested Writing Assignments

1. Imagine yourself an environmental policy-maker. How would you persuade landowners to act in accordance with a land ethic?
2. Leopold asserts that "An ethical obligation on the part of the private owner is the only visible remedy." Write a brief essay expressing the degree to which you agree or disagree with this statement, which is the concluding sentiment of the essay.

SALLIE TISDALE

We Do Abortions Here: A Nurse's Story

The Norton Reader, p. 713; Shorter Edition, p. 426

This essay reflects the intimacy and particularity of caring, as well as, of course, the gendering of the nursing profession. Tisdale is experiential in her approach, and draws on her working experience as she considers the difficult ethical issue of abortion. As she explores it, she moves back and forth in time and also in scale: "I can sweep the horizon with both eyes, survey the scene in all its distance and size. Or I can put my eye to the lens [of a telescope] and focus on the small details, suddenly so close" (paragraph 4).

Although Tisdale does not use the term situation ethics, this essay may exemplify them. Tisdale plainly subscribes to their first principle: contextuality. She judges acts—insofar as she judges them—in context. She may or may not subscribe to their second principle, love, as a standard for judging her own and others' acts. Is it possible to read Tisdale's "We Do Abortions Here" as exemplifying both principles? The first can be demonstrated explicitly as well as implicitly; the second is problematic.

The five sections of the essay are separated by typographical space rather than connected by prose transitions; within each section Tisdale moves back and forth in both time and space. If you ask students to read Scott Russell Sanders's "Looking at Women" (NR 244, SE 147), in the "Human Nature" section, you will be able to introduce and compare two different strategies of accumulation. Sanders gives each of his five sections a narrative focus, whereas

Tisdale repeats within each section the shifting perspectives on time and space. Neither essay follows the conventions of "academic" or "college" writing.

Questions from the NR11

1. Tisdale speaks of taking both broad views—"as if I am standing on a cliff with a telescope"—and narrow views—"I can put my eye to the lens and focus on the small details" (paragraph 4). Choose one section of this essay (such as the second, third, or fourth) and mark the passages you would describe as taking broad views and the passages you would describe as taking narrow views. What is the effect of Tisdale's going back and forth between them? How does she manage transitions?
2. "We are too busy to chew over ethics" (paragraph 21), Tisdale observes. What does she mean by ethics? Does she engage with what you consider ethical issues in this essay? Explain.
3. Although Tisdale takes a pro-choice position, a pro-lifer could use parts of her essay against her. What parts? What are the advantages and disadvantages of including material that could be used in support of the opposition?
4. Write a pro-choice or pro-life essay of your own. Include material that could be used in support of the opposition. You may use Tisdale's essay (with proper credit), but you need not.

Analytical Considerations

1. Some people criticize situation ethics because they are relative rather than absolute. Do students think ethical principles must be absolute?
2. How might situation ethics have provided Tisdale with a framework for a different kind of essay, an analysis or an argument, instead of the associative and accumulative narrative that she wrote?
3. "I don't say 'pain' any more than I would say 'baby'" (paragraph 16), Tisdale observes. Where else in the essay are you aware of her using, as she puts it, "care with my language"? Why is language so important in discussing abortion?

Suggested Writing Assignments

1. In "The Case for Animal Rights" (NR 677, SE 409), in this section, Tom Regan makes a rights case for animals. Can the same case be made for fetuses? Write an essay answering this question.
2. Write an essay in which you have recourse to situation ethics implicitly, like Tisdale, or explicitly. Alternatively, write an essay critical of situation ethics.
3. Tisdale speaks of crisis pregnancy centers advertised in the *Yellow Pages* (paragraph 24). Can you locate one in the *Yellow Pages* of your own or a nearby city? Call them to see what they tell you. Write an account of the experience.
4. Tisdale's most recent book is *Talk Dirty to Me* (1994). Read parts of it and write an essay in which you discuss her recourse to situation ethics with respect to dirty talk.

STEPHEN JAY GOULD

The Terrifying Normalcy of AIDS

The Norton Reader, p. 720; Shorter Edition, p. 433

In this essay, the late Stephen Jay Gould—a biologist, paleontologist, and historian of science—turns his attention to the AIDS "pandemic." Like his regular column in *Natural History* magazine, "The Terrifying Normalcy of AIDS" was written for a lay audience; it appeared in the *New York Times Magazine* in April 1987.

Gould characterizes AIDS as both normal and terrifying. He wants us to see it as occupying a middle position between just another disease for which "medicine will soon generate a cure" and "something so irregular that it must have been visited upon us to teach us a moral lesson" (paragraph 14). Gould also wants to describe and criticize a particular American belief, that technology will solve all of our problems. This belief he embodies in Disney's Epcot Center. His essay, thus, has a double focus: the power of nature (of which AIDS is part) and our false confidence in technological fixes.

Questions from the NR11

1. Gould uses current events, historical information, and scientific data to make his case. Identify examples of each.
2. What case does Gould make?
3. Why is this essay in the section called "Ethics" rather than in the section called "Science and Technology"?
4. Gould uses Disney's Epcot Center in Orlando, Florida, as a symbol of our belief in technology. Find another symbol of this belief and, in a brief essay, describe and interpret it.

Analytical Considerations

1. It is likely that at least some students will have been to Epcot Center. You may want to ask them, before they read "The Terrifying Normalcy of AIDS," to describe it—in discussion or in writing—so that all students can consider what aspects of American culture it embodies. Students who have not been to Epcot Center may be asked, after a discussion of its uses, to locate in their own experience symbols that can be made to carry equivalent meanings.
2. Gould uses current events, historical information, and scientific data to make his case. You may want to ask students to mark examples of each. What are the advantages of including all three?
3. Gould divides "The Terrifying Normalcy of AIDS" into four sections by means of spacing: paragraphs 1–5, 6–9, 10–13, and 14–16. Ask students to consider whether these spatial divisions correspond to units of exposition and argument. You may also ask them, as a class, in groups, or individually, to construct titles for each section of Gould's essay.

Suggested Writing Assignments

1. "The Terrifying Normalcy of AIDS" appeared in 1987. Do library research to ascertain and report on the current state of what is known about the prevention and cure of AIDS. Write an essay in which you organize this information to support Gould's two-part assertion, "AIDS works by a mechanism—and we can discover it" (paragraph 16), to question it, or both.

2. Write an essay using different illustrative material—that is, something other than AIDS—to support Gould's assertion, "The message of Orlando—the inevitability of technological solutions—is wrong, and we need to understand why" (paragraph 10), to question it, or both.

3. Is the current SARS crisis both "terrifying" and "normal"? Study the evidence and argue whether it does or does not follow the patterns Gould describes in this essay.

PAUL FUSSELL

Thank God for the Atom Bomb

The Norton Reader, p. 724; Shorter Edition, p. 437

"Thank God for the Atom Bomb" was originally published in the the the *New Republic* in August 1981. It became the title essay in Fussell's *Thank God for the Atom Bomb and Other Essays*, published in 1988, forty-three years after the bombings of Hiroshima and Nagasaki. Writing on their forty-second anniversary, Fussell says, was prompted "by the long debate about the ethics, if any, of that ghastly affair" (paragraph 1).

Fussell takes on a number of the debaters, mostly those questioning the necessity and the morality of the bombings. You will want students to look at his argumentative strategies, notably his ad hominem arguments (that is, "to the man"). He uses them two ways: in making his own case and in arguing against the cases of others.

In making his own case, Fussell begins by discussing the value of experience, "sheer, vulgar experience" (paragraph 1). He nevertheless embeds his experience in an argument and argues against the cases of others. Fussell sharply and disparagingly contrasts their experience with his—even as he acknowledges the "offensive implications" of what he does (paragraph 9). Those wishing to read what his adversaries have to say will have to search beyond Fussell's essay; sometimes it contains the titles of books and periodicals, but never dates. (Depending on your interests, you might use this essay to consider the advantages and disadvantages of scholarly and popular conventions of annotation.)

Fussell's essay may profitably be discussed in conjunction with Michael Levin's "The Case for Torture" (NR 675, SE 407) in this section. Both Levin and Fussell deal with controversial instances and acknowledge that fact. But Levin deals with an hypothetical instance, whereas Fussell treats a messy and complex historical one. Levin presents himself as detached and magisterial, whereas Fussell is engaged and sometimes irate.

Questions from the NR11

1. Note the places where Fussell includes personal experience in this essay. How much is his own, how much belongs to others? Why does he include both kinds?
2. Fussell dismisses with contempt those who disagree with him. Locate some examples. How do you respond to them? Would you use Fussell's strategies to dismiss those who disagree with you? Explain.
3. Mark some instances of Fussell's "voice." What kind of voice does he adopt? What kind of person does he present himself as?
4. Write a similarly argumentative essay in which you take a strong position. Include your own experience and the experience of others if appropriate.

Analytical Considerations

1. You may want to focus a discussion of Fussell's use of sources by bringing photocopies of the debate between Joseph Alsop and David Joravsky in the *New York Review of Books* to class. This debate, "reduced to a collision between experience and theory, was conducted with a certain civilized respect for evidence," according to Fussell (paragraph 16). Does Fussell fairly summarize the debate? Why does he speak of it as "reduced to a collision between experience and theory"?
2. Fussell ends his essay with "The past, which as always did not know the future, acted in ways that ask to be imagined before they are condemned. Or even simplified" (paragraph 32). Ask students to explain what he means. Is his generalization true with respect to "Thank God for the Atom Bomb"?

Suggested Writing Assignments

1. Rewrite Fussell's essay using the argumentative strategies of Michael Levin in "The Case for Torture" (NR 675, SE 407).
2. August 1995 was the fiftieth anniversary of the bombing of Hiroshima and Nagasaki. As the Smithsonian Institution prepared to commemorate it with an exhibit at the National Air and Space Museum, controversy over the bombing was renewed. Write a narrative account of the controversy using the *New York Times* and the *Washington Post* as sources. (There are various ways of doing this project collaboratively.)
3. After completing the research in Suggested Writing Assignment 2 (above), write an analysis of the issues involved in the controversy.
4. Write an essay in which you consider whether the issues surrounding the debate over the bombing have changed since the 1980s, when Fussell wrote "Thank God for the Atom Bomb."

The Norton Reader, p. 737

Who has not heard the expressions "God helps them that help themselves" or "Remember that time is money" or "Early to bed and early to rise, / Makes a man healthy, wealthy, and wise"? All come from Ben Franklin's *Poor Richard's Almanack*, all represent beliefs deeply engrained in the American psyche, and all are maxims or "apothegms."

Maxims represent, in the words of Sir James Mackintosh, "the condensed good sense of nations"; they convey pithy, often witty observations of people about human conduct. Whether called "apothegms," "maxims," "proverbs," or "aphorisms," wisdom or good sense lies at the heart of these brief statements about human behavior. Unlike ordinary assertions of fact or opinion, which usually concern themselves with particular rather than universal experience, the moral or maxim asserts a universal truth; it is complete and authoritative in its brevity and wit.

The examples in this section include traditional maxims, such as those Franklin collected in the eighteenth century for *Poor Richard's Almanack* or Duc François de La Rochefoucauld collected in the seventeenth century for his *Reflexions ou sentences et maximes morales*, or *Maxims*. We have also included two examples of countermaxims, apothegms that run contrary to conventional wisdom—what William Blake called *Proverbs of Hell* and what Ambrose Bierce included in his *Devil's Dictionary*. And, to give students a sense of this form as ongoing and relevant, we have included three examples of contemporary uses of maxims: on the Internet, on an academic Web site, and on public billboards. Internet advice, whether serious or humorous, frequently circulates in the form of maxims, apothegms, or witty sayings, and you might ask students to bring in their own examples. Stuart Moulthrop's "Pillars of Wisdom" presents guidelines for constructing a Web site in terms of "axioms" and rewrites George Orwell's famous rules in "Politics and the English Language" (NR 540, SE 319), particularly the last: "(vi) Break any of these rules sooner than say anything outright barbarous." The maxims of Jenny Holzer, a conceptual artist, have appeared on billboards, marble slabs, theater marquees, and electronic signs. We have included a selection of her modern, witty maxims, as well as some visual examples of her work.

Questions from the NR11

1. Many maxims represent common sense or conventional wisdom—but stated in clever, unconventional form. Choose several examples that you think represent common sense, and explain why you find their form interesting or appealing.
2. Some maxims represent unconventional wisdom or even advice contrary to common sense. Choose several examples of this sort, and explain what alternative truth they mean to articulate.
3. What makes a maxim memorable? Choose one or two examples that you remember from your reading (or perhaps from childhood) and analyze the features that make it easily recollected.

4. Try writing several maxims. Which features of this form are difficult? Which easy?
5. Choose a maxim with which you agree, and write an essay explaining why it represents good advice. Alternatively, choose one with which you disagree, and write an essay in which you explain why it is incorrect or deceptive.

Analytical Considerations

1. Using the selections from Franklin and La Rochefoucauld, ask students which maxims they have heard or read before, how they learned them, and why they think these sayings have stayed current in the American (or Western) consciousness. What belief or truth do these maxims represent? You might then ask why others have disappeared or become disused.
2. You may want to assign the maxims in chronological rather than in the current alphabetical order. If you do, you might ask how and why the later writers, such as Blake, Bierce, or Holzer, take the form to invert or counter conventional wisdom. What advantages does a form associated with wisdom have for these countercultural writers?
3. Spend some time considering Ambrose Bierce's definitions, perhaps by looking up definitions in a conventional dictionary and comparing them with Bierce's, perhaps by analyzing his extended definitions (e.g., "cemetery," "Christian," "platitude," "saint," "valor") as forms of cultural critique.
4. What difference does *seeing* a maxim—on a billboard or theater marquee—make? How is the experience of seeing Jenny Holzer's maxims different from reading or hearing one? Does the visual experience have impact primarily (or only) because Holzer's displays are countermaxims and go against our expectations?
5. Analyze the forms of maxims that students think are memorable. (They will have prepared answers for Question 3, above.) Point out such features as parallel structure ("Love well, whip well"), contrast ("Romance is tempestuous. Love is calm."), metaphorical language ("Let thy vices die before thee" or "An empty bag cannot stand upright"), irony ("God heals, and the doctor takes the fees"), and qualification ("Three may keep a secret, if two of them are dead"). Then ask students to try writing some modern maxims by using one or more of these features.
6. If you have read selections from the "Fables and Parables" section, ask students about the differences between maxims and these forms—the one that sums up truth in a brief statement, the others that tell a story to capture that truth.

Suggested Writing Assignments

1. Write two or three maxims, either in imitation of one of the writers in this section or as counterstatements to the maxims of one writer.
2. Read one of the parables in *The Norton Reader* (p. 1110). Write a moral that, in your view, sums up the truth of the parable.

HENRY DAVID THOREAU

The Battle of the Ants

The Norton Reader, p. 756; Shorter Edition, p. 450

Taken from the chapter in *Walden* titled "Brute Neighbors," "The Battle of the Ants" is not so much history as natural history. Yet, because Thoreau alludes to historical battles and imitates the conventions of history writing, this brief account provides an opportunity for discussing what constitutes a historical event and how a historical style of writing gives status to some events, and not to others. The battle Thoreau describes would not normally be considered historical: it is, after all, only a struggle between two species of ants. But Thoreau's account leads us to ponder how the human struggles called "wars" become history—is it because historians record their maneuvers in detail, praise their leaders and soldiers, and treat their outcomes as decisive? Thoreau potentially subverts this traditional approach to history by suggesting that "history" is created by historians and that the events they present as "historical" attain this status in large part because we accept the conventions of their style.

Questions from the NR11

1. Thoreau uses the Latin word "bellum" to describe the battle of the ants and follows it with a reference to the Myrmidons, the soldiers of Achilles in Homer's *Iliad*. Locate additional examples of this kind of allusion. How does it work?
2. Ordinarily we speak of accounts of natural events as "natural history" and accounts of human events as "history." How does Thoreau, in this selection, blur the distinction? To what effect?
3. Look up a description of the behavior of ants in a book by one of the entomologists Thoreau refers to or in another scientific text. Compare the scientist's style with Thoreau's. Take another event in nature and describe it twice, once in scientific and once in allusive language. Or write an essay in which you describe and analyze the differences between the scientist's style and Thoreau's.

Analytical Considerations

1. In the long first paragraph Thoreau alludes to two well-known wars: the battles recorded in Homer's *Iliad* and the American Revolution, particularly the battles of Lexington and Concord (where the "shot heard around the world" was fired). What effect does Thoreau intend? By comparing the battle of the ants to classical Greek and American wars, he writes a form of mock heroic that both elevates the actions of the ants and paradoxically deflates the warlike actions of men.
2. This passage comes from a chapter in Thoreau's *Walden* titled "Brute Neighbors." How does the comparison alluded to in the first paragraph,

between the fighting ants and human warriors, amplify the meaning of that title?

3. Why does Thoreau describe the wounds of the ants in such detail? You might think of his description as an example of natural history as well as an imitation of historical writing.

4. In the final paragraph Thoreau alludes to American and European entomologists, also called "natural historians." Thoreau's style in this paragraph, however, is not that of a scientist but is a parody of the historian's. Why? (For a stylistic comparison, you might look at Alexander Petrunkevitch's "The Spider and the Wasp" [NR 595, SE 368] in "Nature and the Environment.")

5. What significance might there be in that Thoreau, at the end of this selection, dates the battle of the ants as occurring five years before the passage of Webster's Fugitive-Slave Bill? In Thoreau's mind, what kind of historical event seems to be genuinely significant?

Suggested Writing Assignments

1. Read an account of the battles of Lexington and Concord (where Thoreau lived), then write an essay analyzing the section of Thoreau's account that alludes to these battles, with attention to how Thoreau's fellow citizens might have responded to his allusions.

2. Look up a description of the behavior of ants in a book by one of the entomologists Thoreau refers to or in another scientific textbook. What are the conventions of scientific description? Why do you think scientists adopt them? Write an essay comparing the style of the scientist with Thoreau's.

BARBARA TUCHMAN

"This Is the End of the World": The Black Death

The Norton Reader, p. 759; Shorter Edition, p. 453

Barbara Tuchman's account of the Black Death, a chapter from her book *A Distant Mirror: The Calamitous Fourteenth Century* (1978), is a brilliant, justly renowned popular re-creation of a famous historical event. Tuchman describes the movement of the disease from central Asia through Europe; creates statistical data to convey its enormous impact on European society; records human responses to the plague, from the horribly selfish to the literally saintly; and explores various medieval explanations for the cause and meaning of the plague. For many students, this essay will represent a classic—and the best—example of narrative history; Tuchman is a master of its conventions and a skilled practitioner.

Questions from the NR11

1. Why does Tuchman begin with the account of the Genoese trading ships?
2. What ways does Tuchman find to group related facts together—in other words, what categories does she develop? Suggest other categories that

Tuchman might have used in arranging her facts. What would she have gained or lost by using such categories?

3. Can you determine a basis for Tuchman's decision sometimes to quote a source, sometimes to recount it in her own words?
4. Write a brief account of a modern disaster, based on research from several sources.

Analytical Considerations

1. For many students, Tuchman's "'This Is the End of the World'" will seem more like "history" than the other selections in this section. Why? What features of her writing signal that this is history?
2. At some point in the discussion of Tuchman's chapter ask students what facts about the Black Death they remember best. Then consider why they remember them, and what techniques in Tuchman's rendering make them memorable.
3. Tuchman begins with a date, October 1347, and initially proceeds in chronological order. At what point does chronology cease to organize the chapter? What other organization supplants it?
4. Ask students to summarize what each section of the essay does and how Tuchman moves from section to section.
5. In the final two sections (beginning "Ignorance of the cause" [paragraph 28] and "To the people at large" [paragraph 34]) Tuchman explores various explanations that medieval thinkers gave for the plague: the scientific and the religious. Ask students which they consider more authoritative, and why. Do contemporary thinkers still use religious explanations? Of the same sort as medieval thinkers?
6. Tuchman quotes an account left by Brother John Clyn of Kilkenny, Ireland, who kept a record of what happened lest "things which should be remembered perish with time and vanish from the memory of those who come after us" (paragraph 11). Discuss this statement as a motive for writing history: how important do students think it was and still is? Are there other motives for writing history?
7. Read Stephen Jay Gould's "The Terrifying Normalcy of AIDS" (NR 720, SE 433). In what ways is our reaction to this twentieth-century plague similar to the fourteenth-century response to the Black Death? In what ways is it different? You might approach these questions by asking students to consider the purposes that Tuchman and Gould have for writing and how these purposes influence their selection and presentation of material.

Suggested Writing Assignments

1. Has human nature changed since the Middle Ages? Do we still respond to disaster in the same ways? Write an essay in which you address these questions by using details from Tuchman's account and from a recent disaster you have witnessed and/or read about.
2. Tuchman gives us the medieval explanations for the spread of bubonic plague. Do research on the topic and write a modern explanation for its spread.
3. Consult one of the sources Tuchman cites at the end of her essay and analyze how Tuchman uses it. What does she quote? What does she paraphrase?

What does she summarize? Write an essay in which you consider how she shapes her material.

4. Read another account of the Black Death in an encyclopedia or a history textbook. Compare that account with Tuchman's, trying to address this question: What does Tuchman hope to achieve in her account of this fourteenth-century event?

5. Write an essay in response to Analytical Consideration 6 (above) using this and other essays in the "History" section as evidence.

Cherokee Memorials

The Norton Reader, p. 772; Shorter Edition, p. 466

The "Cherokee Memorials" of 1829 are a primary source for the history of the Cherokee Nation and the history of the United States' relations with the indigenous population of North America. Like all such documents, they require interpretation and, for interpretation, a context. We cannot but read the "Cherokee Memorials" ironically, certain that their eloquence failed to move the Congress of the United States. See the "Authors" section for the particulars of their context: the discovery of gold in Georgia, the role of President Andrew Jackson in removing the Cherokees, the names of the leaders of the Cherokee Council (the presumed authors of this document), and the aftermath of the "Cherokee Memorials" — the forced removal of 12,000 Cherokees in 1838–39 to what is now Oklahoma, and the forced march along what is known as the "Trail of Tears," which killed one-third of them. What we cannot know — neither the document nor its context will tell us — is whether its Cherokee authors believed in their rhetoric or just adopted it as a persuasive strategy.

Analytical Considerations

1. Identify passages in which the Cherokee memorialists characterize themselves, their land, the Congress of the United States, and the history of their relations with the United States. Which can we assume represent their true sense of things, which seem suspect as rhetoric?

2. "By the will of our Father in Heaven, the Governor of the whole world, the red man of America has become small, and the white man great and renowned" (paragraph 2). Characterize this account of historical causation. Do you think the "Father in Heaven" they refer to is the Christian God?

3. The Cherokee memorialists are themselves interpreters of historical documents — that is, treaties. Explain the logic of their interpretation.

4. Imagine yourself a member of Congress reading the "Memorials" addressed to you. What might your response be?

5. Do you think the Cherokee rhetoric is dated? Imagine, for example, a similar petition written today. What passages would be eliminated or toned down? Why?

Suggested Writing Assignments

1. Write a request to someone for something. Make at least a few statements you don't believe but to which you think the person to whom the request is addressed will respond favorably . Then provide a context: write a brief analysis of who the person is, what you decided to say, and why you thought it would work.
2. Do research on the Trail of Tears. Either describe how this context affects your interpretation of the "Cherokee Memorials" or, if you locate other Cherokee documents, choose one of them and interpret it.
3. The "Cherokee Memorials" refer to "a sweeping pestilence" (paragraph 2). Do research on this "pestilence" (or pestilences) and write an essay in which you compare it with the Black Death as described by Barbara Tuchman in "'This Is the End of the World'" (NR 759, SE 453).

WALT WHITMAN

Death of Abraham Lincoln

The Norton Reader, p. 775; Shorter Edition, p. 469

Whitman delivered this piece as a lecture several times—in 1879, 1880, and 1881, between fourteen and sixteen years after the assassination of Lincoln. He then included it in *Specimen Days* (1882), his collection of journal entries, articles, and other writings on the Civil War. In it he re-creates the scene of Lincoln's death with great immediacy: "probably the facts are yet very indefinite in most persons' minds" (paragraph 7), he observes. Whitman himself was not present at the performance of *Our American Cousin*, but his companion Peter Doyle was. According to Whitman, he re-created the event by reading "from my memoranda, written at the time, and revised frequently and finally since" (paragraph 7).

In this essay Whitman asserts the significance of Lincoln's death for the American imagination: Lincoln becomes the great American hero, as great as or even greater than any character in Homer. If you have assigned Whitman's journal account of the death of Lincoln (NR 104), you may want to compare that journal entry, written two days after the assassination, with this later, retrospective account.

Questions from the NR11

1. Whitman delivered this piece as a lecture. What features suggest a lecture? How might it have differed if he had composed it as an essay to be read rather than a lecture to be heard?
2. The events of the assassination lead Whitman to mention his perception of Lincoln's fondness for the theater. How does he make this observation serve a larger purpose?
3. At the end of this speech, Whitman speaks grandly of Lincoln's significance for far more than the citizens of the United States. As he sees it, what

do all these people have in common that allows for Lincoln's more-than-national significance?

4. How does Whitman convey the sense of horror and confusion in the scene when Lincoln is shot? Using some of Whitman's techniques, write an account of a similar scene that produces a strong emotional effect.

Analytical Considerations

1. Note where Whitman shifts from the past to the present tense in the scene when Lincoln is shot. How long does he maintain the present tense? Plainly, he uses it for immediacy; how well does it work?
2. The lecture/essay divides into four parts: Whitman's first view of Lincoln in New York City, his overview of the Civil War, his account of the death of Lincoln, and his assessment of its significance. As a follow-up to Question 1 (above), ask several students to read aloud one passage from the lecture that they find dramatic. (For most, this passage will be from the third part.) Then ask how they imagine the other parts should be read.
3. Whitman refers to "real history's stage" (paragraph 9) and to "the stage of universal Time" (paragraph 16). Using students' responses to Question 2 (above), discuss how Whitman uses the metaphor of history as a drama to re-create the events of April 14, 1865.
4. Whitman suggests that "the grand deaths of the race" (paragraph 18) are the foundation of nationality. Do you agree? Ask students to remember other "grand" American deaths they have lived through or heard about.

Suggested Writing Assignments

1. Write an essay comparing Whitman's account of the death of Lincoln written two days after the assassination, in the section "Prose Forms: Journals" (NR 88), and his later account.
2. Write an essay comparing Whitman's account of the Civil War in paragraphs 5 to 7 with H. Bruce Franklin's analysis of the same war (in "From Realism to Virtual Reality: Images of America's Wars" [NR 792]) in paragraphs 1 to 13. Why are these accounts different?
3. Whitman never calls the war the "Civil War." Write a brief account of what he does call it—and why.

PAUL S. COLLINS

22,000 Seedlings

The Norton Reader, p. 782

This is a fascinating essay on the Concord grape—the first commercially viable variety of grape that was developed and grown by the Europeans in the United States in the nineteenth century. But along with a history of this grape, Collins gives us his perspective on the American spirit of invention and entrepreneurship. The essay also provides a fine gallery of interesting characters, figures both familiar and unfamiliar in the nineteenth-century cultural and economic milieu. Collins rescues from oblivion the man who painstakingly and doggedly bred the Concord grape and, in the process, offers a brilliant commentary on the values of the times. The circumstances attending the Concord grape's debut and establishment as a money-making crop is a story of American capitalism.

Questions from the NR11

1. Describe the role of the first three of Collins's paragraphs. How do these paragraphs prepare for the rest of the story? Are there signs of an argument in these opening paragraphs?
2. How would you characterize Collins's tone throughout this essay? What characteristics of his style create that tone?
3. Write a brief Collins-like description of a person, using ordinary details but presenting them in the manner Collins does in his essay.

Analytical Considerations

1. Collins tells the story of Ephraim Bull and his invention of the Concord grape; however, he also introduces a number of other tangential figures— Bronson Alcott and Ralph Waldo Emerson, for example. What function do these other people and stories serve? What do they tell us about the process of invention?
2. Examine Collins's attitude toward American entrepreneurship and capitalism. What specific phrases and passages reveal the author's position?
3. What elements of the history of grape-growing and grape-selling in the nineteenth century foreshadow the workings of American business today?
4. What steps, if any, could Ephraim Bull have taken so that he did not die in the poor house? On what or whom does Collins lay the blame for the sad ending to Bull's life?
5. Collins writes about Ephraim Bull's being deprived of the economic benefits of his inventive effort. Henry Bessemer, on the other hand, made sure that no one would discover his process of making bronze powder by closely guarding the details. He made his fortune by making it impossible for anyone else to duplicate the process. Today, there is a great deal of debate on the rights of "inventors" and their intellectual property. Pharmaceutical companies in affluent nations are accused of carefully guarding the formulas of life-saving drugs that are needed in large quantities in developing nations. Some of the epidemics for which these drugs are needed include tuberculosis and AIDS. The companies argue that they invest a great deal of money in research toward new drugs and that therefore they should be permitted to charge prices that enable them to recover their investment. This return on investment would not be possible, they argue, if developing nations were permitted to manufacture cheaper versions of the same drugs. Developing nations argue that health is a human right and that it cannot be held hostage to profit-making motives. What do you think Western pharmaceutical companies should do?

Writing Assignments

1. Research the story of the person who invented some common product that we take for granted—for example, soap, toothpaste, the rubberband, or peanut butter. Write an essay about that individual, spotlighting the characteristics that made it possible for him or her to achieve success.
2. Burning CDs and downloading MP3 song files from the Internet is fairly common practice today. Yet, one could argue that in doing so, one is violating the intellectual-property rights of artists and their recording companies. Make a case either for or against downloading songs off the Internet. Or make your argument for some other area (in addition to pharmaceuticals and music, computer software is also subject to intellectual-property rights.)

H. BRUCE FRANKLIN

From Realism to Virtual Reality: Images of America's Wars

The Norton Reader, p. 792

H. Bruce Franklin, a professor of literature, has written several books on war, including *War Stars: The Superweapon and the American Imagination* (1988). Students may be interested to know that he was fired from Stanford University, despite having tenure, for encouraging students to protest secret military testing on college campuses. (He now teaches at Rutgers University.) They may be asked whether they can guess his attitude toward war from this piece of scholarly writing.

Franklin uses images—photographs particularly, journalistic accounts more generally—to analyze changing attitudes toward American wars. As a pedagogical model, his essay is extremely useful for teaching close reading, not of words but of images. We suggest that for this essay you ask the class to work in small groups, both to analyze Franklin's argument and to find additional images of war that might provide the basis for students' own essays—though these suggestions can be adapted for a large class or for individual students.

Questions from the NR11

1. Franklin tells a double story of technological advances in making war and in making images. Trace each stage of both narratives. Explain, at each stage, how he links them.
2. Franklin includes seven illustrations in this essay. Explain his choice of each. Are there others he mentions that you wish he had included? Why? (Locating them might be a class project.)
3. Take one of the illustrations in this essay and write an essay in which you offer an alternative interpretation of it as a counterargument to Franklin's interpretation.
4. Franklin includes references to literature (fiction, primarily, but also poetry), films, television, and comic books. How does he present the differences

among them? Compare the powers he attributes to words and the powers he attributes to images.

5. Choose a recent United States war (or military action) and reconstruct your sense of it and how you acquired that sense. Locate some of the images you remember, and write an essay comparing your memory of them with the images as you see them now. Or, if you had no sense of the event when it occurred, locate some of the important images of it, and write an essay comparing how you think you would have seen them then and how you see them now.

Analytical Considerations

1. Divide students into groups, one for each war that Franklin analyzes: the Civil War, the two world wars, Vietnam, and the Gulf War. Ask each group to summarize the basic argument Franklin makes about images from that war.
2. Using the same groups, ask students to do their own analysis of one of the images reproduced in the text. (Students covering World War I and World War II will not find an image in the text; ask them either to analyze the text itself or to find one of the images Franklin discusses, perhaps by viewing a film.) Do they see the same things Franklin sees, or do they see different things?
3. Again in groups, ask students to find additional photographs or images from the same war (see Analytical Consideration 1, above), whether in books, magazines, or films. Ask them to consider whether these images confirm or contradict Franklin's account, and if they find contradictions, what modifications they would make in Franklin's argument.
4. Ask students if they have read Stephen Crane's *The Red Badge of Courage*, Herman Melville's *Billy Budd*, and Mark Twain's *A Connecticut Yankee in King Arthur's Court*. Consider Franklin's assessment of them in paragraphs 9 to 13; probably what he writes about Billy Budd is the most controversial.
5. Franklin coins the term *technowar* (paragraph 1); what does he mean by it? What recent wars (or military actions) are *technowars*? Discuss the concept of a *technowar*.

Suggested Writing Assignments

1. Find an image or photograph of war not discussed by Franklin and write your own analysis of the meanings it projects. If relevant, comment on whether your analysis confirms or contradicts his.
2. Write a counterargument to one of Franklin's analyses of a photograph, suggesting alternative interpretations of it.
3. Choose a recent image of a war not involving the United States and analyze it carefully to see if you think it reflects patterns or themes that Franklin discusses. If not, explain why.
4. Read the novel by Stephen Wright that Franklin discusses, *Meditations in Green* (paragraph 27), or look at the film *The Deer Hunter* that he discusses (paragraphs 29–32). Write an essay in which you consider what responses to the Vietnam War you think one or the other asks for and how it tries to evoke them.

HANNAH ARENDT

Denmark and the Jews

The Norton Reader, p. 807; Shorter Edition, p. 477

Perhaps the most important theme of Hannah Arendt's *Eichmann in Jerusalem: A Report on the Banality of Evil* (1963), from which this selection comes, is that of the ordinariness of evil. Adolf Eichmann regarded his role in the infamous Final Solution to the Jewish question as that of a functionary. At his trial in Jerusalem, he most regretted having been ill-used by superiors. According to Arendt, his inability to acknowledge personal blame is not unusual or abnormal, for evil apparently loses its character as evil when it is assimilated into the normal routines of living and working.

Arendt sets her account of the Danish reaction to the Nazi program of destruction against this background: she embeds history in argument. The Danes, she contends, provide the only case we know of in which the Nazis met open resistance to their treatment of the Jews. This point (and others in *Eichmann in Jerusalem*) have been criticized by some readers. Arendt fills her narrative with facts and statistics, which lend authority to her account. However, her controversial interpretation does not concern what happened, but why. Whether or not one wholly accepts them, her views—about the Danes, about the ordinariness of evil—provide engaging points for discussion.

Analytical Considerations

1. What special force does Arendt's expression "the banality of evil" have?
2. "Denmark and the Jews" is partially narrative in organization. Does the narrative have a climax? Where in the essay does it occur?
3. Arendt spells out the meaning she gives her narrative: "One is tempted to recommend the story as required reading in political science for all students who wish to learn something about the enormous power potential inherent in non-violent action and in resistance to an opponent possessing vastly superior means of violence" (paragraph 2). What is the effect of being told the implications of the narrative before actually reading it?
4. Does Arendt regard her subject as primarily ethical, or primarily historical? What elements of "Denmark and the Jews" support your answer?
5. The tendency to think the Danes heroes seems an inevitable effect of this essay. Is there evidence that Arendt tries to temper this effect, to make us see them as something other or less than heroes? (This question should not imply seeing them as villains.)
6. Read this essay carefully for evidence of Arendt's bitterness about the history and fate of European Jews. What are her chief means of controlling this bitterness? Does her controlled bitterness make this essay more or less effective?
7. Evaluate the final paragraph of "Denmark and the Jews." Which statements are matters of fact? Which are matters of interpretation? How well does she prepare for these interpretations in preceding sections of this selection?
8. Why does Arendt describe the Danes as a nation or a group instead of focusing on individuals? In view of her purpose, is there a rhetorical advantage

to describing them this way? For a sense of the difference focusing on individuals makes, see Amitav Ghosh, "The Ghosts of Mrs. Gandhi" (NR 818).

Suggested Writing Assignments

1. If Nazis like Eichmann exhibit the ordinariness of evil, then the Danes exhibit the ordinariness of good. Drawing from your experience, observation, and reading, write an essay in which you support, refute, or qualify this assertion.
2. Write an essay comparing Arendt's ideas on resistance based on principled and nonviolent action with Martin Luther King Jr.'s in "Letter from Birmingham Jail" (NR 889, SE 521) and with Amitav Ghosh's in "The Ghosts of Mrs. Gandhi" (NR 818).
3. Using "Denmark and the Jews" as a basis, construct a code of conduct for non-violent resistance to any unjust authority or unjust policy.
4. Write a historical narrative of some person or group who in some vital or violent controversy held to a principle and proved to be exceptional.

PHILIP GOUREVITCH

After the Genocide

The Norton Reader, p. 812; Shorter Edition, p. 481

The Rwandan genocide of the mid-1990s is a twentieth-century horror that the West in general and the United States, in particular, have been accused of ignoring. Some 800,000 Tutsis were killed, and virtually nothing was done by international agencies to stop it. Philip Gourevitch's book *We Wish to Inform You That Tomorrow We Will Be Killed with Our Families* was published in 1998, and it made known to the world the extent of the world's blindness. Some African leaders intervened, but the West, by and large, first refused to acknowledge that a genocide was occurring, and then attempted to call it something else when the evidence of bodies made it difficult to deny its reality. (Samantha Power, in her book *The Problem from Hell: America and the Age of Genocide* [2002], makes a similar though more sweeping accusation than Gourevitch. The United States is just plain indifferent to genocide, no matter where it occurs, she says.) Gourevitch's essay forces us to acknowledge a specific tragedy of our human world and to confront the disturbing question of just how much cruelty the human race is capable of inflicting.

Questions from the NR11

1. In paragraph 10 Gourevitch says, "So I still had much to imagine . . ." What does he believe he needs to imagine? And why do you think an act of imagination is so important to him?
2. As paragraph 12 opens, the pronouns change, moving from the first person "I" to the second person "you," in a direct address to us, the readers. What

is the effect of this pronoun shift here? Can he "presume" to know why we are reading?

3. This essay has two sections, separated by a white space. How can the two sections be compared? What do they have in common? Do you note any parallels?

4. Plan and then write two different descriptive paragraphs that both lead up to highly significant last lines, as in Gourevitch's paragraphs 14 and 27. Consider what kinds of writing such conclusions might be best suited for.

Analytical Considerations

1. Gourevitch feels compelled to describe the geographical beauty of Rwanda. Where in the essay do these passages occur, and what function do they serve where they are located?

2. In paragraph 12 Gourevitch directly addresses the reader by assuming a second-person narrative voice: "Like Leontius, the young Athenian in Plato, I presume that you are reading this because you desire a closer look, and that you, too, are properly disturbed by your curiosity." Explain what he means by "properly"; what does it mean to be "properly disturbed"? What other reaction does Gourevitch hope to evoke in the reader beyond that of proper disturbance?

3. In this essay we aren't told why the Hutus wanted to exterminate the Tutsis, only that they wanted to. In what ways would knowledge of the historical and political conditions leading up to the genocide have affected your reading of this essay? According to Gourevitch, what forces contributed to the genocide?

4. We learn that for some individuals the unanswerable question of the genocide is "how so many Tutsis had allowed themselves to be killed"; for others, the question is "how so many Hutus had allowed themselves to kill." What is the value of each question? Which is the more useful question for Rwanda to examine in order to recover and move forward from the genocide?

5. James Baldwin's essay "Everybody's Protest Novel" is a scathing critique of Harriet Beecher Stowe's *Uncle Tom's Cabin*. He berates Stowe for having written a novel that evokes from its readers tears and pity for slaves. These are emotional responses that require no action, he claims. In fact, he argues that one can feel absolved of responsibility by shedding tears. Discuss whether Gourevitch's essay might also provoke a similar criticism.

Suggested Writing Assignments

1. Why should we care about genocide in other parts of the world? How is it even possible for us to avert such horrors in other nations?

2. Describe an experience in which you've been drawn by curiosity to witness an unpleasant scene—a traffic accident, for example—and yet felt simultaneously disturbed by your curiosity.

3. Research an episode of mass killing in United States history. In writing your report, indicate whether you had known of this episode prior to the research. How has your knowledge of the incident affected your sense of yourself as a resident of the United States? As a human being?

AMITAV GHOSH

The Ghosts of Mrs. Gandhi

The Norton Reader, p. 818

Amitav Ghosh introduces himself early on in this essay: in 1984—when the violence against the Sikhs that he describes occurred—he was twenty-eight, had completed a doctorate at Oxford University two years earlier, and was teaching at Delhi University and trying to write a novel (paragraph 3). His degree was in anthropology, and he has since written and published a novel as well as several other books. He waited to write about the events of 1984 because, as he puts it, acts in opposition to violence are undramatic and hard to write about (paragraph 85); his essay was published in 1995. He was probably stimulated to write by religious and ethnic violence ("cleansing") elsewhere: it can hardly be accidental that he concludes his essay with a quotation from Dzevad Karahasan, a Bosnian writer who chronicled the siege of Sarajevo (paragraph 86).

Unlike Hannah Arendt (in "Denmark and the Jews" [NR 807, SE 477], who describes the Danes' opposition to violence collectively, Ghosh offers a series of vignettes: the woman on the bus; Mrs. Sen, Hari's mother; the Bawas's cook. Ghosh, as a presence, a participant even, is able to describe actions that would have gone unrecorded were it not for him. He had to do research, however, to inform himself about their context; see, for example, his interview with Veena Das, a sociologist (paragraph 36). Arendt depended on records; the individuals she focuses on are prominent public figures such as Werner Best, the German S.S. commander in Denmark.

Questions from the NR11

1. Throughout this essay Ghosh interweaves personal history with Indian national history. Make an outline or flowchart that shows how this interweaving works.
2. Near the end of the essay Ghosh contends, "Writers don't join crowds" (paragraph 83), yet he meditates on the responsibility of the writer to intervene in political events. What position does he finally reach about the individual writer's relation to—and responsibility in—history?
3. If you have participated in a political or historical event of some importance, write about your experience, interweaving "personal" and the "public" as Ghosh does. You may want to do some research about the event to learn more about the public record of its history.

Analytical Considerations

1. When the marchers, particularly the women among them, confronted the rioters, the rioters dispersed, "confused" (paragraph 77). Why?
2. Ghosh wonders if authors who write about violence fail "to find a form—or a style or a voice or a plot—that could accommodate both violence and the civilized, willed response to it" (paragraph 84). Ghosh's memoir accom-

modates civilized responses to violence; does it sufficiently accommodate violence?

3. When Ghosh joined the march to confront the rioters, they shouted, as he puts it, "hoary Gandhian staples of peace and brotherhood from half a century before" (paragraph 72). For another view of these "hoary Gandhian staples," see Martin Luther King Jr.'s "Letter from Birmingham Jail" (NR 889, SE 521).

Suggested Writing Assignments

1. According to Ghosh, "repugnance" is the "commonest response to violence" (paragraph 85). Do you agree? Write an essay drawing upon your experience, observation, and reading to answer this question.
2. Ghosh, to his surprise, found his involvement in public life effective and meaningful. Are you involved in public life? Write an essay in which you consider your own involvement—or lack of involvement—in public life, drawing upon Ghosh's essay insofar as it suits your purposes.
3. Do research on the partition of India and Pakistan in 1947 and the violence accompanying it, and write an essay in which you assess Ghosh's belief that it "could never happen again" (paragraph 38). Is his response to that episode in Indian national history reasonable?

FRANCES FITZGERALD

Rewriting American History

The Norton Reader, p. 828

Frances FitzGerald is a talented journalist, popularly known for *Fire in the Lake*, an account of the Vietnam War. This essay, "Rewriting American History," is one of three parts of a long essay that appeared serially in the *New Yorker* in the winter of 1979 and was later included in her book *America Revised*. In this part, primarily, she compares American-history textbooks of the 1950s and the 1970s. You will want to ask students if American-history textbooks changed again in the 1980s and 1990s; see Question 2, below. If the students in your class vary in age, the discussion will be enriched by their recollections across decades.

Interesting in its own right, FitzGerald's comparison leads to something even more interesting: a general consideration of the nature of history as a discipline, which accounts for changes in history—in the sense of history as a text—and in our understanding of history—in the sense of history as historical events.

Questions from the NR11

1. What differences does FitzGerald find between the American-history textbooks of the 1950s and those of the 1970s? In what ways—according to what she states or implies—have they been improved? Does she see any changes for the worse?

2. FitzGerald's *America Revised* was published in 1979, and textbooks, she argues, change rapidly (paragraph 15). Have American-history textbooks changed since the late 1970s and, if so, in what ways? What do you remember of the American-history textbooks you used in school—and when did you use them? What kind of American-history textbooks are being used today? On your own or in a group, write a brief essay updating FitzGerald.
3. By "rewriting," FitzGerald does not mean changing the facts of American history. What is the relationship between the facts of history and history textbooks?
4. FitzGerald says that in the new texts "the word 'progress' has been replaced by the word 'change'" (paragraph 8). Write an essay in which you consider the difference between these two words and the changes that the replacement of one by the other reflects.

Analytical Considerations

1. Ask students to summarize FitzGerald's essay in a sentence or two; then ask several students to read their summaries aloud. From the similarities and differences, begin a discussion about the points most easily grasped, those less easily grasped, and why.
2. What is FitzGerald's understanding of "history"? Why does she think human beings need to create history?
3. FitzGerald relies mainly on the mode of comparison (and contrast) to show how American history has been "rewritten." By focusing on two paragraphs in her essay, perhaps the one beginning "Poor Columbus!" (paragraph 4) and the one beginning "The political diversity" (paragraph 10), ask students to discuss how comparison works.
4. Analyze any single section of "Rewriting American History" to show how FitzGerald defines by example. Possibilities include the section on the political diversity of textbooks today and the section on the physical appearance of textbooks today.
5. If we can't know what really happened, then why study history? Does FitzGerald's essay imply that history presents us with relative rather than absolute knowledge? If so, why do we study history?
6. Have students read Katha Pollitt's "Does a Literary Canon Matter?" (NR 1047, SE 618). Can they locate the equivalents for American history of the conservative, liberal, and radical (or ultraradical) positions Pollitt describes for the literary canon? Fitzgerald should provide enough information; some students may know about the recent controversy concerning national guidelines for an American-history curriculum.

Suggested Writing Assignments

1. Choose an event from American history with which you are familiar—either one that FitzGerald mentions or one that you know well. Write an essay in which you compare its presentation in three textbooks, each written during a different decade; be certain to select texts written for the same grade level.
2. Choose an event from American history with which you are familiar—either one that FitzGerald mentions or one that you know well. Write an

essay in which you compare its presentation in three textbooks, each written during the 1990s; be certain to select texts written for the same grade level.

3. To what extent do history textbooks, or any other history books, present "truths"? Use your own ideas as well as ideas from other writers in this section to address this question.

4. The process of rewriting American history has taken away some of its romance and myth. Write an essay in which you consider whether that is good, bad, or both.

5. Read Frances FitzGerald's *America Revised* (1979), and write an essay in which you discuss one or more issues she lays out in the rest of her study. Does she take positions on them? On what kind of evidence? According to what principles?

6. Do research about the recent controversy concerning national guidelines for an American-history curriculum, and write an essay about it. You may want to consider the extent to which FitzGerald, in 1979, laid out issues that are still debated today.

EDWARD HALLETT CARR

The Historian and His Facts

The Norton Reader, p. 834

Edward Hallett Carr's *What Is History?* (1961), a classic in the field of historiography, was originally delivered as the George Macaulay Trevelyan Lectures at Cambridge University in 1961. "The Historian and His Facts," Carr's first lecture, is also the first chapter of the volume; other chapters include "Society and the Individual," "History, Science, and Morality," "Causation in History," "History as Progress," and "The Widening Horizon." Forty years later, "The Historian and His Facts" would be more accessible had Carr revised his lectures for publication with an eye to, if not posterity, at least a wider audience: while the history faculty and students in attendance at his lecture would not have been fazed by his mention of many historians in passing, today readers may well be. The historians he mentions have been annotated; you may want to ask students to list them by century and to guess, by the amount of space Carr gives each, which are more important, which less important. How do they know, for example, that R. G. Collingwood (paragraphs 13–14) is more important than Dr. Kitson Clark (paragraph 5)? (The gingerbread vendor's being kicked to death by an angry mob is probably a historical fact more because of Carr's second mention of him than because of Clark's first.)

If, as Carr asserts, "nineteenth-century historians were generally indifferent to the philosophy of history" (paragraph 12), so too are twentieth-century historians: they would rather be doing research and writing history than theorizing about historiography, that is, the study of historical writing (as opposed to the study of history itself). Carr's philosophy of history is, in application, eminently pragmatic and commonsensical. It is, however, carefully articulated and its theoretical premises laid bare; for these reasons, *What Is History?* is a classic.

In addition, "The Historian and His Facts" illustrates the classical rhetoric of synthesis. With the kind permission of Charles Kay Smith (see his *Styles and Structures* [1974], especially chapter 13), here is a condensed version of Carr's analysis: Carr presents the nineteenth-century assumption that history is a series of self-evident inductions based on all available facts, as a thesis; the twentieth-century assumption that history has no objective facts but consists rather of interpretation, as an antithesis; and, rejecting both, the assertion that history is a tension or process of interaction between fact and interpretation, as a synthesis.

Questions from the NR11

1. How does Carr answer the question "What is history?" Trace the development of his argument, step by step, showing how each section of the essay builds on the one preceding it.
2. Carr's answer to "What is history?" comes at the end of his essay in the form of a definition. Could he have offered this definition at the beginning of the essay? Why or why not?
3. How does Carr distinguish between "a mere fact about the past" and "a fact of history" (paragraph 5)?
4. Imagine yourself about to write a short historical essay on a recent local event. Working on your own or in a group, list a number of facts (about the event) and mark those that will be mere facts, those that will be facts of history. What principles informed your decisions?
5. Read one of the historians represented in this section of *The Norton Reader* and discover what you can about him or her. Then write an analysis of how this historian, in Collingwood's terms, is concerned "neither with 'the past by itself' nor with 'the historian's thought about it by itself,' but with 'the two things in their mutual relations'" (paragraph 14).

Analytical Considerations

1. Locate the historians Carr mentions and list them by century; then assess which are the more important ones. (This exercise can be divided by centuries and assigned to different groups of students. It can also lead to the writing assignment suggested in Question 5, above.)
2. How does Carr define "history" in "The Historian and His Facts"? Is his definition compatible with that of Frances FitzGerald in "Rewriting American History" (NR 828)?
3. If we can't know what really happened, then why study history? What, according to Carr, are the dangers of "the Collingwood view of history" (paragraph 19)? How does he confront them?
4. How does Carr develop and support his thesis, antithesis, and synthesis in "The Historian and His Facts"?
5. One distinguishing feature of Carr's essay is his use of metaphor. Ask students where and how he uses it: e.g., the fish market metaphor, theological metaphors, biblical metaphors. What are the effects of his metaphorical language? What, if any, other historians in this section use metaphor?

6. Carr describes how, when he writes, reading and writing are simultaneous and inseparable (paragraph 21). For students, they are probably sequential. Ask students to consider the virtues of Carr's method and the potential flaws of theirs.

Suggested Writing Assignments

1. Write an essay of definition for an important and disputed term, following the thesis-antithesis-synthesis pattern used by Carr in "The Historian and His Facts."
2. Write an essay about Frances FitzGerald's "Rewriting American History" (NR 828) as a response to Carr.
3. Write an essay comparing FitzGerald's and Carr's senses of "history."
4. Respond to the question "What is history?" in an essay of your own.

POLITICS AND GOVERNMENT

GEORGE ORWELL

Shooting an Elephant

The Norton Reader, p. 851; Shorter Edition, p. 493

"Shooting an Elephant" is a classic example of an author using a personal experience to illuminate a political institution and its social implications: here, the experience of shooting an elephant and the British Raj (the imperial government of India and Burma), and colonialism itself. Orwell carefully and precisely renders setting, action, and character (himself) by developing his responses, feelings, and thoughts with novelistic density. He braids into the narrative the personal responses to the experience: "I often wondered whether any of the others grasped that I had done it solely to avoid looking a fool" (paragraph 14). Orwell, whom students are likely to know as the author of *Animal Farm* and *1984*, served in the British police force in Burma after leaving school. The experience heightened his political consciousness.

You may need to show students that "Shooting an Elephant" is also an essay about how the expectations of others force us to play roles, to behave in ways that we do not choose, and to behave as selves other than the selves we think we are—worse selves, as in this essay, and sometimes better selves as well. Orwell, though he does not use the term, is conscious of what we now refer to as the "social construction of reality." Yet, in "Shooting an Elephant," he both affirms and denies it: that is, he presents role-playing as educative. "I perceived in this moment," he writes, "that when the white man turns tyrant it is his own freedom that he destroys" (paragraph 7).

Questions from the NR11

1. Why did Orwell shoot the elephant? Account for the motives that led him to shoot. Then categorize them as personal motives, circumstantial motives, social motives, or political motives. Is it easy to assign his motives to categories? Why or why not?
2. In this essay the proportion of narrative to analysis is high. Mark which paragraphs contain which, and note, in particular, how much analysis Orwell places in the middle of the essay. What are the advantages and disadvantages of having it there rather than at the beginning or the end of the essay?
3. Facts ordinarily do not speak for themselves. How does Orwell present his facts to make them speak in support of his analytic points? Look, for example, at the death of the elephant (paragraphs 11 to 13).
4. Write an essay in which you present a personal experience that illuminates a larger issue: schooling, or affirmative action, or homelessness, or law enforcement, or taxes, or some other local or national issue.

Analytical Considerations

1. Pose Question 1 (above) to demonstrate the dense rendering of Orwell's narrative and how he constructs it, but also to show that Orwell's realization of his motives comes not precisely at the moment he pulls the trigger, but years later as he writes his essay.
2. Ask students to analyze the opening paragraphs in terms of shifts from narration to commentary. As they will soon see, a personal-experience essay moves frequently back and forth from one to the other. It does not, as students sometimes assume, give all narrative first, all commentary last.
3. How does Orwell reconcile social construction and individual freedom?

Suggested Writing Assignments

1. Rewrite Orwell's "Shooting an Elephant" from the point of view of one of the Burmese.
2. Write an essay in which you consider at least two instances of your own serious (rather than trivial) role-playing, both of worse and of better selves. Is role-playing always educative?

JONATHAN SWIFT

A Modest Proposal

The Norton Reader, p. 857; Shorter Edition, p. 499

"A Modest Proposal" is often anthologized as a brilliant example of sustained irony. It is also shocking: you may want to ask students to read Mark Twain's "Advice to Youth" (NR 647, SE 395), in the "Ethics" section, to contrast the tameness of his irony with the savagery of Swift's. Swift violates one of our strongest and most universally held prohibitions, the prohibition against eating human flesh; Twain merely upsets a prohibition against dishonoring fathers and mothers, a prohibition most of us upset frequently. Moreover, Swift disquietingly juxtaposes the reasonable voice of his putative author (or invented persona) and his horrifying proposals, horrifying to us as readers but apparently not horrifying to the proposer. The author's "modest proposal" can perhaps be entertained as logically consistent, but in moral terms, it is indefensible. Students need to see that Swift's juxtaposition of reasonableness and horror is ironic: while the putative author of "A Modest Proposal" says one thing, Swift means another.

Understanding irony from another era can be difficult. You might provide information about Irish poverty in 1729, when Swift published "A Modest Proposal," and its historical causes. You will want to have students look at paragraphs 29 and 30, Swift's "other expedients," which will suggest some of the things Swift's audience knew that we no longer know. You may also want to remind them that, had Swift been anxious to prevent a literal reading of "A Modest Proposal," he could have included these expedients earlier; they are, after all, the remedies that a "reasonable" Swift himself proposed. But even three centuries after Swift's pamphlet was published, most students will quickly recognize that this satirical essay was not meant to be taken at face value but represents a deeply and bitterly ironic commentary on the state of things in Ireland.

Questions from the NR11

1. Identify examples of the reasonable voice of Swift's authorial persona, such as the title of the essay itself.
2. Look, in particular, at instances in which Swift's authorial persona proposes shocking things. How does the style of the "Modest Proposal" affect its content?
3. Verbal irony consists of saying one thing and meaning another. At what point in this essay do you begin to suspect that Swift is using irony? What additional evidence of irony can you find?
4. Write a modest proposal of your own in the manner of Swift to remedy a real problem; that is, propose an outrageous remedy in a reasonable voice.

Analytical Considerations

1. Ask students to describe how Swift's putative author characterizes himself by his style. If style is the man, what kind of man are we listening to?
2. Although Swift's primary concerns are economic, issues of population control also run through "A Modest Proposal." What do the author's proposals indicate about his views of sexuality and reproduction? Can we infer Swift's proposals and his views of sexuality and reproduction from them? You may want to suggest ways in which time (and changing sexual and reproductive practices) destabilize Swift's irony with respect to population control more than with respect to economic policy.

Suggested Writing Assignments

1. Write an essay in which you consider your responses to "A Modest Proposal." Some readers have found Swift's irony too shocking, so strong as to detract from his really quite sensible proposals for reform. Does his literary form, for you, subvert his purposes or serve them? How and why?
2. Look up a brief proposal written by a contemporary of Swift, Daniel Defoe, in 1702, "The Shortest Way with the Dissenters," and also an account of its reception in a biography of Defoe. Write a brief essay on the risks of irony using this information.

NICCOLÒ MACHIAVELLI

The Morals of the Prince

The Norton Reader, p. 864; Shorter Edition, p. 506

Niccolò Machiavelli, the Florentine whose political treatise *The Prince* was published in 1513, acquired in his time a scandalous reputation: he was

"Old Nick" (or Satan), who held the diabolical doctrine that the end justifies the means. His reputation was largely established by the chapters on "The Morals of the Prince" reprinted here. Students should notice how Machiavelli is aware of making a controversial case, of writing about the *is*—"the way we really live"—rather than the *ought*—"the way we ought to live" (paragraph 1). Political treatises of Machiavelli's time were ordinarily utopian. Machiavelli's is not, and consequently, as he announces, he has something new to say. Today we might speak of his politics as "realpolitik," a word derived from German that means a politics based on practical and material, rather than theoretical and ethical, considerations.

You may want to use "The Morals of the Prince" to exemplify shifting boundaries between idealism and realism, realism and cynicism; we can pretty much agree on their definitions, but when we come to apply them, what one person takes to be realistic, another person takes to be cynical. Nevertheless, Machiavelli appears to present his "realistic" argument with the intention of shocking readers. While it may be realistic to discuss the dangers of virtue in a world in which people are "a sad lot, and keep no faith with you" (paragraph 14), it is surely cynical to argue that the appearance of virtue is better than virtue itself. You can call attention to the antitheses in Machiavelli's argument: the qualities in a prince that elicit praise or blame (paragraph 2) and the chapter headings in which he opposes liberality to stinginess, cruelty to clemency, and love to fear. Part of his shock technique depends upon setting up binary oppositions and arguing for the conventionally pejorative term.

Questions from the NR11

1. This selection contains four sections of *The Prince*: "On the Reasons Why Men Are Praised or Blamed—Especially Princes"; "On Liberality and Stinginess"; "On Cruelty and Clemency: Whether It Is Better to Be Loved or Feared"; and "The Way Princes Should Keep Their Word." How, in each section, does Machiavelli contrast the ideal and the real, what he calls "the way we really live and the way we ought to live" (paragraph 1)? Mark some of the sentences in which he arrestingly expresses these contrasts.
2. Rewrite some of Machiavelli's advice to princes less forcibly and shockingly, and more palatably. For example, "Any man who tries to be good all the time is bound to come to ruin among the great number who are not good" (paragraph 1) might be rewritten as "Good men are often taken advantage of and harmed by men who are not good."
3. Describe Machiavelli's view of human nature. How do his views of government follow from it?
4. Machiavelli might be described as a sixteenth-century spin doctor teaching a ruler how to package himself. Adapt his advice to a current figure in national, state, or local politics and write about that figure in a brief essay.

Analytical Considerations

1. One feature of Machiavelli's style is his use of aphorisms, that is, terse formulations of truths and beliefs. You might ask students to gather a number of them and describe how Machiavelli uses them and to what effect or effects. See also the section called "Maxims and Morals" in *The Norton Reader*.

2. What are Machiavelli's customary sources of examples? How frequently does he use them? How extensively does he explain them? What do they indicate about his audience?
3. Man, in the Renaissance chain of being, stands between beasts and angels. You may want to have students look at paragraphs 14 and 15, in which Machiavelli proposes as models for imitation the fox and the lion. What do these metaphors contribute to his argument?

Suggested Writing Assignments

1. Do library research on the politics of Florence during Machiavelli's life (the way Florentines really lived) and write an essay in which you consider *The Prince* as a response to local conditions.
2. Write an essay defining "Machiavellian" by applying it to and illustrating it with examples from contemporary politics.
3. See Suggested Writing Assignments 2 and 3 for the "Declaration of Independence."

THOMAS JEFFERSON

Original Draft of the Declaration of Independence

The Norton Reader, p. 871

and

THOMAS JEFFERSON AND OTHERS

The Declaration of Independence

The Norton Reader, p. 874; Shorter Edition, p. 513

These two drafts of the Declaration of Independence—the first, Jefferson's preliminary draft, and the second, the final draft as printed—may provoke students into a fresh reading of a text whose familiarity dulls attention. The preliminary draft is a transcription of a copy in Jefferson's hand (in the Library of Congress), with illegible passages taken from a transcription made by John Adams, and missing passages, presumably added later, taken from a copy Jefferson made for George Wythe (in the New York Public Library). We do not know how many drafts and revisions preceded it; we do know that Jefferson consulted with several people, among them Benjamin Franklin and John Adams. This preliminary draft was edited by members of the Second Continental Congress and probably, in large measure, by Jefferson himself.

Students should notice that the three-part structure of the preliminary and final drafts is the same: Jefferson enunciates a series of principles concerning human nature and the function of government, rehearses the offenses against them by George III, and proclaims the political connection between the American colonies and the king of Great Britain dissolved. The structure is derived from the syllogism: a major premise, a minor premise, and a conclusion. The logic is deductive: given the principles—which Jefferson calls "sacred and undeniable" in the preliminary draft, "self-evident" in the final draft—and given the facts, the conclusion follows ineluctably.

These two versions of the Declaration of Independence illustrate the final revision procedures of an experienced writer. With his argumentative structure and his particulars in place, Jefferson revises at the paragraph and sentence level. Chiefly he prunes and tightens: he recognizes that he has been somewhat overinclusive in his exemplification, somewhat clumsy in his sentences, and long-winded in using more words than he needs to say what he needs to say. While his language in the final draft is simpler and more direct, his sentence structure, especially with respect to repetition and balance, is more artful. In addition, the inconsistent spelling and punctuation of the preliminary draft have been regularized.

Questions from the NR11

1. The Declaration of Independence is an example of deductive argument: Jefferson sets up general principles, details particular instances, and then draws conclusions. Locate the three sections of the declaration in both the original and final drafts that use deduction. Explain how they work as argument.
2. Locate the general principles (or "truths") that Jefferson sets up in the first section of both the original and final drafts. Mark the language he uses to describe them: for example, he calls them "sacred & undeniable" in the original draft, "self-evident" in the final draft. What kinds of authority does his language appeal to?
3. Write an essay explaining Jefferson's views on the nature of man, the function of government, and the relationship between morality and political life, as expressed in the Declaration of Independence. What assumptions are necessary to make these views, as he says in the final draft, "self-evident"?

Analytical Considerations

1. You may want to ask students to work on the first or second sections of the Declaration of Independence in the preliminary and final drafts, noting what has been pruned and conjecturing about the reasons for the omissions. This analysis can profitably be done in groups.
2. You may also want to ask them to "modernize" sentences in the final draft with pronounced repetition and balance by loosening both.

Suggested Writing Assignments

1. Jefferson died on July 4, 1826, exactly fifty years after the promulgation of the Declaration of Independence. In ill health, declining an invitation to travel to Washington to participate in the fiftieth- anniversary celebrations, he wrote of the declaration:

> May it [the "Declaration"] be to the world what I believe it will be (to some parts sooner, to others later, but finally to all), the signal of arousing men to burst the chains under which monkish ignorance and superstition had persuaded them to bind themselves, and to

assume the blessings and security of self-government. . . . All eyes are opened, or opening to the rights of man. The general spread of the light of science has already laid open to every view the palpable truth, that the mass of mankind has not been born with saddles on their backs, nor a favored few booted and spurred, ready to ride them legitimately by the grace of God.

Write an essay in which you trace the appearance of the ideas Jefferson singles out as important in this letter in the Declaration of Independence. Does he give them due prominence there?
2. Write a letter to Jefferson from the perspective of today in which you assess the optimism of his letter of 1826. Or do the same in essay form.
3. Write a comparison of Jefferson's positions (in the Declaration of Independence) and Niccolò Machiavelli's positions (in "The Morals of the Prince" [NR 864, SE 506]) concerning the nature of man, the function of government, and the relationship between morality and political life. What assumptions led them to diverge?
4. Are you a Jeffersonian or a Machiavellian? Explain.
5. Write an argument on a topic of your choice in which you use the three-part structure of a syllogism. Is it possible, for example, to recast the arguments of other essays in this section, such as Lani Guinier's "The Tyranny of the Majority" (NR 885) or Martin Luther King Jr.'s "Letter from Birmingham Jail" (NR 889, SE 521), in this mode?

ELIZABETH CADY STANTON

Declaration of Sentiments and Resolutions

The Norton Reader, p. 878; Shorter Edition, p. 516

The first women's rights convention was held at Seneca Falls, New York, July 19–20, 1848. It was called by Elizabeth Cady Stanton, Mary Ann McClintock, Lucretia Mott, and Martha C. Wright. The "Declaration of Sentiments and Resolutions"—or the "Seneca Falls Declaration," as it is often called—is usually attributed to Stanton; she read it at the convention, where, after some emendations, it was adopted. But, according to the *History of Woman Suffrage*, edited by Stanton, Susan B. Anthony, and Matilda Joslyn Gage (1881, reprinted 1969), the genesis of the "Declaration"—and perhaps its writing—was collective: Stanton, McClintock, Mott, and Wright decided "to adopt the historic document [i.e., the "Declaration of Independence"] with some slight changes, such as substituting 'all men' for 'King George.'"

Students will see how the "Declaration of Sentiments and Resolutions" recapitulates the three-part syllogistic structure of the "Declaration of Independence." They will also see how the language of the first and third sections of the "Declaration of Sentiments" is a paraphrase of the language of the first and third sections of the "Declaration of Independence." They will need to split three paragraphs of the second section of the "Declaration of

Sentiments" to come up with the same number of offenses as appear in the second section of the "Declaration of Independence"—eighteen. The collaborators were determined to enumerate at least as many offenses in their declaration as the members of the Second Continental Congress had enumerated in theirs. As George III had been guilty of "absolute Tyranny," so were all men.

Questions from the NR11

1. Stanton imitates both the argument and style of the "Declaration of Independence." Where does her declaration diverge from Jefferson's? For what purpose?
2. Stanton's declaration was presented at the first conference on women's rights, in Seneca Falls, New York, in 1848. Using books or Web site resources, do research on this conference; then use your research to explain the political aims of one of the resolutions.
3. Write your own "declaration" of political, educational, or social rights, using the declarations of Jefferson and Stanton as models.

Analytical Considerations

1. As a supplement to Question 1 (above), ask students to mark examples of how the "Declaration of Sentiments and Resolutions" imitates the "Declaration of Independence" through quotation and paraphrase—that is, by both repeating and changing its words.
2. To what ends do Stanton et al. quote and paraphrase the "Declaration of Independence"? Consider both the political goal and rhetorical means of achieving it.
3. How is the imitation of Stanton et al. different from parody—that is, quotation and paraphrase for comedy or ridicule? (Lewis Carroll's parodies are surefire examples; they are reprinted with originals in *Parodies* [1960].)

Suggested Writing Assignments

1. The "Declaration of Sentiments and Resolutions" concludes with the authors' (and signatories') anticipating "no small amount of misconception, misrepresentation, and ridicule" (paragraph 20). Consult the appendix to volume 4 of the *History of Woman Suffrage* (1881, reprinted 1969), which reprints some contemporary responses to the Seneca Falls Convention. Why was the Convention seen as ridiculous in the nineteenth century? Is it seen as ridiculous today? Explain.
2. Frederick Douglass participated in the Seneca Falls Convention. Do library research on the role he played and write an essay discussing his role and why he felt betrayed afterward by the women he supported.
3. Do library research on one of the women who organized the Seneca Falls Convention: Mary Ann McClintock, Lucretia Mott, Elizabeth Cady Stanton, or Martha C. Wright. According to the *History of Woman Suffrage* (1881, reprinted 1969):

    While they had felt the insults incident to sex, in many ways, as every proud, thinking woman must, in the laws, religion, and literature of the world, and in the invidious and degrading sentiments and customs of all nations, yet they had not in their own experience endured the coarser forms of tyranny resulting from unjust laws or association with immoral and unscrupulous men, but they had souls large enough to feel the wrongs of others, without being scarified in their own flesh.

Write an essay in which you particularize these generalities with reference to the life of one of the organizers.

ABRAHAM LINCOLN

Second Inaugural Address

The Norton Reader, p. 880

Abraham Lincoln's "Second Inaugural Address" is a piece of ceremonial discourse formal in tone and diction, as required by the occasion. Like Martin Luther King Jr., Lincoln assumes Christian belief even while pointing out that, although North and South "read the same Bible, and pray to the same God" (paragraph 3), neither has evidence of God's unqualified favor. Lincoln's strategy is to invite reconciliation with, not alienation of, the South while keeping up the resolve of the North in fighting for a just cause.

If you have chosen to teach some of the speeches in the "Spoken Words" section, you might want to compare John F. Kennedy's "Inaugural Address" (NR 906)—in style, form, and tone—with Lincoln's. What does the modern presidential address owe to Lincoln's seminal speech? Ask students what similarities and what differences they find.

Analytical Considerations

1. You may want to remind students that Lincoln reviews four years of history in the course of this brief address. What events does he select, and what pattern does he see in them?
2. Lincoln uses three types of rhetorical appeal in this address: logical, emotional, and ethical. Ask students to identify examples of each. Which do they find most effective? Which do they think Lincoln's audience found most effective?
3. While Lincoln tries to speak to both North and South, students probably will not find him hypocritical or slippery. You may want to try arguing that he is, that his presentation of himself as honest and his purpose as single-minded is ethical posturing, in order to force close reading. How, finally, do we determine sincerity?

Suggested Writing Assignments

1. Write an essay in which you compare Lincoln's "Second Inaugural Address" with John F. Kennedy's inaugural address of 1961 (NR 906) or some other recent inaugural address. Compare rhetoric, content, and audience.

2. Do research on the events immediately preceding Lincoln's second term as president and write an essay in which you consider his "Second Inaugural Address" as a response to them.

CARL BECKER

Democracy

The Norton Reader, p. 882; Shorter Edition, p. 518

This passage by Carl Becker appeared in a volume called *Modern Democracy*, published in 1941. The United States did not enter World War II until December 1941, after the Japanese attacked Pearl Harbor. But Becker—and his readers—would have been aware of the threat to European democracies by both Hitler's Germany and Stalin's Russia as a result of the German-Soviet Nonaggression Pact signed in 1939. Becker, choosing from a range of definitions of "democracy," elaborately stipulates the meaning he gives to the term.

Questions from the NR11

1. In this excerpt Becker carefully defines an abstract term with multiple meanings, "democracy," using the following strategies: (1) he looks for extreme and paradoxical instances that most people would exclude; (2) he distinguishes between ideal instances "laid away in heaven" (paragraph 2) and real instances; (3) he settles for a common meaning derived "partly from the experience and partly from the aspirations of mankind" (paragraph 2); and (4) he looks at additional instances that provide a test for exclusion and inclusion. How, finally, does he define "democracy"?
2. Machiavelli, in "The Morals of the Prince" (NR 864, SE 506), also draws a contrast between the real and the ideal. What are the particulars of his contrast and Becker's? What is Machiavelli's sense of the relation between the real and the ideal? What is Becker's? What are the differences between them?
3. Guinier, in "The Tyranny of the Majority" (NR 885), argues that "majority rule may be perceived as majority tyranny" (paragraph 10). How might Becker include the instances she describes in his definition?
4. Consult a standard desk dictionary for the definition of an abstract term with multiple meanings; you might consider terms such as "generosity," "love," "sophistication," "tolerance," "virtue." Then write your own definition of the term following the strategy Becker uses to define "democracy," supplying your own instances.

Analytical Considerations

1. Spend some time on Becker's discussion of definition in paragraph 1. You may want to bring in photocopies of the definitions of "democracy" in an unabridged dictionary or even the *Oxford English Dictionary*. Talk about how dictionaries are made and why, in the case of large abstractions like

democracy, stipulative definitions are advisable. Consider this passage from Becker as an extended stipulative definition.

2. Look for evidence of contemporary events in this passage. Because definitions are abstractions from particulars, particulars shape definitions. Or, as Becker concludes, "This I take to be the meaning which history has impressed upon the term democracy as a form of government" (paragraph 3).

3. How would Lani Guinier, in "The Tyranny of the Majority" (NR 885), criticize Becker's concept of "the common will," as in: "A democratic government has always meant one in which the citizens, or a sufficient number of them to represent more or less effectively the common will, freely act from time to time, and according to established forms . . ."? Why does she find "the common will" problematic?

4. If you have given students the parallel writing assignments on Becker and White—Question 3 on E. B. White's "Democracy" (NR 884, SE 520) and Suggested Writing Assignment 2 below—compare the results. Is it possible to succeed in both modes of definition, metaphoric and stipulative? What constitutes success in each mode? What problems does each mode of definition pose?

Suggested Writing Assignments

1. It is possible, Becker indicates, to define actual democratic government as "government of the people, by the politicians, for whatever pressure groups can get their interests taken care of" (paragraph 2). To what extent do you agree with this definition of democratic government? Write an essay in which you express your views of the balance between ideal and actual institutions in this country now. Becker argued for a balance in 1941; would you argue for a tilt to the actual?

2. Using Becker's technique, write a definition of an abstract term; you might consider terms such as "speculation," "obedience," "fear," "argument," "charity."

E. B. WHITE

Democracy

The Norton Reader, p. 884; Shorter Edition, p. 520

In this short essay E. B. White writes on request (he explains the circumstances in the essay) about a well-worn topic. He makes it fresh by providing a series of examples that function as metaphors, technically as "synecdoches," or figures of speech in which a part stands for the whole. He provides images and avoids abstractions. Presumably the War Board, which asked him to write about "The Meaning of Democracy" in 1943 (during World War II), expected a patriotic response. Is White's response patriotic, or is it flip? Or are these alternatives a false opposition? Ask students to be explicit about the grounds for their answers; encourage variety and disagreement.

Questions from the NR11

1. Consult a standard desk dictionary for the definition of "democracy." Of the several meanings given, which one best encompasses White's definitions? What other meanings do his definitions engage?
2. Translate White's examples into nonmetaphorical language. For example, "It is the line that forms on the right" might be translated as "It has no special privileges." Can "It is the don't in don't shove" also be translated as "It has no special privileges"? Consider what is lost in translation or, more important, what is gained by metaphor.
3. Using White's technique, write a definition of an abstract term; you might consider terms such as "generosity," "love," "sophistication," "tolerance," "virtue."

Analytical Considerations

1. White creates his definition with a series of examples. You may want to ask students if they can group them and if they can discern a principle that orders them? Or do they consider them random?
2. Ask students to consider the date of composition, 1943. Do they find any of White's examples dated? Can they suggest contemporary substitutes?
3. Ask students to consider an abstraction they might be asked to define in an examination in another course. Have them, probably in groups, construct answers in the manner of E. B. White and consider their professors' probable reactions. (You might dare them to try such an answer on an examination.)

Suggested Writing Assignments

1. Imagine, for yourself, someone without textual know-how who takes White's metaphors literally and finds White's essay silly. Write an explanation of several of White's metaphors. Can you explain them without giving a general explanation of how metaphor works?
2. Imagine yourself a member of the War Board who finds White's response unpatriotic and write him a letter explaining why the War Board declines to use it. Or imagine yourself a member of the War Board who finds White's response particularly useful and write him a letter thanking him for it. Or write both letters.

LANI GUINIER

The Tyranny of the Majority

The Norton Reader, p. 885

Lani Guinier, a graduate of the Yale Law School and a professor at Harvard, was nominated by President Clinton to be Assistant Attorney General for Civil Rights early in 1993. Opponents of her nomination used five articles she published in law reviews (and later reprinted in *The Tyranny of the Majority*

[1994]) to contest her nomination, which President Clinton withdrew. This essay, written for that volume, serves as part of its introduction.

Opponents of her nomination characterized her views of representation as radical and subversive, and in a political climate in which the Supreme Court has declared parts of the Voting Rights Act unconstitutional, perhaps they are. Certainly her introduction to them calculatedly gives a different impression. Autobiographical material—her own experience, as a Brownie, of unfairness and her son Nikolas's principle of taking turns—suggests that the rightness of her proposals is apparent even to children. Nevertheless, her use of a Founding Father, James Madison, on the despotism of the people (paragraph 11), indicates that the issues of representation she considers are a perennial concern of political philosophers.

Analytical Considerations

1. Why, according to Guinier, did James Madison fear the tyranny of the majority? What are the usual remedies? Why does Guinier think they fail with respect to blacks?
2. Define Guinier's concept of a "Madisonian Majority"?
3. Guinier says that in her legal writing she "pursue[s] voting systems that might disaggregate The Majority so that it does not exercise political power unfairly or tyrannically" (paragraph 22). What does she mean by disaggregating the majority? How might this disaggregation be achieved? If your students do not bring up proportional representation, you will need to remind them of it, or explain it to them.

Suggested Writing Assignments

1. Have you ever encountered a situation in which what Guinier calls a "zero-sum solution" prevailed (paragraph 6)? Were you a member of the majority or the minority? Write about the situation with some reference to what Guinier calls a "positive-sum solution" (paragraph 5). Or imagine yourself in such a situation and write about it.
2. Read one of Guinier's law reviews articles reprinted in *The Tyranny of the Majority* and summarize its argument. Would you describe it as primarily argument or primarily persuasion? How convincing—or how persuasive—do you find it?
3. Read James Madison's Federalist Paper No. 10 on the rule of the majority and summarize his position. Does Guinier do it justice in the brief space she has?
4. Guinier was nominated to be Assistant Attorney General for Civil Rights early in 1993. Write a narrative account of the controversy over her nomination and its withdrawal using the *New York Times* and the *Washington Post* as sources. (Various ways of dividing up this project collaboratively suggest themselves.)

MARTIN LUTHER KING JR.

Letter from Birmingham Jail

The Norton Reader, p. 889; Shorter Edition, p. 521

Martin Luther King Jr. was the most important figure in the American Civil Rights movement before his assassination in 1968, at the age of thirty-nine. He participated in the Montgomery, Alabama, bus boycott in 1955–56 (see paragraph 35) and in the Birmingham, Alabama, demonstrations in 1963, where he was arrested along with many other demonstrators. He wrote "Letter from Birmingham Jail" in response to a published statement by eight Birmingham clergymen who supported the goals of the Civil Rights movement but criticized King for his "unwise and untimely" activism.

King uses Christian doctrine and Christian belief to make common cause with the white clergymen to whom he addresses his letter; see his reference to the Black Muslim movement and its repudiation of Christianity (paragraph 27). You can use his reference to Black Muslim bitterness and hatred to lead into a discussion of his nonviolent activism. Central to his justification of activism — "civil disobedience" — is his distinction between just and unjust laws (paragraphs 15–20). Ask students to summarize his distinction and how he applies it.

Questions from the NR11

1. King addressed the "Letter from Birmingham Jail" to eight fellow clergymen who had written a statement criticizing his activities (see note 1). Where and how, in the course of the "Letter," does he attempt to make common cause with them?
2. King was trained in oral composition, that is, in composing and delivering sermons. One device he uses as an aid to oral comprehension is prediction: he announces, in advance, the organization of what he is about to say. Locate examples of prediction in the "Letter."
3. Describe King's theory of nonviolent resistance.
4. Imagine an unjust law that, to you, would justify civil disobedience. Describe the law, the form your resistance would take, and the penalties you would expect to incur.

Analytical Considerations

1. You can ask students to explain the paradox of King's both urging obedience to the law, namely the 1954 Supreme Court decision outlawing segregation in public schools, and breaking it.
2. Do your students know about recent instances of civil disobedience other than those associated with the Civil Rights movement? You may have to

explain resistance to the war in Vietnam, unless you have older students in your class. More recent instances would include resistance to the use of nuclear power, both peaceful and military.

3. King, who expresses his disappointment with whites who call themselves moderates, alternatively characterizes himself as a moderate and an extremist. Students can look at instances of both and the kinds of behavior to which he attaches these labels. Which characterization of King do they think was more accurate in 1963, which more accurate today?

4. If you have assigned King's speech "I Have a Dream," in the "Spoken Words" section, you might ask students to note the common beliefs and the common rhetorical features of that speech and this letter. What differences in rhetorical form do they note? Do these differences arise from a written text versus a speech designed for oral delivery?

Suggested Writing Assignments

1. If you can't see yourself engaging in civil disobedience, as in Question 4 (above), imagine an unjust law and the form someone else's resistance to it would take, then write a letter in which you try to convince this person to obey rather than to resist.

2. King calls into question, in the context of events in Birmingham, "the strangely irrational notion that there is something in the very flow of time that will inevitably cure all ills" (paragraph 26). Is this an "irrational notion"? Supply two or three other contexts in which the notion might figure and write an essay in which you agree or disagree with King.

3. Do library research on Mahatma Gandhi and his doctrine of nonviolent resistance. Then, on the basis of King's "Letter from Birmingham Jail," analyze similarities and differences between Gandhi's and King's ideas about and uses of nonviolent resistance.

4. Sort out, consulting King's text and the notes, the biblical figures King cites, the Church Fathers and earlier theologians, and the contemporary theologians and philosophers. Do research on one of the contemporary theologians and philosophers and write a brief essay in which you consider why he was useful to King.

PROSE FORMS: SPOKEN WORDS

QUEEN ELIZABETH I

Speech to the Troops at Tilbury

The Norton Reader, p. 905

The speech to the troops on the eve of battle was a well-known genre in Elizabeth I's time; a famous example comes from Shakespeare's *Henry V*, when the king addresses his troops before the Battle of Agincourt. In that time the monarch was fully engaged in military affairs, often appearing at the head of troops, and frequently joining in the battle, especially if it was for the defense of the homeland. This engagement in warfare stemmed from two distinct strands of thought about a king's role: first, the monarch's personal presence at a battle site is a literal embodiment of his (or in this case, her) commitment to the subjects. Second, a monarch's leadership qualities were thought to be tested most fittingly in battle. We can see signs of this ideal of monarch as warrior in later paintings of kings wearing armor, a tradition that lasted well beyond the time they regularly led their troops into battle. Part of the function of Elizabeth I's address is to demonstrate that though the English have a woman for a monarch, their monarch is truly fearless and fully up to the task of directing the nation's defense in a time of immense peril.

We have every reason to believe that Queen Elizabeth I composed this speech herself. Unlike most women of her time, she had a superb classical education, personally overseen by Roger Ascham, one of England's most learned men and author of the *Book of the Schoolmaster*, a highly influential pedagogical treatise.

Students might benefit from knowing the historical circumstances surrounding the speech. At the time it was given, 1588, Spain was the great power in Europe and in the Americas. It was Catholic, pledged to battle the Pope's enemies, like the English. The Spanish monarch, Philip II, also had a reasonable dynastic claim to the English throne, having been married to Elizabeth I's cousin, Mary. Financed by the riches of the South American gold mines, Philip assembled a huge invasion fleet, the Spanish Armada, filled with foot soldiers ready to attack. Elizabeth I's generals assembled troops for the island's defense, and she traveled to address them. As every English child is taught in school, the British fleet led by Sir Francis Drake turned away the Armada, and a vicious series of storms did the rest, scattering and sinking much of the invasion fleet and ending Spain's attempts to conquer England.

Questions from the NR11

1. How does Elizabeth I use the word "we" in different parts of this speech? Does she shift her meanings? How does it contrast with her use of "I"?
2. What reason does Elizabeth I give for her visit to address the troops? Might there be other, unspoken reasons?

3. Write about how Elizabeth I confronts the supposed paradox of a woman at the head of her troops. She does not take the Joan of Arc route and actually lead as a warrior queen. What is the approach she chooses?

Analytical Considerations

1. A summary of this speech will enable one to trace the movement of thought. There is a logic to the speech that is not always apparent at first glance.
2. Why do you think she does not mention her "lieutenant general" by name?
3. Parma and Spain refer not to places but to the titles of the men who oppose her, another way in which the person of the monarch is regarded as the embodiment of the nation-state

Suggested Writing Assignments

1. List the phrases that seem particularly elevated to you, fitting the royal personage giving the speech as well as the importance of the occasion.
2. Compare Elizabeth I's brief speech to Shakespeare's speech in *Henry V* (Act 5, scene 2), noting the main points of similarity.
3. In a brief essay, describe how the parallel constructions Elizabeth I uses are similar to or different from the parallel constructions in another speech. Suggested comparisons: Kennedy's "Inaugural Address" (NR 906) or Lincoln's "Gettysburg Address" (NR 561, SE 339).
4. What seems to be Elizabeth I's purpose in lines 2–5 when she claims she has ignored warnings over possible "treachery"?

JOHN F. KENNEDY

Inaugural Address

The Norton Reader, p. 906

In 1961 many Americans associated John F. Kennedy with youth and modernity, and he was happy to go along with this assumption, saying in this speech, "the torch has been passed to a new generation, born in this century. . . ." He meant that last phrase literally, since Kennedy, born in 1917 and 43 years old in 1961, was the first president born in the twentieth century. In fact, he was the youngest man to be elected president.

Photographs of Kennedy on January 21, 1961 show him wearing formal clothes and a top hat, just like the Presidents of the 1890s. Those clothes, very old-fashioned even in 1961, serve to suggest that Kennedy's speech looks in two directions: strong echoes of the past appear both in his formal garb and in his quite elaborate rhetoric, even though part of the actual burden of the speech is an appeal to America's and the world's youth. Kennedy's phrase "the torch has been passed" also looks both ways: the very traditional metaphor is of a torch of liberty, drawn from classical times, yet that metaphorical torch is being handed from one generation to another. It's the kind of metaphor that had been used for thousands of years in formal speeches, and in employing it again Kennedy is in keeping with the high rhetorical mode he and his writers chose for this address.

Students will benefit from some information about the context for Kennedy's speech, since Kennedy's youth was seen as a potential vulnerability. In the Cold War confrontation between the Communist Soviet Union and the United States and its allies, Kennedy claimed special expertise in foreign policy, and thus his address deals with pressing international issues that were at the forefront of everyone's consciousness. Primary among them was nuclear arms control, since the Soviets and Americans were increasing their nuclear arsenals and Kennedy had campaigned successfully against the Republicans by claiming (incorrectly, it turned out) that America was falling behind. Another pressing international issue was the end of colonialism, as most European powers were relinquishing the remnants of their overseas empires, and the newly liberated nations of Asia and Africa were being courted both by the Communists and the Americans and their allies. Finally there was the new issue of Cuba, where a long-standing U.S.-supported dictatorship had been recently overthrown by Fidel Castro, a leftist with Communist leanings and no feelings of friendship for his American neighbor. All three—arms race, colonialism, and Cuba—were addressed in Kennedy's speech in ways that were obvious to his listeners but are no longer so apparent to today's college students.

The large doses of formal rhetoric here deserve attention. Students will benefit from a metaphor hunt, perhaps starting with the notion of a "torch" being "passed" at the beginning and then moving to the last few paragraphs, where they abound. The notion of the "peroration," the rousing conclusion, is a useful one, since Kennedy and his speechwriters were clearly interested in working up to a grandiose climax.

Individual instructors will have to decide how deeply to investigate the tropes Kennedy and his writers employed. It will come as a surprise to many students that these constructions have names and were part of a speechwriter's repertory of stylistic devices. They will probably not know that word "device," or the term "trope." It seems useful to explain a little bit, but not over much. For instance, all classes will probably concentrate on the hortatory "Let," which begins eight sentences. Other classes will no doubt concentrate some attention on the very obvious rhetorical tropes marking the highly wrought phrases that have become part of our heritage: "Let us never negotiate out of fear. But let us never fear to negotiate" and "ask not what your country can do for you—ask what you can do for your country" (both examples of "chiasmus").

Questions from the NR11

1. Choose three rhetorical devices from this speech and show how they are constructed. What are their common elements? Their differences?
2. On what level of generality is Kennedy operating? When does he get specific?
3. Kennedy was the youngest man to be elected President. Speculate on how that fact might be reflected in this speech.

Analytical Considerations

1. The headmaster of Kennedy's prep school had coined a ringing phrase: "Ask not what Choate can do for you—ask what you can do for Choate." Does this copying make Kennedy's speech any less valuable or admirable?
2. Examine the role of the word "let" in the speech. How often does it begin sentences? What kind of person uses such a word? On what type of occasion?
3. Some analysts use Kennedy's speech as an example of changing tastes in political addresses, pointing out that it was highly respected in 1961 but now seems overdone. Point to specific passages or to general issues like tone that some might regard as too much. Do you think they are overdone, or do they still work for you?

Suggested Writing Assignments

1. Look at contemporary newspaper and magazine accounts to see how Kennedy's speech was regarded in 1961, then write an essay reacting to what you discovered when reading those contemporary evaluations. What did you find that surprised you?
2. Describe what parts of Kennedy's forty-year-old speech now seem dated and what parts still seem to address vital concerns of the twenty-first century.
3. View the video of this speech and then write about the differences between reading it, on one hand, and seeing and hearing it, on the other.

MARTIN LUTHER KING JR.

I Have A Dream

The Norton Reader, p. 909

Many students will be familiar with this speech from high school history classes, where it is a staple. The interesting thing will be to get students to understand it as an example of political oratory, shrewdly calculated to take advantage of the occasion, one of the largest Civil Rights demonstrations ever held. King was a well-trained professional orator, descended from Baptist preachers and highly experienced in moving his audiences. He had given parts of this particular speech on other occasions. The art of this speech deserves very close attention.

Two terms seem essential for talking about King's formal rhetoric: "antithesis" and "anaphora." They both come together in the middle section—"I have a dream"—while antithesis seems to dominate the opening and anaphora ("let freedom ring") the end. It's helpful to introduce both terms with one or two examples (and perhaps the word "antithetical" as well) and then have students find examples on their own. This task works especially well if given out when the reading is assigned, for the quest for the terms will help produce a richer, more intelligent reading.

Similarly, many students will know at least some of the Biblical allusions, and many perhaps need to be told some more. The African American tradition of comparing black slaves in the South to Hebrew slaves in Egypt will be familiar to many. So will King's fondness for terms with a Biblical flavor like "great trials and tribulations," "valley of despair," and "drinking from the cup of bitterness and hatred." This is a language King and his African American audience grew up with, and it resonates particularly well in a speech that is part manifesto, part sermon. The speech is full of Biblical echoes, and operates on a metaphorical level that recalls New Testament parables without ever directly alluding to them.

Questions from the NR11

1. What elements of a sermon do you notice in King's speech?
2. What are the benefits King derives from posing things in the form of a dream? Are there any losses?
3. King's address has a "modular" form, meaning it has distinct, separate parts. Do you note any "modules" in King's speech? What would be changed if some parts were omitted?

Analytical Considerations

1. Note the connections to Lincoln that seem to permeate this speech, from the setting to the actual echoes of his words.
2. Why mention the two prominent Confederate mountain memorials in this speech?
3. Compare King's demands to the attitudes in Garrison's speech on refusal to compromise (NR 912).
4. Examine the figurative language at the opening: "great beacon light of hope," "seared in the flames," "joyous daybreak," "end the long night of captivity." What kind of mood does such language create?
5. Note that within the cascade of figurative language that dominates the speech, King inserts some very specific, heartfelt details into paragraph 8.
6. An African American preacher who would be a national leader needed a common touch as well as a facility with the rich biblical language. Look for evidence of this common touch in the "check" metaphor in paragraphs 3 and 4.
7. "Gradualism" (at the end of paragraph 4) was a powerful and dangerous term, much like "compromise" to Garrison (NR 912). King is arguing against lukewarm supporters who urge caution, much as Garrison was. He stresses "the fierce urgency of now."

Suggested Writing Assignments

1. Listen to a recording (better still, see the video) and describe how adding the sounds and pictures changes your way of understanding this speech. Did people recognize this as a classic speech at the time?
2. Compare the way King uses sentences beginning with "Let" to the way Kennedy does in his inaugural address (NR 906).
3. Examine "I Have a Dream" in light of King's earlier "Letter from Birmingham Jail" (NR 889, SE 521) for the differences between a speech to a large

public gathering and a written document that could indulge in finer distinctions and much greater detail.

WILLIAM LLOYD GARRISON

No Compromise with Slavery

The Norton Reader, p. 912

Garrison's speech is a carefully crafted argument in favor of what he calls "fanaticism." As the title states boldly, Garrison will allow "no compromise." Such directness must be set against terms and phrases every student of American history learns: the "Great Compromise" and the "Compromise of 1850." For Garrison, such compromises, worked out with much wrangling in Washington by eminent statesmen (such as Henry Clay of Kentucky, known thereafter as "the great compromiser"), were inherently evil, since they merely managed and limited the spread of slavery but did nothing to end it. Indeed, Garrison was so opposed to living in a nation permitting slavery that he favored succession of the North, in order to get away from a union with Southern slaveholders. (He did not explain how such a break would help end slavery.)

In a world filled with compromise, it is bracing—and somewhat unsettling—to have a clear voice cutting through all of the "one the one hand" and "on the other." Garrison, who in today's jargon would be termed a "hard-liner," insists on principle, on his side of the fight, and on his own inexorable and inflexible logic. Students need to see that he isn't arguing against the South or slaveholders—whom he regarded as totally beyond hope—but with his Northern friends and allies who were against slavery but not willing to do anything serious about it, who were willing to "compromise." No, says Garrison. Compromise is wrong.

Interestingly, Garrison's next-to-last paragraph is a shrewd analysis of the situation in the 1850s: the South subjugated everything to the principle of maintaining slavery (even though only a minority of southerners held slaves), while the North cowered in fear ("like a plantation slave" as Garrison has it) over a possible fracture of the Union. Thus the South was able to maintain its way of life by threatening to secede, and the North was willing to compromise time after time to keep the Union together. This helps explain Garrison's own feelings about secession, which for him was less to be feared than the status quo.

A speech like this forces students to confront a battle over principle. Garrison's language and style have little in common with the meliorist prose of Martin Luther King Jr.'s "Letter from Birmingham Jail." It's a "Here I stand" document by someone who is convinced he is right.

Analytical Considerations

1. Garrison states that he "insist[s] on the American people abolishing slavery or ceasing to prate about the rights of man." Is there room in between, even if only temporarily?
2. What arguments might Garrison's Northern friends have used against him?

3. Consider how some similar uncompromising stands characterize arguments over present-day issues like abortion or capital punishment. Which side, like Garrison, seems to have the more extreme position, those in favor or those opposed? What might account for this?
4. In what ways are the compromisers of this world vulnerable? How are the fanatics vulnerable?
5. What happens when cold logic replaces human warmth?
6. Does Garrison have a point when he condemns compromise? What is wrong with compromising?
7. Have students trace the way Garrison employs "anaphora" (structured repetition) throughout, a trait he has in common with almost all of the speakers in this section, including especially King and Kennedy.

Suggested Writing Assignments

1. Demonstrate Garrison's approach by making an outline of the main stages of his argument.
2. Compare the way Garrison argues with the argument in Carl Cohen, "The Case for the Use of Animals in Biomedical Research," (NR 687) or with Tom Regan, "The Case for Animal Rights" (NR 677, SE 409). What are the differences between Garrison's approach and Cohen's or Regan's?
3. Describe the way you would choose to argue a strongly held belief, and explain why you'd choose to do it that way. What would you gain from a stark, uncompromising approach? What would you lose?
4. In "Reading Philosophy at Night" (NR 1208) Charles Simic writes, "Only idiots want something neat, something categorical." Write about how Simic's statement conflicts with Garrison, who seems the very essence of a categorical thinker. Could it be that Simic indulges in the luxury of speculation while Garrison must confront an urgent issue of public policy? Or might "neat" and "categorical" thinking be a tactical mistake in any situation, since human affairs are inherently messy and complex?

DAVID McCULLOUGH

Recommended Itinerary

Norton Reader, p. 915; Shorter Edition, p. 488

A recent addition to that massive but lightly read genre, the graduation speech, this example by popular historian David McCullough seems clever, thoughtful, and free from much of the pomposity that characterizes the genre, a pomposity that keeps most such speeches from being taken very seriously.

McCullough, like all graduation speakers, is in the interesting rhetorical position of having to provide a kind of capstone to four years of a college education, and for many of his audience the last formal education they will ever receive. He very shrewdly maneuvers his audience by inviting them to consider travel, something natural to the upper-middle-class Middlebury graduates (to whom he speaks) with a summer before them. He picks up on the old theme—unstated to be sure—of the Grand Tour, the finishing point of every traditional gentleman's education. But this grand tour is different: it starts in one of the usual places, the Ufizzi, moves to Edinburgh (one of the places European gentlemen were getting away from on their tour!) and moves to Meso-America, and then back home to the United States. What McCullough turns to is his own version of a tour through American history. And it's a highly partisan version of history, told in a modest manner but hardly balanced or thorough. It's a private tour offered to the entire graduating class.

Questions from the NR11

1. Are the places McCullough recommends visiting appropriate for graduates of a liberal arts college? Why or why not?
2. Read Vermont resident Jamaica Kincaid's essay "Sowers and Reapers" (NR 156); then write about McCullough's question "What kind of people are we if we turn our backs on the land and the people who have worked it for so long and in all seasons?" What is missing from McCullough's reading of Jefferson's garden diaries?
3. Characterize the books McCullough urges his listeners to read. What do they have in common? Read about McCullough in the "Authors" section of *The Norton Reader* and them write a paper on whether the books seem to fit the kind of person you think McCullough is.

Analytical Considerations

1. What seems to be McCullough's principle of selection for the places to visit?
2. McCullough believes that education doesn't end when school does. Do the places he urges graduates to visit seem too "educational"?
3. What kinds of places are missing from McCullough's list? What kinds of events does he overlook?
4. McCullough is shocked when a journalist for a major newspaper, "a graduate of one of our great universities," has never heard of Antietam. What is his point here? Who is at fault? (Had you ever heard of Antietam?)
5. Is there anything McCullough would be shocked at in the gaps in your own historical knowledge?
6. What kinds of knowledge does McCullough leave out of his itinerary? Be as specific as you can.
7. "As we have a language requirement for the Foreign Service, so we should have a history requirement for the White House." What do you think? How seriously is this meant? Who would benefit from such a requirement?

Suggested Writing Assignments

1. Using McCullough as a model, provide a "Recommended Itinerary" of your own for one of the following:
   for people who want to know what you are like
   of places you'd like to visit
   of places to avoid

2. Compare this speech with the graduation address you get in Maya Angelou's "Graduation" (NR 32, SE 18). What attitudes do both speeches have in common? What are the key differences?
3. Put yourself in the place of that woman journalist whose ignorance McCullough derides. Write your version of her response to his scorn. Or, if you didn't know of Antietam, write your own personal response to McCullough. In each case, you are free to agree with McCullough's attitude or to challenge him.

JAMES VAN THOLEN

Surprised by Death

The Norton Reader, p. 919

Some context for this sermon might help. A Protestant minister has a very clearly defined relationship to a congregation. In most denominations, the congregation appoints, or "calls" the minister, who serves as the congregation's spiritual guide. Nothing is more important for a minister than the sermon, the centerpiece of a Sunday service. Among Christians, the Sunday sermon plays a much more important role for Protestants than it does for Roman Catholics. Van Tholen's church is Christian Reformed, a small, strict off-shoot of the Dutch Reformed Church, based in Grand Rapids, Michigan. All Reformed churches uphold a version of Calvinism, which stresses the radical dependence of humans on God's will; for a member of a Reformed church, the only thing that can lead to salvation is God's Grace. (Van Tholen deals with this issue in paragraphs 6 and 7.)

Van Tholen's concentration on his own situation is both uncommon—the minister's personal life is not often the subject of the weekly sermon—and necessary, since all members of the congregation would be wondering what he would have to say about his illness. He addresses the matter with a nice rhetorical gesture at the very beginning, saying, "I want to ignore my absence, and I want to pretend everybody has forgotten the reason for it." The next paragraph, beginning "But we can't do that . . . ," makes the transition to the personal.

Questions from the NR11

1. Many sermons and speeches have a "modular" form, meaning they are made up of distinct, separate parts. Choose two speeches from this chapter and note the "modules" they use. How are they organized? Why do you suppose the speaker chose this order?
2. Compare the rhetorical devices used in two speeches—particularly strategies that help the listener follow the argument or that move the listener to agree or take action. Consider, for example, repeated key words, pronouns that include or exclude series of sentences with parallel constructions, and quotations from esteemed sources. What rhetorical elements do the two speeches have in common? What are their differences?

3. Listen to a speech, either in person or on television or video. What rhetorical techniques did the speaker use that you noticed in the "Spoken Words" of this section? Write a brief description of the speech, noting its effective techniques.

Analytical Considerations

1. Speculate on why Van Tholen might have chosen to use the word "vacationing" in the opening paragraph. Does that notion of "vacationing" return later in the sermon?
2. Look at some alternative translations of the opening passage to see how they handle the "still." In verse 6, Van Tholen says, Paul's use of "still" is a "repetitious and ungrammatical piling up of his meaning." Do other translations verge on the ungrammatical?
3. How does Van Tholen move from his own situation to the situation of all humans?
4. Note the anaphora in the opening, especially the repetition of "we."

Suggested Writing Assignments

1. Using Van Tholen's sermon and Reinhold Niebuhr's (NR 1141), write about the range of sermon style. For instance, Niebuhr uses a very high level of generality, while Van Tholen is quite specific.
2. Describe how Van Tholen's sermon is formed of distinct parts, with the transitions from section to section marked by the words "but" and "so."
3. This is literally one of those "If you had only a year to live" situations, and Van Tholen tells us he will spend his time serving as pastor. Write about this. Is it the approach you would take in such a situation? Or, if you prefer, write a defense of Van Tholen's decision to continue on in his calling as minister.

SCIENCE AND TECHNOLOGY

JACOB BRONOWSKI

The Nature of Scientific Reasoning

The Norton Reader, p. 924; Shorter Edition, p. 535

Bronowski's "The Nature of Scientific Reasoning" is of a piece with his "The Reach of Imagination" (NR 210), in "Human Nature." In the latter essay he argues that scientific and poetic thinking are essentially the same in that both originate in the imagination. In this essay he extends his argument to their ends: Scientists and poets search for order, which "must be discovered and, in a deep sense . . . created" (paragraph 9). Central to Bronowski's purposes is disabusing readers of the notion that scientists mechanically accumulate inert facts; see, for example, Thomas S. Kuhn, "The Route to Normal Science" (NR 928), paragraphs 10 to 11. Bronowski provides multiple illustrations of scientific discovery ranging from Copernicus to Yukawa and makes them intelligible to nonscientists, that is, if they read them carefully. Students often don't; they skip explanations they expect to be hard to follow or drift away from the text. Making sure they understand Bronowski's examples can be a useful demonstration of active reading: what they have to do to make sense of them, what they have to bring to them, and what strategies, like imagery, are useful.

Questions from the NR11

1. Mark the generalizations Bronowski makes in the course of "The Nature of Scientific Reasoning" and their location; for example, "No scientific theory is a collection of facts" (paragraph 7). Where is the information that supports them?
2. Bronowski tells the well-known story of Newton and the apple (paragraphs 11–12). How many of his generalizations does it exemplify, and how?
3. "The scientist," Bronowski observes, "looks for order in the appearances of nature" (paragraph 9). Is this operation unique to scientists? Consider the operations of "knowers" in humanities and social science disciplines such as history, literature, psychology, and sociology.
4. Bronowski sets up an adversary, a literary person who believes that scientists observe, collect, and record facts, and writes his essay as a refutation. Adapt his rhetorical strategy in an essay of your own: explain your beliefs about something by refuting the beliefs of someone who disagrees with them.

Analytical Considerations

1. You may have students list Bronowski's illustrations and references, perhaps in two columns labeled "science" and "literature." Which illustrations does he explain, which does he simply refer to? What do his illustrations and references suggest about his intended audience?

2. Ask students to list the dates for Bronowski's scientific illustrations. Bronowski turns more extensively to early modern than to modern science, and the example of Yukawa's calculations is less detailed than earlier examples. What does his choice of illustrations suggest about modern science? You may refer students to Thomas S. Kuhn's "The Route to Normal Science" (NR 928): in it Kuhn discusses how and when research reports ceased to be intelligible to laypersons (paragraph 17).

3. Bring to class a copy of a Renaissance drawing of a youth with outstretched arms—you can find one on p. 121 of *Leonardo on Painting*, ed. Martin Kemp (New Haven: Yale University Press, 1989)—and a copy of Blake's *Glad Day*, both of which Bronowski discusses in paragraph 5. Ask students if he gives enough detail for them to visualize these pictures, or is it necessary to see or to have seen them?

Suggested Writing Assignments

1. Write an essay in which you consider the science courses you have taken with respect to Bronowski's assertion "No scientific theory is a collection of facts" (paragraph 7). Were you taught science in such a way as to make Bronowski's assertion meaningful? Do you think you should have been?

2. Do library research on current debates over the teaching of science or conduct interviews with science faculty at your institution. What complaints are made about it, what remedies are suggested? Write an essay in which you discuss these debates. You may want to use Bronowski's essay to focus your own, but you need not.

3. "Science finds order and meaning in our experience" (paragraph 11). Can this statement be broadened to: "All fields of study find order and meaning in our experience"? Write an essay in which you consider a course or courses you have taken in another field of study. Use "I" in a way that seems appropriate to you. How much of your own experience will go into your essay, and how will you include it?

THOMAS S. KUHN

The Route to Normal Science

The Norton Reader, p. 928

Thomas S. Kuhn was a Ph.D. in physics turned historian and philosopher of science; "The Route to Normal Science" comes from his best-known work, *The Structure of Scientific Revolutions* (1962). His concept of a "paradigm" (or a research tradition) and a "paradigm shift" (or the end of one research tradition and the beginning of another) has been widely adopted, which is evidence of his influence. For example, we speak of changes in the teaching of writing—from emphasizing product (or the finished essay) to emphasizing process (or its production through multiple drafts)—as a paradigm shift.

You may begin class discussion of "The Route to Normal Science" by directing students to its first two paragraphs, in which Kuhn briefly and magisterially lays out the concepts that he will illustrate: normal science, the reporting of scientific achievements, the nature of a research tradition, and its relation to scientific practice. He naturally illustrates these concepts with examples drawn from science. You may be able to enlist knowledgeable students to explain current paradigms; they will probably not be able to explain discarded ones—which itself will illustrate their disappearance. To illustrate a current paradigm, you can look at Kuhn's distinction between a textbook and a research report: the references in Henry Wechsler et al., "Health and Behavioral Consequences of Binge Drinking in College" (NR 948, SE 551) point to the tradition these researchers built on and extended. To illustrate a discarded paradigm (Kuhn features Newton's optics and Franklin's electricity), Isaac Asimov's "The Eureka Phenomenon" (NR 223, SE 130), Jacob Bronowski's "The Reach of Imagination" (NR 210) will help.

Questions from the NR11

1. Mark the important terms in this selection from *The Structure of Scientific Revolutions* and Kuhn's definitions of them. How many terms does he illustrate as well as define? Why does he both define and illustrate?
2. What are prevailing paradigms in sciences other than those Kuhn discusses? You might consider biology, chemistry, psychology, and sociology. Are you aware of older paradigms in these sciences, or have they and the work based on them, as Kuhn says (paragraph 15), disappeared?
3. Without a paradigm, Kuhn writes, "all of the facts that could possibly pertain to the development of a given science are likely to seem equally relevant" (paragraph 10). What, according to Stephen Jay Gould in "Darwin's Middle Road" (NR 1011, SE 600), was the paradigm that enabled Darwin to discriminate among his facts? How can he be said to have made a "scientific revolution"?

Analytical Considerations

1. You may want to look at Kuhn's discussion of paradigms in relation to gathering facts and establishing their relevance (paragraphs 10 and 11). Analogies with writing may be useful here: what gets included and excluded from an essay, when, and why?
2. Kuhn speaks of "the unfortunate simplification that tags an extended historical episode with a single and somewhat arbitrarily chosen name" (paragraph 9). Ask students for examples from history and literature and consider the various ways they function. Is simplification always "unfortunate"?

Suggested Writing Assignments

1. If you have encountered the term paradigm in another field of study, write an essay in which you describe what it refers to and how it is used and discuss whether it is used in Kuhn's sense.
2. Kuhn, in "The Route to Normal Science," mentions what happens to scientists who cling to discarded paradigms (paragraph 15). Elsewhere in *The Structure of Scientific Revolutions* he discusses several, including Louis Agassiz, who held out against Darwin. Do research on Agassiz or another

holdout and write an essay about him or her using Kuhn's concept of a paradigm.
3. Kuhn's *The Structure of Scientific Revolutions*, published in 1962, engendered considerable debate that was essentially about definitions. Read his postscript to the second edition (1970) and describe the issues of definition he raises.

STEVEN WEINBERG

Can Science Explain Everything? Anything?

The Norton Reader, p. 936; Shorter Edition, p. 539

Steven Weinberg is a Nobel laureate in physics who teaches at the University of Texas. Focusing primarily on physics, this essay works methodically to answer the questions of its title. Though he offers his answers in simple declarative sentences, most of the essay concerns the precise definitions of the terms in his answer. Early in the essay, Weinberg asserts that "we explain a physical principle when we show that it can be deduced from a more fundamental physical principle." To demonstrate what he means by this, have students list the physical principles that, according to Weinberg, science has successfully explained.

Resisting the philosophical tendency to create special definitions of common words (ironically here exemplified by Wittgenstein), Weinberg attempts to define words according to how they are most commonly used. His essay is difficult. You may want to suggest some strategies for reading and preparing to discuss difficult material.

This essay proceeds along the methods Weinberg himself recommends for science: he explains his answers through a discussion of the meaning of his terms. In defining his terms, he draws upon examples spanning the history of physics, from Aristotle, Kepler, and Newton, through Einstein, to late-twentieth-century physicists Hempel and Oppenheim, James Peebles, and others. Weinberg's essay defines three key terms—"fundamental," "deduce," and "principle." Help students see the arc of his argument by showing them where the discussion of each key term begins. His discussion of deduction takes up the bulk of the essay; help students see why this is central to his claim. How does it connect to their project as writers of analytical prose?

In spite of his interest in defining what science can do, Weinberg insists that science declines to answer teleological questions. Define what "teleological questions" are for your students. Ask them why he sees them as outside the realm of science?

Questions from the NR11

1. Explain how Weinberg enters the conversation (or argument) about the limits of explanation.
2. Weinberg's essay was written for an educated audience of nonscientists. Can someone who doesn't understand issues of quantum mechanics or string

theory get much out of it? What does such a person need to do in order
to understand Weinberg? What help does Weinberg provide for the
nonscientist?

3. In an essay, describe and explain the limits Weinberg acknowledges of our
ability to explain significant physical events.

Analytical Considerations

1. What does Weinberg see as the main difference between physics and
chemistry and other sciences?
2. What is the difficulty with the word "fundamental"?
3. In three consecutive paragraphs of the essay, Weinberg outlines problems
with the process of deduction. Divide the class into groups and assign each
the task of explaining one of these problems with deduction to the class as
a whole.
4. Bring the definition of "explanation," "fundamental," "deduce," or "principle" from several dictionaries—a student dictionary, an unabridged dictionary, and the *Oxford English Dictionary*. Compare them to each other
and to Weinberg's method, discussing the different purposes of each.
5. Review the example from E. M. Forster. Choose an event—the outcome
of an election, your choice of one college over another, or your choice of
a roommate. Divide a sheet of paper into two columns. On one side, describe the event, on the other, explain it. What's the difference between
the two activities? Discuss that difference with your classmates.

Suggested Writing Assignments

1. Write your own definition of a common argumentative term (such as
"basic," "hypothesis," "assumption," "rule," or "theory") and then explain
your definition in a short essay.
2. Choose one of the scientific discoveries mentioned by Weinberg and research its history. What phenomenon did the scientist set out to explain?
Did the explanation lead to unexpected further applications? New questions?

HENRY WECHSLER, ANDREA DAVENPORT, GEORGE DOWDALL, BARBARA MOEYKENS, AND SONIA CASTILLO

Health and Behavioral Consequences of Binge Drinking in College: A National Survey of Students at 140 Campuses

The Norton Reader, p. 948; Shorter Edition, p. 551

This essay, along with "Too Many Colleges Are Still in Denial about
Alcohol Abuse" (NR 397, SE 566), based on the same study, form a natural
pair. It is a scientific paper, written for a specialized, technical audience of
experts who read the *Journal of the American Medical Association*, whereas the
second is an opinion piece, written for the *Chronicle of Higher Education*,
which attracts a wider audience, primarily of college administrators. As such,

these two essays represent the scientific paper and its popularization. There is a clear primacy here: the scientific paper was published first; the popular piece is dependent upon it, and in fact much of the knowledge claimed in the *Chronicle* essay grows out of the scientific study. Without the grounding supplied by the scientific study, the opinion piece would carry a great deal less weight.

The thrust of *The Norton Reader*'s questions on these essays is to involve students more deeply in the knowledge base reported in the research. What seems to many students to be the scientific presentation of cold facts is instead a careful description of an experiment that grows out of plainly stated premises: that "binge" drinking is something that can be clearly defined, that students are accurate reporters of their experiences, and that the survey questions reported in the article provide a useful way of getting at the phenomenon examined in the *Chronicle* essay.

The scientific article is particularly good at laying out all of the questions asked and is exemplary at foregrounding its criteria for definitions. Students need to see how this foregrounding is the very essence of scientific inquiry, since it presents the means by which information was gathered. This article, like all good scientific work, includes plenty of opinion, but this opinion is reasoned, explained, and most of all, carefully delineated for readers to see and judge for themselves. The opinion piece, unlike the original article, moves far beyond the data to make its points.

Questions from the NR11

1. This article's conclusions depend on the wording of the questions asked. A central question is "Think back over the last two weeks. How many times have you had five or more drinks in a row?" What do you think "in a row" means? Do you think the question is precise or fuzzy? Why was it asked this way?
2. How do you and people you know define "binge drinking"? How close is your definition to the definition used by Wechsler et al.?
3. At 44 of the 140 colleges surveyed, more than 50 percent of the students were binge drinkers. Does that sound alarming? Accurate? What might some of those colleges be?
4. Compare this scientific article with the Op-Ed Wechsler and his colleagues wrote for the *Chronicle of Higher Education* (NR 397, SE 566). Note the important changes you see between this article and the Op-Ed. Are they changes in style? In audience? In format? In details? Which changes matter most to the overall impact of the essays?

Analytical Considerations

1. In their conclusion, the writers of the *Chronicle* essay switch from discussing their research to calling for change by directly addressing college administrators. The transition is handled deftly and subtly: note the invocation of "administrators" in paragraph 15, "college officials" in paragraph 19, and "campus authorities" in paragraph 20; by paragraphs 21 and 22 the authors

are using imperatives and, finally, explicit second-person direct address in the last paragraph (paragraph 24).

2. Find parts of the *Chronicle* essay that are not supported by the data in the scientific study.

3. Ask students which article has more redundancy, and whether it seems to be intentional. Is a certain amount of redundancy helpful in some kinds of writing? Which types benefit from redundancy? Which types lose impact?

4. How might "the weekend tour" the authors urge present the drinking situation more impressively than a scientific paper? On the other hand, how might the tour be misleading?

Suggested Writing Assignments

1. Interview a sample of people on your campus about their drinking habits, and write a piece aimed at authorities about whether they are in denial about drinking on their own campus.

2. Explain what would have to change at your college if college officials acted on the warnings in this article. How would campus life be different?

3. Write an essay explaining why college officials have every incentive to keep alcohol-related problems covered up.

4. Write a description of a "problem" caused by drinking. Choose the problem from the list in Table 2 of the scientific article.

5. Dramatize one of the "secondary binge effects" in Table 4 of the scientific article by writing the dialogue that might occur between a drinker and someone affected by the drinking.

MATT CARTMILL

Do Horses Gallop in Their Sleep?: The Problem of Animal Consciousness

The Norton Reader, p. 963

One of Cartmill's goals in this essay is to persuade his fellow scientists of the value of looking at the margins of a discipline—where science and philosophy are allied, where indirect evidence is persuasive. He negotiates a space of inquiry between sentimental anthropomorphism and the overzealous resistance to it. Students are likely to share his skepticism of a too vigorous specialization.

Cartmill clearly believes that animals are conscious, but he is a long way from being able to prove consciousness to the satisfaction of scientists. Instead, he presents several thought-experiments to make his case. While thought-experiments are common in philosophy, they are much less common in biology. Of course, Cartmill wants to straddle the border of these disciplines, so this exemplifies how he, as a scientist, is open to other methods of inquiry. Discuss the merits and demerits of thought-experiments as evidence. How much depends on the discipline in which the author is working?

The section on sleep and sleepwalking offers a model of counterargument that is worth discussing in some detail. Cartmill concedes that "the phenomenon of sleepwalking shows that you can get surprisingly complicated and even distinctly human behavior without consciousness." If this were the end of the story, then his argument would fail. Discuss with students how he turns this seeming objection to his advantage. You might also want to point out how the essay opens with a hypothetical example about sleepwalking, which asks us to think of the phenomenon with distaste. How does this plant the seed for our later reaction?

Cartmill's description of the circumlocutions necessary to avoid attributing consciousness to animals provides an opportunity to discuss the uses and misuses of the passive voice. This might be a good opportunity to review the distinction between passive and active as Cartmill himself makes the standard case in favor of the active voice. If the passive voice sounds silly even to scientists, who regularly insist on it, can students imagine situations in which it would be appropriate?

Questions from the NR11

1. Cartmill has a way of dropping surprising or disquieting facts into this essay. What fact or notion surprised you most? Why do you think Cartmill included it?
2. Do you think that scientists who describe behavior will change their approach as a result of Cartmill's argument? Why might they be resistant to changing their approach to description?
3. Drawing on Cartmill's essay, write a short paragraph explaining what about sleepwalking causes difficulties in defining consciousness.

Analytical Considerations

1. One of the main obstacles to persuading people that animals have consciousness is our investment in the difference between humans and animals. Ask your students if they are invested in this difference. Is it important to them to believe they are different from (higher than) other living creatures? Why or why not? What are the cultural and historic reasons for the persistence of this belief?
2. Ask students to find one of the moments in which Cartmill uses humor to make his point. On their own, have them each write a sentence or two assessing the moment's effectiveness. Discuss their conclusions.
3. Is the conclusion persuasive? Is what a gazelle does when she notices that a lion is hungry thinking? If not, what is it?

Suggested Writing Assignments

1. What makes us different from computers? What makes us different from animals? Read John Hockenberry's "The Next Brainiacs" (NR 982, SE 571). Each essay challenges preconceived ideas about what makes humans different from both machines and animals. Write an essay discussing these differences with reference to Hockenberry and Cartmill.

SANDRA STEINGRABER

Pesticides, Animals, and Humans

The Norton Reader, p. 971

Steingraber received her Ph.D. in biology from the University of Michigan. A cancer survivor, she is the author of a volume of poetry, *Post-Diagnosis*, and two environmental books, *Living Downstream* (1997) and *Having Faith* (2001) (about her experience becoming a mother and the womb as the first environment). She has held many visiting positions (at Radcliffe, Columbia College in Chicago, and others) and awards (including a Woman of the Year award from *Ms.*), and currently holds a research position at Cornell University.

Steingraber is inspired by Rachel Carson, and stands a good chance of being as influential. In this chapter from *Living Downstream*, she combines a discussion of the importance of cancer research on animals (animals with cancer and the more controversial practice of testing new treatments on animals) with her own experience as a cancer survivor. She constantly forces us to move from an abstract data point, such as MCF-7, the name of a human cell line used to study breast cancer, and the person who donated those cells. Not only does she want to know about the cancer, she also asks "Whose breasts did they come from, and what was her fate?" (121).

Steingraber mentions her fight against cancer midway through this essay. Throughout the book from which this chapter is drawn, she links her personal struggle against cancer to the likely environmental causes in her hometown, to biological evidence, and to the need for political action. Rachel Carson, the pioneering environmentalist whom she takes as a model, never once publicly mentioned her own cancer even as she testified in Congress for stronger environmental legislation to ban carcinogens. Carson felt that her credibility, already fragile on account of her sex, would only be further undermined if people knew she had cancer: she believed the appearance of impersonality and objectivity was more persuasive than subjective testimony. Much has changed in the intervening decades. Nonetheless, Steingraber is an unconventional research scientist. This essay affords an opportunity to discuss with students the place of gender and of personal testimony in science. In what situations might Carson's approach be preferable to Steingraber's? How would their experience reading Steingraber differ if she mentioned her own cancer up front? If she left it out?

Questions from the NR11

1. Why does Steingraber insist on the connection between MCF-7 and Sister Catherine Frances Mallon? How does that connection foreshadow the rest of the essay?
2. Steingraber's hospital roommate says, "I think I'm going to stop partying for a while," while Steingraber replies, "I think I'm going to start" (paragraphs 64–66). What do you think of Steingraber's attitude here? Would you do the same? What makes this exchange a natural way to end a segment of the essay?

3. Do research on the impact of Carson's book *Silent Spring*, published in 1962, and ask whether Steingraber's work takes up where Carson left off. (Interestingly, Carson finished her book while suffering through the last stages of cancer. Steingraber obviously knew of this connection.)

Analytical Considerations

1. Toward the end of her essay, Steingraber describes a dream about a giant crab, completing the circle that begins the essay linking cancer the disease and cancer the crab. She says the meaning of the dream is obvious, but she does not spell it out. Ask students to articulate the dream's significance and then discuss with them the connection she's trying to create through this imagery of crabs and cancer.
2. Ask students why "Pesticides, Animals, and Humans" is a good title for this essay.
3. Steingraber clearly meant to be provocative when she asked the researcher "Did you know she was a nun?" Discuss this move with your students: is it a cheap trick or an important humanizing moment? Is there a difference between doing it to one person and reporting on it in writing to many?
4. Steingraber wants to move people to action, to make her readers into environmentalists. She uses all the tools in her arsenal to persuade us: touching descriptions of sympathetic animals and humans, her personal story, scientific research, and accounts of the state of public policy. Help your students identify all of these moments and discuss with them the risks and benefits of this mixed method.

Suggested Writing Assignments

1. The National Cancer Institute maintains an atlas of cancer rates by county on the Web (www.nci.gov). Find a county near your home or school where rates are significantly higher than the national average. Research the reasons for the higher rate and write a short paper reporting on your findings.
2. Steingraber concludes that perhaps a pilgrimage showing people with cancer sites where animals suffer from cancer might persuade people of our interconnectedness and so move them to act. On a subsequent occasion, she helped a university to cease using pesticides on their football field when she informed the team that the pesticide was proven to lower sperm counts. Research an environmental problem in your community and write a paper in which you try to enlist the support of a local group in your call for change.

JOHN HOCKENBERRY

The Next Brainiacs

The Norton Reader, p. 982; Shorter Edition, p. 571

Television correspondent, journalist, and author John Hockenberry writes about how technological innovations have helped the severely disabled communicate and move. That he has been in a wheelchair since a car accident when he was nineteen gives him special insight into the questions his essay raises. His title, "The Next Brainiacs," shows us disabled people as amazing experimenters, living on the border of human and machine, showing us the potential of the human mind to adapt to new and difficult conditions. He writes with delight, energy, and pride in the synergy between himself and his chair, describing how one of his daughters' first attempts at locomotion mimicked his movements in the chair. He writes, too, of the surprisingly moving experience of standing up on his own for the first time in many years: an admission that might seem at odds with the peace he's made with his situation, and one that adds both poignancy and persuasiveness to the hypothesis that there must be some deep, instinctive pleasure in the sensation of standing up and balancing.

Although this journalistic piece does not have an obvious thesis or an analytical conclusion, the body of the essay has a familiar structure: each model of assistive technology is accompanied by the story of a person who makes use of it. Ask your students to deduce a thesis and conclusion from these examples. Then go back to the essay. Although its style is journalistic, there is a clear thesis in the introduction. The conclusion, however, ties things up less conventionally. Since conclusions are so difficult for students, who struggle to find the right place between restating the opening and going off in a wholly new direction, they may be interested in discussing his strategies here. What opportunities does revisiting the puppet metaphor provide? Are there strategies here that they could adapt in their own writing?

Questions from the NR11

1. Hockenberry's large claims come at the end of his essay. What claims does he finally make? Do you think he has prepared readers for them?
2. What is distinctive about Hockenberry's writing style? As a way of answering this question, think about words or phrases that characterize his opening and closing sentences.
3. Write an essay explaining the extent to which you accept Hockenberry's assertion of a new way of being human, a machine-body mixture. How seriously do you think he means us to take this assertion?

Analytical Considerations

1. Hockenberry begins and ends his essay by analogizing himself to a puppet. Discuss the analogy: how is the relation between puppet and puppeteer like that between a disabled person and assistive technology?
2. Hockenberry describes three different research areas for assistive technology (The Cure, FES, and cortical implant technology). Divide the class into thirds, have each group research one area and debate the merits and demerits of each. How would they allocate funds for future research?
3. Throughout the essay, Hockenberry ends paragraphs with the imperative "think" followed by a noun. Discuss the effectiveness of this refrain with your students. What does Hockenberry want to accomplish with it? Is it appropriate for academic writing?
4. What are the lessons of this essay for engineers and designers?

Suggested Writing Assignments

1. Read Nancy Mairs' "On Being a Cripple" (NR 58, SE 36). Both Hockenberry and Mairs write openly and with pride about their life with a physical disability. Compare the two approaches.
2. Research a recent technological invention aiding communication or mobility. Write an essay in which you discuss the different possibilities it offers both people who are disabled and people who are not. Was it developed to aid the disabled? Is it being used in a way that differs from its inventors' projections?

MELVIN KONNER

Why the Reckless Survive

The Norton Reader, p. 995; Shorter Edition, p. 584

Ask students why "Why the Reckless Survive" is in the section called "Science and Technology" rather than in the section called "Human Nature." Melvin Konner poses questions about risk taking and, initially, attempts to answer them in the familiar language of behavioral science. Only later, more than halfway through the essay (paragraphs 23–24), when he brings in the physiological correlates of the risk-taking or sensation-seeking personality, does he attempt to answer them in the language of biological science. Students may need to be alerted to this shift from the psychological analysis they feel comfortable with to the less-familiar biological and evolutionary analysis. Biology and behavior are linked, for Konner, by physical anthropology and, ultimately, by evolution and genetics. Clues to Konner's orientation appear early in the essay, when he suggests there may be "something inevitable—even something good" about taking chances (paragraph 3) and that risk taking is "a conundrum for an evolutionist" (paragraph 6). His final answer, that the risk taking that seems maladaptive now was adaptive in the dangerous environment of our ancestors, relies on Darwinian selection and a drive to reproduce.

Konner, who began as an anthropologist and then went to medical school, is stationed at the cutting edge of interdisciplinary research. As he wrote in an earlier work, *The Tangled Wing: Biological Constraints on the Human Spirit* (1982): "The encroachments of biology on behavioral science have come in two broad, separate areas: evolution and genetics on the one hand, anatomy and physiology on the other. These two areas have a natural link in the science of embryology, but the link—biochemical genetics—has only just begun to be explored." Unlike some sociobiologists, Konner is neither a determinist nor a conservative. "The result of the vastly long evolutionary balancing act," he writes in this essay, "is a most imperfect organism" (paragraph 39)—but one that we can improve, his writing demonstrates, by the exercise of intelligence and compassion.

Questions from the NR11

1. Mark the research and the researchers' disciplines that Konner relies on. How many kinds of studies does he bring together? What are they?
2. Konner is interested in the effects of biology on human behavior. Locate the evidence he draws from biology and explain his uses of it.
3. Konner introduces and concludes this essay with autobiographical material; he stations himself with respect to his subject. What does the autobiographical material contribute to this essay?
4. Write an essay in which you describe your own or someone else's irrational behavior and speculate about its causes.

Analytical Considerations

1. The psychological and biological research Konner cites is not footnoted. This section, "Science and Technology," illustrates degrees of popularization. At one end, Wechsler et al. write in the manner of a scientific report; at the other end, Konner, in "Why the Reckless Survive," and Stephen Jay Gould, in "Darwin's Middle Road" (NR 1011, SE 600), include general references in the text. You can call students' attention to the advantages and disadvantages of each method; you may demonstrate them by assigning reports on the sources Konner and Gould use.
2. Sociobiology, which provides biological explanations of human behavior, is a controversial field of inquiry, especially insofar as it tends toward determinism. How deterministic is Konner's account of risk-taking behavior?
3. You can discuss current debates about Richard J. Herrnstein and Charles Murray's *The Bell Curve: Intelligence and Class Structure in American Life* (1994), perhaps by bringing in a review. Why has it become politically contentious with respect to both its science and its politics?

Suggested Writing Assignments

1. Imagine being told that some achievement, or some failing, or both were genetically programmed and beyond your control. Write an essay in which you describe the traits, the occasion of your discovery, and your response.
2. Read a section of Konner's *The Tangled Wing: Biological Constraints on the Human Spirit* (1982) and describe how psychological and biological explanations intersect.

NEIL POSTMAN

Virtual Students, Digital Classroom

The Norton Reader, p. 1004; Shorter Edition, p. 592

As a veteran educational commentator, Postman has often been in the vanguard of new advances in schooling, so it is unusual to see him sounding reluctant about the promise of technology. But the particular grounds of his complaint make perfect sense: there is a great deal of hype about computers in the classroom, and far too little common sense. Postman takes what he obviously considers to be a practical view of computers and worries that rapid technological adoptions will displace attention from more important questions.

One question for students is what they think the role of computers in the classroom will be in the future. If you break the question down, it gets more interesting. What will the role be in five years? Twenty years? Fifty years? Most will agree that computers will play an enormous role. Some other key questions are: who will control the rate of change? How can computers be introduced equally, so no students are penalized? How can we prepare now for a different future? Students will soon recognize that Postman raises the traditional liberal-arts values of an open mind and an informed citizenry. Does he provide ways of preserving these values in the face of the mechanization of computers?

Postman's other focus seems to be on willpower, on the motivations of the learner. Lively discussion can ensue when a class is asked, who bears the responsibility for learning—the school or the student? Once students get beyond the usual valedictorian clichés (School is what you make it, etc.), they can use Postman's essay to interrogate educational theories and the technology that enthralls so many.

Questions from the NR11

1. In paragraph 10 Postman says that "schools can provide . . . a serious form of technology education" and argues for "making technology itself an object of inquiry." Since this is exactly what Postman does as a writer and professor, is this argument an instance of self-interested special pleading? Why or why not?
2. Consult Postman's biography in the "Authors" section; then look through his essay for evidence of his professional expertise. What kinds of sources does he refer to? What is the range of his reading? Is he writing for a specific community of readers?
3. Write about computers in your own formal education, arguing from your own experiences whether Postman makes a good case or not.

Analytical Considerations

1. In paragraph 10 Postman says "using computers to process information . . . is a trivial thing to do." What is trivial about it? What meaning of "process" is Postman relying on? Are there other meanings of "process" that might make the task seem less trivial?
2. Postman is hard on technophiles, whose prophecies always have "a cheery gee-whiz tone" (paragraph 6). Students might recall some current or past overenthusiastic technophilic statements. Ask them if the technophiles' "cheery gee-whiz" tone is a by-product of an understandable enthusiasm or if it is evidence that they are out of touch with real life, as Postman seems to argue. (See the opening of paragraph 9: "These are serious matters, and they need to be discussed by those who know something about children from the planet Earth. . . .")

Suggested Writing Assignments

1. In an essay, describe another "Faustian bargain" (paragraph 8) society has made, in addition to the automobiles and television that Postman mentions. Potential subjects might include artificial birth control, missile technology, and high-tech agriculture.
2. Use Postman's statement, "Schools are not now and have never been largely about getting information to children" (paragraph 9), as an epigraph for an essay that responds to this statement, drawing on your own knowledge. What in your own experience have schools "been largely about"?
3. Write about someone who is actually using the computer to make learning more effective. This can be a fellow student, a worker learning on the job, or someone learning a subject in his or her spare time. Think about whether this person's activities support or challenge Postman's contentions.

STEPHEN JAY GOULD

Darwin's Middle Road

The Norton Reader, p. 1011; Shorter Edition, p. 600

Stephen Jay Gould was a biologist, a historian of science, and a superb popularizer. "Darwin's Middle Road," like others of his essays, was first published in the column he wrote for *Natural History* magazine. In this essay he introduces Darwin's working toward a theory of natural selection by discussing two opposed views of scientific creativity: "inductivism," or reliance on observation and the accumulation of data, and "eurekaism," or reliance on predictive hunches and synthesis. Today, he observes, eurekaism is privileged; see, for example, Isaac Asimov's "The Eureka Phenomenon" (NR 223, SE 130) in "Human Nature." In Darwin's time, inductivism was privileged. There has been, to use Thomas S. Kuhn's nomenclature, a paradigm shift in accounting for scientific discovery; see "The Route to Normal Science" (NR 928).

Gould, by beginning with this general discussion, is better able to present the particulars of Darwin's achievement, and we are better able to follow not only the particulars of Darwin's achievement but also Gould's disentangling them from Darwin's own account of his achievement. Gould, arguing that Darwin shuttled between induction and prediction, puts one piece of evidence after another in place. The structure of Gould's essay, students should be asked to notice, is predictive (rather than inductive). But rhetorical structure need not reflect the method of discovery. Darwin's thinking and Gould's writing together may lead to a useful discussion of the writing process and the relation of rhetoric to thought. Like Darwin, we shuttle between induction and prediction when we think and frequently use our first and intermediate drafts to clarify what we are doing. Final drafts, however, usually require a predictive structure to prepare readers to follow our thinking.

Questions from the NR11

1. What, according to Gould, constituted Darwin's scientific research? How and why did he depict it falsely in his autobiography (paragraph 8)?
2. Rather than isolating scientific research from social and political experience, Darwin, Gould explains, was influenced by a social scientist, an economist, and a statistician (paragraph 20). Identify each one and explain what he contributed to Darwin's theory of natural selection.
3. Consider a recent experience of writing an essay. Did you, thinking and writing, shuttle between inductivism and prediction as Gould claims Darwin did? Describe your experience using Gould's analytic vocabulary.

Analytical Considerations

1. You may ask students to read one or more of the following essays: Isaac Asimov's "The Eureka Phenomenon" (NR 223, SE 130), Jacob Bronowski, "The Reach of Imagination" (NR 210), and Henry David Thoreau, "Observation" (NR 232), all in "Human Nature," and Jacob Bronowski's "The Nature of Scientific Reasoning" (NR 924, SE 535) and Thomas S. Kuhn's "The Route to Normal Science" (NR 928), both in this section. How does each, describing scientific discovery, present what Gould calls "inductivism" and "eurekaism"?
2. Society writes biology, at least in part, a science writer once claimed. How did society write Darwin's account of the operations of natural selection?
3. Ask students to describe their experience of thinking and writing as they produced a recent essay. Does Gould's account of inductivism and prediction clarify the experience for them? This task is best done in groups.

Suggested Writing Assignments

1. Write an essay about a eureka experience of your own. You may consider, in conjunction with it, Gould's conclusion to "Darwin's Middle Road": he refers to Louis Pasteur's remark that fortune favors the prepared mind.
2. Look at the prescribed form of scientific reporting—abstract, methods, results, discussion, and references—as exemplified by Henry Wechsler et al., "Health and Behavioral Consequences of Binge Drinking in College: A National Survey of Students at 140 Campuses." Write an essay in which you consider the relation of the article's rhetoric to its thought: is its rhetoric primarily inductive or predictive?

LITERATURE, THE ARTS, AND MEDIA

EUDORA WELTY

One Writer's Beginnings

The Norton Reader, p. 1019; Shorter Edition, p. 607

Taken from her best-selling memoir by the same title, this essay turns to the world of Eudora Welty's childhood in Jackson, Mississippi, and offers an adult's reflections on formative early experience. "One Writer's Beginnings" is clearly a chapter from the autobiography of an artist and intellectual. Welty describes the books read to her and the books she read, notes the texts she admired and adored, and talks about reading as she experienced it—and as she hopes her readers will also experience it. Perhaps the most important aspect of "One Writer's Beginnings" comes near the end, when Welty considers "voice." Her five-paragraph treatment of the subject, beginning with her mother's songs and records played on the Victrola, then retracing her own experience of reading and writing, provides a valuable opportunity to define and illustrate this difficult rhetorical concept.

Questions from the NR11

1. In the opening paragraphs Welty speaks of what she later calls her "sensory education." What does she mean? What examples does she give?
2. Throughout her essay Welty lists the titles of books that she and her mother read. What is the effect of these lists? Have you read any of the books on them? Or books like them? How important were they to you?
3. Welty concludes her essay by talking of the writer's voice—of "testing it for truth" and "trust[ing] this voice" (paragraph 24). What meanings does she give the key words truth and trust?
4. Read John Holt's essay "How Teachers Make Children Hate Reading" (NR 420, SE 249). Write an essay of your own, entitled "How Children Learn to Love Reading," drawing your evidence from Welty's "One Writer's Beginnings" and your experience, observation, and reading.
5. Welty grew up before the advent of television. How does television affect a child's "sensory education"? Write an essay comparing a modern child's sensory education with Welty's.

Analytical Considerations

1. Follow up on Question 2 (above) by considering the following: why does Welty devote so much space to describing the books of her childhood? Are they the forces that most powerfully shaped her, or is she, through memory and words, also (re)shaping the self she presents in this autobiography of an artist?
2. Welty obviously loves books and loves to talk about them. Ask students what strategies she uses to communicate her responses to books—not just

adjectives, but metaphors, memories, anecdotes—and what strategies they most respond to.

3. Ask students why this selection has been titled "One Writer's Beginnings." Would they expect different "beginnings" from the autobiography of, say, a painter or politician or businessperson?

4. Welty writes, "Movement must be at the very heart of listening" (paragraph 23). This principle is also true for reading. Ask students to plot the movement of "One Writer's Beginnings" and then to consider what unifies the piece.

5. In what ways is Welty's essay a cultural document reflecting the world of the American South in the early decades of this century? You might begin discussing this question by asking students to note what is different about Welty's childhood from their own—or, perhaps, what details from Welty's childhood they have encountered in stories told by their parents or grandparents.

6. In paragraph 24 Welty offers a description of "voice" in a story or poem. After discussing it, ask students to characterize the voice they hear in "One Writer's Beginnings."

Suggested Writing Assignments

1. In describing her reading of classic tales from *Every Child's Story Book*, Eudora Welty notes: "I located myself in these pages and could go straight to the stories and pictures I loved" (paragraph 12). If you have had a similar experience with stories or books, write an essay about it. If your experience with books was quite different, that, too, will provide the subject of an essay.

2. Welty lists many of the children's tales she read and loved as she grew up. If you have read any of them, reread one and, in an analytical essay, suggest why it continues to appeal to children.

3. "Learning stamps you with its moments. Childhood's learning is made up of moments. It isn't steady. It's a pulse" (paragraph 16). Reflect on your own educational process, both formal and informal; then write an essay in response to Welty's observation about how learning occurs. You may find Alfred North Whitehead's essay "The Rhythmic Claims of Freedom and Discipline" (NR 475) helpful.

VLADIMIR NABOKOV

Good Readers and Good Writers

The Norton Reader, p. 1025; Shorter Edition, p. 613

Although Nabokov is well known to teachers of literature and writing, his work may be unfamiliar to students. In preparation for this essay on reading and writing fiction, you may want them to read a short story by Nabokov, in order to consider connections among his fiction, his theory of fiction, and the writers he prefers.

More generally, you may want to ask students what they expect from fiction: why they read, what pleases them, what satisfies them at a story's end. Nabokov's views on what "good readers" ought to expect from fiction are likely to prove quite different from theirs; indeed, through the mock "quiz" he gives, Nabokov insists that action, emotional identification, and historical interest are not "good" motives for reading. The views of other essayists in this section—Eudora Welty, in "One Writer's Beginnings" (NR 1019, SE 607), and Katha Pollitt, in "Does a Literary Canon Matter?" (NR 1047, SE 618)—will serve to counterpoise Nabokov's views.

Questions from the NR11

1. Make a list of the qualities that Nabokov believes "good readers" should have; then make a list of the qualities he believes "good writers" should have. Do they correspond? Why or why not?
2. Nabokov, as he points out in the conclusion to this essay (paragraphs 14–16), considers the writer from three points of view: as storyteller, as teacher, and as enchanter. He has not, however, organized his essay by these points of view. Where and how does he discuss each one? Why does he consider the last the most important?
3. Take Nabokov's quiz (paragraph 5). Write an essay in which you explain your "right" answers (as Nabokov sees "good readers") and defend your "wrong" ones.
4. How would Eudora Welty (see "One Writer's Beginnings" [NR 1019, SE 607]) and Katha Pollitt (see "Does a Literary Canon Matter?" [NR 1047, SE 618]) do on Nabokov's quiz? Give what you think would be their answers and explain, using information from their essays, what you think their reasons would be.

Analytical Considerations

1. Why does Nabokov use a quotation from the French novelist Gustave Flaubert in the opening paragraph of his essay? Ask students what the quotation tells us about the style, tone, and persona of the writer.
2. Nabokov gives a "quiz" about "good readers" (paragraph 5) that he claims he once gave to students and that Question 2 (above) asks students to take. Why does he give this quiz rather than present his ideas more directly? Does he, in a sense, coerce readers into choosing the "right" answers and shame them for choosing the "wrong" ones?
3. Nabokov distinguishes between "minor" and "major" authors in paragraph 4. Look at the metaphors he uses to describe the "major" (or "real") author.
4. Nabokov also distinguishes between two varieties of imagination in paragraphs 8 to 9. What are they? How are they related to his "good" and, by implication, his "bad" readers?
5. At the end of this essay Nabokov retells the story of the boy who cried wolf. In the standard version of this story, the boy is devoured when a real wolf finally comes along; it is a homily on the virtues of telling the truth. Why does Nabokov revise it? What new meanings does he want us to grasp?
6. The essay ends with an image of an artist who "build[s] his castle of cards," which turns into "a castle of beautiful steel and glass" (paragraph 16). Ask

students to analyze this image, the sense of the artist it conveys, and why Nabokov chose to end his essay with it.

Suggested Writing Assignments

1. Write an argument for or against Nabokov's suggestion that "the good reader is one who has imagination, memory, a dictionary, and some artistic sense" rather than an inclination toward "emotional identification, action, and the socio-economic or historical angle" (paragraph 5).
2. Read a story written by Nabokov and write an essay in which you consider the ways in which his fiction reflects the values expressed in "Good Readers and Good Writers."
3. Write your own essay on the topic "What Makes Good Writers."

NORTHROP FRYE

The Motive for Metaphor

The Norton Reader, p. 1030

This essay, Frye explains, is part of a series of six talks for students and critics of literature. The title of each comes from a different poem (paragraph 19); "the motive for metaphor" occurs in a poem by Wallace Stevens that Frye quotes near the end of this essay, after he has developed a theory of poetic language and an apologia for literature. You can start with the poem: ask students about the relations between the self (Stevens's "you") and the world that he depicts in it. Or you can come to the poem after working through Frye's theory of poetic language—either way works.

At the beginning of the essay Frye poses a number of resonant questions with respect to the value of literature, the identity of poets, and the differences between art and science. Ask students what uses they think literature has. Frye locates the roots of imagination in human desires and mental capacities. Students will grasp his distinction between the world they live in and the world they want to live in (paragraph 7). But they may not care to reconcile them in Frye's visionary, quasi-religious manner: religions, he observes, also "present us with visions of eternal and infinite heavens or paradises" (paragraph 18).

Questions from the NR11

1. At what point in this essay does Frye come to the meaning of his title? What is his conception of the motive for metaphor? Why does he wait to explain it?
2. Frye describes three kinds of English, or, rather, he describes one English and three uses to which we put it. What are they?
3. Frye describes metaphor, forcibly, as nonsense (paragraph 20). How, then, do we make sense of it?

4. Robert Frost, in "Education by Poetry: A Meditative Monologue" (NR 1038), wants to make "metaphor the whole of thinking" (paragraph 14). What kinds of argument do Frye and Frost make? How do their conceptions of metaphor figure in? Write an essay comparing the claims each makes for metaphor.
5. Why, according to Frye, doesn't literature improve the way science does? What happens to old science? Read Thomas S. Kuhn's "The Route to Normal Science" (NR 928), and do additional research if necessary. Then write an essay in which you compare the fates of old literature and old science.

Analytical Considerations

1. How does Frye define three levels of the mind? How does each operate? Why does he take such pains to distinguish among them?
2. In paragraphs 5, 12, and 13 Frye presents his understanding of how science works. Compare his view with that of Jacob Bronowski in "The Nature of Scientific Reasoning" (NR 924, SE 535) or of Stephen Jay Gould in "Darwin's Middle Road" (NR 1011, SE 600), both in "Science and Technology."
3. How does Frye distinguish between the arts and the sciences? Ask students what limitations they see in his distinctions. Ask them also about their own values. Students who plan to choose a "practical" major such as biology or engineering instead of a major such as art history or English (an "impractical" major?) will provide examples on the spot of how modern society acknowledges the importance of science and questions the value of art.
4. How does Frye distinguish between poetry and religion?
5. Frye poses the question "Is it possible that literature, especially poetry, is something that a scientific civilization like ours will eventually outgrow?" (paragraph 14). What answer does he expect us to give? Why?
6. Plot the design of this essay, accounting for its organization, development, and points of emphasis. The concluding paragraph merits special consideration.

Suggested Writing Assignments

1. Write an essay in which you compare Frye and Jacob Bronowski ("The Reach of Imagination" [NR 210]) on the function of the imagination.
2. Analogy, according to Frye, is "tricky to handle in description, because the differences are as important as the resemblances" (paragraph 20). Write a description of something in which you liken it to one or more other things. Then explain the points of resemblance that make the analogy (or analogies) work and the points of difference that must be ignored.
3. Choose an essay from this section in which metaphor is important—for example, Robert Frost's "Education by Poetry" (NR 1038)—and using what you have learned from Frye, analyze its use of metaphor.
4. Frye observes, "We notice in passing that the creative and the neurotic minds have a lot in common" in dissatisfaction (paragraph 17). Write an essay in which you make something of his observation.

ROBERT FROST

Education by Poetry: A Meditative Monologue

The Norton Reader, p. 1038

Robert Frost's personal and rather quirky address to Amherst students in 1930 will acquaint students with one of twentieth-century America's most famous writers, whose poetry they probably have sampled but who looms as a literary figure rather than as a distinct personality. In "Education by Poetry" Frost reveals a lot about himself, not only by what he says but also by how he says it. The best way to approach the rhetoric of "Education by Poetry" would have been to hear Frost deliver it, because to a great extent the form as well as the content of this speech reflect Frost the man—at least the platform man. Since hearing him is no longer possible, you may want to have students read various parts of the speech as they think he might have delivered it.

Frost presents himself as a teacher—he did teach at Amherst College—and as a student. He has been to hear lectures on Virgil: see his praise of one that had "all the colors of an enthusiasm passed through an idea" (paragraph 11). Ask students what kinds of lectures they think he heard. He has been to hear a lecture by Niels Bohr: see his references to Heisenberg's, Einstein's, and Schrodinger's theories (paragraphs 16, 18, and 19). Ask students who have studied physics if Frost got them right; colleagues in physics say he did—but would be startled by his reduction of modern physics to metaphor. Students, Frost argues, should be able to discern metaphor in the world beyond poetry—in history, philosophy, psychology, and science. Indeed, he observes, "I have wanted in late years to go further and further in making metaphor the whole of thinking" (paragraph 14).

In "Education by Poetry," in a voice both humorous and cantankerous, Frost takes us on a circuitous route to make the point that poetry is essential to education because it teaches us to understand metaphor, and "unless you are at home in the metaphor, unless you have had your proper poetical education in the metaphor, you are not safe anywhere" (paragraph 21). This is a large claim; how much of its exaggeration is rhetorical? Frost also claims that poetry, by teaching metaphor, teaches belief—in self, love, country, God—and that belief is the only means of bringing something into being, of living creatively and responsively.

Questions from the NR11

1. Frost admires speech that has "range, something of overstatement, something of statement, and something of understatement" (paragraph 11). Does this spectrum appear in Frost's own speech? Show where and how.
2. What does Frost mean when he says, "unless you have had your proper poetical education in the metaphor, you are not safe anywhere" (paragraph 21)? Mark some of the metaphors Frost examines in this essay. From

what fields does he draw them? What does he say about each? How are they useful to him?

3. Northrop Frye, in "The Motive for Metaphor" (NR 1030), calls simile and metaphor "two crude, primitive, archaic forms of thought" (paragraph 20). Frost, however, wants to make "metaphor the whole of thinking" (paragraph 14). What kinds of arguments do Frost and Frye make? How do their conceptions of metaphor figure in their arguments? Write an essay comparing the claims each makes for metaphor.

4. Choose two metaphors from an essay in *The Norton Reader* about a field other than literature, and write an essay in which you consider the uses to which the author puts them, as well as their effectiveness.

Analytical Considerations

1. In this essay Frost first talks about riding a metaphor and knowing when it breaks down (paragraph 21) and then gives an example (paragraphs 24–34). In "The Motive for Metaphor" (NR 1030), Northrop Frye talks about analogy as tricky, "because the differences are as important as the resemblances" (paragraph 20). Put Frost's and Frye's passages together. Students should be able to see that they are talking about the same properties of metaphor, Frost metaphorically, Frye analytically.

2. Ask students to locate other places in this essay where Frost describes metaphor and to consider his understandings of it.

3. In perhaps a dozen places Frost digresses or becomes parenthetic. Are these digressions distractions or effective rhetorical devices that contribute to his purpose? What might a speech (which this originally was) demand or allow that an essay does not?

4. Ask students to determine if there is order or pattern in this essay. If so, what provides the thread of continuity? Is it Frost's personality? His theme? His imagery? Something else?

5. What does Frost mean when he says, "To learn to write is to learn to have ideas" (paragraph 39)? You may want to connect his statement with current ideas about writing as a mode of discovery.

Suggested Writing Assignments

1. The Latin poet Horace said that poetry should both delight and teach. Would Frost agree? Write an essay in which you answer this question by considering "Education by Poetry" and one or more of his poems.

2. Paul R. Gross and Norman Levitt, in *Higher Superstition: The Academic Left and Its Quarrels with Science* (1994), have attacked humanists who make claims about science without being adequately trained in it. Read their introductory chapter and write an essay in which you either extend their attack to Frost or defend him from it.

3. Write an essay in which you consider Frost's views on what he calls "the marking problem" (paragraph 7). Would you like to be graded by Frost?

4. Write an essay in response to Frost's declaration "We ask people to think, and we don't show them what thinking is" (paragraph 39). Draw examples from your experience and observation.

KATHA POLLITT

Does a Literary Canon Matter?

The Norton Reader, p. 1047; Shorter Edition, p. 618

Katha Pollitt's essay on the literary canon appeared in the *Nation*, of which she was an associate editor. She is a sharp, satirical writer who gives a debater's edge to her nuanced position. Her comment—"I found that I agreed with all sides in the debate at once" (paragraph 1)—is somewhat disingenuous; she also disagrees with all sides at once because she finds their positions too simple.

Pollitt expects her readers to know about the debate over the canon; students may not. However, in the course of this essay she describes three positions and names enough literary works—or "texts"—for students to identify what positions have informed their own literary education. Ask them what they read in school. Ask them what their teachers say are motives for reading. Ask them what term their teachers use for books—"literature" or "texts." Has their literary education reflected a conservative, liberal, or radical (even ultraradical) position on the canon?

Pollitt analyzes similarities as well as differences among the conservatives, liberals, and radicals: for example, they all believe that the books assigned in school are the only books students will ever read. At issue among them is "what books to cram down the resistant throats of a resentful captive populace of students" (paragraph 16). They may of course be right. Ask students about their extracurricular reading—their answers are likely to be depressing to readers. Ask them about their assigned reading.

Pollitt's position on the canon itself is closest to that of the liberals, as students are likely to discern. But, as she observes, "A liberal is not a very exciting thing to be" (paragraph 5). Her argumentative strategy enables her to present a more complex position than those advocated by other sides in the debate and to lend excitement to her liberal and inclusive views.

Questions from the NR11

1. Pollitt's strategy of argument is classification; she enunciates three positions on the literary canon. How many times does this three-part classification appear in her essay? Mark them.
2. What are the points of difference among the three positions? More important to Pollitt's own argument, what are their points of similarity?
3. What are the strengths and weaknesses of Pollitt's finding herself in partial agreement with all three positions? You may want to contrast her style of argument with Michael Levin's in "The Case for Torture" (NR 675, SE 407). Levin, like a debater, argues only his own position and puts down, entirely, the counterarguments of those who disagree with him. Is Pollitt's or Levin's approach more congenial to you?
4. Write a two-part or a three-part essay in which you argue the strengths and weaknesses of all three positions outlined by Pollitt.

Analytical Considerations

1. Conservatives, liberals, and radicals all believe, according to Pollitt, that "the chief end of reading is to produce a desirable kind of person and a desirable kind of society" (paragraph 14). What do students think of this argument? Do they themselves distinguish between medicinal reading and other reading?

2. In paragraph 12 Pollitt counters this simplistic account of reading (see Analytical Consideration 1, above) with a more elaborate one, which, she alleges, conservatives, liberals, and radicals suppress. To what extent does her account reflect students' experience? It may be useful to have students discuss this question in groups.

3. According to Pollitt, "if you read only twenty-five, or fifty, or a hundred books, you can't understand them" and "if you don't have an independent reading life . . . you won't like reading . . . them" (paragraph 11). Ask students to explain what Pollitt means. Even students who are readers are likely to need help in explaining how reading itself makes one a better reader.

4. While Pollitt disagrees with the radicals' argument that reading should enhance self-esteem, she also sees virtue in it. How are paragraphs 5 and 6 typical of her argumentative strategy?

Suggested Writing Assignments

1. Pollitt offers Randall Jarrell's list of "Important" and "Unimportant" books (paragraph 13). Make a short list of your own "Important" and "Unimportant" books and write an essay in which you explain your assignment of books to one category or another.

2. Look again at Pollitt's account of reading (paragraph 12). How many of the goals of reading that she mentions can be served by television adaptations of books? Write an essay in which you either take a position on television adaptations of literary works or stake out two opposing positions and explain your own by moderating between them.

3. The literature Pollitt considers in this essay is primarily fiction. Write an essay in which you explain the differences and similarities between her view of reading fiction and Vladimir Nabokov's (in "Good Readers and Good Writers" [NR 1025, SE 613]) and use their views to help define your own.

NGUGI WA THIONG'O

Decolonizing the Mind

The Norton Reader, p. 1054

Ngugi rails against the mental colonization of African children who as a result of the hegemony of English language education were discouraged and even punished for speaking in their native languages and, worse, made to feel that their language and culture were inferior. The children were fed a continuous diet of English narratives, English characters, and English traditions. The devaluation of African languages and African culture robbed the children of a strong sense of self-worth rooted in the culture of their parents and grandparents.

This essay could be used to spark a discussion about the privileging of English in the educational system in the United States, a policy that deprives many immigrant children of a chance to remain fluent in their native languages while they acquire English and that begins the process of emotionally severing them from the cultural milieus of their ethnic communities. Arguments have been made to support competing views: the position of English-only advocates is that immersion in English is the most effective way to ensure an immigrant child's quick adjustment to the expectations and challenges of life in the United States; opponents of this view cite research that proves that when immigrant children are placed in bilingual programs, where they learn English even as they continue to receive instruction in their native language in some subjects, their academic performance is superior to those who receive all instruction in English. The debate is passionate and divisive, with long-term implications for the United States' understanding of multiple cultures and multiple nations. Social commentators like Margaret Talbot write that Americans' ignorance of languages other than English leads to their misunderstanding the nuances of peoples of other nations.

In many other parts of the world, students routinely receive education in at least two, if not three, languages. Skill with a specific language is the surest way to begin to "enter" and learn about the culture based on that language, because, as Ngugi says, "Culture is almost indistinguishable from the language that makes possible its genesis, growth, banking, articulation and indeed its transmission from one generation to the next."

Questions from the NR11

1. The last paragraphs of Ngugi's essay contain the names of many classic and contemporary European writers. Why do you think he chose to include them? Can you relate their inclusion to the way Ngugi chooses to present himself in this essay?
2. What literary writers did you read in secondary school? Was there any theme or purpose behind that selection? (You may find some help in Pollitt's essay on a literary canon [NR 1047, SE 618]).
3. Write a paper characterizing the writers Ngugi was assigned when he was at the British school. What do they have in common? Who is left out? Then speculate on why such writers were chosen.

Analytical Considerations

1. What does it mean to be "mentally colonized"? Under what circumstances can an individual become mentally colonized?
2. Ngugi notes that when the system of education in Kenya was taken over by Englishmen, not only did knowledge of English become the primary marker of one's "intelligence" and worth, but also England and Europe became the center of the universe. Might it be possible to implement a

system of education in which a language can be privileged without an accompanying privileging of the history, culture, and traditions associated with that language? Could Kenyans have learned English without feeling that their own languages and traditions were unworthy?

3. What languages other than English should students learn in their schools? Why? In several countries, students learn English, the national language, and usually a third language that is commonly spoken in the region. What are the benefits or disadvantages of learning multiple languages?

4. Many of us read about different cultures and study the history of other nations through books written in English. What might we be missing or gaining by viewing these peoples and nations through the lens of English? For instance, how would reading a memoir in English about being an Iranian woman be different from reading the same memoir in Farsi?

5. Since 1986, Ngugi has been writing almost exclusively in his own native language—Gikuyu—although he still makes presentations to international audiences in English. What does Ngugi's command of English allow him to achieve? What does his "return" to Gikuyu allow him to accomplish? Discuss whether Ngugi, in the essay, advocates an outright rejection of English.

Suggested Writing Assignments

1. If you speak with reasonable skill a language other than English, discuss what your knowledge of that language does for you—intellectually, socially, emotionally, professionally, or academically.

2. Ngugi writes that when he was young, he was forced to read English writers and texts that recorded experiences that were unlike anything to which he could relate. One could argue that the classroom is the place where one goes to learn not only about experiences similar to one's own but also about experiences that are dramatically dissimilar. What has your own education been like? What do you feel about reading histories and literature that have nothing to do with your life? You may base your essay on a particular text or texts that you've encountered in the classroom.

ADRIENNE RICH

When We Dead Awaken: Writing as Re-Vision

The Norton Reader, p. 1062

Like Virginia Woolf's "In Search of a Room of One's Own," which follows, Adrienne Rich's essay takes up the problems and possibilities of the woman writer. Rich twice alludes to Woolf's essay in hers—once near the beginning (paragraphs 7–9) and again near the end (paragraph 22)—and if you prefer to work chronologically, you can begin by discussing Woolf's essay and then take up Rich's "re-vision" of Woolf's thought. Rich offers a much more personal consideration of the obstacles that confront women who wish to write.

In the course of this essay Rich tells us a great deal about her career as a poet—at least, about how it felt from the inside. From the outside it looked (and looks) different, for she has had a long, distinguished career as a writer. While she was an undergraduate, her first book of poetry, *A Change of World* (1951), was chosen by W. H. Auden for the Yale Younger Poet's Prize. She went on to write more than twenty books of poetry and prose and, in 1994, to win a MacArthur Award. You might ask students why the outward career, so obviously successful, might have felt different from the inside. Was the problem one of living in "traditional" women's roles—or is there something difficult about being in one's twenties and in the early stages of a career that is a problem for men as well as for women?

Questions from the NR11

1. Rich describes herself as hesitant to use her own experience as evidence and illustration in this essay: it would be "a lot easier and less dangerous to talk about other women writers" (paragraph 9). The dangers are personal—i.e., self-exposure and violating the privacy of others—and rhetorical—i.e., relying on evidence that readers may find limited, unconvincing, and self-serving. Locate instances of the first. Consider the second. What do you think are the advantages and disadvantages of Rich's using her own experience?
2. How does Rich work her own experience into a larger argument about women writers—and all women—at a time when gender and gender roles were being called into question? Find particular instances for analysis.
3. How does Rich describe the experience of writing poetry? How does it follow that her life in the 1950s, as she describes it, was inimical to her writing?
4. Rich refers to "the influence that the myths and images of women have on all of us" (paragraph 11). There are also myths and images of men that influence us. Write an essay in which you consider one myth about either women or men, how it gets internalized, and how it affects the behavior of both women and men.
5. Write an essay on a larger issue in which you focus on your own experience as evidence and illustration.

Analytical Considerations

1. Why does Rich use the hyphen in "re-vision"?
2. The body of Rich's essay depends on quotations from her poetry—from her early years as a student ("Aunt Jennifer's Tigers," written in 1951) to the present ("Planetarium," written in 1971, the year she also wrote this essay). Perhaps in groups, ask students to analyze each poem that Rich quotes in terms of the argument she makes: what evidence does the poem provide—and in support of what point or points?
3. If you have assigned "In Search of a Room of One's Own" (NR 1074, SE 625), ask students how Rich both agrees with and alters Woolf's argument.
4. If you have assigned "In Search of a Room of One's Own," have students look at Rich's characterization of Woolf's tone in this essay: "I was astonished at the sense of effort, of pains taken, of dogged tentativeness. . . . And I recognized that tone. I had heard it often enough, in myself and in other

women. It is the tone of a woman almost in touch with her anger, who is determined not to appear angry, who is willing herself to be calm, detached, and even charming in a roomful of men where things have been said which are attacks on her very integrity" (paragraph 7). How would they characterize Rich's tone? Is she angry? Is she in touch with her anger?

5. Rich ends this essay by speculating about "another story to be told"—that of masculine consciousness. What does she propose about the effect of women's "awakening" on men?

Suggested Writing Assignments

1. Rich wrote this essay in 1971. Write an essay in which you consider whether or not the situation has changed for the woman writer—or, alternatively, for women pursuing professional careers.

2. Compare what Virginia Woolf (in "In Search of a Room of One's Own" [NR 1074, SE 625]) and Adrienne Rich have to say about the problems and possibilities of the woman writer: on what do they agree? On what do they differ?

3. He: "Women take everything personally." She: "The personal is political." Write an essay in which you make a case for or against the personal.

VIRGINIA WOOLF

In Search of a Room of One's Own

The Norton Reader, p. 1074; Shorter Edition, p. 625

This essay is from chapter 3 of Virginia Woolf's *A Room of One's Own*, a central document in twentieth-century feminist criticism. The work began in 1928 as lectures given to undergraduates at two of Cambridge University's women's colleges, Girton and Newnham. Woolf then developed her lectures into a text. "In Search of a Room of One's Own" presents Woolf at her characteristic best: impassioned, witty, learned, and insightful. The essay operates on the historical, imaginative, and personal levels simultaneously, for Woolf writes about the plight of women writers in history—emblematized by the fictitious Judith Shakespeare—which leads to an expression of her concern that women who want to write need to find the means and space to work without distractions.

Questions from the NR11

1. At the beginning of her essay Woolf wonders about the conditions in which women lived that made it difficult, if not impossible, for them to produce literature (paragraph 2). What does she reveal about those conditions in the course of her essay?

2. Throughout her essay Woolf supplies many examples of the obstacles faced by women writers. Choose two or three that you found particularly effective and explain why they are effective.

3. How does the phrase "A Room of One's Own" suggest a solution to the problems Woolf has enumerated for women writers.
4. Has the woman writer of the twenty-first century overcome the obstacles Woolf describes as inhibiting the work of nineteenth-century women writers? Write an essay, based on research and/or interviews, in which you argue yes or no.

Analytical Considerations

1. Ask students what they infer from Woolf's title, "In Search of a Room of One's Own." Does the essay confirm their inferences?
2. Why does Woolf choose to focus on the living conditions of women in England during the time of Queen Elizabeth? What rhetorical effect can she achieve by using the age of Shakespeare rather than, say, the age of Pope, around 1720?
3. Explain what Woolf means when she says that "fiction is like a spider's web, attached ever so lightly perhaps, but still attached to life at all four corners" (paragraph 2). What other images might one use for fiction? Would they serve Woolf's purpose as well?
4. What, according to Woolf, is the image of womanhood gained from studying poetry and fiction written by men? Do you agree with her assessment?
5. What does Woolf mean by saying, "It is one of the great advantages of being a woman that one can pass even a very fine negress without wishing to make an Englishwoman of her" (paragraph 9)?
6. How does Woolf answer the question she poses: "what is the state of mind that is most propitious to the act of creation" (paragraph 10)?
7. Ask students to focus on the last seven sentences of paragraph 6 (about the bishop), and analyze what each sentence does. What is the total effect of the passage? How does Woolf use the bishop again? Does he become a metaphor in this essay?
8. Adrienne Rich (in "When We Dead Awaken: Writing as Re-Vision" [NR 1062]) says of Woolf's tone in this essay: "I was astonished at the sense of effort, of pains taken, of dogged tentativeness. . . . And I recognized that tone. I had heard it often enough, in myself and in other women. It is the tone of a woman almost in touch with her anger, who is determined not to appear angry, who is willing herself to be calm, detached, and even charming in a roomful of men where things have been said which are attacks on her very integrity" (paragraph 7). Ask students if they agree or disagree with Rich's characterization of Woolf's tone and her explanation of it.
9. This essay was once a lecture, shaped by the demands and conventions of spoken performance. After looking for textual clues that characterize the piece as a lecture, look at two other essays by Woolf in *The Norton Reader*—"My Father: Leslie Stephen" (NR 136) and "The Death of the Moth" (NR 1178, SE 697)—both written for publication, not for oral delivery. Ask students how Woolf adapts her techniques and style to an audience of readers rather than listeners. Perhaps even direct the reading and discussion toward the preparation of an essay on this topic.
10. In what ways is "In Search of a Room of One's Own" a personal statement? In what ways is it a cultural document?

Suggested Writing Assignments

1. Write an essay in response to Woolf's description of "that very interesting and obscure masculine complex . . . ; that deep-seated desire, not so much that she shall be inferior as that he shall be superior" (paragraph 14).
2. "Unimpeded" is a key word in Woolf's essay. Discuss what the term represents in political, physical, and psychological terms for the artists—men, women, or both—whom Woolf discusses.
3. Write an essay in response to the question: Do women today have a room of their own?

JOHN UPDIKE

Little Lightnings

The Norton Reader, p. 1085; Shorter Edition, p. 645

and

Moving Along

The Norton Reader, p. 1087; Shorter Edition, p. 647

Updike has written on art throughout his career; most recently, his art essays and reviews have been appearing in the *New York Review of Books*. But the slight, charming pieces here are very different from full-scale reviews or appreciation essays. They seem more like reaction papers, concentrating on a particular aspect of an artwork that strikes him and taking off from there. The discipline here is in the prose style, which is carefully crafted and definitely not the language of cool description and analysis.

It is valuable for students to pay careful attention to the way Updike proceeds. In the four-paragraph "Moving Along" he opens with a long and grand generalization about travel. Paragraphs 2 and 3 each take one of the paintings as an example, using fairly straightforward description that seems ordered simply by what catches his eye. Paragraph 4 wraps up the discussion of the general theme, travel, by listing one or two striking similarities, then linking them again to another kind of travel at the end. The conclusion seems far removed from the notions of jet lag expressed in the opening.

Questions from the NR11

1. One reviewer of *Just Looking*, the book from which these short essays are taken, called Updike a dilettante about art; another said these pieces produced not criticism of art but "an enhanced understanding of the writer and his . . . preoccupations." Using both essays as examples, show how these critiques of Updike are or are not true.
2. On the basis of these two pieces, what seem to be Updike's major interests when it comes to viewing pictures?

3. Compare the painting by Leutze (see www.metmuseum.org/explore/gw/el_gw.htm) to that of de Forest. What kinds of echoes does Updike seem most interested in bringing to our attention? Do you see any other connections?

Analytical Considerations for "Little Lightnings"

1. Now, Updike writes, he sees fireflies rarely, but in his boyhood summers they were everywhere. He wonders aloud about why this should be so, asking a few rhetorical questions, but he doesn't press. Why doesn't he?
2. The distance between the eras is nicely captured in the "exquisite little slatted box" versus the pickle jar. Does that box seem exquisite? Why?
3. Paragraph 3 has a startling sentence beginning "If science can be believed, the signal is erotic. . . ." Why wouldn't science be believed? Is this the artist speaking, invoking separate orders of knowledge? Note how he moves from "notes in class" to the heavy-duty terminology at the end of the paragraph. (Later, in paragraph 4, he reveals his source by saying "as the encyclopedia tells me now.")
4. What determines for us whether we can or cannot believe science?
5. Updike inadvertently kills a firefly and says "this death haunted me in giant proportions." How seriously do we take him here?

Suggested Writing Assignments for "Little Lightnings"

1. Describe the order in which Updike moves around the picture. Why does he choose this approach?
2. What important or interesting points does Updike *not* discuss in this picture?
3. Write your own description of catching fireflies, with either you or someone else doing the capturing. Include some reactions you might have now about the cruelty of the process. Did you think it was cruel then? Now?

Analytical Considerations for "Moving Along"

1. The part of travel that interests Updike here is its "eeriness" (paragraph 2). Can it be argued that most of the modern travel Updike deplores in paragraph 1 isn't anything like the lovely scene depicted in the artwork?
2. For some observers, these two images are very different. Describe the differences that strike you as most significant.
3. The ending seems to suggest that the representations of travel in both artworks are better than the real thing. How strongly do you think Updike means this?
4. Updike suggests that the "Canoe of Fate" has "a suggestion of allegory, of myths to which we have lost the key." Might this be true of "Baz Bahadur and Rupmati" as well?
5. Is this essay about travel or about painting?

Suggested Writing Assignments for "Moving Along"

1. "Men on the move brutalize themselves and render the world they arrow through phantasmal," complains Updike. Write two or three sentences in which you supply a "positive" spin on travel.

2. Find an image of travel that interests you (for example, an ad, a painting, a photograph) and write your own description, either in Updike's style or in a manner of your own choosing.
3. Research the story of Baz Bahadur and Rupmati, which has many variants. Then write a short, impressionistic piece describing which version of the legend this particular artwork seems to depict.

SUSAN SONTAG

A Century of Cinema

The Norton Reader, p. 1090; Shorter Edition, p. 635

Susan Sontag is a cultural and literary critic, a novelist, and a filmmaker: she has written and directed several films. She is also, obviously, a cinephile. Her essay, originally titled "The Death of Cinema," appeared in the *New York Times Magazine*; this slightly longer version of it, "A Century of Cinema," appeared in the small-circulation journal *Parnassus: Poetry in Review*. Sontag, assuming that readers of *Parnassus* would be better informed about European films than readers of the *Times*, added references that American students are likely to find obscure.

Nevertheless, her account of one hundred years of filmmaking is accessible as well as elegant. Questions included in the text ask students to locate themselves in relation to the one hundred years she surveys. Instructors will want to locate themselves as well. Some students will probably be taking or will have taken a course in the history of film; ask them to talk about it. You may also suggest, as a topic for research, investigating when cinema became a serious subject of academic study.

Ask students, too, what attitudes they think are characteristic of people who use the terms "cinema," "film," and "movies." Usually "cinema" signifies art, "movies" entertainment, and "film" somewhere in between. But, Sontag argues, in its beginnings film was entertainment "on a very high artistic level" (paragraph 7); now it no longer is. Where else do we find similar splits between art and entertainment? In literature, in music, in the visual arts? What is the cultural significance of these splits?

Questions from the NR11

1. In her essay Sontag summarizes one hundred years of film history, from 1895 to 1995. Diagram her periodization of this history. Locate her movie-going period (she was born in 1933) and yours on it. Which of the older films Sontag mentions have you seen? If you have seen other films made before you began going to the movies, name some of them. How did you see them—in a film-studies course, for example, or on your own?
2. What is Sontag's definition of a "cinephile"? Are you one? Is Susan Allen Toth one? See her "Going to the Movies" (NR 1097, SE 642).

3. Sontag has harsh things to say about contemporary films: they are "astonishingly witless," "bloated, derivative," "a brazen combinatory or re-combinatory art" (paragraph 1), reduced to "assaultive images, and the unprincipled manipulation of images (faster and faster cutting) to be more attention-grabbing" and, at the same time, "disincarnated, lightweight," and they don't "demand anyone's full attention" (paragraph 6). Write an essay using at least three contemporary films that you have seen in which you agree with, disagree with, or modify her charges.
4. Write an essay in which you compare what Sontag and Toth look for in film.

Analytical Considerations

1. What does Sontag mean when she writes that the "conditions of paying attention in a domestic space are radically disrespectful of film" (paragraph 5)? What are the differences between seeing a film in a theater and seeing it on television or video?
2. What, according to Sontag, are the characteristics of "cinema as industry" (paragraph 10)?
3. Ask students if they have seen any of the great movie houses of the 1930s. What are they like? (Pittsburgh's downtown movie house, for example, now houses the Pittsburgh Symphony Orchestra. You may need some pictures.) Contrast them with today's movie houses. What does each tell us about the place of movies in our culture?

Suggested Writing Assignments

1. Watch the same film in a theater and at home. Write an essay in which you consider differences in the film itself and in your experience of viewing it.
2. Watch for the first time one of the older films Sontag describes as a masterpiece and write an analysis of it. You need not formally compare it with a contemporary film, but you should allude to some features of contemporary film as a way of defining features of the older film.
3. Identify a new film that brings in a large amount of money in the first week it is shown, view it, and write an essay in which you identify features that you think make it a success at the box office.
4. Do research on when film studies (or cinema studies) became a serious subject of academic study and write a paper on the founding of the discipline.

SUSAN ALLEN TOTH

Going to the Movies

The Norton Reader, p. 1097; Shorter Edition, p. 642

In addition to writing books and regularly contributing to newspapers such as the *New York Times*, Toth teaches writing at Macalester College in Saint

Paul, Minnesota. In this short essay she responds to various kinds of films not by analyzing the films but by describing the men with whom she sees them. Because the essay is neatly divided into four sections, it gives instructors an opportunity to show how "classification" and "division" work as rhetorical modes. It may be usefully contrasted with Susan Sontag's "A Century of Cinema" (NR 1090, SE 635), which discusses film much more analytically.

Questions from the NR11

1. Toth describes four kinds of movies by describing the men she sees them with: Aaron, Bob, Sam, and finally no man. Make a list of the adjectives or descriptive phrases she includes for each man. How do such descriptions convey, by implication, her attitudes toward the movies?
2. Which kind of movie does Toth like best—or does she like them all equally? How do you know?
3. Using Toth as a model, write an account of going to some event or participating in some activity by describing the person(s) you go with. Like Toth, convey your response to the event by means of your description of the person(s).

Analytical Considerations

1. Toth's simple arrangement allows for a discussion of the rhetorical techniques of "classification" and "division," and it also allows students to consider how the order in which parts are presented imply a sequence (often less important to more important). Use the students' responses to Questions 1 and 2 (above) to discuss the structure of the essay and to ask whether the sequence from Aaron to Bob to Sam to herself alone implies an arrangement of increasing pleasure.
2. Ask students whether they think the men Toth describes are real, fictional, or composites. Does it make any difference in reading the essay? What advantages may Toth gain by associating men with movies?
3. Do the arts events that we attend reflect our values? Ask students what Toth thinks—and what they think.

Suggested Writing Assignments

1. View one of the movies Toth mentions and write an analytical account of it.
2. View one of the movies Toth lists in the last section and write a brief essay comparing your response with hers.
3. Write an essay in which you compare what Susan Sontag, in "A Century of Cinema" (NR 1090, SE 635), and Toth look for in film. Or, alternatively, write an essay in imitation of Toth's in which you describe going to the movies with Susan Sontag.
4. Write an essay about some literary or artistic subject that uses the rhetorical technique of "classification" or "division."

RICHARD TARUSKIN

Text and Act

The Norton Reader, p. 1100

This essay by a professor of music at the University of California, Berkeley, seems at first to be nothing more than a review of a CD recording of a medieval composer. Taruskin writes with skill about music, employing words and phrases that re-create the sound of the instruments and suggest the emotional significance of the composition. But Taruskin uses this occasion of a new CD release to talk about a twentieth-century audience's relationship to a piece of music from more than five hundred years ago, and then goes from there to posing difficult questions of moral value. This essay, then, is a useful example of how good art criticism does not confine itself to the art object in question, seeking instead to use the art object as a springboard for meditating about the quality of our lives and our conscience.

The printing press, with its ability to provide a permanent version of a story or poem, gradually eroded the value of oral performers, whose strength lay in their ability to alter or embellish a popular poem or story to respond to the exigencies of the moment—the makeup of an audience, the particular circumstances surrounding a performance, social and political forces, or even the weather. So also, the printing press and, later, developments in recording technology, gave a fixed quality to a musical composition that before the advent of mass production was much more likely to vary each time it was performed. Taruskin argues that this move to fix an art object in a definitive way and to make that definitive version sacred, not to be altered, places art above people and robs us of our humanity and concern for those among whom we live.

Questions from the NR11

1. What does Taruskin mean when he states, "music has been objectified as 'art'" (paragraph 2)? Explain this process in your own words, using Taruskin's four stages as a guide.
2. In the third section of the essay Taruskin explains what happened during a typical Renaissance mass. Why does he include this explanation? How does it aid his argument?
3. In the final section Taruskin raises the difficult question of how modern performers should treat "offensive" material (paragraph 24). What position does he take? What arguments might be made on the other side?

Analytical Considerations

1. How does Richard Taruskin go about establishing his credentials as a scholar of early church music?
2. Early in the essay, Taruskin declares, "Our musical difficulties are but the prelude to a moral quagmire." What are the principal musical difficulties he discusses? What is the moral quagmire he poses?

3. Mark Twain's novel *The Adventures of Huckleberry Finn* has been both criticized as a racist text (for its demeaning portrayal of Jim and for its frequent use of the word "nigger") and lauded as a supremely anti-racist novel. Many schools ban it for the deep hurt it causes African American students, but just as many schools consider it a classic of American literature. Taruskin, in discussing Busnoy's anti-Semitism, believes that a conductor today ought to expurgate the offensive language from the choral text and explain the excision. He faults Blachly for treating art with excessive respect and ignoring human concerns. Why would or why wouldn't such a strategy of excision or modification work for classic texts that have language offensive to certain groups of people? Or works of visual art that have offensive images of certain peoples? How should these works be read or viewed? Should they be read or put on public display to be viewed at all?
4. How does one decide what a work of art is? Who decides? What makes a classic?
5. The famous composer Richard Wagner is known to have been an anti-Semite, yet his works continue to be admired and performed. Discuss why an artist with obvious moral flaws deserves our continued consideration, and why we should or should not take into account the composer's anti-Semitic feelings.

Suggested Writing Assignments

1. Taruskin accounts for the persistence of anti-Semitism in part by pointing to anti-Semitic messages embedded in a great deal of "classic" art based on Christian doctrine. Discuss the subliminal impact of art. For instance, how do rap artists affect their listeners' feelings about women? What effect do television images promoting certain ideals of beauty have on adolescent girls? How does violence in the media influence the use of violence in society?
2. The lyrics of rap artist Eminem are considered to be homophobic and misogynistic. Make an argument for the artistic quality of his work and explain why his value as an artist should supersede any distaste the message contained in his lyrics might arouse.
3. Certain groups of people continue to be represented in negative terms in the media. Write about a recent movie, television show, or theatrical performance you've seen that demeaned people of a certain ethnicity, race, religious background, or sexual orientation. Discuss whether this work you saw can be called art.

AARON COPLAND

How We Listen

The Norton Reader, p. 1105; Shorter Edition, p. 650

Aaron Copland, an American composer, writes a cogent analysis of the listening process in "How We Listen." Because he wishes to inform and instruct, he takes pains to be clear. He first splits listening into its component parts (or "planes") through classification; he characterizes this splitting as mechanical but useful in providing clarity (paragraph 1). He then proceeds to analyze each part, and, finally, he reintegrates the three. The structure of his essay, his use of example and analogy, and the simplicity of his language lead readers to understand that they listen to music in multiple ways at the same time. His essay provides a model of how an expert can communicate ideas in a form accessible to a lay audience.

Analytical Considerations

1. Ask students to mark Copland's categories in "How We Listen." Are they mutually exclusive and clearly explained?
2. Copland's categories—or "planes"—are hierarchical and arranged in ascending progression. Why? How does he assign value to each?
3. Consider Copland's judgments. How, for example, is Beethoven "greater" than Ravel (paragraph 6)? And Tchaikovsky "easier to 'understand' than Beethoven" (paragraph 11)? What criteria does Copland use?
4. How does Copland use analogy? Ask students to mark his analogies and consider how they work and how effective they are. This exercise may be done in groups.
5. Copland extends his categories, by analogy, to theatergoing. Can they also be extended to viewing art, reading literature, and reading essays?
6. How do we take Copland's references to "simple-minded souls," one "timid lady" (paragraph 9), and "the man in the street" (paragraph 18)? Do we identify with or distance ourselves from them? How, then, do these labels function as rhetorical devices?

Suggested Writing Assignments

1. Write a rhetorical analysis of "How We Listen," detailing the means by which Copland succeeds or fails in discussing a difficult topic.
2. Apply the categories of listening discussed in Copland's essay to a piece of his own music. Consider a piece that has a theme.
3. According to Copland, "A subjective and objective attitude is implied in both creating and listening to music"; see his explanation in paragraph 25. Write an essay analyzing subjective and objective elements in his three categories of listening.

PROSE FORMS: FABLES AND PARABLES

The Norton Reader, p. 279

The parable and fable are didactic forms, ideal for conveying moral or religious truth, ideal for communicating advice by means of story and storytelling. Parables usually have human characters; fables usually achieve their special effect with birds, mammals, or insects. In writing a parable or fable, a modern writer will continually verge on straight prose narrative but also will, by means of narrative, preserve the essayist's essential commitment to the definition and description of ideas in relation to experience.

Two of the selections in this section, the New Testament parables of Jesus and the Zen parables, represent classic examples of religious teaching using the parable form. Two others, Plato's "The Allegory of the Cave" and Aesop's fable of "The Frogs Desiring a King," show how writers in the Western tradition have long used the form to explain and illustrate philosophical truth. The final two selections, Jonathan Swift's "The Spider and the Bee" and Mark Twain's "The War Prayer," give examples of literary fables and parables that intervene in contemporary issues and debates and, by means of a story, make an implicit argument about an appropriate course of human action.

Questions from the NR11

1. Many parables end with a moral explicitly stated—as in the conclusion to Aesop's fable, "Let well enough alone!" Which parables in this section include such morals? Which do not? Why might some writers choose not to conclude with an explicit statement of the "moral"?
2. For those parables that do not include morals, write your own version of a moral or maxim that might be deduced from the narrative. Is it possible to deduce more than one moral?
3. Write a parable that, while using a narrative form, has a moral or maxim embedded within it.

Analytical Considerations

1. Some fables, like Aesop's, end with a moral. Some parables, like those Jesus told to his disciples, have morals embedded within them. Others, like Plato's allegory and the Zen parables, do not end with explicit morals. Ask students to read the morals they have written for such parables (see Question 2, above), and perhaps write them on the blackboard. Most likely, they will vary in focus and even in meaning. Discuss why this variation occurs: what is it about interpreting a complex parable that makes it difficult to sum up in a single sentence?
2. In pairs or small groups, ask students to read the parables they have written for Question 3 (above), but without including the moral. Then ask the group to write down the moral they derive. Use these morals to help the writer think about where revision might be needed, as well as to discuss how and why some details in a story can lead readers astray.

Suggested Writing Assignments

1. Take one of the ancient parables and write a personal essay in which you use your experience to demonstrate the truth of the parable.
2. Choose one of the modern, literary parables, and instead of a story, write a formal argument in which you advance a thesis and present evidence for a view similar to that expressed by the writer.
3. Write a fable of your own that tells a story about "animals" but implicitly comments on human behavior.
4. Write a parable that tells a story and embed a moral or maxim within it.

PHILOSOPHY AND RELIGION

LANGSTON HUGHES

Salvation

The Norton Reader, p. 1125; Shorter Edition, p. 656

"Salvation" reveals in full measure Langston Hughes's gifts as a storyteller: economy and precision of language, a keen ear for dialogue, a sharp eye for descriptive detail, a detached, ironic voice, and a capacity for seriousness with humor. Hughes's re-creation of a revival meeting in rural America around 1914 or 1915 is an engaging cultural document. It is possible to see it both as an exposé of the sometimes dishonest theatrics of a manipulative preacher in front of a gullible flock of souls and as an account of the efforts of a community of believers to induce a reluctant inquirer to share their experience. It is also an account of an experience with considerable symbolic importance in Hughes's memory; as such, it might be considered a rite-of-passage narrative.

Questions from the NR11

1. Hughes describes how he lost his faith in Jesus at the age of twelve. How did the grown-ups in his life contribute to the experience?
2. Hughes expected to "see" Jesus. How did he understand the word "see"? How did he need to understand it?
3. Hughes was twelve ("going on thirteen") when the event he describes in first-person narration took place. How careful is he to restrict himself to the point of view of a twelve-year-old child? How does he insure that we, as readers, understand things that the narrator does not?
4. Write a first-person narrative in which you describe a failure—yours or someone else's—to live up to the expectations of parents or other authority figures.

Analytical Considerations

1. How do we know that "Salvation" was written by an adult? You will want students to notice the strategies Hughes uses to record the experience of a twelve-year-old and adult reflections on it.
2. The discussion evoked by Analytical Consideration 1 can be extended to a discussion of autobiography as both a record of and a reflection on personal experience with cultural resonance.
3. A rite of passage is a ritual associated with a crisis or a change of status. What are some of the ways the revival meeting changed Langston Hughes?
4. What is the tone of Hughes's first sentence? Of his second sentence? What is the effect of paragraph 12, which consists of one four-word sentence?

5. Ask students to analyze Hughes's techniques as a narrator. Is his narrative effective? Why or why not?
6. Compare Hughes's ability to recapture childhood experience with that of one or more of the following authors whose narratives appear in the section called "Personal Report": Maya Angelou in "Graduation" (NR 32, SE 18), Alice Walker in "Beauty: When the Other Dancer Is the Self" (NR 68, SE 46), and Wallace Stegner in "The Town Dump" (NR 18).

Suggested Writing Assignments

1. Write an essay on the ways in which "Salvation" re-creates a particular time and place. Why, for example, are some characters named but no specific location cited?
2. Write a personal essay in which you recount feeling pressured into doing something you would have preferred to have avoided. Try to convey, as Hughes does, both your feelings at the time and your present attitude toward the experience.
3. Write your own rite-of-passage narrative.

EDWARD RIVERA

First Communion

The Norton Reader, p. 1127; Shorter Edition, p. 658

Born in Puerto Rico, Rivera moved to New York's Spanish Harlem while in elementary school. He recounted his growing up in his 1982 autobiographical memoir, *Family Installments*. This chapter is a comic recounting of his first communion, a rite of passage for him and his family.

Rivera contextualizes his religious memories, reminding us that profound spiritual events and feelings take place in the midst of social, economic, and political turmoil. Here the background to his first communion is the grinding poverty of a welfare family, the nuns' rigidity, the neighborhood changing from Irish and Italian to Puerto Rican, the rivalries between public and parochial school kids, the personal relations between Rivera and his classmates, and even the quest for Puerto Rican independence, as Maestro Padilla's organ playing reminds us. In contrast to traditional narratives of spiritual development, this vivid story of a comic failure presents a lived religion enforced by family, teachers, and church officials while menaced by peers, society, and an eight-year-old's lack of confidence.

Questions from the NR11

1. Rivera (re)creates a conflict between Puerto Ricans and "others" who represent authority. Point out instances where this conflict operates. Does this theme dominate the entire essay? Why or why not?

2. Chart the behavioral conflicts within the young Rivera, who sometimes acts like an impulsive eight-year-old and sometimes acts according to the standards of his parochial school.
3. Describe an experience in which you or someone else was unable to live up to the expectations of parents or authority figures.
4. Write an essay in which you compare the use of first-person narration in this essay and in Langston Hughes's "Salvation" (NR 1125, SE 656).

Analytical Considerations

1. How do we know that "First Communion" was written by an adult? You will want students to notice the strategies Rivera uses to record the experience of an eight-year-old and adult reflections on it.
2. Have students compare Rivera's "First Communion" with Langston Hughes's "Salvation," also in this section, as rite-of-passage narratives. Does Edward Rivera show his first communion changing him as much as Hughes shows the revival meeting changing him? How might the difference in their ages contribute? How about the fact that Hughes's "Salvation" is a stand-alone narrative, while "First Communion" is a chapter in an autobiography?
3. Both Rivera and Eudora Welty, in "Clamorous to Learn" (NR 413, SE 244), mention "deportment." Ask students if the word has any resonance for them. Some will never have heard it, while others are likely to have had it engraved on their consciousness. Ask them if they know the word "conduct." Then ask them the significance of different schools naming these concepts differently.
4. Are there any signs in the depiction of Rivera as an eight-year-old that he will grow up to be an English professor and a writer?

Suggested Writing Assignments

1. Write about two different cultures coming into conflict through the eyes of a younger person. The cultures can be ethnic, as in Rivera's essay, or religious, generational, or geographic.
2. Rivera describes both a community and a family occasion. Write your own account of a community or family event that went wrong. Be sure to give your version a narrator who was also a participant.

JAMES THURBER

The Owl Who Was God

The Norton Reader, p. 1140

Thurber was a master of the brief humorous piece—shorter than an essay but longer than a joke. Like Aesop's fables, Thurber's are animal stories with single-sentence morals; compare this one with Aesop's "The Frogs Desiring a King" (NR 1112), with its moral, "Let well enough alone!" Unlike Aesop's, Thurber's morals are turned upside down (or inside out), and his humor always flirts with the subversive. In this fable, for example, his moral plays off Abraham Lincoln's remark: "It is true that you may fool all the people some of the time; you can even fool some of the people all the time; but you can't fool all of the people all the time."

Analytical Considerations

1. Tone is all-important to Thurber's fables. Ask students to consider his knowing narrative voice. What are its characteristics? Where have they heard it before? What makes it effective?
2. Does the silliness of Thurber's fable imply a serious message? Or is his variation on Lincoln's remark one more joke?
3. What does Thurber's drawing of a large owl add to the fable? Does the illustration (along with the other illustrations in Thurber's book) make the tale look like a children's story? Does that resemblance detract or enhance? Is Thurber paying homage to Aesop and reminding the reader visually of the seriousness of the fable tradition?

Suggested Writing Assignments

1. Invent a three- or four-paragraph animal fable of your own, leading up either to a well-known saying or to a variation on one. Try to achieve the same knowing tone as Thurber.
2. Write an essay explaining why the Thurber fable either does or does not belong in this chapter on philosophy and religion.
3. Read some additional Thurber fables; they are collected, with his line drawings, in *Fables for Our Time* (1940) and *Further Fables for Our Time* (1956). Write an essay about at least three of his fables in which you analyze his strategies; you may also wish to consider what his drawings contribute.

REINHOLD NIEBUHR

Humor and Faith

The Norton Reader, p. 1141

Niebuhr's text is a careful, unhurried, sober consideration of the proper place of humor in relation to Christian religious faith. Humor and faith, he notes, are intimately related: both "deal with the incongruities of our experience"; both "are expressions of the freedom of the human spirit." The difference, he argues, is that humor deals with immediate, obvious, surface issues of experience, while faith deals with ultimate ones. Hence, humor is a healthy precursor to prayer, he concludes, but "It must move toward faith or sink into despair when the ultimate issues are raised."

Students inexperienced with philosophical discourse may need some help interpreting this essay. The author assumes a readership comfortable working at the level of abstraction (life, faith, dignity, incongruity, despair, judgment, mercy, forbearance, justice, existence, irrationality, wisdom, contrition) without concrete supporting examples. Similarly, he assumes his readers are familiar with numerous schools of philosophy (such as asceticism, cynicism, naturalism, materialism, idealism), which he invokes but does not explain, thus leaving readers (or teachers) to supply the contexts by which his comparisons and contrasts among these schools may become meaningful.

The essay serves as a productive model for students in two ways at least. First, it can help students understand the value of looking for what is *not there*, what is missing from their topics. These absences are often the marvelously fruitful places to begin analyses. Niebuhr, for instance, begins by noting there is "not much humor or laughter in the Bible." After locating this ostensible absence, he works to demonstrate the intimate connection between laughter and faith despite their apparent lack of connection at the outset. Students can be encouraged to follow a similar pattern and look for absences when examining their topics, especially when their first attempts at development prove less than fully successful. Second, the essay demonstrates that the comparison/contrast form with which they are so familiar (and may find so restrictive) need not be a simplistic container for thought, but rather can drive deeply meaningful and important work when turned on the proper subject matter, especially when that work finds and elucidates correspondences between things that seem unconnected on the surface.

Questions from the NR11

1. Before reading this essay, did you associate religious faith with humor or laughter? Why or why not? What associations does Niebuhr make?
2. What view of man does Niebuhr convey in this essay? What view of God? How are they related?
3. Using one of Niebuhr's categories of analysis, write about an event in your life or an event in contemporary history in terms of "humor" or "laughter." If you think Niebuhr's category is inadequate to explain the event, say why.

Analytical Considerations

1. How many different kinds of laughter does Niebuhr discuss in this text? How might you characterize each? What is the cultural function of each? Can you think of a specific time in your life when you experienced each of these kinds of laughter? Who was there? When was it? Where, exactly? What happened?
2. Besides those delineated by Niebuhr, how many *other* kinds of laughter are there? How would you characterize these? What are the cultural functions of these kinds of laughter? Can you think of a specific time in your life when you experienced each of these kinds of laughter? Who was there? When was it? Where, exactly? What happened?
3. Of all these kinds of laughter, which ones do you find yourself engaged in most predominantly? Why do you think that is? What might these predilections say about you as a person?

4. Consider the section in which Niebuhr discusses "the profound wisdom which underlies the capacity of laughter in the Negro people." What are your responses to this section? Why do you think you responded to it in these ways? What does this section make you think about the author? What do you find valuable about this section? What do you find objectionable? Is it possible for you to separate the concepts the author is trying to impart from the language in which it is expressed? Why or why not?

Suggested Writing Assignments

1. Niebuhr notes that humor and laughter are not commonly associated with religion and faith. What emotional states *do* you most typically associate with God, religion, or faith? Why? What are the bases of these associations? Where do they come from for you? Write an essay in which you first identify the *single* emotional state you *most* associate with God, religion, or faith, and then explain the bases for that association. Locate and render in specific detail incidents from your past that will demonstrate to your readers why you associate God, religion, or faith with this particular emotional state, which will show and prove that your conceptual linkage between God, religion, or faith and this particular emotional state is a valid one.

2. In his section on "Laughter and the Self," Niebuhr says, "What is funny about us is precisely that we take ourselves too seriously. . . . The less we are able to laugh at ourselves the more it becomes necessary and inevitable that others laugh at us." A more schematic (and darker) expression of the same sentiment might be "We will continue to be humiliated until we learn humility." Write a narrative essay in which you tell the story of your personal realization of this universal fact. Select a singular episode from your past when you, as Niebuhr says, gained a vantage point from which to look at yourself and thus recognized the "ludicrous and absurd aspects of [your] pretensions." Develop the narrative of this experience with enough specific details for your readers to "see" the events and repercussions fully.

ROBERT GRAVES

Mythology

The Norton Reader, p. 1150

Graves was seriously wounded in World War I, wrote a powerful memoir of his experience, *Good-bye to All That* (1929), then turned to writing poetry. He had a lifelong interest in mythology, even claiming that his own poetry could not have been written without the inspiration of a "White Goddess." Late in life he was asked to edit two popular collections: the two-volume Penguin books paperback *The Greek Myths* (1955) and the *Larousse Encyclopedia of Mythology* (1959), both aimed at the general reader. This essay is the introduction to the second. Graves approached myths not as a scholar but as a collector, a writer who used them for inspiration. He was particularly attracted to Greek and Roman mythology, and he made his home in Spain's Balearic Islands, in the midst of the Mediterranean world that was the locus of many of the myths about which he wrote.

Thinkers about myths in this century, such as the Swiss psychologist Carl Gustav Jung and the French social anthropologist Claude Lévi-Strauss, have elaborated various theories about them: Jung regarded them as connected to universals of human consciousness, while Lévi-Strauss thought of them as having a grammar or sign system of their own. Graves regarded them rather more simply as "a dramatic shorthand record of such matters as invasions, migrations, dynastic changes, admission of foreign cults, and social reforms" (paragraph 13). He also regarded them as material to be used, particularly by writers, for, as he concludes this essay, "myths are seldom simple, and never irresponsible" (paragraph 16).

Questions from the NR11

1. Graves begins by defining the term "mythology." How does (or doesn't) his definition fit with your previous understanding of the term? Why does he choose this particular definition?
2. What are the two functions of myths (paragraphs 2–3)? How does Graves illustrate and amplify these functions throughout the rest of his essay?
3. Can stories from a religious text—the Bible, the Koran, the sayings of Confucius—be treated as myths? Using a story from one of these sources, argue the case either for or against this view.

Analytical Considerations

1. Graves introduces his discussion of myths by laying out two functions for them. To what extent does he organize this essay by these categories?
2. The first and last sentences of this essay are examples of Graves's ability to turn a memorable phrase. Ask students to pick out three more such phrases and to note particularly what purpose they serve. (Often these striking statements are summarizing sentences, introducing or concluding detailed listings of particular myths drawn from different traditions.)
3. According to Graves, standard European mythologies omit Judeo-Christian beliefs, while including myths from Persia, Babylonia, Egypt, and Greece, among others (paragraph 1). Is it ethnocentric to call some religious beliefs and not others "myths," in effect, to draw a line around Judeo-Christian beliefs and exclude them? As a follow-up to this discussion, you might ask students to write a response to Question 3, reprinted above.
4. Contrast the way Graves uses the word "myth" with Betty Rollin's use of the same term, in "Motherhood: Who Needs It?" (NR 341), in "Cultural Critique."

Suggested Writing Assignments

1. Write an essay on contemporary understandings of myth after collecting evidence from people you know. Ask them for their definition of "myth" and specific examples. Do their myths answer questions about origins and justify existing social systems?

2. Ask people you know how they differentiate their religious beliefs from myth and write an essay on contemporary understandings of myth and religion.
3. Cast yourself as a narrator unfamiliar with North American life and write an essay describing three myths that seem to animate people in this decade. (Jessica Mitford, in "Behind the Formaldehyde Curtain" [NR 314, SE 194], in "Cultural Critique," does something on this order. She describes American funeral practices as if they were embodiments of odd myths and makes the ordinary seem strange and somewhat preposterous.)

HENRY DAVID THOREAU

Where I Lived, and What I Lived For

The Norton Reader, p. 1155; Shorter Edition, p. 674

This excerpt from *Walden*, which includes many of the best-known quotations from Thoreau, is a touchstone of American philosophical thought. In each paragraph, one can recognize the origins of ideas that now permeate our popular culture. Instructors should be prepared to gloss Thoreau's frequent allusions, but a lecture on transcendentalism shouldn't be necessary before students can begin to work profitably with the text, since Thoreau's prose and imagery are mostly straightforward, and important concepts are approached repeatedly from a variety of angles. While students won't be challenged to understand Thoreau, they will be challenged *by* him: both his rhetoric and his message are confrontational, if not accusatory. Thoreau goads us to follow his lead, to live thoughtfully, simply, and morally, to cast off the illusory, cleave through the surface of things, and seek the reality of life.

Questions from the NR11

1. Thoreau's title might be rephrased as two questions: "Where did I live?" and "What did I live for?" What answers does Thoreau give to each?
2. Throughout this essay Thoreau poses questions—for example, "Why is it that men give so poor account of their day if they have not been slumbering?" (paragraph 7) or, "Why should we live with such hurry and waste of life" (paragraph 11). To what extent does he answer them? Why might he leave some unanswered or only partially answered?
3. Thoreau is known for his aphorisms (short, witty nuggets of wisdom). Find one you like and explain what it means.
4. If you have ever chosen to live unconventionally at some period of your life, even if only briefly, write about your decision, including the reasons and the consequences.

Analytical Considerations

1. Thoreau asks, "What should we think of the shepherd's life if his flocks always wandered to higher pastures than his thoughts?" What, indeed, should we think of a computer scientist, engineer, architect, chemist, etc., whose products at work are the most imaginative things he or she creates? In what ways is that laudable? In what ways is that tragic?

2. Thoreau cites an admonishing inscription on a bathtub: "Renew thyself completely each day: do it again, and again, and forever again." What does this advice mean to you? Why do you think it is so strongly worded? How do you renew yourself? Do you think it is possible to renew yourself *completely*, as is suggested? Why or why not?

3. What do you think Thoreau means when he talks of "our Genius"? For instance, he writes that "After a partial cessation of his sensuous life, the soul of man, or its organs rather, are reinvigorated each day, and his Genius tries again what noble life it can make." Similarly, he says, "Little is to be expected of that day, if it can be called a day, to which we are not awaked by our Genius, but by the mechanical nudgings of some servitor, are not awakened by our own newly-acquired force and aspirations from within, accompanied by the undulations of celestial music, instead of factory bells." What is the nature of our Genius, according to Thoreau? From where does it originate? What is its purpose?

4. "Our life is frittered away by detail," Thoreau contends. How is your life frittered away by detail? How many specific examples of such frittering details can you cite from your daily experience?

5. "We do not ride on the railroad," Thoreau argues, "it rides upon us." Consider some piece of technology you interact with on a daily basis. Discuss how this thing uses you more than you use it.

Suggested Writing Assignments

1. Thoreau goes into great detail about what he can see from his house, eventually noting that "Though the view from my door was still more contracted, I did not feel crowded or confined in the least. There was pasture enough for my imagination." What do you see out of *your* door? Write an essay in which you detail what you see from where you live. Do not stop with simple description; be sure to address how what you see "provides pasture enough for your imagination." How does what you see affect what you think?

2. In perhaps his most famous question, Thoreau asks, "Why should we live with such hurry and waste of life?" In perhaps his most famous maxim, he admonishes us to "Simplify, simplify." Write an essay in which you develop and explain your plan to simplify your life. Be specific. What concrete actions can you realistically take to simplify your life? How, exactly, will each of these steps work to reduce the hurry and waste in your life?

MARTHA NUSSBAUM

The Idea of World Citizenship in Greek and Roman Antiquity

The Norton Reader, p. 1164; Shorter Edition, 683

Martha Nussbaum is an academic trained in classics, philosophy, and law. Recently she has begun to write cultural criticism; in *Cultivating Humanity: A Classical Defense of Reform in Liberal Education* (1997), from which this essay is taken, she turns her considerable erudition to contemporary debates about liberal education and the curriculum. While some argue that multiculturalism is a newfangled form of political correctness, Nussbaum argues that it has its roots in classical antiquity and persists in the legacy of Stoicism.

Nussbaum introduces this essay by setting up two oppositions: one, the natural and normal versus the parochial and habitual; the other, nature versus convention (paragraphs 3–4); she concludes it with a third, multiculturalism as it leads to the affirmation of human identity versus multiculturalism as it leads to the affirmation of minority identities. Her focus in most of the essay, however, is a history of the idea of multiculturalism and multicultural inquiry from classical antiquity to the present. Her challenge: to be clear, engaging, and accurate without becoming bogged down with minutiae and qualifications. Instructors are likely to think she succeeds; students may or may not. It's worth pointing out to them that biography—her sketches of Diogenes and Marcus Aurelius—is one strategy she employs to present ideas in relation to each other.

This essay, compared with others in *The Norton Reader*, is rather heavily annotated and offers an opportunity to discuss the multiple functions of footnotes. Ask students to mark Nussbaum's footnotes (as opposed to the editors' footnotes). Which cite references? Which are explanatory? What kind of statement do her notes make about the range of her reading? How do they buttress her authority? You may wish to bring to class copies of Nussbaum's article in the *Journal of Political Philosophy*, cited in note 5 (NR 1164)—or just its notes—to contrast annotation for general readers with that for specialized readers.

Questions from the NR11

1. What does Nussbaum mean by "world citizen" and "world citizenship"? How does she use the concepts of (or quotations from) other philosophers to work toward a definition? Where does she present her own definition?
2. Why does Diogenes the Cynic play such an important role in Nussbaum's exposition? What concepts or examples from his life contribute to her understanding of a "world citizen"?
3. Write an essay in which you answer the question posed in paragraph 32: "Can anyone really think like a world citizen in a life so full of factionalism and political conflict?" Use examples not only from Nussbaum's essay but also from your own experience.

Analytical Considerations

1. Look at the biographical sketches of Diogenes the Cynic and Marcus Aurelius. How many of Nussbaum's points about multicultural inquiry does each embody? You might follow up this exercise by asking students' responses to Question 2, reprinted above.
2. Contrast the education of the Athenians and the Spartans, as Nussbaum presents them. What might be their contemporary analogues?
3. Citizens of the world are, according to Nussbaum, "philosophical exiles from our own ways of life" (paragraph 15). What are some examples of this exile in her essay? What examples can be drawn from the contemporary world?
4. In the course of this essay Nussbaum quotes Rabindranath Tagore, Kwame Anthony Appiah (both in paragraph 2), and the African National Congress (paragraph 38). Why?
5. Nussbaum acknowledges the force of the local and particular with respect to language and literature. How? Do you agree with her argument?
6. "The task of world citizenship requires the would-be world citizen to become a sensitive and empathic interpreter. Education at all ages should cultivate the capacity for such interpreting" (paragraph 30). Ask students if and how their education has developed this capacity.

Suggested Writing Assignments

1. Choose a custom that some people take to be natural and normal, and write an essay in which you argue that it is parochial and habitual. Or, alternatively, choose a custom that some people take to be parochial and habitual and argue that it is natural and normal.
2. Write an essay in which you characterize your own education or a segment of it (elementary, secondary, or post-secondary) as Athenian or Spartan. Do you agree with Nussbaum's claim that an Athenian education is superior to a Spartan one?
3. Take one or more instances, in school or elsewhere, when you behaved as an empathic interpreter of someone else. Write an essay in which you analyze how you behaved as one and the ease or difficulty of the task.
4. "To understand is to forgive"—so goes the adage. Write an essay in which you consider whether empathic interpretation is always a virtue.

VIRGINIA WOOLF

The Death of the Moth

The Norton Reader, p. 1178; Shorter Edition, p. 697

This essay, one of Virginia Woolf's best-known works of nonfiction, combines narration and description in the service of definition. Woolf writes with feeling but not sentiment, offering her reader a carefully realized observation before speculating about its meaning.

Woolf plays the role of observer and reporter in this essay. What begins as idle curiosity becomes conscious speculation, but no explicit conclusions are drawn. Although she points to possible meaning immanent in the death throes of the moth, she does not overshadow the event itself with analysis. Her technique here might be contrasted with that of other essayists who draw out their meanings more directly; students might be asked to think about how writers' choices interact with discourse conventions to create a range of possibilities in the essay form.

Questions from the NR11

1. Trace the sequence in which Woolf comes to identify with the moth. How does she make her identification explicit? How is it implicit in the language she uses to describe the moth?
2. Choose one of the descriptions of a small living creature or creatures in Annie Dillard's "Sight into Insight" (NR 1180, SE 700) and compare it with Woolf's description of the moth. Does a similar identification take place in Dillard's essay? If so, how; if not, why not?
3. Henry David Thoreau, in "The Battle of the Ants" (NR 756, SE 450), also humanizes small living creatures. How do his strategies differ from Woolf's?
4. Write two descriptions of the same living creature, one using Woolf's strategies, the other using Thoreau's. Or, alternatively, write an essay in which you analyze the differences between them.

Analytical Considerations

1. Ask students what aspects of "The Death of the Moth" they remember best, and why? Imagery will likely be relevant to their responses. If so, have students select several images and describe the primary appeal of each (visual, aural, tactile). Then ask them to determine how each image functions within the essay.
2. Does Woolf provide a thesis statement? Does she have a central point she wishes to make? Or is her essay a speculative exercise, more important for the act of reflecting than for making a point?
3. You may want students to describe the persona Woolf creates in this essay and how she creates it. Call attention to her use of the third person ("one") in much of the essay and her shift to the first person in the last paragraphs. What effects do these pronouns and their sequence create?
4. How and to what effect does Woolf use a kind of triple focus—the world "out there," the moth, and the narrator—in this essay?
5. What is the relationship between the life and death of the moth and the life and death of human beings in "The Death of the Moth"? Does Woolf offer any conclusions about death in this piece?

Suggested Writing Assignments

1. If the death of an animal has moved you to speculate on significant questions concerning life and death, write an essay describing and analyzing the experience.

2. With ironic understatement, Woolf writes: "The insignificant little creature now knew death" (paragraph 5). Yet this little creature was not insignificant. Write an essay explaining why.
3. Observe an insect and describe it from two points of view—one objective and one subjective, as a scientist might describe it and as a poet or a novelist might describe it.

ANNIE DILLARD

Sight into Insight

The Norton Reader, p. 1180; Shorter Edition, p. 700

Dillard is known for personal essays about nature and spiritual experience. "Sight into Insight," which appeared first in 1974 as a magazine essay, was then included in her most famous book, *Pilgrim at Tinker Creek* (1974). Attending to everyday matters at Tinker Creek, she is, without traveling, a pilgrim who awaits illuminations that reveal the timeless and universal.

Dillard accumulates examples and renders them in detail with a showiness and panache that may put students off. You may want to consider a single paragraph or assign single paragraphs to groups of students to consider; paragraphs 3, 4, 5, 6, 11, 12, 19, 27, and 36 will serve the purpose.

Each of this essay's six sections begins with sight. Section two ends with insight, section three with blindness, section four with untutored infant sight, and sections five and six with insight. All the passages describing insight warrant close reading. Dillard claims that the effort to achieve insight "marks the literature of saints and monks of every order east and west, under every rule and no rule, discalced and shod" (paragraph 34). Evelyn Underhill, in *The Essentials of Mysticism* (1911), schematizes the stages of mystic experience as reported by mystics themselves across religions and cultures: they go from an intense and enlarged perception of the natural world to a perception of realities above and beyond it to union with divine presences. The first two stages are present in this essay. Students are likely to need help in understanding and characterizing Dillard's descriptions of insight; contrasting them with her descriptions of sight will help.

Dillard also describes insight as unedited and unlearned (see section four), unverbalized (see section five), and unwilled (see sections five and six). Sight, she implies, is edited and learned, verbalized, and willed. These distinctions afford another way of contrasting her descriptions of sight and insight.

One of Dillard's masters is Thoreau. She quotes him directly (in paragraph 33), and his doctrines and strategies can be found throughout this essay, especially in her terse, apothegmatic general statements. Thoreau is represented in *The Norton Reader* by selections from his journal (NR 102), by "Observation" (NR 232), "The Battle of the Ants" (NR 756, SE 450), and "Where I Lived and What I Lived For" in this section (NR 1155, SE 674).

Questions from the NR11

1. Dillard works by accumulation: she heaps up examples. Sometimes, not always, they are accompanied by a terse, apothegmatic general statement, such as "nature is very much a now-you-see-it, now-you-don't affair" (paragraph 3). Locate other examples of these accumulations; mark the general statements that accompany them. What uses do these accumulations serve? In what kinds of writing are they appropriate, in what kinds inappropriate?
2. How does the kind of seeing Dillard describes at the end of her essay differ from the kind of seeing she describes at the beginning? How does material that appears in the sections on sight help her describe insight?
3. Take one of Dillard's terse, apothegmatic general statements and write your own accumulation of examples for it.
4. Dillard says, "I see what I expect" (paragraph 8). Write a description of something familiar, paying attention to how you "edit" your seeing. Then write a parallel description of it as if you were seeing it "unedited," as Dillard tries to see "color-patches" like the newly sighted do (paragraph 27).

Analytical Considerations

1. How can Dillard's descriptive prose be justified or criticized? How does she bind a series of descriptive statements together? How does she make us see?
2. Contrast two of Dillard's individual pieces of description, one of sight and one of insight. What are the components of each?
3. Identify doctrines and strategies in a selection by Thoreau (see NR 102, 232, 756, 1155; SE 450, 674) that also appear in this essay by Dillard.

Suggested Writing Assignments

1. Write an essay in which you compare Dillard's account of sight and insight with William Wordsworth's account in "Ode: Intimations of Immortality from Recollections of Early Childhood."
2. Dillard takes some ordinary creek water and places it in a white china bowl to look for small creatures. Do the same with some rain, creek, pond, or puddle water and report what you see, first in a plain, factual style and then with elaboration in Dillard's fashion.
3. Read Gilbert Highet's "The Mystery of Zen" (NR 1191, SE 710). Write an essay in which you compare Highet's reflections on the instruction in archery he describes with Dillard's reflections on giving up in order to see in section six of this essay (paragraphs 34–36). What are the similarities between them?

GILBERT HIGHET

The Mystery of Zen

The Norton Reader, p. 1191; Shorter Edition, p. 710

In "The Mystery of Zen," Gilbert Highet, a well-regarded teacher and author of *The Art of Teaching* (1950), writes about a German philosopher, Eugen

Herrigel, who studied archery under a Zen master for six years. Highet is at least as concerned with the method by which Herrigel learned as with the content of what he learned from his lengthy course. At a deeper and more abstract level, the essay confronts the difficulties of describing a dimension of human existence that, Highet concludes, cannot be analyzed but must be lived to be understood (paragraph 12).

In this essay Highet depends heavily upon a single source, Herrigel's *Zen in the Art of Archery* (1953). He credits it explicitly in his own text. He does not quote directly from it; presumably he summarizes and paraphrases. He does not provide footnotes (as this essay originated in a radio broadcast and, as such, did not require a scholarly mechanism). Most important, he brings to it clearly defined interests of his own that guarantee he will rearrange Herrigel's account and reshape it to his own purposes, and that virtually guarantee he will not plagiarize. These features of Highet's essay are worth discussing with students, who in their writing often find themselves relying on a single source and uncertain about what does and what does not constitute plagiarism.

Questions from the NR11

1. In his essay Highet depends heavily on Eugen Herrigel's *Zen in the Art of Archery*. What does Highet himself bring to the essay? Mark passages in which he makes his own contributions and summarize them.
2. "Zen teachers," Highet observes, "seem to deny the power of language and thought altogether" (paragraph 18). How, then, does Highet manage to write about Zen?
3. Highet says Zen is "a religion rather than a philosophy" (paragraph 22). How has he led up to this conclusion? What definition of religion and philosophy does it imply?
4. In his essay Highet addresses criticism of Zen only at the end, while Jean-Paul Sartre, in "Existentialism" (NR 1199, SE 719), defends existentialism as he explains it. Consider the differences these two approaches make in the content, organization, and tone of the two essays. What might Highet's essay be like if he defended Zen throughout, Sartre's if he addressed criticism of existentialism only at the end?
5. Write an essay in which you describe learning to perform a physical action. Pay particular attention to what you learned through language, what through doing.

Analytical Considerations

1. Consider Highet's contrast between philosophical and Zen meditation (paragraph 15). Is Zen meditation a goal you would pursue?
2. Highet's discussion of mystical writers (paragraph 18) is worth considering in detail, for he dwells upon the insufficiency of language "to describe experiences which are too abstruse for words." In what situations and in what ways does language fail them? Why do they "fall back on imagery and analogy"?
3. Would Annie Dillard be a likely candidate for Zen meditation? Use her essay "Sight into Insight" (NR 1180, SE 700) as evidence.

Suggested Writing Assignments

1. Highet refers to D. T. Suzuki's *Introduction to Zen Buddhism* as an authoritative text. Locate a passage in which Suzuki describes from the "inside" something Highet describes from the "outside" and write an essay comparing their strategies. You may wish to consider which description works better for you and why.

2. Highet confuses *The Magnificent Seven*, an American film, with the Japanese film from which it was adapted, *The Seven Samurai*, but he remembers the scene in which the elderly samurai selects his comrades (paragraph 16). View *The Seven Samurai* with particular attention to this scene and write an essay in which you consider the differences between Kurosawa's cinematic representation and Highet's linguistic representation of swordplay.

3. Write an essay comparing *The Seven Samurai* with *The Magnificent Seven*. Consider, in particular, how compatible the Japanese film is with an American western and what notable changes were made in the American version.

4. Write an essay in which you, like Highet, depend heavily upon a single source and credit it in the text. Be sure, again like Highet, to bring your own interests to your source and to reshape it to your own purposes.

JEAN-PAUL SARTRE

Existentialism

The Norton Reader, p. 1199; Shorter Edition, p. 719

Jean-Paul Sartre, one of the most famous twentieth-century philosophers, developed his philosophy of existentialism in the 1940s; this essay is one of his attempts to define it and to refute charges made against it. Sartre enumerates these charges in the course of the essay: existentialism is a counsel of despair; it deprives humans of a standard of conduct; it is too inward-looking. (It was also regarded as a serious threat to religion; as Sartre claims in paragraph 31, existentialism is "nothing else than an attempt to draw all the consequences of a coherent atheistic position.")

The essay's opening is the most difficult part; once past the first few paragraphs, Sartre keeps matters simple and provides drawn-out examples to make his points. However, his opening benefits from close analysis, which the questions below attempt to provide.

Sartre tries to distinguish his philosophy from Christianity on the one hand and Marxism on the other. He shares a great deal with both. Growing up in prewar France and attending parochial schools gave him early exposure to Roman Catholicism. From the 1930s on he was a committed socialist, frequently aligning himself with the Communist party agenda, as a kind of fellow traveler, not a member. He is careful to point out, though, that his political activism stems from his existentialism, not the other way around.

Questions from the NR11

1. "Existence precedes essence": this concept is central to Sartre's existential philosophy. What does he mean by it?
2. Sartre develops his essay by definition: existentialism, he says, enables us to understand the "actual content" of three terms: "anguish," "forlornness," and "despair" (paragraph 4). What are Sartre's definitions of these three terms? How does he distinguish among them?
3. Throughout this essay Sartre defends existentialism against criticism as he explains it, in contrast, for example, to Gilbert Highet, who, in "The Mystery of Zen" (NR 1191, SE 710), addresses criticism only at the end. Consider the differences these two approaches make in the content, organization, and tone of these two essays. What might Sartre's essay be like if he addressed criticism of existentialism only at the end, Highet's if he defended Zen throughout?
4. Sartre says, "when we say that a man is responsible for himself, we do not only mean that he is responsible for his own individuality, but that he is responsible for all men" (paragraph 1). Write an essay explaining how, in the framework of existentialist beliefs, this paradoxical statement is true.

Analytical Considerations

1. The essay opens with large, sweeping statements. A look at the opening and closing of paragraph 1 reveals not a developed argument but a series of provocations. Mark them. Why do you think Sartre adopts this rhetorical strategy? What does he gain? What does he risk?
2. Sartre draws analogies among the patriarch Abraham, a madwoman, and himself (paragraphs 6–9). What dilemma do they share? How does each resolve it?
3. According to Sartre, "No general ethics can show you what is to be done . . ." (paragraph 20). What examples does he provide? What examples can you provide? What counterexamples? Are they sufficient to call his generalization into question?

Suggested Writing Assignments

1. Write a paragraph in which you define "existentialism" without using Sartre's language.
2. Examine the term "existentialism" in at least two dictionaries and two encyclopedias. Write an essay on the commonly accepted meaning of the word. If you find differences in nuance or of substance among the entries, be sure to consider them. Also consider whether the entries appear to fit Sartre's own conception of existentialism.

CHARLES SIMIC

Reading Philosophy at Night

The Norton Reader, p. 1208

In this essay Simic uses writing as a way of thinking down the page. It is an excellent example of the essay as cognition in progress/process. As in the best work of Montaigne, Simic allows the reader to be a fellow traveler as he goes on his mental journey. His adventures in reading philosophy allow us to hear the diverse array of voices that are active in his consciousness one evening, and to follow the sometimes discontinuous ordering of his fragmented thoughts, from "start" to "finish" as they occur to him. He offers a sometimes messy string of personally structured elements, rather than offering us a cleaned-up, systematized, rearranged, and reordered revision of those thoughts.

Students often respond favorably to the highly variegated textuality of the piece, its hybridization of many discourses. It melds philosophical aphorism and quotation, poetic hyperbole and simile with autobiography, stark description, dreamvision, metacognitive jargon, folksong, profanity, and literary and pop cultural allusion in its attempts to render the wholeness and complexity of its subject.

Finally, Simic's text construes philosophy as a grand adventure, a sexy, ludic, poetic, heroic careening from the hyper-concrete to the furthest abstractions and back. It works well to counter students' common presuppositions about the aridity and tedium of philosophy.

Questions from the NR11

1. Early in his essay Simic describes a dream and its variants. What purpose do these descriptions serve? Of what relevance is his statement in paragraph 8, "My effort to understand is a perpetual circling around a few obsessive images"?
2. Throughout the essay Simic quotes philosophers. Choose one quotation and suggest how it illumines a personal moment or experience that Simic has described.
3. The shape of this essay has been described as a journey or a quest. What is the goal of the journey?
4. Write a personal essay about some kind of literature—whether biography or murder mysteries, political philosophy or sports magazines—that you read with a passion. Include details of when, how, and why you read it.

Analytical Considerations

1. Ask students to attend to the many different voices/genres Simic incorporates.
   a. How many different kinds of writing does the author merge together to form this text? How many different voices or genres can you identify? Where does each start and stop? How would you describe or name each?

b. What is your response to this complexity and variation of voices? In what ways do you find it attractive, engaging, effective? In what ways do you find it distracting, difficult, ineffective?

c. Compare Simic's varied textual surface here to the kinds of writing you are required to produce in academic circumstances. How do you think your teachers would respond if your essays featured his kind of multiple voices and genres? Why do you think they would respond this way?

d. Why do you think Simic chose to develop his essay this way? In what ways might the multivoiced style be related to the meaning of the text?

2. Ask students to consider the effectiveness of Simic's introduction.

a. Why do you think Simic chooses to open his essay with epigraphs? What is the effect on the reader of opening with epigraphs?

b. How do these epigraphs work to set us up for what follows? What is the effect on readers of his citing Nietzsche and Magritte at the outset? How does it work to construct our sense of the essay? How does it work to construct our sense of the author?

c. What happens in the first paragraph? What does it mean? Why do you think Simic chose to begin his essay this way?

d. In sum, do you think the epigraphs and first paragraph work together as an effective introduction for this essay? Why or why not?

Suggested Writing Assignments

1. Simic's text is peppered with provocative one-liners, with bold, well-crafted assertions without supporting evidence. He writes, for instance:

"Words are impoverishments, splendid poverties."
"Only idiots want something neat, something categorical."
"Understanding depends on the relationship of what we are to what we have been."
"[The] effort to understand is a perpetual circling around a few obsessive images."

Write an essay in which you mine your own history for the evidence necessary to support one of these claims. Render in depth and detail a specific experience from your own past that proves one of these assertions to be a true statement. You might choose to use Simic's claim as your thesis statement at the beginning of your text; you might also choose to use his assertion as the "moral" to your story, saving it for the end of your narrative.

2. Consider the italicized section of Simic's essay, the part where he says, "here's what went through my head just last night as I lay awake thinking of my friend's argument." As Simic does in this section, try your hand at rendering your actual thought process on paper as you attempt to work through some problem or come to some decision.

This is no easy matter: it will require you to take a mental step back and "watch" yourself thinking. It will require you to attend carefully to what is actually happening in your head as you think, to slow down the rapid-fire of your synapses, to make a slow-motion movie of your mind in action.

You will most probably need to experiment with unusual textual techniques in your effort to render on paper what went on in your head as you worked through that problem or decision-making process. Simic, for instance, portrays the dialogue among the many voices in his head, but he does so in controlled and traditional syntax. Other writers have employed carefully crafted, but seemingly random, "stream-of-consciousness" text blocks in their attempts to render the workings of their minds. You might also want to consider how you might manipulate the visual appearance of the page with special formatting so that it better represents your actual thinking processes on paper.

GREAT IDEAS AND ENDURING QUESTIONS: SAMPLE SYLLABUS

Each of the six units below introduces a question central to human experience that has provoked response from writers and thinkers over many centuries. Each unit is designed to last two weeks. The first week concentrates on readings that can serve to sharpen critical thinking skills through discussion and response. The second week allows time for conducting workshops on the students' essays and discussing additional essays that further reflect on the central question of the unit. To supplement the content of any unit, instructors can invite students to bring in newspaper or magazine articles or other readings that put the central question in a contemporary light.

Identity: What Does It Mean to Be Human?

First week: Readings and draft of an essay. The readings might focus on the concept of identity within a special group, in terms of ethnicity, gender, or sexual orientation, or they might take up general questions of human life and death.

Second week: Additional readings on the concept of identity, plus writing workshops and/or peer-review sessions.

Essays on gender and sexuality:

> Paul Theroux, "Being a Man"
> Harvey Mansfield, "The Partial Eclipse of Manliness"
> Anna Quindlen, "Between the Sexes, A Great Divide"
> Andrew Sullivan, "What Is a Homosexual?"

Essays on race and ethnicity:

> James Baldwin, "Stranger in the Village"
> Zora Neale Hurston, "How It Feels to Be Colored Me"
> Judith Ortiz Cofer, "More Room"
> Sonia Shah, "Tight Jeans and Chania Chorris"

Essays on life and death:

> John Donne, "No Man is an Island"
> Stephen Jay Gould, "Our Allotted Lifetimes"
> Elisabeth Kübler-Ross, "On the Fear of Death"
> James Van Tholen, "Surprised by Death"

Writing Assignment: Draft and revision of an essay, as suggested in the "Suggested Writing Assignments" in the *Guide*.

Learning and Language: What Is the Purpose of Education?

First week: Readings on literacy and education and draft of an essay.

Second week: Writing workshops and peer review, plus additional assignments on education, if desired.

Essays on literacy:

> Frederick Douglass, "Learning to Read"
> Dionne Brand, "Arriving at Desire"
> Eudora Welty, "Clamorous to Learn"

Essays on education:

> John Holt, "How Teachers Make Children Hate Reading"
> Adrienne Rich, "Taking Women Students Seriously"
> Richard Rodriguez, "Aria"
> Maxine Hong Kingston, "Tongue-Tied"

Writing Assignment: Draft and revision of an essay, as suggested in the *Guide*, especially Holt (p. 113), Douglass (p. 108), or Brand (p. 111). A personal literacy narrative could be especially appropriate for this unit.

Memory, Imagination, and Expression: Why and How Do We Interpret Experience?

First week: Readings on interpretation and draft of a writing assignment.

Second week: Writing workshops and peer review, plus additional readings. Instructors may wish to consider both verbal and nonverbal ways of interpreting experience or to use essays, like Updike's "Little Lightnings" or Morrison's "Strangers," that combine verbal and visual elements.

Essays on interpreting personal experience:

> N. Scott Momaday, "The Way to Rainy Mountain"
> George Orwell, "Shooting an Elephant"
> E. B. White, "Once More to the Lake"
> Maya Angelou, "Graduation"
> Wayson Choy, "The Ten Thousand Things"
> (Many other personal essays will work equally well.)

Essays on interpretation in literature, music, art, and film:

> Northrop Frye, "The Motive For Metaphore" (literature)
> Toni Morrison, "Strangers" (photography)
> John Updike, "Little Lightnings" and "Moving Along" (painting)
> Aaron Copland, "How We Listen" (music)

Richard Taruskin, "Text and Act" (music)
Susan Allen Toth, "Going to the Movies" (film)
Susan Sontag, "A Century of Cinema" (film)

Writing Assignment: Draft and revision of a writing assignment suggested in the *Guide*, especially Momaday 2 (p. 50), White 1 (p. 21), or Angelou 1 (p. 10) for personal experience, or Updike (p. 272) for art, Morrison (p. 36) for photography, or Taruskin (p. 277) for music.

Nature and Technology: How Should We Live In Our Environment?

First week: Readings from "Nature and the Environment" and other sections, plus draft of an essay.

Second week: Writing workshops, peer review, and additional readings.

Essays on living in or with nature:

Margaret Atwood, "True North"
Dorothy Wordsworth, "The Alfoxden Journal 1798"
Aldo Leopold, "Marshland Elegy" and "The Land Ethic"
Henry David Thoreau, "Where I Lived and What I Lived For"
Edward Abbey, "The Serpents of Paradise"
William Cronon, "The Trouble with Wilderness"
Joyce Carol Oates, "Against Nature"
Chief Seattle, "Letter to President Pierce, 1855"
Terry Tempest Williams, "The Clan of One-Breasted Women"

Writing Assignment: Write a personal essay that describes an ideal or appropriate relation between human beings and the environment. Alternatives might include: keeping a nature journal, writing about an environmental issue of local importance, or choosing one of the "Suggested Writing Assignments" in the *Guide*.

Freedom, Power, and Justice: What Is the Individual's Relationship to Government?

First week: Readings and draft of a writing assignment.

Second week: Writing workshops, plus additional readings. One topic for group discussion might be the politics of revision in the two versions of the "Declaration of Independence." An alternative topic might be the issue of justice for minority groups, as discussed by Garrison, King, and Guinier.

Classic essays and speeches on government:

Niccolò Machiavelli, "The Morals of the Prince"
Abraham Lincoln, "Second Inaugural Address"
John F. Kennedy, "Inaugural Address"

Thomas Jefferson and Others, "Original Draft of the Declaration
of Independence"
Elizabeth Cady Stanton, "Declaration of Sentiments and
Resolutions"
Carl Becker, "Democracy"
E. B. White, "Democracy"

Essays that reflect on or challenge existing forms of government:

George Orwell, "Shooting an Elephant"
William Lloyd Garrison, "No Compromise with Slavery"
Martin Luther King Jr., "Letter from Birmingham Jail" and "I Have a
Dream"
Lani Guinier, "The Tyranny of the Majority"

Writing Assignment: An essay suggested in the *Guide*, especially Machiavelli 2 (p. 220), Orwell 1 (p. 217), King 1 and 3 (p. 230), and Stanton 3 (pp.
223–24).

Truth and Belief: How Do We Know Right from Wrong?

First week: Readings on ethical issues and draft of a writing assignment.

Second week: Writing workshops, plus additional readings on myth, parable,
and fable as means of conveying moral or ethical teachings.

Essays from "Ethics," as well as the following:

Hannah Arendt, "Denmark and the Jews"
Philip Gourevitch, "After the Genocide"
Sallie Tisdale, "We Do Abortions Here: A Nurse's Story"
Paul Fussell, "Thank God for the Atom Bomb"
William Lloyd Garrison, "No Compromise with Slavery"
Martin Luther King Jr., "Letter from Birmingham Jail"

Parables:
Plato, "The Allegory of the Cave"
Zen Parables
Jesus, "Parables of the Kingdom"

Writing Assignment: Draft and revision of an essay suggested in the *Guide*,
especially Arendt 4 (p. 208), Tisdale 2 and 3 (p. 192), or one of the writing
assignments for "Prose Forms: Op-Eds." An alternative or additional assignment might be to write (or rewrite) a parable that conveys a modern-day
moral lesson.

WRITING ACROSS THE CURRICULUM: SAMPLE SYLLABUS

The second half of *The Norton Reader* is readily adaptable to a writing-across-the-curriculum course, whether one that emphasizes writing to learn or one that focuses on the rhetorical conventions of academic discourse. Instructors might simply choose five or six sections of the *Reader* and use a sampling of essays to construct a syllabus for such a course. We have outlined seven possible units corresponding to sections of the *Reader*. Within these units, we have integrated selections from other sections of the *Reader* so that multiple connections will emerge.

The seven units below are each designed to last two weeks. If an instructor feels the pace is too fast or wishes to give additional reading or writing assignments, any unit can be expanded to three weeks—and, of course, an instructor might choose to use only four or five units.

The first week concentrates on readings that show conventions of critical thinking and writing in the discipline and that might serve, in some ways, as models for the students' own writing. The second week allows time for conducting workshops on the students' essays and for discussing additional essays that reflect on the nature and concerns of the discipline. The content of any unit might be supplemented with articles written by professors at one's own college or university, with visits from such professors to discuss their own work, or with newspaper and magazine articles that address similar issues as they are addressed to a general audience.

Education

First week: Education from the teacher's point of view.

> John Holt, "How Teachers Make Children Hate Reading"
> William G. Perry Jr., "Examsmanship and the Liberal Arts: A Study in Educational Epistemology"
> Wayne C. Booth, "Boring from Within: The Art of the Freshman Essay"
> Adrienne Rich, "Taking Women Students Seriously"

Assignment: See suggestions in the *Guide* for the essays listed above.

Second week: Education from the learner's point of view.

> Frederick Douglass, "Learning to Read"
> Dionne Brand, "Arriving at Desire"
> Eudora Welty, "One Writer's Beginnings"
> Maya Angelou, "Graduation"
> Maxine Hong Kingston, "Tongue-Tied"
> Richard Rodriguez, "Aria"

Assignment: A personal essay about an educational experience or one of the writing assignments suggested in the *Guide*, especially Douglass 3 (p. 108), Welty 1 and 3 (pp. 109–10), Angelou 2 (p. 10), Kingston 1 (p. 127), or Rodriguez 1 (p. 129).

Environmental Studies

First week: Readings in natural history and draft of a writing assignment.

> Alexander Petrunkevitch, "The Spider and the Wasp" (natural history)
> Edward Abbey, "The Serpents of Paradise" (natural history)
> Chief Seattle, "Letter to President Pierce, 1855" (environmental advocacy)
> Henry David Thoreau, "Where I Lived and What I Lived For" (classic American statement of value of nature)
> Rachel Carson, "Tides" (natural history)

Writing Assignment: An essay about something in nature, whether an animal, a plant, or a place, or an argument about an environmental issue, based on suggestions from the *Guide* for these essays.

Second week: Writing workshops and readings about contemporary environmental issues.

> Joseph Wood Krutch, "The Most Dangerous Predator" (preserving Baja California)
> Terry Tempest Williams, "The Clan of One-Breasted Women" (environmental advocacy)
> Aldo Leopold, "Marshland Elegy" and "The Land Ethic" (classic statements of environmental movement)
> William Cronon, "The Trouble with Wilderness" (reflections on American attitudes)
> Joyce Carol Oates, "Against Nature" (controversial anti-statement)

Writing Assignment: Writing workshop or peer review, followed by revision of draft. Because this unit is especially rich and diverse in its forms, it could be divided into two units, one on nature writing, another on environmental issues. Students might then try writing one essay of each kind.

Science and Technology

First week: Readings and draft of a writing assignment.

> Henry Wechsler, Andrea Davenport, George Dowdall, Barbara Moeykens, and Sonia Castillo, "Health and Behavioral Consequences of Binge Drinking in College: A National Survey of Students at 140 Campuses" (scientific report in its standard form)
> Melvin Konner, "Why the Reckless Survive" (social science drawing on scientific research)

Alexander Petrunkevitch, "The Spider and the Wasp" from "Nature and the Environment" (scientific observation of nature)

Assignment: Draft of a writing assignment suggested in the *Guide*, especially those for Wechsler et al. (p. 247), Petrunkevitch (p. 160), or Konner (p. 253). Alternatively, ask students to conduct a survey of drinking habits on campus (of the sort that Wechsler et al. did) and write up their findings in the form of a scientific report.

Second week: Writing workshops, plus additional readings on technology or on the nature of scientific thinking.

Essays on technology:

John Hockenberry, "The Next Brainiacs"
Neil Postman, "Virtual Students, Digital Classroom"

Essays on scientific method:

Jacob Bronowski, "The Nature of Scientific Reasoning"
Thomas S. Kuhn, "The Route to Normal Science"
Stephen Jay Gould, "Darwin's Middle Road"
Steven Weinberg, "Can Science Explain Everything? Anything?"

Assignment: Writing workshop or peer review, followed by revision of draft. Alternatively, students might (1) write an account of the invention of some useful object or (2) do additional readings and a writing assignment on the nature of science and scientific thinking, as derived from the *Guide* entries for Bronowski, Kuhn, Gould, or Weinberg.

History

First week: Readings and draft of a writing assignment.

History essays:

Barbara Tuchman, "'This Is the End of the World': The Black Death" (classic history)
Amitav Ghosh, "The Ghosts of Mrs. Gandhi" (public and personal history)
Hannah Arendt, "Denmark and the Jews" (history and moral philosophy)
Cherokee Memorials (historical document)
Walt Whitman, "Death of Abraham Lincoln" (historical document)

Assignment: Draft of a writing assignment suggested in the *Guide*, especially those combining the students' personal experiences or knowledge of history with official, public history—as in Ghosh's account.

Second week: Writing workshops, plus additional readings on the theory and practice of writing history.

Essays about history:

> Frances FitzGerald, "Rewriting American History"
> H. Bruce Franklin, "From Realism to Virtual Reality: Images of
>   America's Wars"
> Edward Hallett Carr, "The Historian and His Facts"
> Henry David Thoreau, "The Battle of the Ants"

Assignment: Writing workshop or peer review, followed by revision of draft. You might use the second set of readings to help students reflect on the history assignments they are writing. Additional assignments on historical writing can be found in the *Guide* entries for Thoreau 1 (p. 199), FitzGerald 1 (p. 212), or Carr 1 and 3 (p. 215).

Philosophy and Ethics

First week: Readings and draft of a writing assignment.

Philosophy:

> Plato, "The Allegory of the Cave" (philosophical text)
> Martha Nussbaum, "The Idea of World Citizenship in Greek and
>   Roman Antiquity" (modern uses of classical philosophy)
> Gilbert Highet, "The Mystery of Zen" (philosophical discussion)
> Zen Parables (religious document)
> Reinhold Niebuhr, "Humor and Faith" (theological meditation)
> Jean-Paul Sartre, "Existentialism" (philosophical text)

Assignment: Draft an essay that explores one of the above philosophies in greater depth. See writing assignment suggestions in the *Guide*, especially Sartre 1 and 2 (p. 297) or Niebuhr 1 (p. 286).

Second week: Writing workshops, plus additional readings. Because the philosophical positions presented above are so complex, instructors may wish to devote additional discussion to each. Alternatively, one might concentrate on ethical questions such as those raised by the following essays, all but one of which are from "Ethics":

> Paul Fussell, "Thank God for the Atom Bomb"
> Sallie Tisdale, "We Do Abortions Here: A Nurse's Story"
> Michael Levin, "The Case for Torture"

Assignment: Writing workshop or peer review, followed by revision of draft. Students who have chosen to write on the same issue might work together in small groups to test and refine their arguments.

Literature and the Arts

First week: Readings on literature and draft of a writing assignment.

> Vladimir Nabokov, "Good Readers and Good Writers"
> Eudora Welty, "One Writer's Beginnings"
> Northrop Frye, "The Motive for Metaphor"
> Robert Frost, "Education by Poetry: A Meditative Monologue"
> Ngugi wa Thiong'o, "Decolonizing the Mind"

Supplementary reading: A short story by Nabokov, Welty, Woolf, or Ngugi, or a poem by Frost.

Assignment: Draft of an assignment suggested in the *Guide*, especially Nabokov 2 and 3 (p. 260).

Second week: Writing workshop, plus additional readings in other arts. Instructors may wish to divide the readings listed above into two segments, one on fiction, the other on poetry; or they may wish to consider a second art form, such as film or music.

> Susan Allen Toth, "Going to the Movies" (film)
> Susan Sontag, "A Century of Cinema" (film)
> H. Bruce Franklin, "From Realism to Virtual Reality: Images of
>   America's Wars" (war photography)
> Toni Morrison, "Strangers" (photography)
> Nora Ephron, "The Boston Photographs" (photojournalism)
> John Updike, "Little Lightnings" and "Moving Along" (art)
> Richard Taruskin, "Text and Act" (music)
> Aaron Copland, "How We Listen" (music)

Assignment: Writing workshop or peer review, followed by revision of draft. For an assignment on film, see the questions in the *Reader* for Toth and Sontag, as well as the writing suggestions in the *Guide*, especially Toth 2 (p. 275) and Sontag 1 (p. 274). The *Reader* and *Guide* also include questions about photographs.

Politics and Government

First week: Readings and writing assignment (draft).

> Niccolò Machiavelli, "The Morals of the Prince" (political treatise)
> Martin Luther King Jr., "Letter from Birmingham Jail" (political
>   treatise)
> Jonathan Swift, "A Modest Proposal" (parody of political treatise)
> George Orwell, "Shooting an Elephant" (personal essay on
>   colonialism)
> Jamaica Kincaid, "The Ugly Tourist" (personal essay on colonialism)

Assignment: A writing assignment suggested in the *Guide*, especially Machiavelli 1 to 3 (p. 220), Orwell 1 (p. 217), or King 2 (p. 230).

Second week: Writing workshops, plus additional readings on American politics.

> Thomas Jefferson, "Original Draft of the Declaration of
>   Independence"
> Thomas Jefferson and Others, "The Declaration of Independence"
> Elizabeth Cady Stanton, "Declaration of Sentiments and Resolutions"
> Abraham Lincoln, "Second Inaugural Address"
> John F. Kennedy, "Inaugural Address"

Assignment: Workshop on assignment from the first week, with perhaps an additional assignment on Jefferson, Stanton, or Lincoln, as suggested in the *Guide*. Alternatively, this unit might focus on the "Declaration of Independence," its draft forms, and its influence on later documents such as Stanton's.

RACE, CLASS, AND GENDER: SAMPLE SYLLABUS

The Eleventh Edition of *The Norton Reader* lends itself particularly well to extended classroom explorations of race, class, and gender. Many essays that directly address these issues are grouped together in separate sections (such as the end of "Cultural Critique," pp. 341–59 on gender, and 360–86 on race). But since essays in all parts of the book deal with race, class, and gender, we have outlined five possible two-week units. Instructors can assign any number of these units, since the selections do not overlap. Thus in a one-semester course an instructor may wish to assign the two-week unit "Race: A Variety of Perspectives" and the two-week unit "Gender: Women's and Men's Perspectives." A deeper examination of these issues is possible by assigning the additional two-week units on race and on gender.

We present these units as suggestions. If an instructor feels the pace is too fast or wishes to give additional reading or writing assignments, any of the five units could be expanded to three weeks. And the reading selections given in the five units do not exhaust all of *The Norton Reader*'s rich collection of essays touching on race, class, or gender. Instructors can use many additional essays from other parts of the book and may also want to assign other essays and reading selections from current books, newspapers, or periodicals.

In each of the five units, the first week introduces the issue and includes an essay assignment. The second week allows time for workshops, for further drafts of the first week's essay, and for additional reading and writing assignments.

Race: The African American Experience

First week: Readings and draft of a writing assignment.

> Martin Luther King Jr., "Letter from Birmingham Jail" (struggle for equal rights)
> Maya Angelou, "Graduation" (struggle for equal rights)
> James Baldwin, "Stranger in the Village" (confronting racism)
> Gloria Naylor, "Mommy, What Does 'Nigger' Mean?" (confronting racism)

Assignment: Describe whether you think these writers' dependence on their personal experiences strengthens or weakens their cases for racial equality. What does a writer gain from using his or her own experience? What are the potential losses or limitations?

Second week: Writing workshops and additional drafts of week one's writing assignment, along with essays that add complexity to the first week's readings.

> Zora Neale Hurston, "How It Feels to Be Colored Me"
> Henry Louis Gates Jr., "In the Kitchen"
> John Edgar Wideman, "Hoop Roots"
> Jamaica Kincaid, "Sowers and Reapers"

Assignment: Writing workshop or peer review, followed by revision of draft. All three of the second week's essays employ personal experience; however, in each case the arguments in favor of equality take a backseat to celebrations of the special qualities of life in the African American community. (It is useful to have students trace the arguments in favor of equality that are implicit in each essay.)

Race: A Variety of Perspectives

First week: Readings and draft of a writing assignment.

> Shelby Steele, "The Recoloring of Campus Life" (racial divisions on campus)
> Richard Rodriguez, "Aria" (bilingualism)
> Chief Seattle, "Letter to President Pierce, 1855" (Native Americans in search of recognition)
> Judith Ortiz Cofer, "More Room" (Latina concerns)

Assignment: Draft an essay about "making it" in American society and what has to be left behind. Use examples from your own experience, the week's readings, and perspectives of people you know about.

Second week: Writing workshops and additional drafts of week one's writing assignment, along with essays that add complexity to the first week's readings.

> Edward Rivera, "First Communion"
> Brent Staples, "Black Men and Public Space"
> Debra Dickerson, "Who Shot Johnny?"

Assignment: Writing workshop or peer review, followed by revision of draft. These additional essays are about failing to "make it" in acceptable ways. Rivera cannot receive his First Communion, while Staples cannot remain inconspicuous, no matter how hard he tries. The essays, in very different ways, raise questions about exactly what "making it" means.

Class

First week: Readings and draft of a writing assignment.

> Lars Eighner, "On Dumpster Diving" (homelessness)
> George Orwell, "Shooting an Elephant" (colonial rule and subalterns)
> Niccolò Machiavelli, "The Morals of the Prince" (training for aristocrats)

Assignment: Draft an essay on how these authors react to others who aren't of the same standing in society. What is their opinion of people who are higher or lower on the social ladder? How much do they identify with people who are at the same level they are? How do they regard the struggle for power?

Second week: Writing workshops and additional drafts of week one's writing assignment, along with essays that add complexity to the first week's readings.

> Jonathan Swift, "A Modest Proposal"
> Ngugi wa Thiong'o, "Decolonizing the Mind"

Assignment: Writing workshop or peer review, followed by revision of draft. The second week's readings stand in stark contrast to each other (and to the first week's readings as well). Both Swift and Ngugi offer solutions to the problems of colonized peoples, but Swift uses satire, whereas Ngugi uses "straight" argument. Students need to see that Swift, two centuries ago, rejects the meliorist solutions proposed by moderates and instead reacts with barely suppressed rage. (Some students need to be shown that Swift's "solution" is not merely ghoulishly clever but represents a moment of genuine despair about the possibility that any simple "project" can improve the lot of the poor.)

Gender: Women's and Men's Perspectives

First week: Readings and draft of a writing assignment.

> Anna Quindlen, "Between the Sexes, a Great Divide" (woman's observation)
> Paul Theroux, "Being a Man" (male perspective)
> Scott Russell Sanders, "Looking at Women" (male perspective)
> John McMurtry, "Kill 'Em! Crush 'Em! Eat 'Em Raw!" (sports and masculinity)
> Alice Walker, "Beauty: When the Other Dancer Is the Self" (self-esteem)

Assignment: Draft an essay about whether people consider the differences in men's and women's attitudes inherent in human nature or the product of society. Base your essay on the beliefs of those you know and of these writers.

Second week: Writing workshops and additional drafts of week one's writing assignment, along with essays that add complexity to the first week's readings.

> Harvey Mansfield, "The Partial Eclipse of Manliness"
> Betty Rollin, "Motherhood: Who Needs It?"
> Gloria Anzaldúa, "How to Tame a Wild Tongue"

Assignment: Writing workshop or peer review, followed by revision of draft. These three essays can serve as test cases for the writing assignment students have been drafting. Discussion of Mansfield, Rollin, and Anzaldúa will help sharpen the drafts and allow students to evaluate the nature of the evidence they are using.

Gender: Women, Language, and Schooling

First week: Readings on literature and writing assignment (draft).

> Adrienne Rich, "Taking Women Students Seriously" (school)
> Anne Fadiman, "The His'er Problem" (language)
> Amy Cunningham, "Why Women Smile"

Assignment: Using your own experience and the works you have read, describe the particular difficulties women have faced in schools. Then speculate on what it will take to overcome these obstacles, however large or small they seem in the present.

Second week: Writing workshop or peer review, followed by revision of draft.

> Maxine Hong Kingston, "Tongue-Tied" (training for women)
> Lord Chesterfield, "Letter to His Son" (training for men)
> Mary Wollstonecraft, "A Vindication of the Rights of Women"
>   (women's education)
> Lady Mary Wortley Montagu, "Letter to the Countess of Bute, Lady
>   Montagu's Daughter"

This follow-up lends itself particularly well to anecdotal evidence from class members about parental advice, warnings, and examples. Such testimony may not have much impact singly, but can be overwhelming when taken as an indication of broad cultural values transmitted from generation to generation.

An alternative is to have class members recall clichés and common sayings that embody male/female stereotypes.

PERSUASION AND ARGUMENT: SAMPLE SYLLABUS

The Norton Reader lends itself to a course emphasizing persuasion and argument by including many essays that illustrate a range of argumentative strategies and personae. The sections "Ethics," "Politics and Government," and "Nature and the Environment" are the most concentrated sources of persuasive and argumentative essays: in the Regular Edition, "Ethics" has eight, "Politics and Government" seven, and "Nature and the Environment" nine; while in the Shorter Edition, "Ethics" has six, "Politics and Government" five, and "Nature and the Environment" three. In addition, in the Regular Edition (though not in the Shorter Edition), "Op-Eds" has seven, and a new section, Spoken Words," has six. Appended to this syllabus are the argumentative and persuasive essays in the Regular Edition listed by section; those that also appear in the Shorter Edition are asterisked.

At the same time *The Norton Reader* includes other kinds of essays that provide material for persuasive and argumentative essays and suggests assignments using them. Typical assignments for persuasive and argumentative essays, in both the *Reader* and the *Guide*, ask students to take a position and support it by drawing on their experience, observation, and reading.

This syllabus is set up for a fourteen-week semester. It contains five units of two weeks each and a four-week unit on a longer paper with attention to library research and documentation. It assigns students five papers in two drafts: a paper analyzing an essay, a personal report, two persuasive/argumentative essays, and a longer persuasive/argumentative paper using library research. It also assigns them a third draft of one of the persuasive/argumentative essays and, at the end of the course, in first draft only, an analysis of their experience in writing persuasion and argument. Any of these units can be repeated using additional essays; any of them can be dropped.

Class discussion should focus on purpose, evidence, personae, and audience, both in the essays assigned from *The Norton Reader* and in students' own writing. Both editions of *The Norton Reader* offer a rich variety of all these.

First week: Reading assignment: Read the following selections in the "Op-Eds" section.

> Molly Ivins, "Get a Knife, Get a Dog, but Get Rid of Guns"
> Brent Staples, "Why Colleges Shower Their Students with A's"
> Jack Hitt, "The Battle of the Binge"
> Kenneth Bruffee, "Binge Drinking as a Substitute for a 'Community of Learning'"

In-class: Analyze, for several of these selections, the author's purpose and evidence, the kind of persona the author creates, how, and for what audience. How effective is the author's evidence and persona?

Writing assignment (draft): Draft an essay about one of the selections in the "Op-Eds" section not discussed in class. Analyze what the author's evidence is, how it is deployed, what kind of persona the author creates, how, and for what audience. How effective do you find the author's evidence and persona?

Append a paragraph in which you consider whether you, as a student, could adopt a similar persona or, if not, what kind of persona would be suitable to the audiences you will be addressing as a writer in college.

Second week: Reading assignment.

> Michael Levin, "The Case for Torture" ("Ethics")
> Katha Pollitt, "Does a Literary Canon Matter?" ("Literature and the Arts")
> William Lloyd Garrison, "No Compromise with Slavery" (spoken words)

In-class: Discuss logic, evidence, and persona in the Levin, Garrison, and Pollitt essays.

Writing assignment (revision): Divide into groups for peer review of drafts; revised drafts to be handed in at the next class.

Third week: Reading assignment.

> Scott Russell Sanders, "Under the Influence" ("People, Places")
> Andrew Sullivan, "What Is a Homosexual?" ("Human Nature")
> Sallie Tisdale, "We Do Abortions Here: A Nurse's Story" ("Ethics")
> Nora Ephron, "The Boston Photographs" (Ethics)

In-class: Discuss several of these essays as narrative or exposition, and consider how they provide material that could be used in arguing a controversial issue.

Writing assignment (draft): Draft a personal essay based on an experience or experiences that will provide material to be used in arguing a controversial issue.

Fourth week: Reading assignment.

> Maya Angelou, "Graduation" ("Personal Report")
> Lars Eighner, "On Dumpster Diving" ("Personal Report")
> David Guterson, "Enclosed. Encyclopedic. Endured: The Mall of America" ("People, Places")

In-class: Discuss how one or more of these essays could be used as evidence in taking a position or in arguing for a social change or changes.

Writing assignment (revision): Divide into groups for peer review of drafts; revised drafts to be handed in at the next class.

Fifth week: Reading assignment.

> "Cherokee Memorials" ("History")
> Lani Guinier, "The Tyranny of the Majority" ("Politics and Government")

Martin Luther King Jr., "Letter from Birmingham Jail" ("Politics and Government")

In-class: Discuss evidence and personae in the "Cherokee Memorials" and the Guinier and King essays.

Writing assignment (draft): Draft a persuasive or argumentative essay that uses as evidence experience, observation, and reading of one of the essays above or any other essay in *The Norton Reader*.

Sixth week: Reading assignment.

Tom Regan, "The Case for Animal Rights" ("Ethics")
Carl Cohen, "The Case for the Use of Animals in Biochemical Research" ("Ethics")

In-class: Discuss the principles and values that underlie the disagreement between Regan and Cohen.

Writing assignment (revision): Divide into groups for peer review of drafts; revised drafts to be handed in at the next class.

Seventh week: Reading assignment.

Thomas Jefferson, "Original Draft of the Declaration of Independence" ("Politics and Government")
Thomas Jefferson and Others, "The Declaration of Independence" ("Politics and Government")
Elizabeth Cady Stanton, "Declaration of Sentiments and Resolutions" ("Politics and Government")

In-class: Discuss syllogistic argument: a major premise, a minor premise, and a conclusion.

Writing assignment (draft): Draft an essay on animal rights or some other controversial topic that highlights the major premises (or principles and values) about which you and your opponents cannot agree.

Eighth week: Reading assignment.

Wechsler et al., "Health and Behavioral Consequences of Binge Drinking: A National Survey of Students at 140 Campuses" ("Science")
Wechsler et al., "Too Many Colleges Are Still in Denial about Alcohol Abuse" ("Science")

In-class: Discuss the conventions of reporting scientific research and the rhetoric of Wechsler et al. as they report their research in the *New England Journal of Medicine* and argue from it in *The Chronicle of Higher Education*.

Writing assignment (revision): Divide into groups for peer review of drafts; revised drafts to be handed in at the next class.

Ninth week: Reading assignment: Read through the essays in either "Nature and the Environment" or "Ethics" or "Politics and Government," and begin library research in preparation for writing a persuasive or argumentative essay on an issue that appears in one of them.

In-class: Introduction to print and electronic resources in the library.

Writing assignment (draft): Brainstorm, make notes, list, free write—whatever works best to get you started—about what you know and what you need to know, where you are in your research, where you are going, and where you think you will come out.

Tenth week: Reading assignment: Continue library research.

Writing assignment (draft): Divide into groups for peer review of brainstorming, etc. Begin to draft a persuasive or argumentative essay that incorporates library research.

Eleventh week: In-class: Discuss the purposes of bibliography and notes, and review their form.

Writing assignment (draft): Divide into groups for peer review of drafts.

Twelfth week: Writing assignment: Divide into groups for peer review of bibliography and notes; final draft of essay that incorporates library research due.

Thirteenth week: Reading assignment: Read persuasive and argumentative essays in either "Cultural Critique" or "Education."

> Anthony Burgess, "Is America Falling Apart?" ("Cultural Critique")
> Betty Rollin, "Motherhood: Who Needs It?" ("Cultural Critique")
> Brent Staples, "Black Men and Public Space" ("Cultural Critique")
> Caroline Bird, "College Is a Waste of Time and Money" ("Education")
> Adrienne Rich, "Taking Women Students Seriously" ("Education")

Writing assignment (draft): Draft an essay in which you review the papers you wrote this semester and analyze your strengths and difficulties in writing persuasion and argument.

Fourteenth week: Writing assignment (draft). Divide into groups, share drafts, and report to class the issues concerning persuasion and argument that emerged in the groups.

Assignment (revision): Revise one of your earlier papers from this course and hand it in; append a paragraph in which you describe what you aimed for in your revision.

Essays Exemplifying Persuasion and Argument (by section)

Human Nature

> Stephen Jay Gould, "Our Allotted Lifetimes"

Cultural Critique

> Anthony Burgess, "Is America Falling Apart?"
> Betty Rollin, "Motherhood: Who Needs It?"
> Brent Staples, "Black Men and Public Space"

Op-Eds

> Molly Ivins, "Get a Knife, Get a Dog, but Get Rid of Guns" (in "Cultural Critique")
> Brent Staples, "Why Colleges Shower Their Students with A's"
> Russell Baker, "American Fat"
> Jack Hitt, "The Battle of the Binge"
> Kenneth Bruffee, "Binge Drinking as a Substitute for a 'Community of Learning'"

Education

> Caroline Bird, "College Is a Waste of Time and Money"
> Adrienne Rich, "Taking Women Students Seriously"

Nature and the Environment

> Carl Sagan, "The Abstractions of Beasts"
> Chief Seattle, "Letter to President Pierce, 1855"
> William Cronon, "The Trouble with Wilderness"
> Joseph Wood Krutch, "The Most Dangerous Predator"
> Terry Tempest Williams, "The Clan of One-Breasted Women"

Ethics

> Lord Chesterfield, "Letter to His Son"
> Jonathan Rauch, "In Defense of Prejudice"
> Michael Levin, "The Case for Torture"
> Tom Regan, "The Case for Animal Rights"
> Carl Cohen, "The Case for the Use of Animals in Biochemical Research"
> Nora Ephron, "The Boston Photographs"
> Stephen Jay Gould, "The Terrifying Normalcy of AIDS"
> Paul Fussell, "Thank God for the Atom Bomb"

History

> "Cherokee Memorials"
> Hannah Arendt, "Denmark and the Jews"
> Edward Hallett Carr, "The Historian and His Facts"

Politics and Government

Jonathan Swift, "A Modest Proposal"
Thomas Jefferson, "Original Draft of the Declaration of Independence"
Thomas Jefferson and Others, "The Declaration of Independence"
Elizabeth Cady Stanton, "Declaration of Sentiments and Resolutions"
Abraham Lincoln, "Second Inaugural Address"
Lani Guinier, "The Tyranny of the Majority"
Martin Luther King Jr., "Letter from Birmingham Jail"

Spoken Words

Elizabeth I, "Speech to the Troops at Tilbury"
John F. Kennedy, "Inaugural Address"
Martin Luther King Jr. "I Have a Dream"
David McCullough, "Recommended Itinerary"
James Van Tholen, "Surprised by Death"

Science

Henry Wechsler et al., "Too Many Colleges Are Still in Denial about Alcohol Abuse"
Stephen Jay Gould, "Darwin's Middle Road"
Sandra Steingraber, "Pesticides, Animals, and Humans"

Literature and the Arts

Katha Pollitt, "Does a Literary Canon Matter?"
Ngugi wa Thiong'o, "Decolonizing the Mind"
Richard Taruskin, "Text and Act"

Philosophy and Religion

Reinhold Niebuhr, "Humor and Faith"

IN PROCESS: A COLLABORATIVE APPROACH TO READING AND WRITING: SAMPLE SYLLABUS

Contributed by Dawn Rodrigues, Empire State College

The breadth of selections in *The Norton Reader* makes it easily adaptable to a collaborative approach to reading and writing. The units below are designed to last for two to three weeks each. If an instructor feels the pace is too fast or wishes to give additional reading or writing assignments, any unit can be simplified or expanded. The first week of each unit concentrates on reading the essays, finding a topic, and keeping an informal learning log; the second and third weeks focus on writing drafts and conducting workshops on the students' work.

I recommend that students keep a learning log, a three-ring notebook in which they record their in-class writing and homework writing exercises; a folder for all of their completed papers, including rough drafts; and a writing portfolio of their best work. At the end of the semester, the portfolio might include an expository essay, a documented research paper, a piece of the student's own choosing (a journal entry, a collage of brief free writings, or another essay or research-based paper), and a cover letter in which the student explains and reflects on the contents of the portfolio.

Paper 1: Autobiographical Essay

First week: Readings and learning log assignment.

> Zora Neale Hurston, "How It Feels to Be Colored Me"
> Nancy Mairs, "On Being a Cripple"
> Alice Walker, "Beauty: When the Other Dancer Is the Self"
> Henry Louis Gates Jr., "In the Kitchen"
> Langston Hughes, "Salvation"
> Edward Rivera, "First Communion"

Learning log assignment: For each reading, select one of the two questions below:

1. Write about a personal memory triggered by the reading assignment.
2. Write about how your experiences are similar to or different from those described in the selection you read.

After students have responded in their learning logs to all of the essays, they should draft an autobiographical essay of their own.

Second week: Additional autobiographical essays, writing workshops, and second drafts.

> Scott Russell Sanders, "Looking at Women"
> Debra Dickerson, "Who Shot Johnny?"
> Frederick Douglass, "Learning to Read"
> Dionne Brand, "Arriving at Desire"

Assignment: Write an autobiographical essay, using one or more of the selections you have read as inspiration. If none of the essays you have read provides that inspiration, you can choose another text—from a book you have read, from the feature section of the newspaper, or from another source—and use that as the basis for your essay.

Third week: Writing workshop or peer review, followed by revision of draft.

Paper 2: Synthesis Essay

This assignment calls for an argumentative essay in which students choose a single issue of interest to them, synthesize the viewpoints of several readings, find at least two additional readings from other sources, and then take a stand on the issue.

First week: Readings and learning log. For groups of argumentative essays, see "Persuasion and Argument: Sample Syllabus," pp. 315–20.

Learning log assignment: For each reading, do the following:

1. Summarize the main points of the selection.
2. Write a personal response or reaction to the selection.

Second week: Additional, outside readings chosen by students on an issue that both interests them and is connected to the assigned readings. Students draft analytical essays in which they synthesize different points of view and argue the position they think is most convincing.

Assignment: Find two selections from *The Norton Reader* or from other sources that relate to an issue in one of last week's assigned essays. Draft an essay in which you synthesize the argument of each essay, state your opinion on the issue, and try to persuade readers to think as you do or to take action along the lines of your opinion.

Third week: Writing workshops and revisions.

Paper 3: Synthesis of Group-Selected Readings

This assignment calls for students to write a paper with several classmates, synthesizing several readings from the *Reader*. The group can produce one traditional paper, or if they choose, they can produce a collection of individual pieces along with a summary of the group's consensus on an issue or their continuing dissensus. The paper can be revised as desired by students who wish to use it in their portfolios.

Each group proposes its own collection of readings and its own work plan. Each group presents its work to the class in the form of skits, panel discussions, or readings. In any case, the group's presentation should be more than simply turning in a completed paper.

First week: Selecting a subject area and getting into groups. The subject areas might be drawn from the following sections of the *Reader*:

Cultural Critique
Education
Language and Communication
Nature and the Environment
Politics and Government
Science and Technology
Literature, the Arts, and Media
Philosophy and Religion

Assignment: After selecting a subject area, get together with a group of students interested in pursuing the same general issue or topic. You should not formulate your specific paper topic until you have all read several essays. In your groups, you should:

1. Develop a list of readings relevant to your topic.
2. Determine how you would like to share readings (for example, by writing log entries and sharing them with one another or by assigning different group members the task of leading group discussion on a specific essay).
3. Turn in your plan so that the instructor will have a record of what you will be reading.

Second week: Group discussion on how to draft the essay, followed by actual draft.

Assignment: Devise a plan for drafting your group's essay. You might ask each person to do one section; you might all write drafts on the issue and then combine parts from each into one whole; or you might assemble around one computer and start drafting with one person typing while the others talk.

After you decide how to collaborate, decide how to share your responses to the readings. You might have each person write down one or two points that he or she thought interesting; or you might talk for a while, then write down your personal response to the discussion. You could then read one another's responses. Don't start working on your draft, however, until you come up with a working plan.

Third week: Groups revise their draft in their groups before turning in their final work.

Paper 4: Individual Papers Based on Another Group's Readings

Working with a group, students write individual papers based on the readings chosen by one of the other groups in the previous unit and in response to that group's final paper or papers. Students also write a summary and response for at least two additional essays related to the readings for this assignment.

Paper 5: Individualized Research Paper

The final research paper should grow out of students' personal interests in issues addressed during the term, either raised during class discussion or by one of the readings.

First week: Readings and learning log assignments. For suggested thematic groupings, see the sample syllabi in this *Guide* for "Great Ideas and Enduring Questions," pp. 301–04; "Writing Across the Curriculum," pp. 305–10; and "Race, Class, and Gender," pp. 311–14.

Assignment: Choose four new readings from *The Norton Reader* or from outside sources on a topic you would like to pursue in a research paper. Write learning log entries for each selection and try to arrive at a question you would like to pursue further. Then, find two additional outside sources on that question and write learning log entries for them.

Second week: Additional readings and draft of essay.

Assignment: Once you arrive at a question you wish to pursue, consult three to five additional sources. Draft an essay, using MLA style to document all sources you have consulted.

Third week: Writing workshop or peer review, followed by revision of draft.

THE MODERN ESSAY: SAMPLE SYLLABUS

This syllabus explores forms of the modern essay. Each unit asks students to read classic and contemporary examples and then to draw on their personal experience and knowledge to write in the same form. The essay forms are loosely grouped: the personal experience essay, the biographical portrait or character sketch, the essay about a place, an analysis of a cultural phenomenon or "cultural critique," and an Op-Ed piece that makes a contribution to an issue of public concern.

The emphasis in each unit is on writing the essay—hence the detailed writing assignments. Essays that fit the mode are listed, but many other examples can be found in *The Norton Reader* and in local and national newspapers and journals. The readings provide "models" in the sense that they suggest ways that professional writers have explored their personal experience or analyzed a contemporary phenomenon or argued a case in the public realm. But the "models" are plural, multiple, and complex—not simple or singular, as in the traditional rhetorical "modes."

I. Interpreting Personal Experience

Assignment: Write an essay, based on personal experience, in which you both narrate and interpret the significance of a personal experience. In common with the essays read in this unit, focus your essay on a single story or event (although it may include earlier or peripheral incidents if you wish) and aim to make a single, public point. In other words, you should not only tell your story, but you should seek to affect the way your readers will think about the specific problem or issue you raise in telling it.

Readings:

> George Orwell, "Shooting an Elephant"
> Langston Hughes, "Salvation"
> Terry Tempest Williams, "The Clan of One-Breasted Women"
> Debra Dickerson, "Who Shot Johnny?"
> Brent Staples, "Black Men and Public Space"
> Joan Didion, "On Going Home"
> Chang-Rae Lee, "Coming Home Again"
> Alice Walker, "Beauty: When the Other Dancer is the Self"
> E. B. White, "Once More to the Lake"

II. Portraying a Person

Assignment: Write an essay that portrays a person in his or her typical context. Whether you write about a person you know well or someone you know only slightly or through the media, gather new, additional information about that person, whether through interviews or research or both, and incorporate it into your account. If you write about a family member, interview other family members who know (or knew) the person. If you write about someone local, interview your subject and others who know—or work with—him or her. If you write about a public figure, find ways to gather information and interpret it in a new way.

Readings:

> Tom Wolfe, "Yeager"
> Annie Dillard, "Terwilliger Bunts One"
> Scott Russell Sanders, "Under the Influence"
> Judith Ortiz Cofer, "More Room"
> Debra Dickerson, "Who Shot Johnny?"
> Gary Soto, "The Guardian Angel"
> Thomas Jefferson, "George Washington"
> Nathaniel Hawthorne, "Abraham Lincoln"

III. Understanding a Place

Assignment: Write an essay for a wide audience that describes, creates the essence of, and interprets the meaning of a place. The place may be as small as a room, the size of a campus building, or as large as a town. Choose a place that you can observe as you write this essay or that you know so well you need not observe it anew. Incorporate not only observations from the present or memories from the past, but information about the place that will help you convey its "meaning" to your readers (possibilities: its history; its inhabitants; responses of people who see the place for the first time or who live or work there; information about its founding, its changing fortune, or its demise).

Readings:

> Henry Louis Gates Jr., "In the Kitchen"
> Fatema Mernissi, "The Harem Within"
> Judith Ortiz Cofer, "More Room"
> Edward Abbey, "The Serpents of Paradise"
> Margaret Atwood, "True North"
> Mary Austin, "The Land of Little Rain"
> Aldo Leopold, "Marshland Elegy"
> Fred Strebeigh, "The Wheels of Freedom: Bicycles in China"
> Dave Guterson, "Enclosed. Encyclopedic. Endured: The Mall of America"

IV. Cultural Critique

Assignment: Write an essay that analyzes and comments on a specific feature of modern culture. Your focus should be on a concrete, recognizable object or phenomenon, not on some broad historical or political trend (even though you may want to use history or politics to analyze your object of choice). Look closely at your object or phenomenon: describe it, describe who uses it, think about why it has become popular, explain the values or beliefs it embeds or conveys.

Readings:

Roland Barthes, "Toys"
Daniel Harris, "Light-Bulb Jokes: Charting an Era"
Sonia Shah, "Tight Jeans and Chania Chorris"
Henry Louis Gates Jr., "In the Kitchen"
Susan Allen Toth, "Going to the Movies"
Jessica Mitford, "Behind the Formaldehyde Curtain"
Malcolm Gladwell, "The Sports Taboo"
Adam Goodheart, "9.11.01: The Skyscraper and the Airplane"

V. Op-Eds and Public Debates

Assignment: Write an Op-Ed (a short persuasive essay or argument) meant to influence a wide audience, following the lines of the opinion pieces and editorials read during this section. Your Op-Ed may use any of the types of evidence that appear in the readings, including personal experience, statistical data, authoritative opinion, expert testimony, and so on. Try to make your argument engage some important public issue of current interest, possibly taking a position against some already published essay.

Readings:

Op-Eds on binge drinking:

> Harold Wechsler et al., "Too Many Colleges are Still in Denial about Alcohol Abuse"
> Jack Hitt, "The Battle of the Binge"
> Kenneth A. Bruffee, "Binge Drinking as a Substitute for a Community of Learning"

Other Op-Eds or short arguments:

> Michel de Montaigne, "That One Man's Profit Is Another's Loss"
> Molly Ivins, "Get a Knife, Get a Dog, but Get Rid of Guns"
> Brent Staples, "Why Colleges Shower Their Students with A's"
> Anna Quindlen, "Evan's Two Moms"
> Russell Baker, "American Fat"
> Betty Rollin, "Motherhood: Who Needs It?"